Canada in Decay:
Mass Immigration, Diversity,
and the Ethnocide
of Euro-Canadians

Ricardo Duchesne

Canada in Decay:
Mass Immigration, Diversity, and the
Ethnocide of Euro-Canadians

Ricardo Duchesne

ISBN-13: 978-1-912759-98-9

Copyright © 2021 Black House Publishing Ltd

1st Edition published August 2017.
2nd Edition published November 2018.
3rd Edition published April 2021.

Black House Publishing Ltd
Kemp House
152 City Road
London
United Kingdom
EC1V 2NX

www.blackhousepublishing.com

Email: info@blackhousepublishing.com

Contents

Preface

In the last few decades Canada has been governed by a left-right coalition determined to diversify the racial character of the nation through mass immigration. As late as 1971, when Prime Minister Pierre Trudeau announced multiculturalism as an official government policy, over 96 percent of Canada's population was European in origin.

Today, the proportion of Canadians with a European ethnic origin has declined to about 75 percent. Statistics Canada has projected that the visible minority population could represent between 31.2 percent and 36 percent of the Canadian population by 2036, and the working age population (ages of 15 and 64) could be as high as 40 percent. By 2031 visible minority groups are estimated to comprise 63 percent of the population of Toronto, 59 percent of Vancouver, and 31 percent of Montréal. Eric Kaufmann, a professor at the University of London, thinks it can be reasonably estimated that Canada will be "20 percent white, 65 percent non-white, and 15 percent mixed race by 2106"[1]

There is no example in history of a people or a nation promoting its own replacement by foreigners from other races, religions and cultures.

The establishment will tell you that "this experiment of major proportions", as Pierre Elliot Trudeau characterized it some decades ago, has been incredibly successful in creating a freer, more tolerant, and inclusive Canada that is now a beacon of hope and admiration across the world, "a brilliant prototype for the moulding of tomorrow's civilization", to use the words of Trudeau again.[2] What the Canadian

---

1   As cited by Douglas Todd, "Almost 7 in 10 Metro residents will be non-white in two decades" (*Vancouver Sun*, June 7, 2017). On Stats Canada's projections, see its 2016 census: https://www12.statcan.gc.ca/census-recensement/2016/dp-pd/index-eng. cfm and "Study: A look at immigration, ethnocultural diversity and languages in Canada up to 2036, 2011 to 2036", http://www.statcan.gc.ca/daily-quotidien/170125/dq170125b-eng.htm

2   Pierre Trudeau, "The New Treason of the Intellectuals". This essay, to be discussed at length in chapters 17 and 18, was originally published in *Cité Libre* in 1962, and is now available online, https://docs.google.com/document/d/1CChvPQwRJWj02WN3nur7j Kr9nwj8aBgPKzSliSIbMpY/edit?pli=1#heading=h.gwl098qh9ien

establishment will not tell you, and this book will explain, is that the elites of most Western nations are making very similar claims about their own uniqueness as nations founded by "immigrants from diverse cultures". While a key aim of this book is to explain the origins and nature of the ideology of "immigrant multiculturalism" in Canada, this explanation will be constructed in such a way that it also explains generally the emergence of the same ideology across the West. It is impossible to explain why our elites embraced with such dogmatic fervor the idea that "diversity is Canada's strength" while ignoring the spread of this same fervor in most European-created countries.

This book is divided into four major parts. Part I, "Statistical Reflections on the Pioneers, Settlers, and Indigenous Euro-Canadians who Created Canada", demonstrates that the constantly repeated claim that "Canada is a nation of immigrants" is actually not supported by the historical demographic evidence, but is simply one of the many deceptions our elites have been employing to generate support for what can only be described as "an experiment of major proportions" to create a Canada of diverse immigrants that never existed in the past. Students are being deceived by our major historians when they are taught that "from the very beginning, the land that became Canada was a multiracial place, the destination of a constant flow of new immigrants of varying ethnicities". [3] The facts are amply clear: Canada's immigration experience was not only overwhelmingly European from the beginning until the 1960s/70s, but the Canadians who founded this nation were actually indigenous pioneers and settlers newly born in the hard cold soils of this nation. The Quebecois and the Acadians were a people created through the fecundity of the women, not immigration. The Loyalists, too, were not immigrants but settlers native to the soils of British North America. Before Confederation in 1867, as will be documented in the first chapter, there were only "two quite limited periods" of substantial arrivals of "immigrants" and these "immigrants" were "overwhelmingly of British origin".

Part I will also question the way the word "immigrant" has been deviously extended to include actual settlers. Almost all the men and women who came to Canada from the British Isles and elsewhere in Europe before 1914 were settlers seeking survival in a land sparsely

---

3   J. M. Bumsted, *Canada's Diverse Peoples: A Reference Sourcebook* (ABC-CLIO, 2003), p. 326.

populated and devoid of modern development. Equating the indigenous Canadians who pioneered and settled Canada with the immigrants who came to a ready-made nation after 1921/1945 is part and parcel of the ideological effort of our elites on both the right and the left to destroy the national identities and heritages of European peoples in order to create a new global order dominated by corporations and human rights concepts concocted by well-off academics and "experts" out of touch with their own people. While Amerindians were native to the soils that came to constitute the nation of Canada, they were not the "first nations" of Canada since they were living in tribal units when Europeans arrived, and once Europeans took over they were gradually marginalized and relegated to reserves. The very act of creating a nation-state is a modern European phenomenon.

Part II will show that the "theory of multicultural citizenship", which was articulated in the main by Canadians, principally by Will Kymlicka and Charles Taylor, is not really a "liberal theory of minority rights", but a cultural Marxist effort to undermine the historic rights of the majority population of Euro-Canadians. Multicultural citizenship affords immigrants minorities with special group rights backed by the philosophical argument that "humans have a deep need" to have their culture and ethnic identity recognized, while categorizing Euro-Canadians who affirm their ethno-cultural collective identities as "racist" and "Nazis" in need of suppression. Kymlicka's argument that Western nations must be civic in character, based on liberal values alone, without any ethnic and deep cultural identity, will be rejected as historically inaccurate. It will also be argued in Part II that mass immigration is not a normal and inevitable affair happening across the globalizing world, but is instead a policy that is being imposed in Western countries by transnational elites on both the right and the left without open dialogue in backhanded ways under the weight of legal threats and loss of employment against Canadians who dissent. The claim that immigration is economically beneficial to Canadians will be subjected to empirical refutation.

Part III, "Refuting the Assimilationist Argument", will question the conservative argument that mass immigration would work better as long as immigrants are encouraged to assimilate to "Canadian values". It rejects the conservative argument that any immigrant group is capable of disaggregating itself into abstract individual units to become average Canadians with the proper encouragement of Canadian values. The view advanced will be quite different: if we are interested in preserving and enhancing the ethnic interests of Euro-Canadians, it is better to work within the existing framework of multiculturalism than to promote assimilation. What we should demand is group rights (or majority cultural rights) for Euro-Canadians rather than just individual rights. The arguments of Neil Bissoondath, Salim Mansur, Janet Ajzenstat, and Jack Granatstein, key proponents of the assimilationist view, will be rejected as fundamentally wrong in their misinterpretation of Canada's history and their lack of awareness of the science of ethnic identity. Ajzenstat will be refuted for claiming that the Fathers of Confederation envisioned Canada as a nation based on mere political values rather than as a nation with a strong British identity in acknowledgment of an ethnic French majority in Quebec. Ethnocentrism is not a dysfunctional malady that needs to be removed from human behavior; it is, rather, a disposition selected for its evolutionary advantages. While Europeans are uniquely individualistic, they still have ethnocentric tendencies that should be nurtured rather than suppressed. As it stands now, Europeans are facing a situation in which people with stronger collective interests are populating their lands, encouraged to do so by Europeans blindly promoting "multicultural rights" while excluding themselves from any form of collective identity. Mass immigration by non-Europeans involves ethnic displacement by people with different genetic interests.

Part III will also explain why Liav Orgad's argument for "majority rights" for Europeans, notwithstanding its welcomed effort to go beyond the liberal obsession with minority rights, is insufficiently protective of the deeper cultural and ethnic attributes that are unique to Europeans and cannot (and should not) be universalized. It will also question the widespread presumption that mass immigration and diversification are somehow fundamentally connected to the liberal way of life. There is nothing in the core principles of liberalism that requires Europeans to reduce themselves to a minority in their own homelands. Diversification without open dialogue is, to the contrary, an illiberal ideology rooted in cultural Marxism. Cultural Marxism is an outgrowth of Marxism which focuses on radically altering the cultures and ethnicities of the West rather than persisting in developing communistic economies which have been proven to be a failure.

Finally, part IV, "Canada Spiraling Out of Control", will address the most important and most difficult question of our times: Why did the entire Western establishment came to the view that white nations had to be diversified and open to mass immigration? It will be argued, to quote words used in Part IV, that "a new set of normative claims with an in-built tendency for further radicalization suddenly came to take a firm hold over Western liberal nations in response to the Nazi experience, and that once these norms were accepted, and actions were taken to implement them institutionally, they came to entrap Westerners within a spiral that would push them into ever more radical policies". The four norms to be discussed are:

1) That racism is the worst evil of modern times, and that a national identity in which a race, or even a cultural group, lays a privileged claim over the nation state is, accordingly, a form of evil inherently inconsistent with the ideals of liberal democracy.

2) That race is a social construct without biological basis, all humans are the same, it does not matter if whites become a minority in their homelands; what matters is whether individuals are "free" to construct their identities.

3) That whites should feel ashamed for enriching themselves by colonizing and enslaving Third World peoples with innate goodness and "authentic traditional lifestyles", and that whites should be morally committed to the achievement of racial equalization.

4) That all humans in the world have human rights to life, liberty, and economic wellbeing, and if Westerners are to live up to these rights they should focus on improving the lives of peoples lacking them by granting them, among other things, citizenship rights in Western lands.

These norms came to "entrap" Westerners within a spiral of radicalization because they have an in-built tendency for never-satisfied "solutions" since ethnic identities cannot be utterly dissolved given the inescapable inclination of humans to identify with their own ethnic group. The political situation will always be seen by proponents of these norms as insufficiently equal given the natural inequalities in talents and achievements exhibited by different ethnic groups.

Moreover, since this drive for racial equality is being carried out in overwhelmingly white countries, it has entailed the arrival of endless masses of immigrant minorities in need of continuous equalization programs, group rights, coupled with ever growing assertions by ever larger "minorities" of their ethnic interests.

The spread of these norms will be assessed in the context of a historical overview of the process by which Canadian elites decided to transform Canada from a nation with rules that restricted immigration from non-white countries, before WWII and right through the 1960s, to a nation today obsessed with racial diversification and with stamping out any form of white identity. The question will also be asked: Was there something within the ethnocentric liberalism of the pre-WW II era which made it susceptible to the promulgation of these norms and their rapid radicalization thereafter? To answer this question, Part IV will bring up Carl Schmitt's argument that liberal states tend to lack a strong concept of the political, that is, liberal nations have an inherent weakness as political entities because they imagine themselves to be contractual creations by abstract individuals with natural rights rather than what they actually have been in the course of their historical creation and consolidation: nations created by ethnic groups against other groups with different ethnic and territorial interests. Liberal leaders have great difficulty thinking of their nations as a collectivity of people laying sovereignty claim over a territory that distinguishes between friends and enemies, who can belong and who cannot belong in the territory. This is why Canadian leaders succumbed so easily to the radicalization of these norms.

Among the many topics to be discussed in Part IV are the ethnic nationalism and liberal values of Canadians evident in the years of the Immigration Act of 1910 and the Immigration Act of 1952, the attack on "British liberties" in the human rights legislation of the 1950s, the normative arguments in favor of the Immigration Regulations of 1962 and 1967, and Pierre Trudeau's assault on Canada's "bicultural" identity and his vision of a Canada as a "polyethnic prototype" for the solution of ethnic conflict in nations across the world. Multiculturalism will be portrayed as an idea that would have made sense, and has made sense, in reference to the coexistence of historical minorities within a nation state. However, insofar as multiculturalism was conceived as a project for the future, entailing the endless promotion of mass immigration, it is one of the most pathological programs ever implemented in history. It will intensify, not lessen, ethnic conflicts. The Charter of Rights (1982) will be interpreted as a document intended to encode legally the transformation of Canada according to the human rights expectations of "experts" against the customary beliefs of Canadians. A long chapter will examine the meaning of multiculturalism in sections 27 and 15 of the Charter, as well as court cases during the 1980s and after dealing with these sections. The argument will be made that the ethnic composition of Canada, the demographics of different ethnic groups, will determine the meaning of these sections rather than the "static" arguments of jurists.

George Grant's assessment of the end of Canadian nationalism will be sympathetically expanded beyond his concern for the impossibility of conservatism in a Canada dominated by the globalizing dynamic of American corporate capitalism to include as well the ways in which conservatives relinquished the cultural nationalism intrinsic to Toryism in favor of a post-Fordist regime of global accumulation consistent with the celebration of multicultural citizenship and cheap labour mobility across borders. To the role of the norms outlined above, will be added the role of global capitalist accumulation, not as entailing necessarily the diversification of Western lands, for otherwise non-Western capitalist nations would have embraced mass immigration as well, but as illustrating how conservatives in the West came to endorse cultural Marxist precepts as useful to the interests of corporate expansion. It will be shown, accordingly, that the right and the left have converged across the West in their globalist support for open borders and racial diversification of white nations.

In the last chapter, Justin Trudeau's announcement that Canada is a "postnational state" will be interpreted as the culmination of the end of all forms of nationalism, not just ethnic and cultural nationalism, but civic nationalism as well. With post nationalism, the radicalizing spiral reaches its end point: the obliteration of any form of identity among whites including an identity based on "Western values". Post nationalism means that Canada has no identity other than the values chosen by individuals from many diverse cultural, religious and racial backgrounds in a diluted way as affluent consumers. The idea that Canada is a "Western liberal nation" is rejected by post-nationalists as a form of Western supremacism that still makes distinctions between "good" and "bad" Muslims, "less" and "more" Canadians. Distinctions can only be made in reference to individuals who make good and bad choices in their path towards tolerance and inclusiveness. This form of hyper individualism and construction of globally deracinated characters, without historical roots and collective identities, will fail. While ethnic, cultural, and sexual identities are not fixed, they are substantive enough to preclude endless reconstructions according to the whims of isolated individuals. This book is an attempt to facilitate the failure of this "experiment of major proportions" in Canada, and to encourage Euro-Canadians to affirm their sovereign ethnic right to govern this nation as uniquely theirs.

Just to avoid unnecessary nitpicking by members of an academic establishment unaccustomed to critical thinking, I use the term "Euro-Canadians" in a descriptive way, to refer to Canadians who have a European ancestry, without intending to say that Canadians have consciously identified themselves as such. I make it evident throughout this book that the majority of Canadians have identified themselves as "British", "English", "Anglo", "French Canadians", or "Quebecois". While sometimes I use "Euro-Canadian" interchangeably with the term "White Canadians", I much prefer "Euro-Canadian" because this term captures both the racial and cultural aspects of a group that is uniquely ancestral to the land of Canada. In this sense, "Euro-Canadian" is an ethnic term rather than a purely biological or racial category. It is a term that includes cultural, historical, racial, religious, and territorial identifiers. Therefore, by "ethnocide of Euro-Canadians", I mean what the United Nations also means by "cultural genocide" and "ethnocide", that is, the deliberate destruction of the ethnic heritage of a people. I do not mean the deliberate killing or extermination of Euro-Canadians, which is also part of the definition of "ethnocide". I mean the deprivation of Euro-Canadians of their integrity as a people with a distinctive culture and ethnic identity in possession of their own nation-state.

However, as I make clear in Part IV, I do not believe that immigrant multiculturalism was implemented initially with the deliberate intention of bringing about the ethnocide of Euro-Canadians. It is only in the last two or three decades, in consequence of the in-built radicalizing tendencies of the ideology of diversity, that Euro-Canadians have been deliberately made to feel that they must accept their eventual reduction to a subdued minority in Canada, as well as the decoupling of their Anglo-Quebecois culture from the nation-state in the name of a "multicultural form of citizenship". It is only recently that the entire establishment has been deliberately compelling Euro-Canadians to believe that any affirmation of their ethnic identity is racist and that they must welcome the supremacist idea that diversification through immigration improves the racial and cultural aspects of all European nations including Canada.

Let me state in this updated edition that *Canada in Decay* was a best seller at Amazon in various key subjects the moment it was released in August 2017. There were months in 2018 when it was ranked # 1 as a 'Best Seller' in numerous categories on Amazon, and never below the top 5. In December 2019 about 70 five star reviews on Amazon suddenly disappeared. In August 2020 the book was even suppressed by Amazon for a few months, making the book difficult to find.

Decide for yourself whether you want to read this book. The book received long reviews with high praises in dissident magazines and journals, but the academic world has ignored it, preferring to use close-minded labels rather than to engage with its arguments. This is the nature of our corporate-feminist controlled universities, where promoting diversity, combating "white supremacy" and denigrating the far superior intellectual culture of the West, has become the main "educational" mission.

Part One

Statistical Reflections on the Pioneers, Settlers, and Indigenous Euro-Canadians Who Created Canada

---

History must be defended against attempts to abuse it in the cause of change; we should constantly be on our guard against theories which either dismiss the past or give it a drastically new interpretation...to sanction a major program of change. From this the path to historical propaganda is short and easy....A nation that repudiates or distorts its past runs a grave danger of forfeiting its future. — Donald Creighton

CRIMESTOP means the faculty of stopping short, as though by instinct, at the threshold of any dangerous thought. It includes the power of not grasping analogies, of failing to perceive logical errors, of misunderstanding the simplest arguments if they are inimical to Ingsoc, and of being bored or repelled by any train of thought which is capable of leading in a heretical direction. CRIMESTOP, in short, means protective stupidity... orthodoxy in the full sense demands a control over one's own mental processes as complete as that of a contortionist over his body. — George Orwell

Facts are stubborn things; and whatever may be our wishes, our inclinations, or the dictates of our passions, they cannot alter the state of facts and evidence. — John Adams

1

"A Nation Created by Diverse Immigrants"

One of the most powerful memes in our times is that "Canada is a nation of immigrants".[1] Many individuals have indeed migrated to Canada since John Cabot first claimed either Newfoundland or Cape Breton Island for England in 1497. But the intended meaning of this phrase goes well beyond this simple observation. This phrase, continuously repeated by the media and pushed into the brains of unsuspecting students from primary to higher education, seeks to fashion an image of Canada as a nation populated from the beginning by peoples from diverse cultures and racial backgrounds, in order to portray the immigration patterns we have been witnessing since the 1970s as a natural continuation of past migration patterns, rather than as what these patterns are: a radical departure aimed at the termination of Canada's deep-seated Anglo-European ethnic character.

It is obvious that this meme is inaccurate. Canada's immigration experience has been overwhelmingly European since the sixteenth century, and for the first 100 years since Confederation in 1867 until 1962/67, the immigration policies were ethnically oriented to keep the country European. Not long ago everyone in Canada, the media, schools, political parties, took it for granted that "Canada was a British nation", or "an English-French nation" or simply "a White nation". No one challenged Prime Minister Mackenzie King when he said in Parliament in 1947, just a few decades ago, that Canada should remain a white man's country. No one rose in arms with accusations of racism when King insisted earlier in his career, in 1922, that to allow immigration by "the races of the Orient" would bring whites "face to face at once with the loss of that homogeneity which ought to characterize the people of this country if we are to be a great nation".[2] This "White Canada" meme, as will become clear in the next

---

1   This phrase, in quotation marks, brings up over 28,000 links from Google Canada, and over 99,000 links from Google USA.

2   As cited in Ninette Kelley, Michael Trebilcock, *The Making of the Mosaic. A History of Canadian Immigration Policy* (University of Toronto Press, Second Edition, 2010), p. 206.

chapters, was taken for granted and accepted for its historical accuracy by Canadians generally as late as the 1960s.

Yet, for some decades now, professional historians have been pushing the "we are all immigrants" meme for its "historical accuracy" against the supposed "myth" that Canada was "founded" by Anglos or Europeans generally. How can an idea, a catch phrase, devoid of historical veracity be accepted by the upper echelons of our society without questioning and counter-narrative? The historical record, the facts we have about the people who came to Canada, the racial makeup of the immigrants, the proportion of whites to non-whites, the birth rate of Euro-Canadians, the rates of immigration versus the domestic fertility rates, demonstrate, to the contrary, that Canada was a nation created from top to bottom by immigrants from Europe and by Euro-Canadians born in Canada, with next to zero contributions by non-Europeans.

What is so odd about this spectacle of lies is that, once we look past the ideological manipulations, the texts promoting this grand deception contain the historical facts disproving it. Let's start with two authoritative books on this topic: J. M. Bumsted's *Canada's Diverse Peoples: A Reference Sourcebook*, and Ninette Kelley and Michael Trebilcock's *The Making of the Mosaic, A History of Canadian Immigration Policy*. Bumsted is a highly regarded historian of Canada, the author of an impressive two volume survey, *The People's of Canada: A Pre-Confederation History* (2003) and *The People's of Canada: A Post-Confederation History* (2004). Kelley and Trebilcock are less well known, but their book, *The Making of the Mosaic*, is clearly the most exhaustive study today of immigration history: close to 700 pages long, it includes 133 pages of notes and 45 pages of references.

These authors are multiculturalists who play up the typical pro-diversity tropes mandated by our totalitarian culture. I will go over these tropes first, or commonly recurring ideological devices in their texts, with the intention of driving home my main objective, to show that despite the generalized presence of these motifs, these scholars cannot but bring out some crucial facts available in the records, which demonstrate the opposite of what they would like to say: Canada was a nation founded by white settlers indigenous to Canada. The more ideological academics who write about such topics as the internment of the Japanese or the "oppression of blacks" in Canada may have the luxury to ignore these inconvenient facts, but any exhaustive study about immigration patterns would find it difficult not to divulge them.

The title of Bumsted's book speaks for itself; it is part of a series on "Ethnic Diversity within Nations" intended to help readers "better appreciate" diversity in order to enable "all of us to interact more effectively" with multiple races.[3] Right in the opening paragraph, Bumsted questions the notion that Europeans "were the first to discover this land and the first to settle it".[4] He writes:

> From the very beginning of human settlement of this continent... North America was sheer diversity. This land was a veritable quilt of peoples and tongues. The ultimate arrival of Europeans complicated, but did not really alter, this pattern.[5]

He uses quotation marks in reference to "the French and the English as the 'founding peoples' of Canada" as it "completely ignores the previous presence of the aboriginals".[6] He bemoans the restrictive racial immigration policies of the past, and constructs a history progressively moving toward a multiracial society in which everyone is accorded full equality, concluding:

> By the year 2000 it was abundantly clear that Canada had won its campaign to impose the concept of multiculturalism upon the nation.[7]

This passage comes from the last chapter, revealing titled "The Future", which announces:

> *From the very beginning*, the land that became Canada was a multiracial place, the destination of a constant flow of new immigrants of varying ethnicities.[8]

---

3   J. M. Bumsted, *Canada's Diverse Peoples: A Reference Sourcebook* (ABC-CLIO, 2003): xvi.

4   *Ibid.* 1

5   *Ibid.* 14

6   *Ibid.* 24

7   *Ibid.* 330

8   *Ibid.* 326; my italics.

Did you get this? The cultural Marxists have "won". Canada is now fully diverse, and don't complain about your culture being swamped, for Canada was from the very beginning multiracial. It has always been this way, and there is nothing you can do about the inevitable future which has already transpired. But we will see below that this is a historical fabrication; Canada was almost totally European from the beginning through to the 1970s. *It was still more than 96% white in 1971 when multiculturalism become official policy.*

A similar pattern characterizes *The Making of the Mosaic*, starting with its endearing title, which projects an image of a country created by colored children happily working together except for the racist white kids who are finally learning to get along with different races. The introduction claims alliance to the "idea" expressed by the political theorist Joseph Carens, who insists that it is not enough to grant citizenship "immediately" to children born of parents who have settled illegally. If Westerners are to be morally true to their liberal values, they must take the perspective of "the most disadvantaged in the world" and accept immigration from the entire world with "very few restrictions".[9] Without any qualms about the insanity of this idea, Kelley and Trebilcock then recite the usual instances of racially discriminatory policies and practices in Canada, framing the entire history of immigration as a progressive movement to overcome

> the atrocities committed over the course of history as a result of tribalism, ethnocentrism, 'ethnic cleansing', religious fanaticism, and ideological collectivism.[10]

Yet, for all these ideological recitations, these two books, *Canada's Diverse Peoples* and *The Making of the Mosaic*, have excellent statistical statements demonstrating beyond a shadow of a doubt that Canada was almost 100 percent European "from the beginning" until very recent times. At one point, Kelly and Trebilcock actually taunt their readers about the inaccuracy of calling Canada an immigrant nation, since throughout most of its history, they admit, the vast majority of

---

9   Carens has earned a very lucrative career promoting these crazed ideas, five book awards, including the 2014 David Easton award from the APSA and the 2014 C. B. Macpherson award from the CPSA. The basic message of his books can be summed up in one sentence: anyone who wants to gain entry to Canada has a "moral right to stay".

10   *The Making of the Mosaic*, p. 471.

Canadians were born in the country. Some may wonder why they would do this if they really want to promote the "immigrant nation" meme. Well, I would say, they also want to make Euro-Canadians feel guilty about having a nation that was not immigrant enough and that they still have work to do if they wish to make Canada the greatest immigrant nation. This is how the mind of the left operates.

The best way to convey to Euro-Canadian patriots that the evidence is totally on our side is to lay out in point form the main statistical statements found in these books. We can make the most of this evidence by offering the correct interpretative framework for these facts.

1. In 1871, according to the first census after Confederation, of the total population of 3.2 million, 32 percent were of French ancestry, 24 percent Irish, 20 percent English, 16 percent Scottish, and 6 percent German.[11] The Irish percentage of total immigration was 68.5 percent in 1825-9, 64.2 percent in 1830-9, 64.2 percent in 1840-9, 41.1 percent in 1850-9, and 22.4 percent in 1860-9.[12] There were only 21,500 blacks and 23,000 natives in 1871;[13] by contrast, there were 202,991 persons of German origin.[14]

2. Canada cannot "accurately be portrayed at Confederation as a nation of immigrants". In 1867, 79% percent had been born in Canada. Over the 400 years before Confederation, there were only "two quite limited periods" of substantial arrivals of immigrants:

---

11 *Ibid.* 23

12 *Canada's Diverse Peoples*, p. 110

13 *The Making of the Mosaic*, p.23 Kelley and Trebilcock are correct in adding that this number about the Native population ought to be "accepted with caution". But their statement that the Native population may have been "substantially higher," "closer to 100,000," is not a cautious one. First, let it be said that the 1871 census does say that the native population was 23,000. However, this figure is for the four original provinces: Ontario, Quebec, New Brunswick, and Nova Scotia. The census was counting the population of these 4 provinces because these were the provinces that came to constitute Canada a few years earlier in Confederation in 1867. Manitoba and Northwest territories joined in 1870, and British Columbia in 1871. While there were many Natives in these new provinces and territories, most Natives in these newly acquired lands were outside the federal government's jurisdiction, and therefore inhabitants of external societies. Moreover, by the same token, this 1871 census is not counting the European population in the other provinces and territories apart from these four provinces. The European population in BC was about 36,000 in 1871.

14 *Canada's Diverse People's*, p. 123

from 1783 to 1812, and from 1830 to 1850. In these two periods, the immigrants were "overwhelmingly of British origin".[15] Immigration was not a major factor in population growth from 1850 to the end of the nineteenth century. From 1871 to 1891, "a high rate of natural increase allowed the population of Canada to grow from 3.7 million to 4.8 million".

3. From 1608 to 1760, immigration to New France consisted of only 10,000 settlers, and thereafter it was "almost non-existent". The French-speaking population numbered about 90,000 by 1770s, and thereafter, until the late 1800s, the population expanded rapidly with women having 5.65 surviving children on average.[16] The increase in population in Lower Canada from 330,000 in 1815 to 890,000 in 1851 "was mainly attributable to the continuing high birth rate within the French-speaking community". By 1950, the Quebec population was almost 4 million. This increase was not a result of immigration, but primarily of the still continuing high fertility rates. It was only in the 1970s that Montreal saw an increasing inflow of non-European immigrants.

4. Between 1896 and 1914, Canada experienced high immigration levels with more than 3 million arriving within this period. However, the ethnic composition of the nation remained 84 percent of British and French origin, while the European component rose to 9 percent.[17] Between 1900 and 1915, the high mark in "Asian immigration" before the 1960s, 50,000 immigrants of Japanese, East Indian and Chinese descent arrived, but this number comprised less than 2 percent of the total immigration flow.[18] In contrast, in 1914, there were nearly 400,000 Germans in Canada,[19] the largest ethnic group apart from the British (which includes the Irish and Scots) and French.

5. The total intake of immigrants between 1946 and 1962 was 2,151,505. Between 1941 and 1962, during more or less the same

---

15 *The Making of the Mosaic*, p. 23

16 *Canada's Diverse Peoples*, p. 42.

17 *The Making of the Mosaic*, p. 115

18 *Ibid*, p.145

19 *Canada's Diverse Peoples*, p. 175

period, the population of Canada increased from 11.5 million to 18.5 million, "largely accounted" by Canada's "extremely high domestic birth rates".[20] Ninety percent of all immigrants who came to Canada before 1961 were from Britain.[21]

6. It was only after the institutionalization of official multiculturalism in 1971 that immigrants from Africa, the Caribbean, Latin America, the Middle East and Asia at large started to arrive in large numbers. During the 1970s the proportion originating in Europe was cut by half, whereas the proportion coming from Asia almost quadrupled. Of the 1.5 million who came between 1971 and 1981, 33 percent came from Asia, 16 percent from the Caribbean and South America and 5.5 percent from Africa. In the period 1991-2001, immigrants of European origin fell below 20 percent at the same time that Asian immigration soared above 58 percent.[22] Canada's visible minority population has been growing much faster than its total population: 22 percent growth from 1996 to 2001 versus 4 percent growth in the general population. Today, roughly one out of every four people in Canada is a member of a visible minority.

It is a historical falsehood, therefore, to say that Canada has always been a diverse nation. Canada was created by Europeans, all the institutions, legal system, educational curriculum, transformation of wilderness into productive farms, all the cities, the parliamentary traditions, the churches, the entire infrastructure of railways, ports, shipping industries, and highways, were created by hardworking Europeans.

There is a standard reply to these truths, and it is that "diverse from the beginning" means that Canada was populated early on by diverse ethnic groups from Europe, combined with Aboriginals. But, as is typical with cultural Marxists, this is yet another form of deception inflicted daily on our students. Why call Canada "diverse from the beginning" in lieu of its diverse immigrants while at the same time decrying the exclusionary immigration policies of "white supremacist"

---

20   *The Making of the Mosaic*, pp. 316-18

21   *Ibid*, p. 467

22   *Ibid*.

Canada? Why not say that "diverse and mosaic Canada" was racist against "diverse and mosaic" immigrants?

We will see in future chapters that the implementation of immigrant multiculturalism in the 1970s was intended to be, as Prime Minister Trudeau said openly, "an experiment of major proportions", an effort to undermine the historic European character of Canada by transforming the nation into a multi-ethnic place in which old ethnic nationalisms would be discredited. This is the context in which to evaluate the "Canada is a nation of immigrants" meme. This meme was designed to manipulate Euro-Canadians into believing that immigrant multiculturalism was not really an experiment but a natural progression out of Canada's past experience, by creating an image of Canada as always diverse and multicultural. Ever since Trudeau announced in 1971 that "biculturalism does not properly describe our society; multiculturalism is more accurate",[23] quite a few Canadian historians have been hard at work erasing the Anglo-European character of Canada's founding history.

Multicultural Revisionism = Fake History

The falsification of the historical record for the purpose of creating a past that fits with the ideological goals of the present has been a common characteristic of revolutionary regimes seeking to legitimize themselves by portraying their actions and goals as if they were conterminous with the aims of history or the venerable beliefs of the past. Perhaps the most egregious example of "illegitimate historical revisionism", as contrasted to the legitimate re-assessment of the past on the basis of improved evaluation of records,[24] is the complete re-

---

23   Cited in Hugh Donald Forbes, "Trudeau as the First Theorist of Canadian Multiculturalism", in Stephen Tierney, *Multiculturalism and the Canadian Constitution* (UBC Press, 2007), p. 30.

24   Questioning older interpretations, "orthodox views", has been a common feature of historical writing in the West since the Enlightenment, if not the Renaissance. Westerners have always been a polemical people who relish overturning dogmas that strike them as faulty, lacking in empirical credentials, and superseded by new reflections and methodologies, and this has been for the good. But a very insidious and misleading form of revisionism has been happening in recent years associated with the re-writing of the history of all Western nations as "immigrant nations", or as nations that were diverse from the beginning, a revisionism that is intended to justify the transformation of Western nations into racially diverse places. I have written at length about this revisionism in the field of world history, how the achievements of the West

writing of the history of Russia by the Communist Party of the Soviet Union, particularly during the reign of Stalin in the mid-1920s to early 1950s; history was not only written according to the "correct" Marxist theory, but state officials commonly went about erasing major historical figures from documents, books, and even photographs the moment they were deemed to be "enemies of the people".[25]

This illegitimate revision of the historical record is also happening in Canada, but in a difficult to detect way, for it does not involve any book burning, outright denials of certain events, or use of forged documents. It is taking place in a rather calmed, seemingly reasonable way, ostensibly in accordance with the protocols of "verifiability", "peer review", and "openness to criticism". Let me be clear: I am not referring here to intentionally polemical books about the "suppressed" history of Canadian women, the "inhumane" treatment of natives, and the like. The books I have in mind are general surveys intended to be summations of the existing state of knowledge, not polemical exegeses, that is, surveys for undergraduate courses read by thousands of impressionable students across the nation. These surveys are now dominated by the dictates of the multicultural agenda, however neutral they may appear at first sight.

Basically what has happened, and is happening, is that historians have been expected to view the older Anglo-Saxon narrative of Canada, or the "two founding races" narrative, as "monolithic mythologies", as "models" that were "violently imposed" on history against "the other", against the actual "complexity" of Canada as a nation created by multiple ethnic groups, to cite the words of John Ralston Saul, the putative philosopher of Canada. "Monolithic", in the establishment world Saul inhabits, means a view that "denies complexity" and holds the "illusion of racial unity or cultural unity". "Mythology" means that it is not truly reflective of the actual historical realities. Saul expresses these thoughts in his superficially contrived *Reflections of a Siamese Twin: Canada at the Beginning of the Twentieth Century* published in 1998.[26] Academics

---

have been downplayed in order to bring about a narrative in which all the races and nations of the world are seen to be "co-equal" participants in the making of the major epochs of Western history. See *The Uniqueness of Western Civilization* (Brill, 2011), and *Faustian Man in a Multicultural Age* (Arktos, 2017).

25 See "The Airbrushing of History", https://s3.amazonaws.com/accredible_card_attachments/attachments/60608/original/CNL_Week_3_Version_04_XIII-vii-31.pdf

26 John Ralston Saul, *Reflections of a Siamese Twin: Canada at the Beginning of the Twentieth Century* (Penguin Canada, 1998), pp. 3-15, 140.

love to use these words when they describe their ways of thinking. Portraying Canada as "richly diverse", a "complex cultural mosaic" from its origins,[27] means that one can grasp complexities, one is "subtle" and "nuanced". By contrast, writing that Canada was fundamentally a British nation bespeaks of crudeness and simple mindedness.

What about the facts? Well, historians have further learned from the more ideologically oriented social scientists that the "old style of history", which took for "granted" Canada's Anglo identity, was a discourse "socially constructed" by dominant Anglo men. The claim that Canada was founded by the British and French was "constructed by white males" to justify their subjugation of minorities. Historians know better now. They are more "sensitive" to the long suppressed diverse voices of Canada's past, and, in this vein, they have constructed a "new discourse" that better captures the "complexity" of Canada as a "multicultural nation" from its beginnings.

This concept of a "discourse", with its notion that the way we think about history and social reality cannot be understood in the language of the natural sciences, because thinking is always a product of the "disciplinary structures of knowledge and power", comes from a school of thought known as "New Historicism". [28] This school emerged in the 1980s under the heavy influence of the French philosopher and historian, Michel Foucault (1926–1984), though the term "new historicism" stands today for a number of postmodern perspectives that focus on the ways race, class, and gender influence our knowledge of nature, history, and society. New Historicists question the whole notion that historians are driven by a sincere disposition to tell it "as it really was". Historical narratives in the Western world, they insist, are best viewed as social constructs enforced by dominant white heterosexual males who control the production of knowledge. They claim that we can rewrite the past more accurately by bringing out the "repressed" historical roles of "marginalized" groups. But if white males

---

27 These words are taken from Craig Brown, ed., *The Illustrated History of Canada* (Key Porter Books, 2000), p. 29.

28 See: Harold Aram Veeser, ed. *The New Historicism* (Routledge, 1989), and Catherine Gallagher, Stephen Greenblatt, *Practicing New Historicism* (University of Chicago Press, 2000). On the meaning of the term "disciplinary structures of knowledge and power", see Michael Arribas-Ayllon and Valerie Walkerdine, "Foucauldian Discourse Analysis", In: Willig, Carla and Stainton-Rogers, Wendy, eds., *The Sage Handbook of Qualitative Research in Psychology*, London: Sage, pp. 91-108.

did in fact play a dominant role in the making of Canada, why would "provincializing" their role be a more accurate rendition of history?

New Historicists can't have it both ways: claim, on the one hand, that there are no facts outside a dominant discourse (the "old historical narratives" are best seen as "mythological" accounts expressing the power of certain elites), while, on the other, claim that they are finally coming up with a "new historicist" discourse that is more accurate in its narrative because it reveals the "disciplinary structures of power". Are they more accurate because they are empirically bringing to light the actual roles of hitherto "marginalized" groups, or because they are politically "liberating" these groups from the oppression of dominant elites? In regards to the surveys of Canadian history I will be examining in the next chapters, we are dealing with historians who, unlike their social science colleagues, tend to avoid convoluted discussions about "discourses", even though they are loosely in agreement with the claim that past histories of Canada have ignored the roles of "marginalized" minorities. Even though they are not overtly political, these historians are still operating within the currently dominant multicultural discourse. They want to be "good citizens" working for, rather than against, a harmonious multicultural society in which, as the Government of Canada instructs them, "the value and dignity of all Canadian citizens regardless of their racial or ethnic origins, their language, or their religious affiliation" must be affirmed.[29] The thought of emphasizing the overwhelming influence of Anglo Canadians, or French Canadians in Quebec, strikes them as impolite and unwelcoming to their increasingly diversified students, never mind how white students may feel about having the history of their ancestors denied.

For some decades now, Canada's history is being re-written as a history of "diverse immigrants" with the Anglo and the French portrayed as immigrants no less than current immigrants. The true founders are the "First Nations" and everyone else, the Acadians, the Loyalists, the Irish and Scots, the British and Germans, are portrayed as immigrants not that much different from the West Indians, Haitians, Pakistanis, Filipinos, Sikhs, and Chinese who have been arriving in the last few decades. But we will see that, as much as current historians claim to

---

29   "Canadian Multiculturalism: An Inclusive Citizenship", Government of Canada, https://web.archive.org/web/20140312210113/http://www.cic.gc.ca/english/multiculturalism/citizenship.asp

be setting the historical record straight, the actual truth is that they are imposing a new dominant discourse that is less accurate than the old "white male" discourse. Over and above what the evidence allows, they are imposing a new image of the past intended to fit with the ideological requirement of a multiracial Canada. Much like Winston Smith, the central character in George Orwell's *1984*, historians today work in the Ministry of Truth, our universities, where they are paid to alter historical facts to fit the needs of the Multicultural Party.

In Chapters 2 to 5, we will see that this new discourse is a pure fabrication. The first generations of English and French speaking Canadians were hardly immigrants; rather, they were discoverers, pioneers, and settlers, mostly *indigenous* to Canada. Before Confederation only a minority of Canadians were immigrants, and after Confederation many Euro-Canadians were born in Canada, and the immigrants were really settlers.

2

A People Created Through the Fecundity of Women

Quebec's motto, which appears on the license plates of vehicles registered in Quebec, is *Je me souviens* ("I remember"). What the Quebecois remember, it is often said, is the English conquest and their determined struggle to maintain their identity in the face of relentless pressure to assimilate to English Canada. But deep down, or so I would say, what they actually remember is that New France was entirely their creation, that they are a unique people newly born in the soil of Quebec along the edges of the St. Lawrence river in the 1600s. They remember that they built themselves through their own natural procreation with minimal immigration.

The people remember — but the elites want them to forget. They want the Quebecois to cease identifying themselves as a unique race. They want them to remember only the French language. The treacherous elites now tell the Quebecois that their culture is about "diversity-born-in-immigration".

"The Revenge of the Cradles"

For two centuries, or from about 1670 to 1850, the Quebecois enjoyed fertility rates "nowhere to be found" in other Western nations. But starting in the 1960s, the fertility rates began a rapid decline, collapsing in the 1980s and 1990s, below replacement and below the Canadian national level. The old loyal elites, with the Catholic Church in the front lines, always believed that "strength in numbers" was the best strategy of French settlers to survive in an English continent. The Church was an ardent promoter of *la revanche des berceaux*, the revenge of the cradles, that is, a pronatalist strategy of survival.

This all ended in the early 1960s. Having reduced their sense of peoplehood to the French language alone, the current elites have been brainwashing the population into believing that the Quebecois are just one group among many "francophone" peoples in the world, one more country in a list of Muslim, Asian, African, and Caribbean nations where French is spoken.[1] Survival, they are now told, hinges on the importation of millions of French-speaking Haitians, Moroccans, and Algerians.

Defenders of Europeans in the world must remember that the Quebecois were a whole new people born in the soil of Canada, without much immigration. Jacques Cartier discovered and explored Canada's great arterial highway in the 1530s, the St. Lawrence, but New France really began when Samuel de Champlain planted the first permanent settlement at Quebec in 1608. Champlain was the first governor of New France vested by the French Monarchy with the authority to defend the colony, dispense justice, regulate the fur trade, and legislate.

By 1627, despite Champlain's appeal in 1617 to the French Chamber of Commerce to "undertake a major colonization program", and after almost 20 years of formal government, there were only 65 colonists in New France.[2] By 1645, the population was still only 400, and fifteen years later, in 1660, it had grown to 3,215 settlers spread tenuously along the edges of St. Lawrence River, of which approximately 1,250 were Canadian-born. Life was incredibly hard for these scattered settlers, threatened by constant Iroquois raids; France had to send them supplies to keep them alive.[3]

Efforts by France and the chartered companies had failed to entice French immigrants to settle in New France. In 1665, the Monarchy commissioned Jean Talon to find a way to increase the population of New France. In 1666, Talon conducted a census of New France, the first census conducted in North America. According to Talon's census, which showed that there were 3,215 people in New France,

---

1   See the Wikipedia entry on the "List of territorial entities where French is an official language", https://en.wikipedia.org/wiki/List_of_territorial_entities_where_French_is_an_official_language

2   W.J. Eccles, *France in America* (Harper and Row, 1972).

3   In coming up with these population numbers, and others to follow in the next paragraphs, I have relied on a number of sources with varying estimates, some of which will be cited in the next footnotes, including H.H. Herstein, L.J. Hughes, R.C. Kirbyson, *Challenge & Survival: The History of Canada* (Prentice-Hall, 1970). J.M. Bumsted, *Canada's Diverse Peoples* (ABC-CLIO, 2003), pp. 35-42. "Early French Settlements (1605-1695)" Statistics Canada, http://www.statcan.gc.ca/pub/98-187-x/4064812-eng.htm

there was a marked imbalance in the number of men at 2,034 versus 1,181 women. This Census also showed that there was a high number of unmarried settlers, and that the largest single age group consisted of 21- to 30-year-olds.[4]

With these facts at hand, Jean Talon devised a population policy that would lead to the creation of a distinctively *Canadien* people almost wholly native-born. First, he encouraged early marriages, gave baby bonuses, offered pensions to fathers of large families, and fined young men who refused to marry. Second, he called for France to send young healthy girls to New France to make up for the male-female imbalance. These policies were a success; by the time Jean Talon departed in 1672, a mere few years later, the population of New France had risen to about 6, 700.[5]

They were fortunate replenishing themselves with these fertile immigrant girls, "filles du roi"[6] (the King's Daughters), most of whom were married and pregnant within a year of arrival. After immigration reached a peak of 1,698 in the decade of 1660-1669, with the arrival of the filles du roi, it declined to an average of about 500 immigrants per decade up until 1750-59, when it increased to 1,751. Yet, despite this low influx of immigrants, the population continued to increase steadily; by the first years of 1700s, it has been estimated that the number of settlers along the Saint Lawrence and the Acadian peninsula was around 15,000 to 16,000. By 1730, it increased to 42,700, by 1754 to 55,000, and by the time of the conquest in 1763, the French-speaking population numbered about 70,000.[7]

---

4   See "Jean Talon, 1624-1694", *Statistics Canada*, http://www.statcan.gc.ca/pub/98-187-x/4064814-eng.htm

5   See "Early French Settlements (1605-1695)" Statistics Canada, http://www.statcan. gc.ca/pub/98-187-x/4064812-eng.htm Although the native born French as a proportion of immigrants really began to grow after the 1650s, Barbara Messamore misleads when she writes of the "arrival of six thousand or so French immigrants who formed the nucleus of New France by the 1650s", see "Introduction: Canada and Migration: Kinship with the World", in Messamore, ed., *Canadian Immigration Patterns From Britain and North America* (University of Ottawa Press (2004), p. 1.

6   Silvio Dumas, Les Filles du roi en Nouvelle-France. Étude historique avec répertoire biographique (Québec : Société historique de Québec, 1972).

7   For slightly different estimates, see Cole Harris and John Warkentin, *Canada Before Confederation: A Study in Historical Geography* (Oxford University Press, 1974). According to this book, in 1712, 20,000 people lived in French Canada; in 1739, 40,000 (p. 36).

Demographic Rise of a New White People

The total number of immigrants from the time of Samuel de Camplain's settlement at Quebec in 1608 up until the conquest in 1763 was only about 10,000. In other words, roughly speaking, immigration contributed one seventh (1/7) to the total population growth of New France from its beginning to its conquest. In Peter Moogk's words, "it was natural increase rather than migration that increased the white population of the St Lawrence valley sevenfold between 1681 and 1765". Moogk says that traditional estimations of the number of immigrants that arrived between 1608 and 1760 vary from just 12,000 to as low as 7500 immigrants.[8] In the words of a high school textbook published in 1970, when Canadians could still express themselves freely: "The population of New France…was almost wholly a native-born population and distinctly *Canadien*".[9]

After the conquest, Quebec saw the arrival of some American British loyalists and during the early 1800s a few thousand immigrants from England and Ireland arrived. The population continued to increase at an accelerating rate, to 113,012 by 1784 in Lower Canada, exploding to 335,000 by 1814 and to 890,000 by 1851.[10] This increase "was mainly attributable to the continuing high birth rate within the French-speaking community". From the 1660s through the 1800s, women in New France had 5.6 surviving children on average, 30 per cent more children than comparable women who remained in France.[11]

By 1950, the Quebec population was almost 4 million. While it is true that "by the early part of the 1900s, there had been some fertility declines, the fertility rate of Quebec still exceeded that of Canada by a notable margin" up until 1960.[12] Explaining this decline, however, is not the

---

8   Peter Moogk, "Emigrants from France in Canada before 1760", in Gerald Tulchinsky, ed., *Immigration in Canada. Historical Perspectives* (Copp Clark Longman, 1994), p. 9.

9   H.H Herstein, L.J. Hughes, and R.C. Kirbyson, *Challenge & Survival: The History of Canada* (Prentice Hall, 1970), p. 70.

10 "Demographic History of Quebec", https://en.wikipedia.org/wiki/Demographic_history_of_Quebec

11 Bumsted, *Canada's Diverse Peoples*, p. 42. See also, Georges Sabagh, "The Fertility of the French-Canadian Women during the Seventeenth Century", *American Journal of Sociology*, Vol. 47, No. 5, 1942.

12 Catherine Krull and Frank Trovato, "Where Have All the Children Gone? Quebec's Fertility Decline: 1941-1991", *Canadian Studies in Population* Vol. 30 (1), 2003

subject of this chapter. It is simply that Quebec was fundamentally created by a new people born through natural procreation. The current meme that Quebec was created by immigrants is a malicious act of deception intended to manipulate ordinary Quebecois into believing that the post 1960s high levels of immigration do not constitute an abrupt break with their history.

We must remember that the creation of Quebec through high fertility rates was a conscious plan of the once loyal authorities. From the first permanent settlement at Quebec in 1608 "until the early 1960s", as a recent demographic study says:

> Government officials and the Roman Catholic Church promoted an ideology of "strength in numbers", often referred to as la revanche des berceaux — the revenge of the cradles. Held to be a means to overcome Québecois subordination to English Canada, this pronatalist strategy was essentially successful. As Henripin and Peron (1972) have noted, between 1760 and 1960, despite losing approximately 800,000 people to emigration, French Canada's population multiplied 80 times. In the same period, the world's population increased only 4 times, while that of Europe grew just 5-fold. Moreover, Quebec's exceptional reproductive rates caused concern in English Canada, for "if the French continued to reproduce at the current rate, they would eventually overrun the country".[13]

The success of this domestic pronatalist policy was largely made possible by the simultaneous promotion of seigneurialism, the system of land distribution and land holding in New France. While the intention was to transplant to New France the feudal system of the mother country, this system developed in the colony along very different lines. The Crown granted a large tract of land to a seigneur, who would then subdivide the land into smaller parcels to tenant farmers in exchange for rents and services. The objective of the Crown was to encourage cultivation as well as orderly settlement by granting the seigneur with administrative, military, and judicial authority at the local level, justice over disputes between his tenants, or *habitants*, as they came to be known.

---

13   *Ibid.*

In contrast to France, these tenants enjoyed considerable rights and privileges, with very manageable rents, allowing them to prosper as long as they worked hard. Seigneurs could no lived off their rents in idleness but were obligated to cultivate their lands no less than the *habitants*, "many of them labouring beside their tenants".[14] The economic difference between these two classes was not significant. The image academic Marxists like to convey about oppressed *habitants* burdened with seigneurial dues is belied by the observations of contemporaries from France about the "spirit of independence", the "happy, cheerful", "very comfortable" lives of the *habitants*.

Obviously, hard work was a given; but overall the standard of living of the *habitants*, once they were settled with their farms, was reasonably good. They had a fairly varied diet consisting of cabbage, carrots, celery, beans, lettuce, peas and onions, with most houses having their own bread oven, a variety of animals, with cows giving them milk, butter and cheese; chickens and eggs, pigs and bacon, with nearby forests abounding with wild berries and wild animals.

This agrarian order was the foundation from which the *Canadiens* emerge as a new people right from the soil, through large families, traditional family values, hard work and self-reliance. This order is what made possible the high fertility rates of the Quebecois, which at one point brought fears to the English commercial elites in Montreal; who feared that if the French continued to reproduce at such high rate, "they would eventually overrun the country".

We are now a long way from this world. A newly released study by Charles Gaudreault has estimated that ethnic French Canadians will become a minority in their Quebec homeland by the year 2042. This demographic replacement has come at the behest of a traitorous elite determined to destroy the Quebecois as a people for the sake of an allegedly superior raced-mixed species without roots and loyalty to anyone other than to generic global corporations.[15]

---

14   Mason Wade, *The French Canadians, 1760-1945* (Macmillan, 1955), p. 35. The obligations of the seigneurs were exacting; as historian W. J. Eccles notes, "If a seigneur failed to settle censitaires on his land, and left it to a wilderness; if he failed to build a mill for the use of his tenants; or if he did not live on his seigneury himself, then his concession was taken away from him and given to someone else. On the other hand, if a censitaire failed to clear and cultivate the land allotted to him, he too lost his land". See *The Ordeal of New France* (The Canadian Broadcasting Corporation, 1969), p. 31.

15   Charles Gaudreault, "The impact of immigration on local ethnic groups' demographic representativeness: The case of ethnic French Canadians in Quebec". *Nations and*

University Texts on Canada's "Diverse" History

The current portrayal of Canada as a nation populated from the beginning by peoples from diverse cultures and racial backgrounds should be seen as nothing more than an act of deception orchestrated by academics in willful disregard of the historical evidence. Before the conquest, from Canada's origins up until the 1760s, immigrants played a very small role demographically in the making of Canada, not only in the case of the Quebecois, but in the case of the Acadians, as we shall soon see. These two ethnic groups were *indigenous* to the soil of North America. Native born Quebecois and Acadians were the main historical protagonists in the settlement of Canada for almost the first two hundred years.

Don't believe current historians who tell you that "New France was a multicultural society, with a considerable First Nations population and an African community". This is the message advocated by one of the most widely used texts in Canadian universities, consisting of two volumes, *Origins: Canadian History to Confederation*, and *Destinies: Canadian History since Confederation*, by Richard Jones and Donald B. Smith.[16] This very successful two volume text, now in its seventh edition,[17] claims that it is a major improvement over "the older texts" in incorporating "new historical research" and in showing that "anyone seeking to understand our diversity today must first examine the pre-Confederation era".[18]

Needless to say, Amerindians were the first inhabitants of territories that came to be identified as "Canada" through the establishment of French

---

Nationalism (Vol. 26, Issue 4: 2019). For one example of countless publications and bulletins promoting the blessings of diversifying Quebec's school, see: https://durhamcatholic.wordpress.com/2015/04/20/students-at-st-wilfrid-catholic-school-journey-back-in-time-to-learn-about-new-france/

16   Richard Jones and Donald B. Smith, *Origins: Canadian History to Confederation* (Harcourt Canada, Fourth Edition, 2000) and *Destinies: Canadian History since Confederation* (Harcourt Canada, Third Edition, 1996).

17   I am using the fourth edition of *Origins*, and the third edition of *Destinies* because these are the copies I have in my great library at home and the university office. I compared these two editions to the newer editions and no changes have been made regarding the points I bring up about diversity and immigration. Actually, these issues have been accentuated insofar as the newer editions bring up recent years in Canada's glorious diversification. Note: in all subsequent citations of these two texts, I will simply mention the short titles, *Origins* and *Destinies,* with the page number.

18   *Origins*, pp. 108, viii.

and Anglo institutions during the 1600s to 1800s. But the "first peoples", the Hurons, Algonquins, Cree, Iroquois, and others, were organized in tribes spread over territories that can in no way be identified as part of "Canada" before Europeans arrived. Indian territories were actually contiguous with the United States rather than neatly located within Canada. Only in retrospect, through the European science of geography, can Amerindian territories be demarcated in the continent of North America for pedagogical instruction, but not as actually existing tribal nations with definite geographical boundaries, since none of these tribes were organized as nations with marked boundaries.

European geographers, not the Amerindians, have classified the natives of Canada in terms of six cultural areas, "Northwest Coast", "Plateau", "Plains", "Subarctic", "Arctic", and "Northeast". Amerindians had an intimate knowledge of the land, the soil, migration pathways of animals, weather, location of rivers, lakes, mountains, upon which the first European settlers and fur traders relied for survival. It was the Europeans, however, who mapped these territories and eventually created our modern institutions from the ground up.[19]

It is extremely anachronistic and misleading to tell students that these tribal groups were members of a multicultural Canada. The French and English, for one, inhabited separate cultural lives, and in respect to the Amerindians, they inhabited totally different worlds. Their interactions with Amerindians are best described as interactions between separate peoples, commercial and military interactions, which affected both sides, but which essentially involved the modernizing encroachment of the Anglo-French side upon the Amerindian cultures, leading to a situation in which, by the time of Confederation in 1867, only 1 percent of the population of Canada was Amerindian. This reduction was of course tragic for the Aboriginals. But we can acknowledge their distinctive heritage only by identifying them as a separate people,

---

19 Some academics today are confusing some geographical diagrams Native Americans prepared in their encounters with the Europeans with "the making of maps" itself, even speaking of a science of "cartography". See *Cartographic Encounters, Perspectives on Native American Mapmaking and Map Use*, ed., G. Malcolm Lewis (Chicago University Press, 1998). Yet, when one reads Lewis's own chapter contribution to this book, we learn that "Evidence of maps that were made largely independent of European influence, however slender, consists of rock art and man-made structures such as mounds, representing mainly celestial and cosmographical subjects" (p. 51). Properly speaking, this cannot be identified as mapmaking and certainly not as cartography, which is a science.

instead of falsely assimilating them into a "multicultural Canada" as co-creators of a nation that only became multicultural in 1971. It is outlandish for *Origins* and *Destinies* to tell students that "in 1867" the Natives peoples were one of the three "major groups" that made up "Canada's multicultural society".[20] How can one percent of the population living in "lands reserved for Indians" — to use the official designation of the British North America Act — be identified as a "major" cultural group in Canada, equal to the French and the British, which made up 92 percent of the population?

The historians of these volumes want to have it both ways: an image of a European Canada that "decimated" the Natives through diseases, and an image of "First Nations" as co-partners in the creation of Canada's parliamentary institutions, legal system, schools and universities, churches, and modern economy. They want students to believe that the Natives were the "first peoples", followed by the French and English, as the next two "major groups", followed by the arrival of "non-British and non-French immigrants", as a fourth major group. This fourth group is portrayed as a multiracial lot, even though the statistics contradict any such picture.

The facts about the ethnic composition of immigrants, which this text cannot hide altogether, show that, at the time of Confederation, the English constituted about 60 percent of the population, the French 30 percent, and the remaining "non-British and non-French immigrants" about 7 percent.[21] The non-British and non-French were all whites from Europe and the United States.

There was no "considerable" African community in New France. The facts stated in *Origins*, which are the only facts that can be legitimately used, contradict this contrived interpretation: from its origins to 1759, only about 1,200 African slaves were brought to New France.[22] Another source says that "from 1681 to 1818 there were approximately 4100 slaves in French Canada, representing less than one per cent of the population".[23]

---

20 *Destinies*, p. 1

21 *The Making of the Mosaic*, p. 115.

22 *Origins*, p. 111.

23 Kenneth Donovan, "Slaves and their Owners in Ile Royale, 1713-1760", *Acadiensis*, XXV (1), 1995.

The facts *Origins* has to rely on, since they are the only historically documented facts, contradict not only its claim that Canada was created by diverse racial groups but also the claim that the Europeans generally were "immigrants". In the case of New France (and let us not forget that the history of New France is basically the history of Canada up until 1763), the text offers a detailed table on the number of French immigrants "by decade" from 1608 to 1759, from which we learn that the total number of immigrants throughout this period was only 8,527.[24] By contrast, the population of New France in 1759 was about 60,000. These numbers are consistent with the numbers I offered in the previous chapter.

Since the French were the first Canadians, and the English proportion in Canada as a whole, before the Conquest of 1763, was scattered and incidental, it behooves us to conclude, on the basis of the above numbers, that immigrants played a minimal role from the time Samuel de Champlain planted the first permanent settlement at Quebec in 1608 up until 1763. This odd combination of interpretative pronouncements (French Canada was created by immigrants from diverse ethnicities) standing in direct contradiction to the actual facts (all the inhabitants were French and most were newly born in the soil of New France) can only be explained by what George Orwell designated as the practice of "CRIMESTOP" or "the power of not grasping analogies, of failing to perceive logical errors, of misunderstanding the simplest arguments if they are inimical to Ingsoc". Alan Simmons, to give another example, tells us that "by the end of the 1700s...only 12,000 immigrants in total had been attracted to New France".[25] If we take the year of 1790 as the point of measurement, when the population of Canada had ballooned to about 191,000, we have to conclude that only about 15.9 percent of the population had been made up by immigrants. Yet Simmons persists in saying that "with the exception of Native peoples" all Canadians are immigrants or descendants of immigrants. Why not say that most are descendants of a newly created people that first came to be known as "original *Canadiens*"?[26]

---

24   *Origins*, P. 93.

25   Alan Simmons, *Immigration and Canada, Global and Transnational Perspectives* (Canadian Scholar's Press, 2010), p. 52.

26   Henri Bourassa (1868-1952) was right observing in 1902: "How thoroughly and exclusively Canadian the French-Canadian is should never be forgotten by those who contemplate any change in the constitutional or national status of Canada...As a matter of fact, he constitutes the only exclusively Canadian racial group in the Dominion. A

The Acadians

This point can be further accentuated through a consideration of the Acadians. In the calculation of the demographic history of French Canadians, the Acadians are sometimes included without a clear identification of their own demographic identity. The Acadians were another newly created people in the soil of America, not in present day Quebec, but in the maritime part of New France, or in the province of present day Nova Scotia.

The beginnings of the Acadians closely resembles that of the Quebecois; they too began as a small colony of men and wooden buildings constructed in Port Royal in 1605 by Champlain, but these colonists were forced to return to France in 1607. In 1611, 20 new colonists, including a family, were brought back to Acadie, but this settlement failed as well. It was only in 1651 that a demographic dynamic was set in Acadie, when about 50 families, or about 500 settlers, were brought in. After 1671, 40 more families were recruited from France, leading to a population of 800+ by 1686.[27] By 1710, there were around 2,000 Acadians, "most of them born in North America".[28] The text *Origins* informs us that the "average Acadian couple usually married in their early twenties and had ten or eleven children, most of whom survived to adulthood".[29]

Without any more French immigration, "the Acadian population multiplied by nearly 30 times between 1671 and 1755". By 1750, "there were more than 10,000", and "in 1755, more than 13,000 (excluding Louisbourg)".[30] J.M. Bumsted tells us that Louisbourg's Acadian population was 3,500 in the 1750s.[31]

---

constant immigration from the British Isles has kept the English-speaking Canadian in close contact with their motherlands; so that even now they still speak of the 'Old Country' as their 'home', thus keeping in their hearts a double allegiance. On the soil of Canada, his only home and country, all the national aspirations of the French Canadian are concentrated. 'Canadian' is the only national designation he ever claims; and when he calls himself 'French-Canadian', he simply wants to differentiate his racial group from that of his English, Scotch, or Irish fellow citizens, who, in his mind, are but partially *Canadianised*". Henri Bourassa, "The French-Canadian in the British Empire", in H.D. Forbes, ed., *Canadian Political Thought* (Oxford University Press, 1985), pp. 177-8.

27   Sally Ross, *The Acadians of Nova Scotia* (Hignell Printing, 1992).

28   J.M. Bumsted, *Canada's Diverse Peoples* (ABC CLIO, 2003), p. 39.

29   *Origins*, p. 140.

30   *Origins*, pp. 141-44.

31   J.M. Bumsted, *A History of the Canadian Peoples* (Oxford University Press, 2011), p. 67.

The British gained control of Acadia in 1713, and in 1749 some 2,500 British Americans were recruited, and then in 1750-51 about 1,500 German Protestants settled at Lunenburg. This population, however, has not been counted in the above Francophone numbers. We will be writing about British immigration/birth rate patterns in later chapters.

In the context of a full-scale war between France and Britain, and the refusal of the Acadians to give a formal pledge of loyalty to the British rulers in Acadia, in 1755-58 the British deported about three-quarters of the Acadian population. By 1762, they had expelled another 3,000. However, in 1764, the British allowed about 3,000 Acadians to resettle back in Nova Scotia, and by 1800 the Acadians numbered 4,000.

It should be noted that in the 1740s there were about 700 Acadians in Prince Edward Island (PEI), then known as Île St-Jean, and categorized as part of Acadia (Nova Scotia). In 1757, approximately 2,000 Acadians had fled to PIE as refugees, which increased the population to about 4,500, but the British expelled many of these Acadians in 1758. A census of 1803 showed a population of nearly 700 in PEI. In New Brunswick, a territory carved out of former Nova Scotia in 1784, there was a population of 4,000 Acadians in 1803, a "result of high birth rates rather than the return of more exiles".[32]

The conclusion we must reach is quite self-evidential: the Acadians began as a small group of immigrant families, only to grow into a people with blood ties firmly set in Acadia, through a very high fertility rate, with its own unique Francophone identity, with speech patterns quite different from the Quebecois, in a very harsh environment that required the harvesting of salt from the salt marshes, the clearing of forested uplands, the building of dikes to reclaim land from the Bay of Fundy's strong tides; yet establishing themselves with a "far higher standard of living than all but the most privileged French peasants",[33] coupled with a spirit of independence and refusal to submit to external authorities, which led to their expulsion, though not their demise, constituting today about 11,000+ in Nova Scotia, and 25,000 in New Brunswick.

---

32   *Origins*, p. 153; Bumsted, 2011, p. 109.

33   R. Cole Harris, John Warkentin, *Canada Before Confederation: A Study on Historical Geography* (Oxford University Press, 1974), p. 30.

The claim that Acadians were just immigrants no less different to the making of Canada than Sri Lankan Tamils, corrupt Chinese real estate millionaires[34], and Somalis[35] is patently absurd, a discreditable claim that only academics out of touch with historical reality would make, shamelessly unburdened by their determination to downplay the fact that native born whites were responsible for founding the nation of Canada, rather than "diverse immigrants".

---

34 "In Vancouver, there are lots of kids of corrupt Chinese officials. Here, they can flaunt their money" *Calgary Herald*, (April 13, 2016).

35 "Why so many Somali-Canadians who go west end up dead" *Globe and Mail* (June 22, 2012).

3

Canada Anglicized and Whitened

The Loyalists Were Not Immigrants but British-Canadian Founders, 1763-1815

We have seen that up until the British Conquest of New France in 1763, the vast majority of Canadians were francophone, Quebecois and Acadians, born in the soil of North America. The total number of immigrants who came to Quebec and Acadia, from the first settlements Samuel Champlain established in the first decade of the 1600s until 1763, was very small. In Quebec, only 8,527 immigrants arrived during this entire period (from 1608 to 1759). In Acadia, a few hundred settlers arrived in the first half of the seventeenth century, and thereafter it was the high fertility rates of Acadians that gave birth to a *native* population of roughly 13,000 by the 1750s.

How about the role of immigrants from "diverse" places after the Conquest? Was not the English-speaking Canada that emerged after the Conquest, in Ontario and Nova Scotia, created by immigrants "from many ethnic backgrounds", as standard college textbooks religiously inform their students today?

The immigration time line from 1760 to 1815, which is the subject of this chapter, and which includes the Loyalists as the principal new settlers in Canada, can only be categorized as a period of "many new diverse immigrants" through the manipulation of words.

What this period actually witnessed was:

1. a massive growth in the population of Quebec through the continuation of high fertility rates with zero francophone immigration, and minimal arrival of British individuals.

2. an internal migration of New Englanders and Loyalists from

some regions of British North America to other regions of British North America, principally to Upper Canada and Nova Scotia. Both New Englanders and Loyalists were long established native born British settlers in the American colonies, not immigrants.

3. the arrival of immigrants from the British Isles (with the exception of some whites from Germany) should also be identified as movement by internal migrants, from the British Isles to other British lands.

1. The English population in New France/Quebec numbered about 500 in 1765. When the British conquered Quebec they anticipated that significant English-speaking families would move from the British American colonies to the British Canadian colonies. They hoped that in this way Quebec would be gradually Protestantized and Anglicized. But only "a few hundred English-speaking, Protestant immigrants, largely merchants" had arrived by 1774.[1] The number of English has been estimated at 2000 in 1780. In the 1780s, a few thousand Loyalists did arrive. There are no precise estimations as to how many Loyalists settled in Quebec proper, rather than what would become Upper Canada or Ontario, which was carved out from the western side of New France in 1791. In any case, when this partition occurred, the English population in Quebec proper, or Lower Canada, was about 10,000. Meanwhile, the total non-Aboriginal population of Quebec in 1791 had increased substantially since the Conquest from about 70,000 to about 160,000.

Now, assuming that all the 10,000 English speaking inhabitants were immigrants, we can safely say that Quebec's francophone population increased by 150,000 souls through a high fertility rate without any immigration. It has been estimated that the English population in Lower Canada/Quebec reached 30,000 by 1812. The francophone population, meanwhile, increased to 335,000 by 1814. Again, assuming that the 30,000 English speakers were all immigrants (hardly the case, since after the Loyalist influx of the 1780s there was little immigration from the English world), it follows that the history of one of the two founding peoples of Canada, the Quebecois, was a history without any significant immigration from 1608 up until 1814.

Between 1758 and 1762, before the arrival of the Loyalists, about 7000 to 8000 New England "Planters" settled in Nova Scotia in the lands

---

1   *Origins*, p. 184.

previously occupied by the Acadians who had been expelled in the 1750s. But half of these Planters left within a few years, finding Nova Scotia too scarce in resources and good lands. These New Englanders were British-Americans who moved from one British-ethnic land (New England) to another British-ruled land (Nova Scotia), which was fast becoming Anglicized after the expulsion of Acadians.

2. The estimated number of Loyalists who came to Canada has been estimated at 50,000. Taking into account natural increases, the Loyalist population by 1811 is said to have numbered about 60,000. About 14,500 Loyalists went to the new territory of New Brunswick, which was partitioned from Nova Scotia in 1784. About the same number went to Nova Scotia, 400 to Cape Breton, and some 500 to PEI. Roughly about 14,000 Loyalists went to Lower and Upper Canada, mostly to the latter territory, during the 1780s and 1790s.[2]

The popular textbook, *Origins: Canadian History to Confederation,* refers to the Loyalists as immigrants who came "from many ethnic backgrounds".[3] It notes that "as many as 500" "black Loyalists"[4] were brought to Upper Canada and some 3000 to Nova Scotia. *A History of the Canadian Peoples*, by Bumsted, likewise refers to the Loyalists as "quite a disparate group" that included "well over 3000 blacks", as well as 2000 Aboriginal "loyalists", who settled in Upper Canada.[5] He notes, though, that nearly half of the blacks soon emigrated to Africa.

It cannot be denied, as the text *Origins* eventually admits, the "overwhelming majority of the Loyalists were *white*". Even if we were to accept the rather wishful claim that blacks and Aboriginals were "Loyalists" (American colonists who remained loyal to the British Crown during the American Revolutionary War), the total non-white proportion was only 7 percent.

---

2   For these facts and numbers, I am relying on standard texts and books already cited here by Bumsted, and by R. Douglas Francis, Richard Jones, and Donald B. Smith, as well as by J.M.S. Careless, *Canada: A Story of Challenge* (St Martin's Press, 1965), including Peter Marshall's "American in Upper Canada, 1791-1812: 'Late Loyalists' or Early Immigrants?" in Barbara Messamore, ed., *Canadian Immigration Patterns From Britain and North America* (University of Ottawa Press (2004), p. 34. See also the informative entry "Loyalists" in *The Canadian Encyclopedia*, http://www. thecanadianencyclopedia.ca/en/article/loyalists/

3   *Origins*, p. 233.

4   *Origins*, p. 237.

5   *A History of the Canadian Peoples*, 2011, p. 101

Moreover, it is more accurate to identify Loyalists as "internal migrants" rather than immigrants, since they actually moved from colonies that were thoroughly British to territories ruled by Britain that were becoming, Nova Scotia and Upper Canada, increasingly Anglicized. It was essentially a movement by Brits "between regions" of the British world of North America.[6]

Some may reply that this argument only holds for the New England "Planters" but not for the Loyalists, since the Loyalists were leaving the newly independent American lands of post-1776. They were Americans rather than British. But this is not a good argument for a number of crucially deciding reasons: First, the Americans were not only a new people created in the soil of North America, but they were still racially and culturally British, and, secondly, the Loyalists were called "Loyalist" precisely because they remained loyal to British rule, rather than American rule in the thirteen colonies. Thirdly, as Carl Berger has persuasively shown in his much admired work, *The Sense of Power: Studies in the Ideas of Canadian Imperialism*, the descendants of loyalists were the one ethnic group that nurtured "an indigenous British Canadian feeling". The following passage is worth citing:

The centennial arrival of the loyalists in Ontario coincided with the fiftieth anniversary of the incorporation of the City of Toronto and, during a week filled with various exhibitions, July 3 was set aside as 'Loyalist Day.' On the morning of that day the platform erected at the Horticultural Pavilion was crowded with civic and ecclesiastical dignitaries and on one wall hung the old flag presented in 1813 to the York Militia by the ladies of the county. Between stirring orations on the significance of the loyalist legacy, injunctions to remain faithful to their principles, and tirades against the ancient foe, patriotic anthems were sung and nationalist poetry recited. 'Rule Britannia' and If England to Herself Be True were rendered 'in splendid style' and evoked 'great enthusiasm.' 'A Loyalist Song,' 'Loyalist Days,' and 'The Maple Leaf Forever,' were all beautifully sung.[7]

---

6   I am using the *Oxford Dictionary of Sociology* (1998) definition of "internal migration" as a movement between regions as opposed to "external migration (between countries)".

7   Carl Berger, *The Sense of Power: Studies in the Ideas of Canadian Imperialism* (university of Toronto, [1970] 2013), pp. 78-9.

Connected to this point, it should be noted that before Confederation most immigrants from the British Isles were Irish (850,000), not English (300,000). It was only between 1900 and 1930 that English immigrants (1.6 million) surpassed the Irish (175,000).[8] It can be argued, accordingly, that the Loyalists, an indigenous people of British ethnicity born in the soil of British North America and Canada, played a most important role in giving Canada its national Anglo identity.

3. Regarding immigrants from the British Isles, the texts I have examined don't always provide consistently precise numbers, but indicate only that from 1790 to 1815 immigrants from the "British Isles" came to Upper Canada, mainly from the Scottish Highlands and Ireland. One estimate has it that between 6000 and 10,000 immigrants came in the early 1800s from the Highland to the Maritimes and Upper Canada. Another text says that in the 1760s and 1770s Nova Scotia saw some 2000 settlers arrived from Ireland, 750 from England, and, in 1773, 200 Scots.

Before these immigrants from the Isles, Nova Scotia saw the arrival of some 1500 German Protestants in the early 1750s. Taking into account these immigrants, Bumsted portrays Nova Scotia in the late 1760s, that is, before the arrival of the Loyalists, as a land characterized by ethnic and religious diversity.[9] He sees the arrival of Loyalists as adding more to this diversity, with the "black Loyalists". But we already saw that Blacks were a very small proportion of the total population, and that the Americans, both the New England "Planters" and the Loyalists, were "white" internal migrants.

It can also be added that the immigrants from the Isles were all English-speaking, very closely related genetically and culturally, moving from the British Isles to an increasingly Anglicized Nova Scotia and a newly-created Anglicized Upper Canada. The Acadians added, and I suppose all the different groups did as well, an *intra-European* ethnic diversity, a French-British diversity combined with some German Aryans.

---

8   Bruce Elliot, "Regional Patterns of English Immigration and Settlement in Upper Canada", in Barbara Messamore, ed., *Canadian Immigration Patterns From Britain and North America* (University of Ottawa Press (2004), p. 53.

9   *A History of the Canadian Peoples*, 2011, p. 86

The most reasonable conclusion we can reach about immigration patterns in Canada's history from 1763 to 1815 is that it was an internal migration movement within a British world in mainland North America, and across the Atlantic from the British Isles to British North America. The demographic growth that Upper Canada experienced from the 1760s, when it was barely populated by Europeans, to 1815, was quite substantial, from 14,000 inhabitants in 1791, to 70,718 in 1806, to 95,000 in 1814. The Loyalists undoubtedly played a key role in this demographic expansion. American inhabitants, or Canadians with American ancestry, made up about 80 percent of the population of 136,000 in Upper Canada, in 1812, for example. It is no exaggeration to say that the Loyalists were the original founders of Ontario, and the original internal migrants who did the most in the introduction of British culture and political institutions to Canada.

Similarly, in Nova Scotia, immigration from the British Isles, and internal migration from British/America contributed, to the demographic growth of Nova Scotia after the expulsion of the Acadians. We will see below that immigration from the British Isles was to increase substantially after 1815, and that these immigrants are best identified as pioneers or settlers. Outside the francophone communities, Anglo pioneers were creating a world of Canadian Anglo ethnicity, British rule of law, language, and religions, not a world of multiple cultures and races.

Immigration from 1815 to 1867: Did Immigrants from the British Isles Increase Canada's Diversity?

It was in the period from 1815 to 1867 that Canada finally saw "large scale immigration" when an estimated 1 million immigrants arrived. This scale of immigration did play a significant role in the "phenomenal growth in population" witnessed during this period, from 600,000 to more than 3.5 million inhabitants. However, outside Quebec, Canada was Anglicized, not diversified; and, inside Quebec, immigration had no impact.

Two key points must be made about this first period of large scale immigration to Canada.

1. Lower Canada or Quebec saw a negligible number of immigrants, and yet the population of this francophone region increased

tremendously, from 335,000 in 1814 to 553,000 in 1831 to 1.12 million in 1861.[10] This increase was driven overwhelmingly by the high fertility rate of the racially homogeneous francophone population. It should be noted that this increase occurred in spite of the emigration of a high number of francophones to the United States: more than 40,000 in the 1830s, 90,000 in the 1840s, and 190,000 in the 1850s.

2. The overwhelming number of immigrants between 1815 and 1867 came from the British Isles and so instead of increasing Canada's diversity "they made the North American colonies more British than they had ever been before", to use the apt words of J.M.S. Careless, who narrated history as it was suggested by the evidence, in his book, *Canada: A Story of Challenge*, first published in 1959, before history was thoroughly polluted by cultural Marxism.[11]

Yet, despite this solid evidence, J.M. Bumsted, possibly the foremost current historian of Canada,[12] interprets immigration between 1815 and 1867 as an experience that reinforced the diversification of Canada. The immigrants who came from the British Isles, he says, did not come from a "homogeneous anglophone group of people". Britain was a nation of diverse dialects, religions, and historic minorities, and this was manifested in the people who moved from the Isles to Canada.

Through this period of immigration, he observes, there was a strong Irish presence, ranging from 30 to 70 per cent of the total number of arrivals, many speaking "the Irish tongue", and, after the mid-1840s, "huge numbers of Catholics" were included among these Irish immigrants. There were also Scottish immigrants, amounting to 10-15 percent of the total throughout this period, almost all of them speaking Gaelic as a first language. Immigrants also originated from other "dialects and linguistic variants" and "distinctive regions" within England proper and "distinctive peoples in Wales".[13]

---

10 "Demographic History of Quebec" https://en.wikipedia.org/wiki/Demographic_history_of_Quebec

11 J.M.S. Careless, *Canada: A Story of Challenge* (St Martin's Press, 1965), p. 147.

12 There is "an inventory of his papers at The University of Manitoba Archives and Special Collections", https://umanitoba.ca/libraries/units/archives/collections/complete_holdings/ead/html/Bumsted_07.shtml

13 *A History of the Canadian Peoples*, 2011, p. 134

Bumsted wants to imprint upon students the idea that this internal-British diversity was in line with the diversity Canada is currently experiencing, when peoples of very different races, totally different religions and cultures, are arriving in the millions. But one has to wonder if he believes, then, that all European nations, not just Canada, were uniquely diverse from the beginning insofar as they were not "homogeneous" but were populated by people with different dialects, regional customs and folkways, which was the case before the standardization of national languages and the full integration of regions through modern communications in the nineteenth century.

Take France, for example: late into the 1800s, regional dialects such as Breton, Gascon, Basque, Catalan, Flemish, Alsatian, and Corsican, prevailed across the nation, notwithstanding France's reputation as a nation centralized since the absolutist days of Louis XIV or the French Revolution. Different folkways, heroes, provincial loyalties superseded any notion of a homogeneous nation before 1900.[14] Are we to conclude that France was also uniquely multicultural (and immigrant) from its origins?

Bumsted does not ponder over these questions. All academics are for diversity, and diversity academics avoid any question that threatens their mirages. The rationale underlying Bumsted's argument about Britain's inherent diversity is now standard fare among the promoters of immigration in both the settler nations of America and Australia and the nations of Europe at large. Deceptive academics and politicians are exploiting the presence of different dialects, ethnic minorities, and different Christian denominations in the past to push onto unsuspecting students the notion that these nations have always been diversely shaped by migratory waves of peoples from all over the world.[15] The sudden arrival of millions of Muslims and Africans to England, France, Italy, Sweden...is nothing to be alarmed about, so

---

14   Eugen Weber, *Peasants into Frenchmen: The Modernization of Rural France, 1870-1914* (Stanford University Press, 1976).

15   Dianne Abbot, a black British Labour Party politician who was appointed as Shadow Home Secretary in October 2016, has indeed argued in an article for BBC, "Multiracial Britain", that England was a multiracial society from its beginnings, never uniquely white British, while at the same insisting that if the British are to overcome their imperial legacy they must overcome their past racial homogeneity and open their borders to African migrants. http://www.bbc.co.uk/history/british/modern/dabbott_01.shtml

they tell naive white girls[16]; it is consistent with the ethnic histories of these nations.

Canada's Britishness: Genetic and Cultural

In the same chapter that Bumsted deals with this large scale immigration, there is a concluding inbox with the subheading "How History Has Changed", in which students are informed that one of the most important changes in the writing of Canada's history is the detailed research historians now give to immigration. Right.[17] A few decades ago, before the 1970s, historians wrote about immigration as one factor among many others without losing track of the inescapable reality that Canada was founded by the French and English.

Bumsted tries to create the impression that due to "recent research" we can't "assume" any longer that these British immigrants came from a "homogeneous" Britain, as if the English, Welsh, Irish, and Scots were unaware of their differences, and as if anyone has ever said that the British Isles were not diverse in dialects, regional identities, and religious beliefs. What new research is revealing, actually, which the academic world is hiding from students, is that all these groups from the Isles have a common genetic background. The genetic makeup of Britain has barely changed in the last 1400 years; its ancestral people consisted basically of different Celtic populations and Anglo-Saxons, with a bit of Viking blood.[18] There is no genetic similarity between this

---

16   Spencer Quinn, "The Battle of Britain: The Muslim Mass-Rape of British Women and Girls" in *Counter Currents* (May 24, 2016). This is a review article of Peter McLoughlin's book, *Easy Meat: Inside Britain's Grooming Gang Scandal* (New English Review, 2016).

17   *A History of the Canadian Peoples*, 2011, p. 163.

18   Recent years have seen an incessant campaign to instill on British people the notion that they are immigrants just like the Africans and Muslims. The fake *New York Times* (March 9, 2017) announced that "Britain is an immigrant nation". This article, by Rachel Shabi, deceitfully equates the migratory flows of Vikings, Romans, Normans, and French Huguenots, in the 17th century with the immigration patterns today. Yet the scientific evidence has been mounting over the last few years showing the exact opposite. A paper, "The fine-scale genetic structure of the British population" (*Nature*, vol. 519, 2015), reports that there has been very little genetic structure (differentiation) within the native British population. Only in the 20th century has the migratory flow increased substantially: "Between 1900 and 1950, the foreign-born fraction of the population rose, but never exceeded 5%. By the early 1990s, it was well above 5%. In 2011, it was around 13%. And today, it is probably above 15%. Thus, contemporary levels of immigration into Britain are historically unprecedented". Moreover, the genetic impact of the Normans and French Huguenots on the British-Celtic stock was negligible: "Estimates for the fraction of the population that Normans comprised,

ancestral population and the immigrants arriving in the millions now.

The "large scale immigration" between 1815 and 1867 (really up to 1850) did not reinforce Canada's diversity, but instead ensured the Anglicization of Canada, the further development of British forms of government. One of the important historical happenings of this period was the emergence of "responsible government". In 1830, Canada saw an executive that was responsible to an elected legislative assembly, with laws and taxes levied through the support of the elected assembly; and then, by 1848, an executive that was governed by the leader of the party that held a majority in the elected legislative assembly, a leader who would also choose the members of the executive council or cabinet from the elected assembly.

While the French continued to increase as homogeneous as ever, reaching over 1 million by the 1860s, the rest of Canada, concentrated in Upper Canada, became more Anglo, in the strong racial sense, notwithstanding the secondary differences between the Scots, Irish, and Brits.

To this French-Anglo racial stock was added a strong dose of Germanic blood, as thousands of Germans also arrived in this period, so that, by 1871, about 203,000 persons in Canada were identified as German in origin, 6 percent of the population. Meanwhile, the combined number of blacks, Aboriginals, and Asians amounted to less than 2 percent, declining in relative numbers, and thus demonstrating that Canada's first large scale immigration made the country whiter and more Anglo, rather than more diverse.

---

following the Norman conquest in 1066, range from 1% to around 5%.
Between 1066 and the turn of the 20th century, it is unlikely that the foreign-born fraction of the population ever exceeded 2%. French Huguenots, for example, are unlikely to have constituted more than 1% of the population". In another article which sums up these new findings we learn that the contribution of Romans and Vikings to the genetics of Britain was also marginal: "The Romans, Vikings and Normans may have ruled or invaded the British for hundreds of years, but they left barely a trace on our DNA, the first detailed study of the genetics of British people has revealed. The analysis shows that the Anglo-Saxons were the only conquering force, around 400-500 AD, to substantially alter the country's genetic makeup, with most white British people now owing almost 30% of their DNA to the ancestors of modern-day Germans". See, "Genetic Study Reveals 30% of white British DNA has German ancestry" *The Guardian* (March 18, 2015). Peter Donnelly, in "The Secret History of Britain is written in our genes", *The Telegraph* (March 20, 2015), reports on the "remarkable local stability of the British population over many centuries", but in obedience to PC dictates he adds "that everyone descends, at some point or other, from migrants to these shores". By this definition everyone is an immigrant, which would make this term worthless for historical analysis.

Atlantic Provinces: Immigration
1815-1867, and Today

"The Atlantic provinces" include the four smallest provinces of Canada: Nova Scotia, New Brunswick, Prince Edward Island, and Newfoundland. Barely anyone outside Canada knows a thing about these provinces. These lands stand out as part of the ever shrinking areas of the world still very white, though the elites have targeted them for relentless diversification.

According to the Canada 2006 census, Prince Edward Island (PEI) is 97.4 percent white. The total non-Aboriginal visible minority population is 1.4 percent. The Aboriginal population is 1.3 percent. The largest ethnic groups, according to a 2011 National Survey,[19] are of "British Isles origins" (Scottish, English, and Irish), followed by French and other Europeans.

The same 2006 census informs us that Nova Scotia is 93.2 percent white. This racial situation has remained almost the same according to a 2011 census: the population grew by only 0.9 percent, and 91.8% of the population reported English only as mother tongue, 3.4% reported French only, and only 4.1% reported a non-official language.[20]

New Brunswick, where I have lived for the past 22 years, is 95.7 white. The total Aboriginal population is 2.5 percent, and the total visible minority is 1.9 percent. The situation in this province has barely changed in racial composition since these numbers were collected in the 2006 census. If we go by mother tongue, the 2011 Canadian census showed a population in which the most commonly reported mother tongues were English (65.58%) and French (31.98%).[21]

Newfoundland (and Labrador) is 94.2 white. The total Aboriginal population is 4.7 percent, and the visible minority population is 1.1 percent. This situation has barely changed since the 2006 census.

---

19   "Prince Edward Island 41 St Annual Statistical Review 2014", http://www.gov.pe.ca/photos/original/2014statsreview.pdf

20   http://www12.statcan.gc.ca/census-recensement/2011/as-sa/fogs-spg/Facts-pr-eng.cfm?Lang=Eng&GC=12

21   New Brunswick, of course, with its Acadian population, was not Anglicized in the same degree.

So, given these white facts in the Maritimes, how is it possible for current historians of Canada to claim that this region was created by ethnically heterogeneous immigrants since the early 1600s through the next centuries until the present? Answer: By manipulating words, employing deceptive images, and misusing the evidence.

Let's look at Nova Scotia first. We saw earlier that the Acadians were the original founders of Nova Scotia, a people born in the soil of Nova Scotia through their love of big families. We saw that before their expulsion in the mid-1750s they constituted the majority of the population.

In 1767, when a detailed census was taken, after the arrival of some 1500 Germans in 1749-50, some 2500 British Americans in 1749, and about 7000 to 8000 New England "Planters" between 1758 and 1762, the ethnic composition of the part that became Nova Scotia proper in 1784 (leaving aside the relatively few inhabitants of the part that became New Brunswick, though including the population of Cape Breton, which for some years was identified as separate from Nova Scotia), was English (756), Irish (2000), Scottish (149), American (5968), German (1883), and Acadian (921).

J.M. Bumsted uses these numbers as a demonstration that Nova Scotia was racially diverse early on in its history, ignoring the fact that Acadians were the ones who founded the province and that all these immigrants were white.[22]

Thousands of Loyalists come to Nova Scotia in the early 1780s, but most of them settled in the part that became New Brunswick in 1784. Many of the Acadians who returned from exile also settled in New Brunswick. After 1815, immigration to Nova Scotia picked up, with 40,000 Scots arriving between 1815 and 1838, though some of these moved to PEI. Together with the 1500 blacks who came as "Loyalists" in the early 1780s, a few more thousand blacks arrived between 1815 and 1867.

The population of NS was 68,000 in 1806, increasing to 120,000 in 1825, to 168,000 in 1831, to 277.000 in 1851, and to 331,000 in 1861. Clearly, while 40,000 Scots is a high number, the population growth

---

22   *A History of the Canadian Peoples*, 2011, p. 86.

of NS was mainly driven by the domestic fertility rate. The historian, J.M.S. Careless, had it right when he observed that "there was not much immigration to" Nova Scotia, and indeed to the Maritime provinces at large, after the Loyalist wave.[23] He meant relatively speaking, of course, compared to the steadily increasing size of the population.

Yet the text *Origins: Canadian History to Confederation*, in describing immigration patterns to the Maritimes between 1815 and 1867, offers separate sections with the headings "The English and Welsh", "The Acadians", "The Scots", "The Irish". "The Blacks", and "The First Nations" — to create an image of racial immigrant diversity.[24] Amazingly, the section on "The English and Welsh" is the shortest, whereas the sections on "The Blacks" and "First Nations" are the longest!

But when we look at the proportions of these groups relative to the total population for the year 1871, in the case of NS (though the same applies to the other Maritime provinces, as we will see below), we find that the First Nations constituted a meagre 0.4%, and the blacks only 1.6%. The rest were all whites, most of them born in Nova Scotia, and most of the "immigrant" ancestors consisting of internal migrants who had moved from one region of British North America to another (the New England Planters and Loyalists), or from the British Isles to British Nova Scotia.

Yet, despite these facts, without any sense of historical veracity, the Canadian Museum of Immigration announces to millions of visitors in its website that Nova Scotia has been a province of people of "African descent" "for over 300 years" no less than people of European descent.[25]

How about New Brunswick and Prince Edward Island? When NB was partitioned from NS in 1784, the population essentially consisted of the Acadians who had moved to this former region of NS after their expulsion, and of Loyalists, most of who had settled in what became NB in 1784. In 1806, the population of NB was 35,000. It can be safely

---

23   *Canada, A Story of Challenge* (St. Martin's Press, 1965), p. 122.

24   *Origins*, pp. 388-393.

25   Lindsay Van Dyk, "Shaping a Community: Black Refugees in Nova Scotia", https://www.pier21.ca/research/immigration-history/shaping-a-community-black-refugees-in-nova-scotia-0

stated that this population consisted of the founding people of this province, the native born Acadians, and the Loyalist internal migrants, who had been native to the British Empire in the American colonies.

This population increased to 94,000 in 1831 and to 194,000 in 1851. The big wave of immigration to NB occurred between 1842 and 1848 when 38,000 Irish arrived. These Irish immigrants, together with the native born Anglo-French inhabitants, accounted for the demographic patterns of NB. In 1871, the Irish became the major ethnic group, 35.3%, followed by the English (many of these likely the descendants of the Loyalists) at 29.2%, the French Acadians at 15.7%, and the Scots at 14.3. The Amerindians made up only 0.3% and the blacks 0.6%.

The claim that NB's heritage has been one of multiple immigrant races does not hold an ounce of water.[26]

Tiny PEI had a non-white population of 1 percent in 1871 consisting of Aboriginals. The rest were all whites, Scots, English, Irish, and Acadians.

The situation has been and is similar today in Newfoundland. Through the first half of the 1600s a number of unsuccessful attempts at permanent settlements were made by the British, and it was only by 1650 that Newfoundland contained about 500 English residents, rising to some 2000 by 1680. There was a French settlement as well with a population of about 900, but these were killed and imprisoned by the British in 1697.

In 1730, the permanent residents amounted to 2300, growing to 20,000 by 1800, and to 40,000 by 1830. The initial English settlers, and then Irish immigrants, played a significant role in this demographic growth. In the 1720s and 1730s, a few thousand Irish immigrants arrived. During the 1770s, the Irish residents numbered between 3,000 and 4,000.[27] By 1815, 19,000

---

26   This is the impression that the provincial New Brunswick tourist likes to give, see: http://www.tourismnewbrunswick.ca/Do/OurCulturalHeritage/ NewBrunswickCulture.aspx. See also the news release, "Government celebrates diversity during Black History Month", http://www.gnb.ca/cnb/news/pg/2007e0135rs. htm

27   I have been relying on the same texts I am criticizing for some of the demographic statistics used, the text *Origins*, books by Bumsted and Careless; but for this particular point, see publications by Heritage Newfoundland and Labrador, "Immigration", http://www.heritage.nf.ca/articles/exploration/immigration.php, and "Voluntary Settlement: The Peopling of Newfoundland to 1820", http://www.heritage.nf.ca/

of the residents were Irish immigrants and their descendants. However, an extensively documented study, *A Reader's Guide to the History of Newfoundland and Labrador to 1869*, by Olaf U. Janzen, observes that:

> Ironically, significant migration to Newfoundland from the British Isles came to an end just as the "Great Migration" to British North America began. By the late 1830s, patterns of population distribution in Newfoundland had therefore become fixed, and growth thereafter was derived largely through natural increase.[28]

The growth based on "natural increase" was substantial: by 1836, the total population numbered 70,000; by 1857, 124,000; by 1869, 147,000; and by 1884, 197,000.[29]

Newfoundland was not only a racially homogeneous province of English and Irish, but its population of 197,000 in 1884 was mostly native born.

Promotion of Diversity in Atlantic Provinces Today

It is impossible to understand this falsification of the historical records in isolation from the current effort to diversify the Atlantic region though mass immigration. Google the words "immigration in New Brunswick", or in Nova Scotia, Newfoundland, or PEI, and multiple links will come up, official documents from the government, all committed to the diversification of these provinces. See the "Statement of Mandate, 2014-2015" from the "Nova Scotia Office of Immigration", for example.[30] It is all about attracting "greater numbers of immigrants each year", making them feel "welcomed", contributing "to their success" and seeing that "the benefits of immigration spread among

---

articles/exploration/voluntary-settlement.php

28   Olaf U. Janzen, *A Reader's Guide to the History of Newfoundland and Labrador to 1869*, http://www2.grenfell.mun.ca/nfld_history/index.htm

29   Historical Statistics of Newfoundland and Labrador Vol. I. Population and Vital Statistics, http://www.stats.gov.nl.ca/Publications/Historical/PDF/SectionA.pdf

30   Nova Scotia Office of Immigration, Statement of Mandate, 2014-2015, http:// novascotia.ca/government/accountability/2014-2015/2014-2015-Immigration-Statement-of-Mandate.pdf

all of our communities". Look at the "Cultural Plan" for the City of Moncton, New Brunswick, the plan for 2016 to 2026; it is about deceiving the majority French speaking inhabitants that their city culture must be "an expression of diversity and inclusiveness". [31]

The obsession with promoting diversity in the Atlantic Provinces is pervasive. Document after document, discussion papers and partnerships[32] spread across Canada with links to the world, at every government level, municipal, provincial, federal, are doing everything they can to persuade the public that immigration is part of the "DNA of residents in the Maritimes" and that Africans, Muslims, and Asians have always been part of the history of this region. The list of institutions, universities, agencies, and corporations determined to bring about a radical alteration in the ethno-cultural heritage of the Atlantic Provinces is endless.[33] This is why they are rewriting history, making students believe that diverse races were responsible for the creation of the Atlantic Provinces and that only "white racism"[34] has stood in the way of acknowledging this history.

---

31   MDB Insight: City of Moncton Cultural Plan, http://www5.moncton.ca/docs/ City_of_Moncton_Cultural_Plan.pdf

32   "Atlantic Region", *Our Diverse Cities*, Number 5 (Spring 2008), http://www. metropolis.net/pdfs/ODC_spring2008_e.pdf

33   And why should we be surprised this is happening in the Atlantic? Canada is filled with organizations dedicated to the promotion of the idea that racial diversity is the "foundation of Canadian identity", as we are informed in John Biles, et al., *Integration and Inclusion of Newcomers and Minorities across Canada* (McGill-Queen's University Press, 2011). This book reveals to us the "burgeoning number of agencies, think tanks, and institutes taking an active interest in immigration", including the Institute for Research on Public Policy Forum, the Maytree Foundation, the Mowat Institute, the Metropolis Project, the Canada West Foundation, and the Fraser Institute. There is also the Social Sciences and Humanities Research Council, Citizenship and Immigration Canada, Canadian Heritage, Human Resources and Social Development Canada, Public Safety Canada, Public Health Agency of Canada, Royal Canadian Mounted Police, Canada Mortgage and Housing Corporation, Statistics Canada, Atlantic Canada Opportunities Agency, Canada Economic Development for Quebec Regions, Canada Border Services Agency and the Rural Secretariat of Agriculture and Agri-Food Canada. This book is a collection of articles by some 25 academics, where we are also informed of "an enormous increase in the resources directed toward the settlement of newcomers, with Citizenship and Immigration Canada more than tripling its expenditures since 2006" (4). The small Atlantic region is quite prominent in the chapters, "Immigration and Diversity in New Brunswick", "Immigration, Settlement, and Integration in Nova Scotia: Provincial Perspectives", Newfoundland and Labrador: Creating Change in the Twenty-First Century", "Perspectives on Integration and Inclusion in Prince Edward Island". The one on tiny PEI is 60 pages long, possibly because this is the whitest region of Canada.

34   See the Report of the Standing Senate Committee on Social Affairs, Science and Technology (June 2013) "In from the Margins, Part II: Reducing Barriers to Social Inclusion and Social Cohesion", http://www.parl.gc.ca/Content/SEN/Committee/411/ soci/rep/rep26jun13-e.pdf

White Canada Forever: Immigration 1867-1914/1921

The period from 1867 to 1914 is generally seen as the time when Canada truly became a nation of diverse immigrants. It is said that immigration not only provided "much of the population growth" for this period, but produced a nation no longer British and French, a nation with a "wide variety of ethnic origins". From this point onward, we are told, the equal "contributions of the other ethnic groups" to Canada's history became undeniable.[35]

Facts barely support this interpretation, and, what is worse, the historians who write eloquently about this diversification inform us, rather incoherently, that this was a time when Canadians imposed immigration restrictions against "any race deemed unsuited to the climate or requirements of Canada", a time when WASPs were unwilling to share Canada with races deemed to be very different, excluding them altogether by the early 1900s. It was a time, they teach students, when dominant Anglo elites forced back to India the Komagata Maru ship[36] (in 1914) amid cries of "White Canada forever".

Of course, some may argue that actual diversification is what prompted these immigration restrictions and that the arrival of thousands of Asians and blacks was indeed creating a new Canada that was only stopped in its tracks by "racist" whites. But we will see, to the contrary, that Canada became more white during this period and that it was the threat, rather than the fact, of diversification that brought immigration restrictions.

Current diversity promoters want to have it both ways: find justification in the past for the intense racial diversification that is going on today, as a way of normalizing its radical nature, while condemning this past

---

35   This is the view held by the standard texts we have been citing, as we will see below, and by all the establishment sources; for example, according to the Canadian Museum of Immigration at Pier 21, "thousands of diverse immigrants came to Canada between 1867 and 1914", https://www.pier21.ca/research/immigration-history/settling-the-west-immigration-to-the-prairies-from-1867-to-1914

36   For two articles that challenge the official interpretation everyone in Canada has to accept about this incident, see Dan Murray, "The Komagata Maru Incident: Don't Apologize to the Sikhs" *Council of European Canadians* (May 18, 2016). Thomas Jones, "The Komagata Maru Apology Fest" *Council of European Canadians* (May 20, 2016).

for marginalizing minorities and excluding non-whites. They act as the moral arbiters of a Canada that apparently failed to live up to ideals that only they are bringing to actualization now.[37] But we have seen in preceding chapters that the evidence stands in the way of such moral grandstanding. What stands revealed are academics accustomed to the manipulation of historical evidence.

Immigration from 1867 to 1896

After the arrival of Anglicizing immigrants from the British Isles between 1815 and 1850, there was relatively little immigration. With the creation of a unified Canadian state in 1867, the pulling together of resources at the hands of a federal government, and the immediate efforts to build up a nation-wide railway system, the government consciously set out to attract immigrants in order to settle the western prairies and ensure Canada's sovereignty over this huge area. These efforts, however, were disappointing. As Robert Craig Brown and Ramsay Cook have observed:

> In the years prior to 1896, nothing had been more disheartening than the country's failure to attract and keep the large number of people necessary to fill up [western Canada].[38]

In fact, thousands had emigrated out of Canada; in 1870 there were 493,464 Canadians living in the United States, and, all in all, between 1871 and 1891, more emigrated from Canada to the United States than had come from abroad.[39]

---

37 These are the opening words of a recent collection of articles by numerous academics: "Multiculturalism existed demographically in Canada at the time of confederation when the country was formed in 1867". Then, in the next sentence the editors of this text add that "the situation in 1867 was one of inequalitarian pluralism". See Lloyd Wong and Shibao Guo, Revisiting Multiculturalism in Canada: An Introduction", in Lloyd Wong and Shibao Guo, eds. *Revisiting Multiculturalism in Canada. Theories, Policies, and Debates* (Sense Publishers, 2015), p. 1.

38 *Canada, 1896-1921: A Nation Transformed* (McClelland and Stewart, 1974), p. 54.

39 Barbara Messamore observes that "from Confederation to the mid-1890s, immigration did not even keep pace with the outflow of population to the United States". See "Introduction: Canada and Migration: Kinship with the World", in Messamore, ed., *Canadian Immigration Patterns From Britain and North America* (University of Ottawa Press (2004), p. 3.

On the surface, it all seems rather diversifying as we are informed that 8000 "Russian Mennonites" settled in Manitoba in 1874, that over 15,000 Chinese arrived to work on the transcontinental railway in 1879-80, and that 247 Jews came to Saskatchewan. But arguing that immigration accounted for "much" of Canada's population growth on the basis of these numbers is quite misleading.

The population of Canada grew from 2,414,519 in 1851 to 3,174,442 in 1861 to 4,009,000 in 1876, and to 4,833,000 in 1891.[40] The population of Quebec grew from 890,000 to 1,489,000 through this period. However, most of the Quebec growth was due to the continuing high fertility rate of the French population. And it is also a fact that immigration played a relatively small role in the overall growth of the Canadian population during this period.

Demographic and Cultural Impact of Immigration - 1896 to 1914/21

When all is said, the historians agree that it was really in the period between 1896 and 1914 that Canada saw a high influx of immigrants, "more than 3 million". There is no doubt that immigrants, particularly if we correctly include their children, did play a very important role in the population growth Canada experienced from 5,074,000 in 1896 to 7,879,000 in 1914.

Mind you, if you compare the estimation of "more than 3 million" immigrants to the numbers on population growth, the increase in population from 1896 to 1914 stands lower than the alleged number of immigrants, which leads one to think that the immigration numbers have been exaggerated, since the number of Canadians should have been considerably higher in 1914 if we take account of the domestic fertility rate, even assuming that some of these immigrants emigrated to the US, and that some died.

The "more than 3 million" figure comes from the authoritative book, *The Making of the Mosaic* by Kelley and Trebilcock.[41] It looks like

---

40   Statistics Canada, "Estimated Population of Canada, 1605 to the Present", http://www.statcan.gc.ca/pub/98-187-x/4151287-eng.htm

41   *The Making of the Mosaic*, p. 113.

J.M.S. Careless, in his book, *Canada: A Story of Challenge*, has the more accurate number of "about two-and-a-half million people"[42] entering Canada between 1896 and 1914. It appears that current historians, in their eagerness to portray Canada as a "nation of immigrants", are inflating the numbers and misleading their students.

Bumsted's figure of "nearly 2.8 million immigrants" arriving in the "peak" decade of 1904-1914 also appears to be inflated.[43] The population between these years grew from 6.1 million to 7.89 million, which is lower than the supposed number of immigrant arrivals. The *Canadian Encyclopedia* article on "Population", likely has the more accurate number in stating that "between 1901 and 1911…Canada experienced its highest recorded wave of immigration. During this period more than 2 million immigrants arrived to this country, mostly from Europe".[44]

The next question is whether the immigrants who came during this period added to the ethnic diversity of Canada. The answer is yes, insomuch as the number of Canadians with a European ethnicity other than English and French increased. However, the white racial homogeneity of Canada was increased, and Germans, which made up about 6% of the Canadian population in 1871, remained the largest proportion of "other Europeans".

Reading the standard texts, including the *Report of the Royal Commission on Bilingualism and Biculturalism*, Book IV, *The Contribution of the Other Ethnic Groups*,[45] students may think that diversification after 1896 was the order of the day. We are told that 7500 Doukhobors, members of a sectarian Quaker-like movement from Russia, arrived on and after 1898, and that between 1896 and 1914, 170,000 Ukrainians settled in the prairies. We are informed that, by 1921, 15 percent of the Canadian population was non-British and non-French, that the Polish population increased from 2,800 to 32,000 between 1901 and 1921,

---

42   Careless, *Canada, A Story of Challenge*, p. 304.

43   *A History of the Canadian Peoples*, 2011, p. 262

44   http://www.thecanadianencyclopedia.ca/en/article/population/

45   *Report of the Royal Commission on Bilingualism and Biculturalism, Book IV, The Contribution of the Other Ethnic Groups (Queen's Printer for Canada, 1970)*, pp. 17-31. This publication can be found in Government of Canada Publications, http://publications.gc.ca/site/eng/472354/publication.html

that Hungarians numbered 13,200 in 1921, that Italians increased from 11,000 in 1901 to 67,000 in 1921, that Jews increased from 16,100 to 126,000 in the same period, and that more than 5,000 Sikhs came during 1905-07. We are also told that, in 1921, the Chinese numbered 40,000, the Japanese 16,000, East Indians 5,000, and the Lebanese 4,134; and that the German population in the prairies increased from 46,800 in 1901 to 148,000 in 1911, and that Canadians of Scandinavia origin in the prairies increased from 17,300 in 1901 to 130,000 in 1921.[46]

Many of these immigrants settled in the under populated prairies, Manitoba, Alberta, Saskatchewan, and so it is quite accurate to say that "cultural diversity" became a "striking feature of prairie society" during this period.[47] Yet we must keep in mind some key facts, starting with the intra-European character of this diversity. We must also realize that these numbers are relatively low compared to the total number of immigrants who came during this period, even though some of these numbers take into account children of immigrants.

When we look at total number of immigrants coming to Canada as a whole, assuming that "more than 3 million arrived between 1896 and 1914", we find that 1.25 million came from the British Isles, including 50,000 "home children", and 1 million from the United States. Most of the Americans were Canadians returning from the US some years after they had emigrated from Canada. Careless, who says that 2.5 million came between 1896 and 1914, also says that "close to a million" were from the British Isles, "more than three quarters" from the United States, and "well over half a million" from continental Europe.[48]

The number of blacks who came in 1871 was 21,500, but after this peak the numbers decline; less than 1500 blacks came from 1901 to 1911, or only 1000+ blacks came to the prairies between 1909 and

---

46   See Robert Craig Brown, and Ramsay Cook, *Canada, 1896-1921: A Nation Transformed*, pp. 61-70; Gerald Friesen, *The Canadian Prairies: A History* (University of Toronto Press, 1984), pp. 242-273; Bumsted, 2003, pp. 157- 167; *Report of the Royal Commission on Bilingualism and Biculturalism, Book IV, The Contribution of the Other Ethnic Groups* pp. 17-31.

47   Gerald Friesen, *The Canadian Prairies: A History*, p. 242.

48   Careless, *Canada, A Story of Challenge*, p. 304. Bruce Elliot, "Regional Patterns of English Immigration and Settlement in Upper Canada", in Barbara Messamore, ed., *Canadian Immigration Patterns From Britain and North America* (University of Ottawa Press (2004), p. 53.

1911.[49] Thereafter, as a result of immigration restrictions, hardly any blacks came until the 1960s. Similarly, the Asian population peaked in the early 1900s, but Asian immigration was stopped altogether by the Chinese Immigration Act of 1923. Immigrants from India were completely prohibited after 1907. In 1931, the total Chinese population in Canada, which was the largest Asian population, was only 46,519.[50]

Multicultural or Racist?

You cannot have it both ways, tell students that immigration and diversity have been an unique feature of Canada's history hidden by past historians, and now uncovered by current historians, while insisting simultaneously that the very period, 1896 to 1914, which supposedly saw the "greatest immigration boom yet known", was a period in which "virtually no Canadians", to use the words of the popular text, *Destinies*, "thought in terms of a culturally pluralistic society".[51]

Was this the period in which Canada saw "record" numbers of immigrants from a "variety" of nations, or was it instead a period in which the government "sought to create a homogeneous culture based on British Canadian customs and the English language"?[52] Was this a period in which "racist" immigration acts were introduced prohibiting Asians and blacks from entering Canada, or was it a period when Canadians from many ethnic backgrounds increasingly made equal contributions to Canadian society?

Remember, when the establishment decided to identify Canada as a multicultural nation in the early 1970s, rather than a bicultural nation, it did so on the grounds that this term was a more accurate description of the "contributions made by the other ethnic groups" through Canada's history. But having examined the history of immigration from the origins of Canada in the early 1600s up until 1921, we have

---

49   *The Canadian Encyclopedia*, "Black Canadians", http://www.thecanadianencyclopedia.ca/en/article/black-canadians/

50   *The Canadian Encyclopedia*, "Chinese Canadians", http://www.thecanadianencyclopedia.ca/en/article/chinese-canadians/

51   *Destinies*, p. 69.

52   *Ibid.*

seen that only in this late period can we identify "other Europeans" as a growing proportion of the Canadian population.

These "other Europeans" came to participate mostly as farmers and workers within a Canada that was politically, economically, and culturally dominated by English speakers in 1921, and a Quebec that continued to be racially homogeneous. During this sequence of centuries, the Aboriginal population was continuously reduced, consisting of only 1 percent of the population by 1867, and declining further in absolute numbers until the early 20th century.

There is no way around the reality that Canada was created, and continued to be created through to 1921, almost entirely by indigenous whites and by internal white migrants from British North America and the British Isles, with a late incoming contribution by other Europeans after 1896. The country, in fact, became whiter during this period: 96 percent of the population was of European origin in 1901; 97 percent in 1911, and 97.5 percent in 1921.[53]

Historians who tell you today that, "from the very beginning, the land that became Canada was a multiracial place, the destination of a constant flow of new immigrants of varying ethnicities",[54] are violating a most basic principle of their profession: the formulation of arguments by carefully considering the evidence.

---

53 I obtained these numbers from a publication by the Canadian Council for Refugees, "A hundred years of immigration, 1900-1999", http://ccrweb.ca/en/hundred-years-immigration-canada-1900-1999

54 *Canada's Diverse Peoples*, 2003, p. 326.

4

Pioneers, Settlers, and Discoverers

Leftist Newspeak

Leftists have been winning the war of words and setting the terms of political discourse for decades. Their discursive power was quite evident three years ago in the decision of the Associated Press to drop the term "illegal immigrant" from its style guide as an "offensive" term that did not accurately describe migrants who enter the United States without documentation. "Islamophobia" is another term used to shut down discussions over Islam's incompatibility with Western values. The Left has been so successful in projecting insidious motives on anyone disagreeing with their totalitarian views that conservatives now devote considerable time playing up their "good intentions" or singing the same tune by targeting "two-faced liberals" caught making sexist or racist remarks. Vladimir I. Lenin (1870-1924) once commanded his comrades:

> The communists must be prepared to...resort to all sorts of cunning schemes and stratagems to employ illegal methods, to evade and conceal the truth....to evoke hatred, aversion, and contempt...not to convince but to break up the ranks of the opponent, not to correct an opponent's mistake but to destroy him, to wipe his organization off the face of the earth. This formulation is indeed of such a nature as to evoke the worst thoughts, the worst suspicions about the opponent.[1]

This tenet of Leninism continues today with improvisations, not just through the use of Orwellian doublespeak, which we know too well, but through the use of bellyfeel words that carry a blind yet enthusiastic acceptance of an idea. They are quite apt at distorting the older meanings of words, even to the point of turning them upside

---

1   Barron J. *KGB — The Secret Work of the Soviet Secret Agents* (Reader's Digest Press, 1974), p. 224.

down. "Discoverer" and "explorer of Canada" were once terms used in admiration; now they are used in quotation marks as untrue and laughable. This chapter is about the replacement of the words "pioneer" and "settler" with the word "immigrant".

Dictionary Definition

The replacement of the words "pioneers" and "settlers" to describe the founders of Canada with the word "immigrant" happened gradually without barely anyone noticing it. In the preceding chapters I have used the term "immigrants" in reference to the French, British, European men and women who arrived in Canada from the 1600s to 1914/21. I did so to show that even on its own terms the established interpretation that Canada is "a nation of diverse immigrants" is false, since most Canadians were either native born with strong ancestries in Canada or internal migrants from within the British world of North America and the British Isles. But it is time to question the way the word "immigrant" has been deceptively extended to include actual pioneers and settlers. Almost all the men and women who came to Canada from the British Isles and elsewhere in Europe, and, if you like, from British America, before 1914, were pioneers or settlers, not immigrants.

Immigrants started to arrive in Canada mostly after WWII. I am saying this in accordance with all the dictionary definitions I have examined. The *New Oxford English Dictionary* is very clear. Immigrant is "a person who comes to live permanently in a foreign country". Settler, however, is "a person who settles in an area, typically with no or few previous inhabitants". Pioneer describes "a person who is among the first inhabitants to explore or settle a new country or area". "Pioneering" means "to be the first to use or apply a new method, area of knowledge, or activity, open up a terrain as a pioneer".

Samuel Huntington: Settlers Before Immigrants

The one academic I know who has addressed this distinction is Samuel Huntington in his book, *Who Are We? The Challenges to America's National Identity* (2004). He writes:

Settlers and immigrants differ fundamentally. Settlers leave an existing society, usually in a group in order to create a new community...Immigrants, in contrast, do not create a new society. They move from one society to a different society.[2]

What Huntington says about American settlers applies to the Canadians who came to Canada more or less before 1914/21. Huntington says that America's "core culture" was created by the settlers who came in the seventeenth and eighteenth centuries. This core culture consisted of the:

> Christian religion, Protestant values and moralism, a work ethic, the English language, the British traditions of law, justice, and the limits of government power, and a legacy of European art, literature, philosophy and music.[3]

While the early settlers were responsible for this core culture, future settlers were responsible for the extension of this core culture into the "American frontier" or the "Great West". These men and women who opened the West were not immigrants. Immigrants only began to arrive in large numbers after the 1820s into the already created towns and cities.

In Canada, it can be said that the "core culture" was created by the time of Confederation in 1867, with French and English as the major languages, Catholic and Protestant values, French civil law and British parliamentary institutions and law. The "non-French and non-British" men and women who arrived in the 1800s and early 1900s were also settlers, insomuch as many of them settled in the new Prairie Provinces and British Columbia, or in new areas in Upper Canada and the Maritimes.

This distinction between settlers/pioneers and immigrants, which was recognized (at least implicitly) by past historians, has been explicitly obfuscated by current historians. The two standard history textbooks I have referenced often in the preceding chapters, *Origins: Canadian History to Confederation*, and *A History of the Canadian Peoples*, avoid

---

2   Samuel Huntington in his book, *Who Are We? The Challenges to America's National Identity* (Simon and Schuster, 2004), p. 39

3   *Ibid*, p. 40.

the use of the words "settler" and "pioneer", but always use the words "immigrants" or "diverse immigrants". In fact, "immigration" enjoys the longest entry in the index of another text I have been referencing regularly, Bumsted's *A History of the Canadian Peoples*, after the words "Canada" and "Aboriginal Peoples".

It is not that historians did not use the word "immigrants" or "immigration" in the past. George Bryce's book, *A Short History of Canada*, published in 1914, a solid book of 600 pages, uses immigrants often, but he also regularly uses "settlers" and "colonizers" (without the negative connotation this term currently carries). The same is true of Donald Creighton's, *Dominion of the North: A History of Canada*, first published in 1944, revised in 1957, which I greatly enjoyed reading in a tiny room at summer residences in the University of Toronto in 2016. Both these books portray Canada as a nation fundamentally shaped by the French in Quebec and the English, not as a "nation of immigrants". J.M.S. Careless's book, *Canada: A Story of Challenge* (originally published in 1959), subtitles the first period of large scale immigration to Canada as "Immigration, Development and the Pioneer Age, 1815-1850".

Canada's Pioneers

If I may disagree a bit with Huntington, it is more accurate to identify the settlers who created the core culture as "pioneers", in contrast to those who extended this culture into new areas in the West, who should be identified as "settlers" proper. The word "pioneer" carries two key meanings; one is very close to the meaning of "settler", that is, a person who first enters or settles a region. But another meaning is uniquely about pioneering in the sense of being the earliest in any field of inquiry, enterprise, or cultural development. The French and the English were the earliest settlers and originators of Canada's core culture and therefore the true pioneers, while the Europeans, including English, who settled the West from about 1867 to 1914/21, were settlers both in the sense of extending farming to the prairies, as well as extending Canada's political culture to this barely settled area of Canada.

The earliest settlers, say, up until Confederation, were the ones who pioneered Canada's institutions, churches, legal system, curriculum, and basic infrastructure. They brought with them the customs, values, and know-how of Europe, and in this sense they were not originators of what we have come to identify as British representative government, Protestant values, French civil law and Catholic doctrine. But there is no question that they adapted these values and institutions to Canadian conditions. This is most evident in the rural and urban landscapes that pioneers created in Canada. R. Cole Harris and John Warkentin explain well what was uniquely new about Canadian pioneers (and settlers). Writing about the period from 1800 until about the 1860s, they note:

> In only three generations the whole peninsula of Southern Ontario was occupied by people of European [British] descent. During this time the forest was cut; the geometry of roads, fence lines and fields was stamped across the land; and the prosperity achieved by many was reflected in ample brick farmhouses and in bustling towns. Everywhere the human landscape was new. In the most recent frontier regions settlers still lived in tiny cabins on patches of cleared land; in the older areas there were still some stumpy fields and many people alive who had known the first pioneers. Whereas the human landscape of Western Europe often reflected centuries of human toil, this landscape reflected the recent arrival, the energy, and the apparent wastefulness of its creators. That Europeans had created the landscape there could be no doubt — the architectural forms, for example, were entirely of European origin. But although components of it existed in the British Isles, the human landscape of Southern Ontario could not be found anywhere in Europe.[4]

Edwin Guillet's *Pioneer Days in Upper Canada* (first published in 1933, with new editions in 1963, 1966, 1968, 1970, 1973, and 1975, but now discarded), is quite entertaining in bringing to light how the first settlers pioneered the very meaning of "Canadian living", starting with the immediacy of clearing up heavily forested lands, lumbering against huge oaks, umbrageous elms and stately pines, to open up lands for settlement. Indeed, the clearing of land involved a new co-operative principle of work known as "bees" in which neighbors would gather together to help each other, as no one family could do the work alone in many instances. These bees were also organized for house building, barn raising, and making quilts. The log and sod houses pioneered by

---

4   *Canada Before Confederation: A Study in Historical Geography*, p. 164.

these settlers were adapted to local materials in order to withstand long harsh winters.

The first settlers also pioneered many types of home-made foods using local products, including buckwheat cakes, rich batter puddings, berry pies, molasses, gelatin, ciders. The diet of the settlers — wild asparagus and berries, chestnuts, ducks, partridges, cucumbers, celery and turnips, roasted pig, boiled mutton, rice pudding, fishes of several kinds — was superior to the current overrated food of "ethnic" restaurants with their rootless globalist menus. They also pioneered city halls, fire-fighter's organizations, theatres, Temperance Societies, sports and inter club games (curling, bandyball, lacrosse, softball, hockey, horse racing), public libraries, debating societies, mechanics' institutes, agricultural associations, literary societies, private schools and colleges, circuses, brass bands.[5]

Don't believe the mainstream press and academic books that state "we are all descended from immigrants and refugees".[6] The goal of the globalist left and corporate right is to destroy the national identities and heritages of European peoples. They want to equate the Canadians who pioneered and settled Canada with the immigrants who came to a ready-made nation after 1921/1945. However, as we will see in the next chapter, the immigrants who came between 1921/45 and 1971 were mostly Europeans who worked really hard and assimilated without any ulterior motives. The immigrants who have been coming since multiculturalism was announced in 1971 are very different, arriving into a Canada that is under the tutelage of an ideology that celebrates their non-European traditions and encourages them to affirm their group rights in ways that are undermining Canada.

Europeans Discovered Canada

David Hackett Fisher observes that "in the last generation, too many scholars have been writing about Indian saints and European savages".[7] Hard to disagree. I can't think of a university survey course

---

5   Edwin Guillet, *Pioneer Days in Upper Canada* (University of Toronto, 1970).

6   John Friesen, "demographic reporter" of *The Globe and Mail* (June 26, 2011), is fundamentally wrong when he says that "Canada has always thought of itself as a nation of immigrants". By "immigrants" Canadian past leaders understood something very different from what we are expected to understand today; they generally meant "white" immigrants or "white settlers".

7   David Hackett Fisher, *Champlain's Dream: A Visionary Adventurer Who Made a New*

of Canadian history in which the first lessons do not portray "First Nations" peoples in a very positive light, sometimes with judgements about their moral superiority, contrasted to the diseases Europeans brought, the capitalist greed that drove Europeans to "discover" Canada (in quotation marks), the intolerance of Christians towards Native beliefs — backed by inbox sections on topics such as "the matriarchal egalitarian Iroquoian society".

Standard survey textbooks are supposed to be evenhanded, avoid strong interpretative angles, offer the consensus view or fairly present different viewpoints. The survey texts I have chosen to focus on, because they are the most widely used in recent years, and because they are otherwise the best current surveys, *A History of the Canadian Peoples*, by Bumsted, and the two volume text by R. Douglas Francis, et al., *Origins, Canadian History to Confederation, Destinies: Canadian History Since Confederation*, are not books with an overtly Marxist, feminist, environmentalist, or postmodernist approach. They have all the scholarly trappings of consensus books intended for first year students, based on the "advice and suggestions of many Canadian historians", incorporating research across the spectrum of (established) ideas.[8]

Nevertheless, from their opening pages, white students are made to feel their ancestors stole this country from the "First Nations" and that there is no reason for them to feel any pride in their past. The opening sentence of Bumsted's text reads:

> At one time, a history of Canada typically would begin with the arrival of the European 'discovery' at the end of the fifteenth century.[9]

The text *Origins* also places quotation marks on the word "discovered". Current texts start with chapters on the history and culture of

---

World in Canada (Vintage Canada, 2009), p. 10.

8   I should make the qualification here that, however strong I have been, and will continue to be, against the interpretations of the authors of these two surveys, I do not mean to be disrespectful personally against them. If I may borrow the language of the once famous French Marxist Louis Althusser, I view academics today as "bearers" of the "roles" and "functions" assigned to them by the cultural Marxist formation of our times. Academics can only "think" the "problems" "already actually posed" by the formation they inhabit. See Louis Althusser and Etienne Balibar, *Reading Capital* (New Left Review, [1968] 1979).

9   *A History of the Canadian Peoples* (1914), p. 4.

Aboriginals, whereas, as this quote says, texts before the 1950s started with the European discovery of Canada, without quotation marks.

George Bryce's *A Short History of the Canadian People*, published in 1914 when historians could write freely without having to meet a political agenda, opens with a few pages on European exploration generally and with a section "Jacques Cartier Discovers Canada".[10] Arthur Lower's *A History of Canada, Colony to Nation,* first published in 1946 (though the copy I am citing is the 1964 edition) when historians were still not obligated to interpret Canada's past with a view to promoting racial diversification and when European males could still be proud of their heritage, opens with the paragraph:

> The history of Canada must begin, as it were, pre-natally. The country of today was not born until generations of Europeans had tramped across the surface of the New World, had fought each other in its fastnesses, had given themselves toil against the wilderness and had debated in their new homes the great questions that lie at the base of society. These men from overseas and that northern region into which they came, thrown together through four centuries of effort, brought to birth Canada, child of European civilization and the American wilderness.[11]

Donald Creighton's *Dominion of the North*, first published in 1944, revised in 1957, opens with the "Norsemen who first discovered the giant stepping-stones which link Europe with northern North America".[12] Then it mentions the discoveries (without quotation marks) of the other Europeans who followed, repeating this word often in the opening pages. This book was also written at a time when historians were free to narrate history according to the facts. J.M.S Careless's *Canada: A Story of Challenge* (1965), opens with the geography of Canada, followed by a short section on "The Indians and the Land», and thereafter the discovery of Canada, without quotation marks.[13]

---

10   George Bryce's *A Short History of the Canadian People* (1914) 4

11   Arthur Lower, *A History of Canada, Colony to Nation,* 1964), p. 1.

12   Donald Creighton, *Dominion of the North: A History of Canada* (Macmillan, 1957), p. 1

13   See also W. J. Eccles, *The Ordeal of New France* (1969), published by The Canadian Broadcasting Corporation (as a written version of a radio program; the first chapter is entitled "The Discoverers, 900-1600". "Discoverer" is no longer used in CBC today. David Hackett Fisher actually notes that "some apostles of political correctness even tried to ban the word 'discovery' itself. Historian Peter Pope met this attitude on the

But it is not as if these books ignored the interactions of Europeans and Indians. Creighton, for example, gives the Huron and Iroquois a prominent role in the creation of the St. Lawrence fur empire. He refers to the canoe, the toboggan, the sledge, the snowshoe, the mocassin as "all examples of the useful tools and devices which the French borrowed from the Indians".[14] The difference is that, unlike the authors of *Origins*, he does not say that Indian tools "were superior to what the Europeans could offer".[15] While *Origins* refers rather curtly to the "metal tools and weapons" of the Europeans, Careless explains in a realistic way how the Indians in fact "became dependent upon" the goods of the Europeans, and "were eager" to trade for European guns, iron traps, kettles, steel knives, blankets, all of which had become essential in the perennial power struggles of Indian tribes.[16]

The name "Canada" originated from the Iroquoian word "kanata" or "canada", meaning "village" or "settlement". But it was the Europeans who then applied this name way beyond a singular settlement to the totality of the lands they were settling through the 1600s along the St. Lawrence River and beyond.

Despite varying definitions as to what constitutes a nation, there is agreement that a tribe is not a nation. The natives of Canada were organized in tribes, and a tribe consists of people with a distinct set of cultural and linguistic traits occupying territories that are not yet integrated into a nation with clear boundaries and a centralized authority. You need a hierarchical order, a cohesive territorial army, and a unified state corresponding to a people with a shared ethnicity, to speak of a national people, though there may be other ethnic groups living under the rule of a territory controlled by a people with a shared ethnicity.

There is a lot of debate[17] whether the ancient Athenians, the Romans,

---

500th anniversary of John Cabot's northern voyages of discovery. He recall: 'I was asked by a servant of the P.R industry in June 1996 to summarize Cabot's achievement without using the term discovery. She told me it had been banned...Any talk of discovery is understood as an endorsement of conquest'" *Champlain's Dream*, p. 8.

14   *Ibid*, p. 82.

15   *Origins*, p. 42.

16   Careless, pp. 21-28.

17   See my article, "The Greek-Roman Invention of Civic Identity Versus the Current

the English in the medieval era, the ancient Egyptians and other peoples, were nations, but one thing is certain, no one claims that there were nations before certain characteristics we identify with a civilized state of living were in place, such as a written language, a legal code, a network of communications, a reasonably centralized army, a bureaucracy capable of enforcing state authority over an extended territory with some boundaries. This is what the French and the English did in Canada, create a nation state, and this is why it is correct to say they discovered Canada, a land inhabited by Indian tribes.

Tough Indians or Effeminate "First Nations"?

David Hackett Fisher also observers that "two generations ago, historians wrote of European saints and Indian savages". [18] Here I have to disagree somewhat with this great historian. My sense, without being an expert, is that current cultural Marxists have exaggerated the negativity of the term "savages" and the overall picture white historians offered of Indians before the PC establishment imposed its language codes and infantile imaginations. From the very beginning of their encounters with Indians, Europeans exhibited keen curiosity and appreciation for the customs and hardiness of Indians, even as they made obvious observations about their sometimes savage ways. This is certainly the image conveyed in one of the first major works touching on Canadian history, Francis Parkman's multi-volume history of the European colonization of North America, titled *France and England in North America*, written between 1865 and 1892. It is also the portrayal one finds in the long established and still, in my estimation, best overview, *The Indians of Canada*, by Diamond Jenness, first published in 1932, with new editions running until 1977, and then reprints through the 1980s until 1996, never revised.

France and England in North America was released in 1983 as a two-volume unabridged version by the Library of America. It provides a full chapter on the "Native Tribes", in addition to many other pages and paragraphs spread over the two volumes. I would say this chapter and these pages exhibit a deeper ethnographic grasp of the natives, based

---

Demotion of European Ethnicity" *The Occidental Quarterly* (vol. 15, no. 3, Fall 2015).

18   *Champlain's Dream*, p. 10.

on a wide array of primary accounts by Europeans who had intimate relations with Indians, a face to face curiosity about their customs and beliefs in North America the moment they established contact with them in the 1600s. It is true that Parkman, like the old fashion historians I mentioned above, called them "savages". By this term they meant that Amerindians were at a lower level of historical development, not living in societies with complex irrigation systems, large cities, written languages and wide networks of trade. They were also voicing what we now know with certainty: people living in tribal units were in constant feuds with other tribal units, without a centralized authority to keep order, quite violent and savage-like in their constant wars with each other, living closer to the Hobbesian state of nature, without policing powers and rules of "civilized" behavior imposed among inhabitants co-existing within a larger territorial state.[19]

Mind you, many Europeans idealized primitive peoples as "noble". Parkman, for his part, while believing that the Iroquois never "have developed a civilization of their own", still admired how "spirits so fierce, and in many ways so ungoverned, lived in peace, without law and without enforced authority".

There were towns where savages lived together in thousands with a harmony which civilization might envy. This was in good measure due to the peculiarities of Indian character and habits. This intractable race were, in certain external respects, the most pliant and complaisant of mankind. The early missionaries were charmed by the docile acquiescence with which their dogmas were received; but they soon discovered that their facile auditors neither believed nor understood that to which they had promptly assented. They assented from a kind of courtesy, which, while it vexed the priests, tended greatly to keep the Indians in mutual accord. That well known self-control, which, originating in a form of pride, covered the savage nature of the man with a veil, opaque, though thin, contributed not a little to the same end. Though vain, arrogant, boastful, and vindictive, the Indian bore abuse and sarcasm with an astonishing patience. Though greedy and grasping, he was lavish without sting, and would give way his all to soothe the manes of a departed relative, gain influence and

---

19   Lawrence H. Keeley, *War Before Civilization: the Myth of the Peaceful Savage* (Oxford University Press, 1996).

applause, or ingratiate himself with his neighbours. In his dread of public opinion, he rivalled some of his civilized successors.[20]

This passage is filled with insights treating Indians with respect as real men, rather than as victims in need of fake praises by male academics who have no sense of what it means to struggle for one's survival with their 10 hour work-weeks and inflated salaries. Most of what we hear today is about how the "Aboriginal peoples lived in a reciprocal relationship with nature" and how "virtually everything written about the indigenous population of Canada was produced from a European perspective" until recent decades.[21] In my estimation it is the other way around: Parkman was European with his own standards, to be sure, but he at least wrote without treating the Indians as ideological pawns to serve contemporaneous political agendas.

Diamond Jenness's book, *The Indians of Canada*, was replaced as the "best survey" by Olive Dickason's *Canada's First Nations: A History of the Founding Peoples from the Earliest Times*, published in 1992. Dickason's text is now seen as a corrective to the Eurocentric biases of past surveys, a more appropriate rendition of the "complex" and "rich society" of the peoples who "founded" Canada and that "composed fifty-five individual nations" before the Europeans arrived. In truth, Jenness's account has not been surpassed in its accurate, dignified, and fair portrayal of Canada's Indians. He graduated from the University of Oxford, conducted numerous ethnographic studies, particularly of the Inuit and Eskimos, was Chief of Anthropology at the National Museum of Canada for many years, and authored more than 100 works (!) on what they now call the "First Nations people". In his survey, he wrote in a matter of fact way that Indians, for example, "had no conception of hygiene, they seldom washed…their homes were squalid and often filthy". [22] But I take these words as testimony of a survey written with a scientific appreciation of the facts of life. This is a survey that carefully describes and tries to explain every facet of Indian life, languages, hunting and fishing, dress and adornment, dwellings, social and political organization, religion, traditions, and art. Every single illustration in the book is consciously intended, in my view, to convey the inner dignity of the Indians as

---

20   Francis Parkman, *France and England in North America*, p. 368-369.

21   *A History of the Canadian Peoples*, 2011, pp. 5, 22.

22   Diamond Jenness, *The Indians of Canada*. (National Museum of Canada, Queen's Printer, 1967), p. 99.

humans and not as subjects to be exploited by leftists looking for political agendas. The book abounds with recognition of their talents within the limits of their stage of development: "They knew the life-histories of the animals they hunted, the different stages of their growth, their seasonal movements and hibernation haunts, and the various foods they sought for sustenance". [23] But today this book is not read, barely known, but seen as an example of a "white colonialist discourse".

Bumsted and the authors of *Origins* are all white males, and the presumption that they have escaped the biases of their time by treating Indians delicately is hard to swallow. The fact is that every single book and article these white historians rely upon to tell us about how we are now finally hearing the "authentic voices" of Amerindians (and *Origins* has a long list of sources) was authored by a European! More accurately, by a European leftist academic pretending to speak for Natives when in fact s/he is just projecting Eurocentric leftist notions onto them.

Cosmopolitan Academics Without Ethnographic Grasp

Bumsted writes dismissively of "whatever technological glitter Europeans had, it would prove relatively useless in the wilderness of the New World".[24] This statement is obviously wrong — for how did Europeans manage to take over the entire non-European world with useless tools? The intriguing question, however, is why Europeans, and only in our current times and never before, put down their ancestors while celebrating the cultures of others? This attitude is unique to Europeans in our times, it is not a generic state of being of the "human race".

Ethnography, like every other discipline taught in our universities, is an invention of Europeans.[25] But only recently have they turned this field against their own culture. Europeans have always shown a Faustian ambition[26] to learn about the unknown, including why different societies have different morals and styles of life. What we must ponder over is why

---

23   *Ibid*, p. 53.

24   *A History of the Canadian Peoples*, 2011, p. 22.

25   Joseph E. Skinner, *The Invention of Greek Ethnography: From Homer to Herodotus* (OUP, 2012).

26   Ricardo Duchesne, *Faustian Man in a Multicultural Age* (Arktos, 2017).

this age-old curiosity, uniquely spacious mind, which led Europeans to invent the disciplines of archaeology and anthropology, and to write the entire history of Asians and Africans and Aboriginals, is uniquely European? Why are Europeans the only people who realized that humans make history, that the course of historical time is not mere repetition, endless cycles, but characterized by cumulative development, that the earth has a geological history, that biological organisms evolve, and that it is possible to trace a sequential development in human history? The answer is that Europeans were the only people to witness true historical development, major transitions, revolutions, sequential scientific discoveries, radically new artistic styles, persistent improvements in mathematics, in technology, and in many other endeavors.[27]

Bumsted says that Europeans "found it impossible to grasp that inanimate objects in nature could be considered to be alive".[28] Well, Europeans used to grasp objects this way until they came to the understanding that there was such a thing as a "mind", a faculty separate from the body and the emotions of humans, which could be objectively employed, in disassociation from the body, to explain observable patterns in the universe through inductive generalizations and deductive inferences from axiomatic definitions.[29]

There is something contrived in the way Bumsted goes on and on trying to persuade students that Natives were superior in all respects, writing that "Europeans were thoroughly disoriented" by the fact that "First Nations religion had no buildings, no clerical hierarchy". Actually, history shows that Aboriginals had no sense of the geographical contours of the world's land masses, where they were located, whereas it was Europeans who went about classifying and explaining the

---

27 Historians should know this, but they refuse to. They think it is reprehensible to attribute to whites only a sense of historical time, and yet the closest to historical awareness we find outside the West are the "Historical Records" of the court historian Sima Qian (145–90 BC), which subsequent Chinese "historians" used as a model. But writing a chronology is not the same as having a sense of cumulative historical changes, which is possible only if a culture actually advances in knowledge and technology, and has a comprehensive sense of world history, which Europeans acquired in the Renaissance era. Other cultures only managed a chronological sense tied to the names and doings of ancestors; and why should we be surprised since non-Western civilizations, as I show in *The Uniqueness of Western Civilization* (2011), were characterized by stasis and repetition?

28 *A History of the Canadian Peoples*, 2011, p. 27.

29 Ricardo Duchesne, "Discovering the European Mind". *Radix Journal* (October 2016).

geographical features of Canada and mapping the entire world. The natives obviously had an intimate sensory and instinctive knowledge of their environments, but we cannot deny the European contributions to the cartographic understanding of these lands.

Bumsted writes: "Tolerance for alternative spiritual values and belief systems was hardly one of Europe's strong suits". If Europeans had shown the tolerance students today are expected to show for millions of immigrants while putting down their own beliefs and barely learning anything about their history, they would have been eaten in no time by the Iroquoians. As it is, the historical record shows, as Perez Zagorin has explained in *How the Idea of Toleration Came to the West*, that:

> Between the sixteenth and twentieth centuries a huge and enormously significant shift of attitudes and values regarding differences in religion gradually occurred in Western societies. Instead of the age-old assumption that it is right and justifiable to maintain religious unity by force and to kill heretics and dissenters if necessary, the opposite assumption came to prevail that it is wrong and unjustifiable to use force and to kill in the cause of religion, and, moreover, that religious toleration and freedom are morally and politically desirable and should be given effect in laws and institutions.[30]

Students would be better educated with a lesson about how the Jesuits in New France employed a far more tolerant method of conversion than the Spaniards had earlier in South America. The Jesuits, members of a male religious order which first arrived in New France in 1611, settled in Huron villages and learned the Huron languages as a way of carrying their message, and rather than rejecting outright all Huron beliefs, recognized certain beliefs that were comparable to Christian beliefs. They also tried to impress the Hurons with their technological superiority and greater knowledge of nature as a way of convincing them of the superiority of Christianity. All this talk about how "First Nations exhibited none of the negative features of capitalistic society" and how "Aboriginals had a strong sense of love and community"[31] is nothing more than virtue signaling by academics who would not last a week living in a real community of tough Indians.

---

30   Perez Zagorin, *How the Idea of Toleration Came to the West* (2003), p. 3.

31   *A History of the Canadian Peoples*, 2011, p. 28.

Why Did Canadians Decide "Never Again" to be a White Nation?

Bumsted claims that "from the beginning" Canada was "a multiracial place, the destination of a constant flow of new immigrants of varying ethnicities". [32] Yet he knows it was only after 1967/1971 that Canada began to accept non-white immigrants, and this is why he accuses them of being racist in their immigration policies prior to this period. *A History of the Canadian Peoples* is quite blunt in its assessment of Canadians in 1945:

> The Canadian government and the Canadian people were, by and large, exclusionist, racist, and not very humane in their attitudes towards immigration. [33]

He refers to a "Gallup poll in April of 1946" indicating "that two-thirds of Canadians opposed immigration from Europe", and to another poll a few months later in which Canadians ranked the "Japanese first and the Jews second" in response to the question, "what nationalities they would like to keep out of Canada?"[34] It is not just ordinary Canadians without a "proper" education who stand condemned before the altar of diversity today but every prominent member of the political elites before the 1960s. Here are some known expressions from the most educated politicians of the past. R.B. Bennett, Prime Minister from 1930 to 1935, told a British Columbia audience in 1907:

> We must not allow our shores to be overrun by Asiatics, and become dominated by an alien race. British Columbia must remain a white man's country. [35]

George Foster (1847-1931), who served in the cabinets of seven Prime Ministers, wanted "to keep British stock dominant". Henri Bourassa, arguably the major politician of Quebec in the first four decades of the 1900s, told the House of Commons in 1904 that

---

32 *Canada's Diverse Peoples*, 2003, p. 326.

33 *A History of the Canadian Peoples*, 2011, p. 370

34 *Ibid*, p. 372.

35 Cited in *Canada 1896-1921, A Nation Transformed*, p. 68.

it was never in the minds of the founders of the nation, it never was in the minds of the fathers of confederation...that in order to be broad...we ought to change a providential condition of our partly French and partly English country to make it a land of refuge for the scum of all nations.[36]

Even the literary minded held similar views. Ralph Connor, author of the popular novel *The Foreigner*, published in 1909, envisioned Canada as a European melting pot:

Out of breeds diverse in traditions, in ideals, in speech, and in manner of life, Saxon and Slav, Teuton, Celt and Gaul, one people is being made. The blood strains of great races will mingle in the blood of a race greater than the greatest of them all.[37]

In contrast to Connor's intra-European melting pot, Stephen Leacock, writing in 1911, lamented the "racial character of the [non-British] immigrants" of his day, that is, Eastern European immigrants, writing: "They no longer consist of the strenuous, the adventurous, the enterprising". [38] I already cited the words of Mackenzie King from 1922 about how "the races of the Orient" would bring whites "face to face at once with the loss of that homogeneity which ought to characterize the people of this country if we are to be a great nation". He would continue to hold similar views right into his tenure as Prime Minister, announcing in the House of Commons in 1947 that:

The people of Canada do not wish as a result of mass immigration to make a fundamental alteration in the character of our population. Large scale immigration from the Orient would change the fundamental composition of the Canadian population.[39]

---

36 *Ibid*, p. 74.

37 *Ibid*.

38 Stephen Leacock, "Canada and the Immigration Problem" in Howard Palmer, ed. *Immigration and the Rise of Multiculturalism* (Copp Clark Publishing, 1971). McGill University's main humanities and social sciences building is "named after Stephen Leacock, a Professor of Economics from 1901 to 1944 and a well-known Canadian humorist and author". If the ignoramuses who attend this university knew they would call for a change in the name.

39 William Lyon Mackenzie King, "Statement of Canada's Immigration Policy", in Howard Palmer, *Immigration and the Rise of Multiculturalism* (Copp Clark Publishing, 1975), pp. 58-61.

Canadians were in agreement with Mackenzie King through to the 1960s. Gallup polls in the 60s showed that only about one third of Canadians thought that Canada should bring any immigrants, and over 60 percent thought that the very low levels of Asian immigration (at the time) were already too high.[40]

So, why did Canadians suddenly agree to open Canada's borders to mass immigration from the Third World? How could an entire nation, from the people to the leaders, undergo such a dramatic change in attitudes within one generation? Bumsted actually addresses this question:

> The conversion within the space of a single generation, from a very insular and parochial nation to one that was relatively sophisticated and cosmopolitan, much more capable of toleration of ethnic differentiation, has been one of the most remarkable and underrated public changes in Canadian history.[41]

But, clearly, the way he poses this change in attitude is extremely biased, and yet it is the standard answer today; Canadians in the past just didn't know any better, they were too parochial; but thanks to a better education, more cosmopolitan surroundings, they learned the truth about the blessings of racial mixing. He holds four factors responsible for nurturing a more "tolerant" Canada:

1. WWII gave millions of Canadians "foreign experience" as soldiers spending years in Europe, 50,000 of whom married foreign girls.

2. The very arrival of more than 3.5 million immigrants between 1946 and 1972, many of whom were neither British nor French, accustomed Canadians to people with different cultures, coupled with the fact that these immigrants came to live in cities rather than in isolated farmstead, mingling with each other and with traditional Canadians.

3. The wave of modernization and urbanization that swept the country during these years; the world of electricity, stoves, refrigerators, radios, televisions and stereos all worked to create an

---

40 Freda Hawkins, *Critical Years in Immigration: Canada and Australia Compared* (McGill-Queen's University Press, 1991, p. 63.

41 *A History of the Canadian Peoples*, 2011, p. 428.

urban, connected, cosmopolitan culture, dissolving the parochial attitudes of the past.

4. Finally, Bumsted says, that the new communications media, particularly the rapid spread of television across the nation after 1950 "increasingly plugged Canadians into the world [...] helped forced them out of their narrow insularity...into the international world previously beyond their ken". [42]

We can hardly underestimate how influential this line of reasoning has been in portraying the diversification of Canada as a development led by people who are more open minded and educated than the previous "parochial" generations. It is incredible how much this argument has helped legitimise the current establishment, this whole idea that supporters of mass immigration are cosmopolitan characters with broad knowledge of the cultures of the world, humane and tolerant; whereas critics of mass immigration are limited in outlook, xenophobic, leftovers from an insular past that no longer makes sense in our global age. Yet, a far stronger argument can be made that Canadians changed their attitudes about Third World immigration during the 1970s only because they were compelled to do so without any open discussion and proper education. Canadians before the 1970s were not racist, but merely ethnocentric, that is, a people with a natural and normal preference for their own ethnic traditions. The research we have, based on objective assessment of the evidence, which I will be summarizing in future chapters, shows that ethnic groups throughout the world exhibit a preference for their own culture and a disposition to judge other cultures by their own standards. This preference is a healthy and practical evaluation of one's ethnic identity and interests consistent with evolutionary theory and cultural sophistication.

Bumsted's argument is contrived and illiberal. It does not allow for Canadians to express their natural ethnocentric attitudes but carries the clear threat of ostracism if one does not blindly accept mass immigration as a blessing. The argument is flawed to its very core. First, there is a clear time lag between the modernization wave Bumsted sees after WWII, in the 1950s, and the supposed change in attitudes of Canadians, which only came after the 1960s, since, as Bumsted himself notes, and as Gallup polls in the 1960s show, Canadians were

---

42   *Ibid,* p. 430.

still a "racist" lot well into the 1960s. The growth of large cities, which can be dated to earlier decades, and the spread of mass communication technologies, which were also quite evident from the 1920s onward, though these really spread in the 1950s, did not engender tolerant attitudes, it seems, on their own, or at least they took some time to have an effect on the minds of Canadians.

When this critical observation is connected to the very powerful fact that "tolerance" for diverse immigrants and prejudicial attitudes against minorities are still pervasive in current hyper modern countries such as Japan, South Korea, Taiwan, and in huge cities in China and India today, and, indeed, in all non-white modernized countries, we can see that there is a fundamental flaw in Bumsted's standard argument. This argument presumes that racism declines as people of diverse ethnic backgrounds live together and "learn" from each other.

But the evidence we have so far is that only in the case of intra-European mixing do we have evidence of successful assimilation to a common "American" or "Canadian" culture. Canadians in the 1960s from different European backgrounds were well assimilated, despite their ethnic differences, to Canada's Anglo heritage. Once we look at the data for black and white integration, in the case of the United States,[43] for which we have the most data, or, for that matter, white and Indian integration in Canada, Australia and the US, we find that tensions, ethnic segregation in places of living, where children go to schools, and in cultural activities, have not declined one bit, even though all blacks and Aboriginals now enjoy the same civic rights. The evidence shows, to the contrary, that the closer to each other different races live, the less tolerant they are of each other.

This leads me to another critical point; did Canadian attitudes really change with modernization, or was this change imposed from above by Canadian elites without democratic approval? Bumsted notes that by 1957 there were 44 radio stations and almost 3 million televisions in Canada. He also notes that in the 1940s and 1950s

---

43   Jared Taylor, *Paved With Good Intentions: The Failure of Race Relations in Contemporary America* (Carroll & Graf Publishers, 1993). See also Stephan and Abigail Thernstrom, *America in Black and White: One Nation, Indivisible* (Simon and Schuster, 1997), written by two civil rights admirers who nevertheless follow the facts in showing that despite billions spent on projects to integrate blacks, particularly in education, the results have been dismal.

secondary education was extended to all, and that by 1961 there were nearly 4 million children in provincially controlled schools. Should we assume that these novelties in-and-of-themselves cultivated pro-mass immigration attitudes? Or should we wonder whether they were instead powerful tools of mass ideological indoctrination? Why only Western elites, not the elites of any non-Western modern country, employed these new means of communication and universal education to portray their past as racist and in need of diversification?

Freda Hawkins informs us indeed that the 1967 immigration regulations emphasizing skill and education, rather than racial origins, were not brought on by popular demand or even parliamentary debate and initiative, but by senior Ministers and Cabinet officials who "did not trust the average Canadian to respond in a positive way on this issue".[44] I already made reference to Gallup polls in the 1960s. But it was not just in the 1960s; we are informed in the text *Nation: Canada Since Confederation*, authored by a prominent list of historians, first published in 1983, that "all the historical evidence – including almost every public opinion poll done over the past 50 years – indicates that most Canadians...do not want any substantial increase in the number of people admitted into the country". [45] Yet, in complete disregard to Canadian popular wishes, the borders of Canada were set wide open from the 1970s under the directives of all the major parties, the media, tenured academic radicals, and business elites. Why? In Parts II and III I will examine the theoretical justifications, from both the Left and the Right, for this undemocratic decision, and in Part IV I will offer an answer.

---

44   Freda Hawkins, *Critical Years in Immigration: Canada and Australia Compared* (McGill-Queen's University Press, 1991, p. 63.

45   J.L. Granatstein, Irving Abella, T.W. Acheson, David Bercuson, R. Graig Brown, and H. Blair Neatby, *Nation: Canada Since Confederation* (McGraw-Hill Pearson, 1990), p. 337.

Part Two

Refuting the Theory of Multicultural Citizenship

*O, what a tangled web we weave when first
we practise to deceive!* — Walter Scott

*Community (Gemeinschaft) means genuine, enduring
life together, whereas Society (Gesellschaft) is a transient
and superficial thing.* — Ferdinand Tönnies

5

Theoretical Deceptions of Will Kymlicka

Karl Mannheim's concept of free-floating intellectuals engaged in the production of knowledge unconcerned with personal motives and interests has long attracted liberal academics uncomfortable with Karl Marx's argument that knowledge is ultimately a reflection of one's class interest, because it offered an image of themselves as self-sacrificing men pursuing truth objectively for the sake of humanity.[1]

This self-image grew in spades when the post WWII age of universal human rights afforded liberals with an airy sense of transnational dedication standing above the prejudices of particular cultures. Will Kymlicka, the most influential advocate of the "exceptional" Canadian model of "immigrant multiculturalism", is generally seen in this light, an academic who produces research for the benefit of everyone in the world, ostensibly standing above petty motives and national interests. His research, relied upon by all the mainstream political parties, universities, and NGOs, is possibly the best funded in Canada, with papers regularly commissioned by government agencies and corporations, including Forum of Federations,[2] International Council for Canadian Studies,[3] Citizenship and Immigration Canada[4] and the Transatlantic Council on Migration.[5]

Mainstream readers have criticized him from the left as a centrist who defends liberal institutions, and from the right as a collectivist who advocates special rights for minorities. He is the man in the

---

1   John Heeren, "Karl Mannheim and the Intellectual Elite" *British Journal of Sociology* (Vol. 22, No. 1, 1971).

2   http://www.forumfed.org/

3   http://www.iccs-ciec.ca/index_en.php

4   Kymlicka's report, "The Current State of Multiculturalism in Canada and Research Themes on Canadian Multiculturalism 2008-2010" was "commissioned by the Department of Citizenship and Immigration to determine which multiculturalism issues are important nationwide and require the development of further research". http://www.cic.gc.ca/english/pdf/pub/multi-state.pdf

5   http://www.migrationpolicy.org/programs/transatlantic-council-migration

middle.[6] In this chapter I will show that Kymlicka's liberal theory of minority rights is bedeviled by a double standard in the way it recognizes the "deep bond" that minorities, as "human beings", have to their culture and ethnicity, at the same time that it categorizes any form of ethno-cultural identity by Euro-Canadians as racist and illiberal. I will show, moreover, how Kymlicka deceptively sneaks in a program of mass immigration and group rights for foreign immigrants under the aegis of a theory of minority rights that was initially designed for *historically established minorities* within European nation states. He claims to be developing a theory of rights for long established minorities in Western nations when he is really pushing a radical program of mass migration and miscegenation in Canada (and the West generally) aimed at destroying the rights of majority indigenous white Europeans.

Kymlicka holds, currently, the Canada Research Chair in Political Philosophy at Queen's University in Kingston. Since the mid-1980s when he was a grad student, he has received, every single year without interruption, highly lucrative grants and awards, including the Premier's Discovery Award in 2009 ($250,000), the Trudeau Foundation Fellowship in 2005-2008 ($225,000), and the Killam Prize in Social Sciences in 2004 ($100,000). He has held visiting professorships and fellowships outside Canada every year since coming to Kingston in 1998. His books have been accepted as part of the official consensus on multiculturalism in Canada and the world, translated into 32 languages. Although he fashions himself as an outsider fighting the dominant Eurocentric discourse, he is Canada's premier government-sanctioned ideologue of multicultural citizenship.

---

6   Did you see that man in the limousine
With the pretty doll, he is fifty and the girl's only seventeen [...]
Did you see that man with a fat cigar He just left his lunch with a belly full of lobster and caviar
[...] 'Cause he's the man in the middle, knows the way to diddle
He's never bothered by his conscience Deals with the Devil, 'cause he wants to be Man in the middle, the middle, the middle
In the middle (in the middle, in the middle)
ABBA - Man In The Middle Lyrics © Universal Music Publishing Group

Theory of Multicultural Citizenship

Kymlicka is said to have articulated a theory showing that minority rights (or group rights) are compatible with the enhancement of individual rights. The essence of his thinking is contained in *Multicultural Citizenship: A Liberal Theory of Minority Rights* (1995).[7] His other books and papers are generally preparations, extensions, and repetitions of the ideas contained in this 240 page book.[8] The logic of his theory can be summed up in a few lines: individuals can only make choices and cultivate their capacities for autonomy and moral agency so long as they have access to a "societal culture" that "provides its members with meaningful ways of life across the full range of human activities, including social, educational, religious, recreational, and economic life". [9] This is not a novel theory. What Kymlicka advocates is known as liberal communitarianism, a philosophical outlook first articulated by Amitai Etzioni, Charles Taylor, Michael Walzer, Allen Buchanan, and Michael Sandel.[10]

He observes that every country has a "societal culture", a set of institutions, government bureaucracies, schools, laws, and official languages within which its inhabitants grow and perform their lives as public citizens. He accepts the prevailing liberal idea that the most important end of an individual is autonomy from coercive structures, but, unlike libertarians, he believes that individual choices can only find fulfillment within communities. Society is no mere aggregation of isolated individuals living private lives. "Individual choice is dependent

---

7   *Multicultural Citizenship: A Liberal Theory of Minority Rights* (Oxford University Press, 1995).

8   *Multicultural Citizenship* has been Kymlicka's most discussed book, the one which has occasioned a number of full critical papers, not just standard book reviews, addressing its arguments, though invariably from a leftist perspective; see Eric Metcalfe, "Illiberal Citizenship? A Critique of Will Kymlicka's Liberal Theory of Minority Rights", *Queen's Law Journal* (Fall 1996); Iris Marion Young, "A Multicultural Continuum: A Critique of Will Kymlicka's Ethnic-Nation Dichotomy", *Constellations*, vol. 4, no.1 (1997); Brian Walker, "Plural Cultures, Contested Territories: A Critique of Will Kymlicka", *Canadian Journal of Political Science*, vol. 30, no. 2 (1997); Triadafilopoulos, Triadafilos, "Culture vs citizenship? A review and critique of Will Kymlicka's multicultural citizenship", *Citizenship Studies*, vol. 1, no. 2 (1997). In this chapter, and particularly the next, I will be referencing many other articles and chapter publications by Kymlicka.

9   *Multicultural Citizenship*, p. 76.

10 References to these authors can be found in chapter 8, which deals with Charles Taylor theory of multiculturalism.

on the presence of a societal culture, defined by language and history". Individuals are always born inside a pre-established culture, and "most people have a very strong bond to their own culture". [11]

The communitarian thesis, then, is that liberal rights presuppose the existence of communities; individuals can self-create themselves only within a cultural context. Free market libertarians hold an excessively individualistic or abstract conception of the self. The very possibility of individual self-development presupposes a community with a culture. As Kymlicka expressed it in his first book, *Liberalism, Community, and Culture*:

> ...liberalism couldn't be based on (abstract individualism]...If abstract individualism [was]...the fundamental premise, there'd be no reason to...suppose that people are being made worse off by being denied the social conditions necessary to freely and rationally question their commitments.[12]

Kymlicka employs this theory to argue that minorities in Canada need communitarian supports to develop as individuals. Anglos in Canada already have a community, and it is one that privileges them. The national English majority (outside Quebec) constitutes, in Kymlicka's eyes, the dominant societal culture of this country. While Kymlicka barely identifies this majority culture as "English", it is evident that he has in mind "the larger Anglophone culture" when he writes about the main societal culture of Canada. One of the essential components of this English societal culture is the principle of individual rights. These rights, however, are not abstract, but are made possible by the cultural and institutional supports of the wider society.

Kymlicka thus employs liberal communitarian concepts to develop a theory of multicultural citizenship in Canada. He writes of two key forms of group-rights: i) national or self-government rights, and ii) polyethnic rights. He welcomes the current federal division of power in Canada in which the province of Quebec and Aboriginal territories enjoy extensive national/communal rights over issues essential to the cultural survival of the French and Aboriginals. The members of these

---

11   *Ibid*, p. 8.

12   *Liberalism, Community, and Culture* (Clarendon Press, 1989), p. 18.

national minorities, Kymlicka insists, have a shared sense of history, territory, language and culture. To maintain this shared culture, they need, and currently have, access to their own societal culture within their own territories, self-government rights and institutions – within the framework of the larger federal government and in accordance with the principle of individual rights. In contrast, Kymlicka explains, immigrant groups do not need their own societal culture: immigrants do not wish to become a separate, self-governing nation; they typically wish to "integrate into, and thereby enrich, the culture of the larger society".[13] By "larger society", Kymlicka means both the English societal culture and the Quebec national minority culture that immigrants typically inhabit.

Kymlicka carefully distances himself from ethnic-group rights that limit the rights of individuals within their group, such as coerced marriages, female circumcision, or any practice that is inconsistent with integration into a liberal society. What he welcomes are group rights that afford immigrant minorities "external protections" against majority decisions and that provide minorities with the resources to enhance their opportunities for individual success within the "dominant" societal culture. These include policies that end discrimination, affirmative action, exemption from some rules that violate religious practices, and public funding of cultural practices.

These group rights, he avers, are compatible with liberalism, for they are intended to open up individual opportunities for ethnic minorities. The point is not for immigrants to develop their own homelands and societal cultures within Canada, but to allow them to maintain their communal distinctiveness "in their family lives and in voluntary associations" while still participating "within the public institutions of the dominant culture".[14] Ethnic minorities, Kymlicka maintains, in a paper co-authored with Keith Banting, will be able to meet the Canadian/Western liberal ideal of individual self-development "if they feel their ethnic identity is publicly respected". [15] Immigrant minorities will develop "a sense of attachment and belonging to the country" to the extent to which Canadians see immigrant minorities

---

13   *Multicultural Citizenship*, p. 94.

14   *Ibid*, p. 14.

15   Keith Banting and Will Kymlicka, "Canadian Multiculturalism: Global Anxieties and Local Debates", *British Journal of Canadian Studies*, vol. 23, no. 1 (2010), p. 61.

with group identities as a "constituent part of the nation". Immigrants "do best, both in terms of psychological wellbeing and sociocultural outcomes, when they are able to combine their ethnic identity with a new national identity". [16]

Fundamental Flaws

There are three fundamental flaws in Kymlicka's theory. The first one is that Kymlicka ignores altogether the cultural identity and the national rights of the majority English Canadians. He discusses only the cultural rights and ethnic attachments of national minorities and immigrant groups. He rarely uses the term "English Canadians" in reference to the majority societal culture. While national minorities and "polyethnic" groups are distinguished by culture and by ethnicity, "the majority Anglophone culture" is identified only through its language and certain modern amenities. The English societal culture is portrayed as a deracinated, neutralized sphere consisting of modern conveniences – economic, educational, and social institutions – intended "in principle" to serve anyone regardless of cultural background. The English are mere possessors of individual rights, whereas every other ethnic group enjoys both individual and group rights.

Kymlicka often asserts that "most people have a very strong bond to their own culture". [17] This is possibly the most important unexamined assumption in Kymlicka's theory. He clearly means that forcing immigrants to "shed their distinctive heritage and assimilate entirely to the existing cultural norms" would amount to the suppression of "a very strong" disposition "in the human condition". [18] Under the "Anglo-conformity model" this inclination among non-Anglos was suppressed, and some immigrants were not allowed entry into Canada because they were seen as "unassimilable". Under multiculturalism this inclination among immigrants should be allowed and celebrated. European Canadians should make multiculturalism an intrinsic part of their culture so minorities feel respected. In one publication he actually justifies "legitimizing and acknowledging ethnicity", the

---

16   *Ibid.*

17   *Multicultural Citizenship*, pp. 8, 84.

18   *Ibid*, p. 90.

ethnic identity of immigrant groups, "as a component of Canadian identity", while at the same time insisting on "combining" this "ethnic accommodation with antiracism", that is, with campaigns against whites who seek to affirm their Anglo identity.[19]

He solemnly writes: "If a culture is not generally respected, then the dignity and self-respect of its members will also be threatened"[20]. But whenever Kymlicka identifies the English/Europeans by history and culture, it is scornfully as "colonizers", "racists", and "conquerors". The only thing European Canadians are allowed to celebrate is multiculturalism. Not a single positive word can be found in Kymlicka's writings about the settlers who founded Canada. The words "pride", "cultural particularity", and "culturally meaningful lives" are reserved exclusively for ethnic immigrant groups. He unambiguously says that multiculturalism cannot succeed as long as "native born [ethnic European] citizens with a strong sense of national identity or national pride"[21] are allowed a voice in the public arena, regularly labelling those who disagree with mass immigration as "xenophobic", "manifestly unjust", and "intolerant".

The second major problem in Kymlicka, and with the entire project of immigrant multiculturalism, is the assumption that Western nations, if they are to live up to their liberal principles, must be open to mass immigration and diverse ethnic groups. Kymlicka develops his theory of multicultural minority rights under this assumption. He traces the "historical relationship between liberalism and minority rights" and insists "there was widespread support for minority rights amongst liberals in the nineteenth century".[22] He questions the claim that liberals in the past were preoccupied only with rights to property, free speech, and representative institutions, while ignoring questions of cultural and linguistic rights. Liberals then, and in the early twentieth century, he notes, were also concerned with national rights of minorities to self-government. He mentions, for example, a scheme implemented by the League of Nations

---

19 "The Three Lives of Multiculturalism", in Shibao Guo and Lloyd Wong, eds., *Revisiting Multiculturalism in Canada: Theories, Policies and Debates* (Sense Publishers, 2015), pp. 23-4.

20 *Ibid*, 89.

21 Keith Banting and Will Kymlicka, "Canadian Multiculturalism: Global Anxieties and Local Debates", *British Journal of Canadian Studies*, vol. 23, no. 1 (2010), p. 60.

22 *Multicultural Citizenship*, p. 7.

…for various European national minorities, which provided both universal and individual rights and certain group-specific rights regarding education, local autonomy, and language.[23]

The problem here is that Kymlicka is misleadingly advancing a theory of group-differentiated rights under a program of mass immigration imposed from above as a natural continuation of past trends in the liberal tradition. While such liberal nationalists as Camillo di Cavour (1810–1861) and John Stuart Mill (1806–1873), for example, did emphasize a form of nationalism compatible with liberal values, they were firm supporters of national identities at a time when a "non-xenophobic nationalism" was meant to acknowledge the presence of centuries-old European ethnic minorities within European nations. These classical liberals were not calling for minority rights for the purpose of integrating masses of immigrants from non-European cultures. They were advocating civic rights for their own people, including historic minorities already established inside the nations of Europe. Never would they have advocated the suppression of the rights of the majority while celebrating the rights of foreigners-to-be-immigrants.

Civic Versus Ethnic Nationalism

Connected to this second flaw is Kymlicka's unquestioned supposition that, while ethnic group rights for immigrants are consistent with liberalism, majority ethno-cultural rights, as well as any form of European ethnic nationalism, contradict the liberal principles of the West. Western nations, he wants us to believe, were meant to have only a civic identity:

What distinguishes 'civic' from 'ethnic' nations is the fact that anyone can integrate into the common culture, regardless of race or colour.[24]

This interpretation, which Kymlicka asserts as if it were obviously true without explanation, is wrong. To start with, the historical record on the origins of liberal nations does not support this view. Western

---

23   *Ibid*, p. 51.

24   *Multicultural Citizenship*, pp. 23-24.

liberal nations were not founded in the absence of an existing ethnic collectivity, and certainly not for the purpose of mixing the races of the world within one state. Modern states emerged in Europe in the nineteenth century as liberal states within ethnolinguistic boundaries and majority identities. The widespread claim that Western nations are based on universal ideas which any human being can assimilate was initiated by Hans Kohn and then extended by three key authors: Benedict Anderson in *Imagined Communities: Reflections on the Origin and Spread of Nationalism*, Ernest Gellner in *Nations and Nationalism*, and Eric Hobsbawm in *Nations and Nationalism since 1780: Programme, Myth, Reality*. These authors exerted an enormous influence in academia, erroneously arguing that the nation states that emerged in nineteenth century Europe were not created by a people sharing a common history, a sense of territorial belonging and habitation, similar dialects, folkways and physical appearances. Rather, the nation-states of Europe were "socially constructed" entities, "invented traditions", "imagined" by people perceiving themselves as part of a "mythological" group in an unknown past.[25]

It is not that these writers denied that people in the premodern era had a sense of communal kin affinities within their respective tribes or localities. Their focus was on the modern nation states of Europe, and their argument was that these nation states, and the corresponding ideology of nationalism, were "artificial historical constructs" designed by political elites interested in forging powerful territorial states among previously scattered and loosely related rural communities lacking a sense of national-ethnic identity. "Imaginary national identities" were imposed on groupings of European people hitherto lacking a strong ethnic core. Nationalism was nothing more than an ideological weapon employed by state-elites seeking to create states with mass appeal, a national infrastructure, official languages, centralized taxation, national currency

---

25 I am grouping the ideas of these authors, but readers should be aware that they differ in other respects, such as the dating of the origins of modern states, the reasons for their creation, the roles of particular elites, and their own ideological inclinations. For key works and articles about these works, see Hans Kohn, *The Idea of Nationalism: A Study in Its Origins and Background* (New Brunswick, NJ: Transaction, 2005 [1944]); Ken Wolf, "Hans Kohn's Liberal Nationalism: The Historian as Prophet", *Journal of the History of Ideas* vol. 37, no. 4 (October–December 1976); Ernest Gellner, *Nations and Nationalism* (Ithaca, NY: Cornell University Press, 1983); Brendan O'Leary, "On the Nature of Nationalism: An Appraisal of Ernest Gellner's Writings on Nationalism", *British Journal of Political Science* vol. 27, no. 2 (April 1997); Eric Hobsbawm, *Nations and Nationalism Since 1780: Programme, Myth, Reality* (Cambridge: Cambridge University Press, 1990).

and laws, through the modern era, culminating in the nineteenth century. The exhortations of nationalists in the 19th and 20th centuries about the kin-ethnic roots of their nations were mere rhetorical ploys to induce mass support for elite efforts at extending their power nationally over an otherwise disparate, never ethnically conscious, population consisting of multiple dialects, ancestries and local loyalties. With the experience of World War I and II, both within liberalism and Marxism, this critique of nationalism turned into a concerted critique of ethnic nationalism, which came to be associated with German militarism in WW I and Fascism thereafter. While Marxists, such as Hobsbawm, started advocating working class internationalism, liberal theorists such as Kohn and Gellner began to formulate a strictly civic form of nationalism. All of them discredited ethnic nationalism as an artificial construct and as the source, in the words of Hobsbawm, of "demotic xenophobia and chauvinism" with no basis in reality.

According to Kohn, Western nation-states were civic from their beginning in the late eighteenth century. "Illiberal ethnic nationalism" was a phenomenon of Eastern Europe, Russia, and Fascism, places that hyped up the ethnic character of the people while suppressing individual rights. Civic nationalism came out of western-north European countries where a solid middle class had developed; the members of this class were inclined to a conception of the state as a voluntary association of individual wills. This was a progressive class, or so argued Kohn, in wanting a form of citizenship based on laws originating out of the free reasonings of individuals; this class did not like states that impose an ethnocultural identity on its members. Ethnic nationalism, by contrast, come out of cultures lacking a middle class, driven by regressive classes suspicious of free willing individuals, and preferring states that impose on their people an irrational sense of ethnic collective identity inspired by emotions rather than by factual historical realities.

Kymlicka never engages the ways in which these ideas have been seriously challenged by the extensive work of Anthony Smith on the ethnic origins of nations.[26] Smith's main contention is that modern nations were not created ex nihilo on the basis of civic values alone, or because the ruling elites wanted to augment their authority through modern infrastructures; rather, nation states were created on the basis of pre-existing ancestral ties and sense of historical continuity. A sense

---

26   Anthony D. Smith, *The Ethnic Origins of Nations* (Blackwell Publishers, 1986).

of nationhood predated the modern era and could be traced as far back as ancient times and throughout the world. The nations of Europe were not mere "inventions" or functional requirements of modernity, but were factually rooted in the past, in common myths of descent. While the rise of modern industry and modern bureaucracies allowed for the materialization of nation-states in Europe, these nations were primordially based on a population with a collective sense of kinship.

Smith's work was undoubtedly fruitful in challenging the notion that Western nations were inherently civic. Yet, for all this, Smith's concept of ethnicity was more about the importance of past communities, a rough territory, a language, artistic styles, myths and symbols, states of mind, than about emphasizing any form of identity along blood lines—actual common lineage and consanguinity. To be sure, an ethnic group cannot be categorized as a race, but Smith's concept of ethnicity followed the mandated social science prohibition against the inclusion of biological references, physical characteristics, and other features that have a racial dimension. For this reason, ethnicity was defined by Smith in terms of cultural traits, linguistic, historical and territorial traits. But more recently, Azar Gat, Professor of Political Science at Tel Aviv University, has offered a stronger biological conception of ethnicity, in his book *Nations: The Long History and Deep Roots of Political Ethnicity and Nationalism*.[27] This book is said to be written from a "sociobiological perspective". The opening chapters and the conclusion definitely state that nations "are rooted in primordial human sentiments of kin-culture affinity, solidarity, and mutual cooperation, evolutionarily engraved in human nature".[28] Agreeing with "much" of what Smith says, Gat still finds wanting his lack of emphasis on human nature, evolutionary theory, and unwillingness to break away from a culture-oriented perspective. He writes that "ethnicity is by far the most important factor" in national identity and that through history nations "overwhelmingly correlate with and relate to shared kin-culture traits".[29] Welcoming the application of evolutionary theory to explain human behavior, he observes that "people tend to prefer closer kin, who share more genes with them, to more remote kin or 'strangers'". [30]

---

27   Azar Gat, Nations: *The Long History and Deep Roots of Political Ethnicity and Nationalism* (Cambridge University Press, 2013).

28   *Ibid,* p. 380.

29   *Ibid,* p. 24.

30   *Ibid,* p. 27. However, in my estimation, Gat fails to be consistent in his sociobiological perspective particularly in his unwillingness to defend contemporary European ethnic

The only reason Western academics insist to this day that Western nations are civic only is that this historical misinterpretation works wonders for the justification of mass immigration. If Western nations never had an ethnic core, and if their identities are pure constructs based only on values that can be assimilated by any individual regardless of race and cultural background, then there is no substantive reason why Western nations cannot be open to individuals from diverse lineages as long as they accept civic liberal values. Indeed, civic liberals insist that ethnicity should be a matter of individual choice and that a "truly liberal" community has no business identifying itself with any ethnicity. The only political/collective identity a liberal state can encourage among its citizens is a civic identity based on values alone.

The presumption that Western nations are inherently civic, and that a civic identity is inherently inclusive, whereas ethnic nationalism is inherently exclusive in treating the nation as part of one extended ethnic family where minorities do not enjoy the same rights, is implicit throughout Kymlicka's writings. Yet, history shows, to the contrary, that those states possessing a high degree of ethnic homogeneity, where ancestors had lived for generations – England, France, Italy, Belgium, Holland, Sweden, Norway, Finland, and Denmark – were the ones with the strongest liberal traits, constitutions and institutions. That is why minority rights became a legitimate component of these liberal nations. By contrast, those states (or empires like the Austro-Hungarian Empire) composed of multiple ethnic groups were the ones enraptured by illiberal forms of ethnic nationalism and intense rivalries over identities and political boundaries. A state divided among many ethnic groups will find it far more difficult to develop a sense of common national identity and therefore inspire a sense of citizenship and self-sacrifice in the nation's members. This is an argument well made by Jerry Muller in his essay "Us and Them: The Enduring Power of Ethnic Nationalism". As Muller succinctly puts it,

> Liberal democracy and ethnic homogeneity are not only compatible; they can be complementary.[31]

---

identity in the face of mass immigration. He simply capitulates to the current notion that Western nations were meant to be multicultural, founded without an ethnic core. It looks like only Israel can be both "Western liberal" and ethno nationalistic. See Ricardo Duchesne, "The Greek-Roman Invention of Civic Identity Versus the Current Demotion of European Ethnicity" *The Occidental Quarterly* (vol. 15, no. 3, Fall 2015).

31   *Foreign Affairs* (March/April 2008). J. S. Mill said as much: "It is in general a necessary condition of free institutions that the boundaries of governments should coincide

In fact, as we will emphasize in later chapters, the British North America Act, 1867, already accommodated collective claims by denominational communities, English and French linguistic minorities, Aboriginal treaty rights, and the national minority of Quebec. Current multicultural liberals tend to downplay these constitutional claims for the sake of playing up the "transformative" effects that human rights legislation after WW II had upon the making of the 1982 Charter of Rights and Freedoms, as the one document that "repudiated" a Canadian history of "discrimination and prejudice against those of non-Anglo-Saxon origins". [32] But they also like to say that the Charter, in its fuller recognition of collective rights for aboriginals, national rights for the Quebecois, and group rights for immigrant minorities, was continuous with the BNA Act, which they like to identify as a unique constitutional act among Western nations in its enshrinement of certain collective identities. They like to say that the BNA Act "differs in a number of significant respects from like documents of other lands"[33] What the multiculturalists don't like to tell you is that the BNA Act was a liberal document which recognized the equality of all subjects under the law, majoritarian rule, and basic liberties in religious and political expression, while recognizing the ethnic identity of the Francophones as a distinct nation, a distinct collectivity of people, within Canada, in combination with the strongly held idea that Canada, in John A. Macdonald's famous words, was to be "a British nation, under the British flag and under British institutions". [34]

---

in the main with those of nationalities". See *The Collected Works of John Stuart Mill, Volume XIX – Essays on Politics and Society Part II*, ed. John M. Robson, Introduction by Alexander Brady (Toronto: University of Toronto Press, London: Routledge and Kegan Paul, 1977), p. 236. Even the influential commentator David Goodhart, once a supporter of open borders in England, has now admitted that the extensive welfare programs that socialists cherish require high levels of ethnic solidarity — the very cohesion he has seen seriously eroded in Britain with the frenzied promotion of immigration; see his book, *The British Dream: Successes and Failures of Postwar Immigration* (Atlantic, 2013).

32 Jack Jedwab, "To Preserve and Enhance: Canadian Multiculturalism Before and After the Charter", in Magnet et al. *The Canadian Charter of Rights and Freedoms: Reflections on the Charter After Twenty Years* (Butterworths, 2003), p. 314.

33 Brian Dickson, "The Canadian Charter of Rights and Freedoms: Context and Evolution" in Gerald-A. Beaudoin and Errol Mendes, Eds. in *The Charter of Rights and Freedoms* (Carswell, 1996, Third Edition), Chapter 1, p. 13.

34 As cited in P.B. Waite, *The Life and Times of Confederation, 1864-1867* (Toronto: University of Toronto Press, 1962), p. 22.

We need to start thinking, as we move forward in this book, why the ethnic nationalism of English Canadians came to be demonized as illiberal, even as this nationalism was increasingly sensitive to minority identities, in the same breath as the collective ethnic identities of minorities and immigrants came to be acknowledged. Why is ethnic identity among Euro-Canadians viewed as inherently illiberal, whereas ethnic identity among non-European immigrant minorities is celebrated as the culmination of liberalism?

The Great Deception

What may well be the most egregious and unethical (third) flaw in Kymlicka's theory is the claim that his theory is about protecting the rights of minorities when in truth it is an effort to justify the growth of foreign minorities in Canada through mass immigration in order to bring about a situation in which Euro-Canadians will be reduced to a minority without group rights. He repeatedly insists that his theory of multicultural citizenship is "first and foremost" about "overcoming" persisting racial inequalities in the West that are inconsistent with minority rights. But this is not true. His theory is essentially a dishonest program to end "typically white" nations.

He has persuaded impressionable students to view multiculturalism as a lofty endeavor "designed to contest the lingering presence or enduring effects of older...ethnic and racial hierarchies" in the Western world after World War II.[35] The Western nations that defeated Fascism in the Second War, he explains, were liberal democratic states in their recognition of equal civic rights for all white citizens, but they were still illiberal in their "exclusion and oppression" of racial (and sexual) minorities. Eliminating this "lingering" racial oppression, he says, is what his theory of minority rights is all about — or so he would like us to believe.

Kymlicka's theory aims at a radically new form of national citizenship that is multiracial and "never again" "typically white and

---

35 Will Kymlicka, "Liberal Multiculturalism and Human Rights" in Ferran Requejo and Miquel Caminal, eds., *Political Liberalism and Plurinational Democracies* (Routledge, 2011), p. 76. This chapter is taken from an earlier publication by Kymlicka, *Multicultural Odysseys: Navigating the New International Politics of Diversity* (Oxford University Press, 2007).

Christian". His principle of minority rights entails the opening of liberal nations to multitudes of minorities from foreign nations. This can be demonstrated through a careful analysis of some key passages in the widely promoted, government approved and printed article, "Multiculturalism: Success, Failure, and the Future", published for the Transatlantic Commission on Migration.[36] Let's start with this passage:

> Multiculturalism is part of a larger human-rights revolution involving ethnic and racial diversity. Prior to WWII, ethnocultural and religious diversity in the West was characterized by a range of illiberal and undemocratic relationships of hierarchy, justified by racialist ideologies that explicitly propounded the superiority of some peoples and cultures and their right to rule over others. These ideologies were widely accepted throughout the Western world and underpinned both domestic laws (e.g., racially biased immigration and citizenship policies) and foreign policies (e.g., in relation to overseas colonies).[37]

There is no question that a few decades ago racialist ideologies were expressed in the West in citizenship and immigration laws that excluded certain races and in the colonial practices of Europeans over Third World countries. While I don't think that racialist ideas as such are inconsistent with liberalism, a country cannot be classified as liberal-democratic if different races therein enjoy different rights of citizenship. Likewise a country cannot be said to be acting according to liberal ideals if it sanctions the subjugation of "inferior races" and precludes different cultures/nations from enjoying national self-determination. If multiculturalism were to amount to no more than the elimination of laws treating people differently and the rejection of colonization, it would be consistent with liberalism. Minority rights for historic minorities are consistent with liberal values. This is not what Kymlicka's theory is about, however.

He continues:

> After WWII, however, the world recoiled against Hitler's fanatical and murderous use of such ideologies, and the UN

---

36   Will Kymlicka, "Multiculturalism: Success, Failure, and the Future" Migration Policy Institute, Reports (February 2012).

37   *Ibid*, p. 5.

decisively repudiated them in favor of a new ideology of the equality of races and peoples. And this new assumption of human equality generated a series of political movements designed to contest the lingering presence or enduring effects of older hierarchies. We can distinguish three 'waves' of such movements:

1. the struggle for decolonization, concentrated in the period 1948-65;

2. the struggle against racial segregation and discrimination, initiated and exemplified by the African-American civil-rights movement from 1955 to 1965; and

3. the struggle for multiculturalism and minority rights, which emerged in the late 1960s.[38]

Although there is a lot of room for debate about the ways the civil rights movement in the United States brought forth policies that were inconsistent with such key liberal principles as freedom of association and property rights, one can make a reasonable argument that these three movements, taken by themselves, are consistent with the principle of equal individual rights. Likewise, one can agree that the principle of equal rights under the law, and the principle of national self-determination, are both liberal principles entailing the right of all peoples to decide their own destiny, rather than to be ruled by outsiders, even if said people inhabit nations with illiberal constitutions. Decolonization, non-racial discrimination within Western liberal states, and minority rights within liberal states, are all presupposed by the principles of liberalism. Liberal nationalism involves equal treatment of individuals regardless of race as well as "the equal recognition of different national identities". [39]

So far so good. But here is the key passage, along with other passages to be cited soon, in which Kymlicka surreptitiously introduces a program that has nothing to do with liberal minority rights for "previously excluded groups" and everything to do with imposing a multiracial identity "across Western democracies" by bringing millions of foreigners:

---

38   *Ibid*, p. 6.

39   Margaret Moore, "On National Self-Determination" *Political Studies* (vol. XLV, 1997).

The case of *immigrant* multiculturalism is just one aspect of a larger ethnic revival across the Western democracies, in which different types of minorities have struggled for new forms of multicultural citizenship that combined both antidiscrimination measures and positive forms of recognition and accommodation.[40]

It all seems innocuous enough when he adds that, just as indigenous peoples and historic minorities should be granted minority (multicultural) rights, so should "permanently settled immigrant groups". But he is not talking about rights for a static group of settled immigrants. He is formulating a theory of "immigrant multiculturalism" and then calling, as he says next, for the "construction" of a "new" "multicultural form of citizenship in relation to immigrant groups".[41] And he is not just making these arguments in reference to Canada, or so-called "immigrant nations" like Australia and the United States. He is formulating a theoretical program for the total transformation of the national identities of all Western nations by mandating that these nations be open to millions of foreigners.

Kymlicka portrays his theory as if it were "first and foremost about developing new models of democratic citizenship...to *replace earlier uncivil and undemocratic relations of hierarchy and exclusion*",[42] when in fact his theory has never been about the past but always about the future. His "theory of minority rights" has barely been about language rights for established minorities, or about self-government rights for aboriginals, or even about equal treatment of "settled" immigrant minorities. He knows that "in most Western countries, explicit state-sponsored discrimination against ethnic, racial, or religious minorities had largely ceased by the 1960s and 1970s".[43] He also knows that Western nations were already legislating, through the 1970s to the 1990s, a variety of laws and policies designed to afford cultural self-determination and territorial rights to minorities such as the Quebecois, Basques, Catalans, Welsh, and Aboriginals.

---

40 Kymlicka, "Multiculturalism: Success, Failure, and the Future", p. 7.

41 *Ibid*, p. 8.

42 *Ibid*.

43 *Ibid*, p. 6.

Kymlicka, who completed his PhD under the supervision of the renowned Canadian Marxist Gerald Cohen, is one of many members of the New Left who infiltrated the Western liberal tradition in order to push the most radical agenda imaginable: the total eradication of white identity across the West by means of a "long march through the institutions", a phrase he enjoys citing regularly.[44] Like many Marxists in recent decades, he realized that the Leninist language of class struggle and communist ownership was no longer credible and that the best way to transform Western countries was to infiltrate and subvert its liberal language and concepts, camouflaging his true intentions.

Overtly, he wants students to think that his theory is about eliminating "those deeply rooted traditions, customs, and symbols that have excluded or stigmatized minorities" (p. 9). But what he is calling for is a "profound transformation", to use his words, in the identities of whites by restructuring their nations as "immigrant nations". Establishment conservatives have missed entirely this goal in their preoccupation with the ways Kymlicka's theory allows immigrants to retain customs that may be illiberally inconsistent with Western ideals. But, as Kymlicka has insisted, particularly in his later publications, the policies of multiculturalism he advocates, such as ethnic representation in the media, multicultural curricula, dual citizenship, are meant to facilitate integration into the West's political atmosphere of civil-rights and democratic constitutionalism. Both immigrants and whites are supposed to forego their racial prejudices in the process of merging into a new form of multicultural state of being.

---

44   *Ibid*, p. 9. This phrase, now associated with Antonio Gramsci's emphasis on the importance of undermining Western culture rather than capitalism alone, is described in Wikipedia as follows: "The long march through the institutions (German: *der lange Marsch durch die Institutionen*) is a slogan coined by student activist Rudi Dutschke to describe his strategy for establishing the conditions for revolution: subverting society by infiltrating institutions such as the professions. The phrase «long march» is a reference to the prolonged struggle of the Chinese communists, which included a physical Long March of their army across China", https://en.wikipedia.org/wiki/The_long_march_through_the_institutions. It cannot be underestimated the many times that Kymlicka uses this phrase throughout his writings; as far as I remember: "Disentangling the Debate", in *Uneasy Partners: Multiculturalism and Rights in Canada*, eds., Janice Stein, et. al., (Wilfrid Laurier Press, 2007), p. 139; Keith Banting and Will Kymlicka, "Canadian Multiculturalism: Global Anxieties and Local Debates", *British Journal of Canadian Studies*, vol. 23, no. 1 (2010), p. 52; *Multicultural Odysseys* (2007), p.? "The Three Lives of Multiculturalism", in Shibao Guo and Lloyd Wong, eds., *Revisiting Multiculturalism in Canada: Theories, Policies and Debates* (Sense Publishers, 2015), p. 18; "The Rise and Fall of Multiculturalism", *International Social Science Journal* (vol. 61, issue 199, 2010), "Ethnocultural Diversity in a Liberal State: Making Sense of the Canadian Model(s)", http://www.couchichinginstitute.ca/history/2007/Kymlicka.pdf

Multiculturalism-as-citizenization is a deeply (and intentionally) transformative project, both for minorities and majorities. It requires both the dominant and historically subordinated groups to engage in new practices, to enter new relationships, and to embrace new concepts and discourses — all of which profoundly transform people's identities.[45]

It is indeed a theory that is "intentionally transformative" in calling for Western nations to embrace mass immigration and enact policies designed to make the integration of multiple races into Western nations "successful". The policy aspects of his theory are all about "civic integration" measures, *not* for historic minorities or long established immigrants, but for masses of newcomers. Indigenous Euro-Canadians will thusly be obligated to enter into "new relationships" and "embrace new discourses" that will "profoundly transform" their "identities". The policies he suggests are about providing assistance and extensive language training programs for incoming immigrants, encouraging broadcasters to reflect on the increasing cultural diversity that comes with the arrival of new peoples, offering grants to them and affirmative action, as well as a citizenship tests to demonstrate knowledge of multicultural liberal values.

It is no accident that Kymlicka generally uses the term "immigrant multiculturalism" rather than just "multiculturalism", for he is not speaking about Canada's historical diversity, about the minorities that co-existed with the Anglo-Quebecois before Third World immigration accelerated after official multiculturalism was introduced in 1971.

This is not all there is to Kymlicka's deceptive maneuvers against Indigenous Euro-Canadian students, workers and well-meaning middle classes. When news about the failures of multiculturalism in Europe come out, he plays up the "distinctive" Canadian character of his theory, even though his theory has always been about creating a totally new identity across the entire West. It is no accident that Kymlicka has spent most of his academic career lecturing in Europe, hardly ever in Canada, touting the "successful model of Canadian multiculturalism". He believes that all Western nations must become multiracial. He never says this explicitly, for he knows that citizens would democratically reject what can only be described as a genocidal

---

45   "Multiculturalism: Success, Failure, and the Future", p. 9.

program. But the meaning is always there in-between the lines:

> This is obvious in the case of the historically dominant majority group in each country, which is required to renounce fantasies of racial superiority, to relinquish claims to exclusive ownership of the state, and to abandon attempts to fashion publish institutions in its own (typically white/Christian) image.[46]

He is condemning by implication Europeans nations that disagree with mass immigration and miscegenation as having "fantasies of racial superiority". He does not say this about all the other non-Western nations that reject mass immigration. His theory is only for the West. It is premised on the manipulation of the liberal values of Westerners to push without democratic debate a complete alteration in the ethnic and cultural character of Western nations.

Millions of students have been wrongly made to believe that the liberal constitutions of Western nations make it mandatory to grant citizenship and group rights to endless masses of foreigners. This is why he calls the program "a long march through the institutions", in quotation marks. There is nothing liberal about this march, which is a term coined by cultural Marxists to describe a strategy for bringing about a profound transformation of Western cultures by infiltrating and subverting the institutions, ideas, and the professions. The strategy Kymlicka came up with, along with others, was to infiltrate and subvert liberal thinking by manipulating the concept of "minority rights" to mean that Western nations must open their border to millions of foreigners until whites are forced to relinquish their homelands.[47]

The deception does not end here. Kymlicka, like all supporters of mass immigration, likes to pretend that his theory is a realistic response to the realities of globalization and the movements of peoples across national borders. He teaches that "massive numbers of people are moving across borders, making virtually every country more

---

46 *Ibid.*

47 Kymlicka's longs for a world in which Euro-Canadians will be "a constantly shrinking minority" and Canada will "never again... be white...a British country". See *Multicultural Citizenship* (1995), and *Finding Our Way, Rethinking Ethnocultural Relations in Canada* (Oxford University Press, 1998), p. 57.

polyethnic in composition".[48] But this statement cannot be described as other than a fabrication. Mass immigration is not a normal and inevitable affair happening across the globalizing world. While the absolute number of migrants in some countries has increased in the last decades, and an estimated 244 million migrants worldwide were said to be living abroad in 2015, "the share of migrants in the global population reached 3.3 per cent in 2015, up from 2.8 per cent in 2000". [49] This is a minuscule proportion of the world's population. Moreover, if one considers only the population of less developed regions, which account for 5.2 billion of the world's 6.4 (2005), immobility is typical for the vast majority of the world's population.[50] In the case of highly globalized Asia, immigrants have accounted for a mere 1.4-1.6% of Asia's population over the past twenty years – despite fertility rates well below replacement levels in Japan, Singapore, South Korea, Taiwan, and other Asian countries.[51]

Kymlicka has become rich, a member of the top two percent income bracket, promoting this illiberal theory. Meanwhile, Europeans have experienced mass sexual assaults by immigrants,[52] endless terrorist incidents, massive welfare costs[53] to support barely educated

---

48   He said this in his 1995 book, *Multicultural Citizenship*, p. 193

49   See *Sustainable Development* (January 12, 2016), http://www.un.org/ sustainabledevelopment/blog/2016/01/244-million-international-migrants-living- abroad-worldwide-new-un-statistics-reveal/

50   Alan Simmons, *Immigration and Canada, Global and Transnational Perspectives* (Canadian Scholar's Press, 2010), p. 121. Simmons further notes that "by 2005, only 1.4 percent of the population of less developed countries were foreign born" (p. 123). Most migrants who actually become citizens in another country are migrants coming to Western countries. Unfortunately, such sources as UN statistics do not make this clear. The article I just cited above from Sustainable Development, which draws on UN sources, obscures the fact that the migrants coming to Europe and North America are coming from a) outside the Western world, and b) are becoming permanent citizens, whereas almost all the migrants going to Asia are "intra-regional", from one region of Asia to another. Also, many of these intra-regional migrants are temporary migrants who eventually return to their original homelands. In the case of the "migrants" going to United Arab Emirates, they are not getting citizenship but come as temporary workers. The establishment, however, enjoys misleading Europeans about these facts.

51   "Asia's wasted migration opportunities" Asian Century Institute (August 11, 2014).

52   Among the multiple articles that can be easily found in the internet on this topic, see Soeren Kern, "Germany's Migrant Rape Crisis Spirals out of Control. Suppression of data about migrant rapes is 'Germany-wide phenomenon.'" *Gatestone Institute* (August 9, 2016).

53   Virginia Hale, "Politicians Admit Migrants To Cost Germany More Than 30 Billion Euros A Year" *Breitbart* (August 4, 2016).

immigrants[54], coupled with constant harassment for their alleged racist past, indoctrination rather than learning, outright lies about how Africans and Muslims were long participants in the making of Western civilization,[55] under the constant threat of ostracism and loss of employment if they ever question this "profoundly transformative" form of multiracial citizenship.

---

54   "Most refugees are young males lacking qualifications", RT (May 20, 2016), https://
      www.rt.com/news/343753-germany-refugees-males-statistics/

55   Ricardo Duchesne, "Was Socrates a Muslim" *Salisbury Review* (Vol. 33, Issue 2, 2014).

6

Empirical Refutation of Will Kymlicka

Kymlicka is continually telling Europeans that Canada's model of multiculturalism has been a "striking success". Yet he confesses that it was only in the 1990s — twenty years after its official implementation — that multiculturalism became a subject of academic inquiry in Canada, and that "for much of the 1990s", publications on multiculturalism were

...dominated by political philosophers who developed idealized theories of a distinctly liberal-democratic and egalitarian form.[1]

To this day, over 20 more years after the early 1990s, Kymlicka's evaluation of Canada's multiculturalism still remains an idealized account about why diversity should be good, with very few empirically-oriented studies backing his claims about its success. Among his numerous publications, only a few address directly the costs and benefits of multiculturalism. Below are three that seem to be focused on this question alone rather than addressing it in passing:

* *Testing the Liberal Multiculturalist Hypothesis: Normative Theories and Social Science Evidence.*[2]

* *Canadian Multiculturalism: Global Anxieties and Local Debates.*[3]

* *The Rise and Fall of Multiculturalism? New Debates on Inclusion and Accommodation in Diverse Societies.*[4]

These three articles were published in the same year, 2010, and it shows; they examine the same evidence, with very similar wording. Moreover, even in these empirically intended articles, the total number

---

1   "Testing the Liberal Multiculturalist Hypothesis: Normative Theories and Social Science Evidence", Canadian Journal of Political Science, vol. 43, no. 2 (2010).

2   *Ibid.*

3   Co-authored with Keith Banting, "Canadian Multiculturalism: Global Anxieties and Local Debates" (2010). *British Journal of Canadian Studies*, vol. 23, no. 1 (2010).

4   "The Rise and Fall of Multiculturalism? New Debates on Inclusion and Accommodation in Diverse Societies", *International Social Science Journal*, vol. 61 (2010).

of (original) pages Kymlicka dedicates to the factual costs and benefits of Canadian multiculturalism are not many; I would say fewer than 15 pages.[5] His evidential assessment can be categorized under three headings: i) integration, ii) xenophobia, and iii) cultural enrichment.

Integration

On the question of integration: on the surface, it appears that immigrants are integrating into Canada insofar as a very small number of them have engaged in terrorist activities or illiberal practices posing an immediate threat to our liberal values. Immigrants are acquiring citizenship, learning one of the official languages, getting involved in Canadian politics, with some intermarrying outside their ethnic group, getting jobs, and participating in Canada's educational institutions.

But these facts do not say much; they merely show that the majority of immigrants are quite glad that they are inhabiting a Canada officially defined as a multicultural place committed to immigrant diversity in which the traditional Anglo culture is no longer accepted as the official culture, in which immigrants are afforded affirmative action programs and financial support to open businesses, and in which they are economically better off than they were in their backward nations. As it is, the evidence offered in these matters is flimsy and intrinsically subjective, based solely on the answers immigrants have offered in surveys created by proponents of immigrant multiculturalism.

He happily informs us that "no major immigrant organization has demanded the right to maintain illiberal practices". "The Somalis [have] not demanded exemption from laws against female genital mutilation. Pakistanis [have] not demanded exemption from laws against coerced marriages".[6] But Kymlicka sidesteps, in a rather disingenuous way,

---

5   Kymlicka occasionally canvasses material evidence in other publications; for example, in *Finding Our Way, Rethinking Ethnocultural Relations in Canada* (1998), he offers four pages on the "domestic [Canadian] evidence". In a chapter, "The Canadian Model of Diversity in a Comparative Perspective", in Stephen Tierney, ed., *Multiculturalism and the Canadian Constitution* (UBC, 2007), he offers a few paragraphs on the "successful" accommodation of immigrants.

6   "The Canadian Model of Diversity in a Comparative Perspective", p. 73. See also "The Three Lives of Multiculturalism", in Shibao Guo and Lloyd Wong, eds., *Revisiting Multiculturalism in Canada: Theories, Policies and Debates* (Sense Publishers, 2015), pp. 29-30.

widespread illiberal practices by Muslims in Europe, by arguing that Muslims are a small percentage of the population in Canada. Does this mean that Canada can only tolerate so many Muslims? Not at all. The truth is that it does not matter to Kymlicka if illiberal practices spread in Canada, as they have in Europe, since he is a major promoter of immigrant multiculturalism in Europe, has never condemned the systematic rape of white girls by Muslims across Europe and has always excused terrorist attacks, or, in fact, has attributed these crimes to lack of support for Muslim integration by European tax payers. He only uses the exceptional model of Canadian multiculturalism as a trope to manipulate Canadians into believing that Europe's problems cannot be expected in Canada.

He says there is little evidence of "entrenched racial concentration in poor ghettos", yet studies do show that Chinese migrants "tend to settle in established Chinese neighbourhoods". In Richmond, BC, where six out of ten residents are new immigrants, and where half do not speak English in their homes, Chinese-language signs, unaccompanied by English, can be seen everywhere, with multiple incidents of Canadians protesting the lack of visible English signs.[7] There is also a comprehensive study of 17 ethnic groups in 12 Canadian cities by Eric Fong and Rima Wilkes (2003) offering reasons for residential segregation among different ethnic groups in Canada.[8] In February of 2012, the *National Post* contained an article, "As Immigration Booms, Ethnic Enclaves Swell and Segregate", with the following finding:

> In 1981, Canada had only six neighbourhoods with ethnic enclaves...Now, that number has mushroomed to more than 260.[9]

Another study, which looks into the future, published by Citizenship and Immigration Canada in July 2012, "A New Residential Order? The Social Geography of Visible Minority and Religious Groups in Montreal, Toronto, and Vancouver in 2031", predicts that

---

7   Just Google the words "Richmond Chinese-language only sign controversy", and numerous articles will come up.

8   Eric Fong and Rima Wilkes, "Racial and Ethnic Residential Patterns in Canada" *Sociological Forum* (vol. 18, issue 4, 2003).

9   Tristin Hopper, "As Immigration Booms, Ethnic Enclaves Swell and Segregate" *National Post* (February 11, 2012).

...in Toronto and Vancouver, the degree of separation between whites and Visible Minorities is projected to rise considerably, beginning to approach that in the average US city in 2010 between whites and African Americans. While in Montreal the visible minority population is predicted to be spread out across "neighbourhoods of all types" (including ones mixed with whites), it is anticipated that in 2031 "about nine out of ten whites will live in white-dominated areas.[10]

Amazingly, Kymlicka has very little to say about the economic benefits other than general remarks one finds in the mainstream media. This is a big issue that requires a lot of analysis. I will address it by tackling the claims Jonathan Tepperman makes in a recent article, "How Canada Got Immigration Right", which succinctly sums up the pro-immigration economic argument. [11] Tepperman brims with confidence about how Canadians have shown themselves to be a most "pragmatic" people in coming to terms with the "necessity" of finding new sources of immigrant labor once sources dried up in Europe in the 1950s. He thinks Canadians devised a highly impressive system of immigrant selection based on a points system wherein applicants for residency are selected on their educational, linguistic and labor skills and their overall suitability in meeting Canada's economic needs. By picking most immigrants based on their ability to make material contributions, Canada produced one of the most successful immigrant populations in the world. Referring to the OECD, Tepperman claims that Canadian immigrants are better educated than any other country's foreign-born population (53% of them enter Canada with college degrees, compared with 39% in the U.S.). Their employment rate is among the highest in the developed world, and without them, Canada's workforce would be shrinking and aging. Tepperman concludes that Canada's immigration experience has been "spectacular — a record for politicians everywhere to emulate".

Tepperman appeals to other Western nations to imitate the Canadian model as the right way for Westerners to relive labor shortages facing their aging and low fertility populations. There is nothing new in

10   Daniel Hiebert, "A New Residential Order? The Social Geography of Visible Minority and Religious Groups in Montreal, Toronto, and Vancouver in 2031", Government of Canada (July 2012), http://www.cic.gc.ca/english/resources/research/residential.asp

11   *Wall Street Journal* (September 16, 2016).

Tepperman. We hear this every day in Canada. Now, before challenging his claims, it is important to keep in mind that the evidence produced in favor of immigration is part of an establishment that does not allow any dissenting views. Almost 100 percent of the academics in Canada are committed to research that is from the beginning about "facilitating immigrants' integration and inclusion into Canadian society". There has been "an enormous increase in the resources directed toward the settlement of newcomers", as one academic noted with great joy in a 2011 publication in which some 40 other academics participated. It is openly stated in this publication that there is a "burgeoning number of agencies, think tanks, and institutes taking an active interest in immigration, including the Institute for Research on Public Policy Forum, the Maytree Foundation, the Mowat Institute, the Metropolis Project, the Canada West Foundation, and the Fraser Institute". [12] By contrast, there are hardly any individuals doing research on the drawbacks of this model, never mind research backed by grants, and for good reason. As Herbert Grubel, Professor of Economics (Emeritus), at Simon Fraser University, has observed:

> The atmosphere of political correctness existing in Canada suppresses any negative comments in the fear that they could be interpreted as evidence that the person expressing them is a racist...As a result, negative results of immigration are debated rarely in public. By contrast, the idea that immigration brings positive results is politically correct and gets much exposure in public discourse.[13]

Grubel is indeed one of a rare few who questions the economic merits of mass immigration, and it is from his work that I have benefitted most in making some of the arguments below. While Grubel is careful not to stray too far from the establishment when it comes to cultural politics, he produces solid facts against the claim that mass immigration is economically beneficial. Here are some of the statistical highlights he has produced:

---

12 John Biles, et al., *Integration and Inclusion of Newcomers and Minorities across Canada* (McGill-Queen's University Press, 2011), pp. 2-7.

13 Herbert Grubel, "Canada's New Immigration Policies 2016: Good Politics, Bad for the Country" *Optimum Online: The Journal of Public Sector Management*, vol. 46, Issue 2 (June 2016).

- The costs in services and benefits, in the year 2002 alone, incurred by the 2.5 million immigrants who arrived between 1990 and 2002, exceeded the taxes they paid by $18.3 billion.[14]

- "Recent immigrants on average paid less than half the taxes paid by the average Canadian, while at the same time immigrants consumed roughly the same amount of government services as other Canadians".[15] As a result, the average immigrant since 1986 has imposed an annual fiscal burden on Canadian taxpayers of $6000, for a total of $25 billion annually for all immigrants.[16]

- The total fiscal burden resulting from immigration "has risen from $16 to $24 billion in 2005, to $20 to $28 billion in 2010, to $27 to $35 billion in 2014".[17]

Grubel explains that these numbers are "the result of these immigrants having low average incomes and paying correspondingly low taxes while they are entitled to all the benefits offered by Canada's welfare state".[18] He observes, furthermore, that "a significant part of this burden originates with the parents and grandparents who join their families in Canada [and who] pay virtually no taxes and consume large amounts of government services, especially health care».[19] But what about Tapperman's point that Canada's points system ensures that most immigrants are chosen for their ability to make an economic contribution? Well, on the surface

---

14　Herbert Grubel, "Recent immigration and Canadian living standards", in Herbert Grubel, ed., *The Effects of Mass Immigration on Canadian Living Standards* (Fraser Institute, 2009), p. 106.

15　Herbert Grubel, "Canada's New Immigration Policies 2016: Good Politics, Bad for the Country" *Optimum Online: The Journal of Public Sector Management*, vol. 46, Issue 2 (June 2016).

16　Herbert Grubel, "A population of 100 million comes with a price; are Canadians willing to pay it?" Fraser Institute, https://www.fraserinstitute.org/article/population-100-million-comes-price-are-canadians-willing-pay-it

17　Patrick Grady and Herbert Grubel, "Immigration and the Welfare State Revisited: Fiscal Transfers to Immigrants in Canada in 2014" Fraser Institute (November 10, 2015), https://www.fraserinstitute.org/studies/immigration-and-the-welfare-state-revisited-fiscal-transfers-to-immigrants-in-canada-in-2014

18　Herbert Grubel, "A population of 100 million comes with a price; are Canadians willing to pay it?" Fraser Institute, https://www.fraserinstitute.org/article/population-100-million-comes-price-are-canadians-willing-pay-it

19　Herbert Grubel, "Canada's New Immigration Policies 2016: Good Politics, Bad for the Country" *Optimum Online: The Journal of Public Sector Management*, vol. 46, Issue 2 (June 2016).

it seems that since the points system was established a few decades ago, "economic" immigrants with skills have constituted around 60 percent of the total, whereas family-class immigrants have constituted around a third of the intake, and refugees about 10-15 percent. But included in the "economic class" are also the spouses and children of the principal economic applicants. For example, it was estimated that in 2005 only 39% of the immigrants classified under the "economic class" were principal applicants selected according to their language skills, level of education, and work experience. As a percentage of *all* the immigrants granted permanent residency in 2005, only 19.5% were directly selected on the basis of their skills and education.[20] In other words, over 80 percent were not economic immigrants.

It should also be noted that many immigrants hold Canadian citizenship but work abroad, paying no taxes in Canada, and only returning to Canada to use expensive government services. About 11 percent of immigrants have citizenship in Canada and one other country. It has been estimated that 8 percent of Canadian citizens, including those with dual citizenship, or 2.7 million people, live outside Canada.[21]

Moreover, the so-called "highly trained immigrants" have come primarily from countries with educational systems and training standards that are either unfamiliar or lower than Canadian standards. Many have arrived with weak skills in English and/or French, and have not exhibited the credentials, education, and work experience required in high-level Canadian jobs. A survey carried out in 2003 by The International Adult Literacy and Skills Survey on some 18,000 individuals (of whom 3,700 were immigrants) showed that the "cognitive skill distribution of immigrants was much lower on average than that of Canadian born individuals".[22] Immigrants from countries in Africa, Asia, Caribbean, and Latin America obtained lower scores on cognitive skills and tests.[23]

---

20   Alan Simmons, *Immigration and Canada: Global and Transnational Perspectives* (Canadian Scholar's Press, 2010), p. 93.

21   Alan Simmons, *Immigration and Canada: Global and Transnational Perspectives*, p. 190.

22   Alan Simmons, *Immigration and Canada: Global and Transnational Perspectives*, p.159.

23   A Statistics Canada 2006 Census report, "Earnings differences between immigrants and the Canadian-born – The role of literacy skills", noted that "in terms of educational attainment, clear differences are apparent, with immigrants, especially males, being more likely to have completed a university degree – 31% in the case of male immigrants compared to 18% of Canadian-born men. Similarly, a larger proportion of immigrant

Data also shows that immigrants have not found jobs as quickly as anticipated. Labor market studies in 2006-07, for example, indicate that immigrants who had arrived in the previous five years were less likely to be actively employed, and that higher percentages were unemployed compared to Canadian born workers.[24] Data shows as well that "Canadian workers' purchasing power remained flat or unchanged from 1980 to 2005". [25] According to the 2006 census, the median earnings of Canadians (in inflation-adjusted 2005 dollars) have increased by 0.1% since 1980. Not only that, but the earnings of the poorest fifth fell dramatically in that time, by 20.6%, while the top 20% of earners saw their incomes rise by 16.4%.[26]

As Grubel argues, there is no such thing as a labor shortage in Canada. There is an unwillingness to work for undercut wages due to cheap immigrant labor and imported contract labor. Canadian workers are proud of their political and economic gains against the harsh working conditions of the past, serfdom, peonage, or coolie labor. They do not wish to see an importation of these low-wage, anti-working class values from the non-Western world just to keep the profits of global corporations high. Grubel also refers to a study estimating that for immigration to actually overcome the problem of an aging population in Canada, the number of immigrants would have to increase "so much that by 2050 Canada's population would have to be 235 million", that is, about 200 million more "Canadians" than the current

women had a university degree (21%) than was the case for Canadian-born women (17%). *Nevertheless, Canadian-born men and women scored significantly higher than their immigrant counterparts in prose literacy, document literacy, numeracy and problem-solving.* Large differences are apparent when immigrants who received part or all of their education in Canada are compared to those who received all of their education abroad (my italics), http://www.statcan.gc.ca/pub/81-004-x/2008005/article/10798-eng.htm#a

24   Alan Simmons, *Immigration and Canada: Global and Transnational Perspectives*, p. 142 There are many revealing statistical studies cited in Simmons but they are marred by the usual habit academics have interpreting negative facts about immigrant earnings, education, and employment levels as products of white discrimination, and rarely as products of low immigrant skills, shoddy educational degrees, and the downward pressure placed on wages by higher supplies of cheap labor. He notes, however, the declining earnings of immigrants since 1980, and that "many arrive with weak skills in English and/or French...they may not have the excellent skills that are required for the high-level jobs" (p, 149).

25   *Ibid*, p. 150.

26   Statistics Canada "2006 Census: Earnings, income and shelter costs", http://www.statcan.gc.ca/daily-quotidien/080501/dq080501a-eng.htm

population![27] Needless to say, the congestion, pollution, and need for new infrastructure would be enormous. Yet, amazingly, none of the leftist enthusiasts for mass immigration have ever made a connection between population growth through immigration and deterioration of the environment and overall decline in the quality of city life.[28]

I have always been perplexed by the celebration of a model predicated on a system designed to entice the most educated individuals from the poorer nations where they are in higher need. This is known in Economics as "human capital flight", a form of "brain drain imperialism". As any undergraduate can find out in Wikipedia,

> Countries in Sub-Saharan Africa have lost a tremendous amount of their educated and skilled populations as a result of emigration to more developed countries, which has harmed the ability of such nations to get out of poverty. Conservatively speaking, "Brain drain has cost the African continent over $4 billion in the employment of 150,000 expatriate professionals annually". [29]

This goes to show how immoral and hypocritical the Canadian "humane" model of mass immigration really is; on the one hand, calling upon Canadians to cherish other cultures, while, on the other, promoting policies that weaken the economic well-being of these cultures.

---

27   Herbert Grubel, "Canada's New Immigration Policies 2016: Good Politics, Bad for the Country" *Optimum Online: The Journal of Public Sector Management*, vol. 46, Issue 2 (June 2016).

28   Ricardo Duchesne and Tim Murray, "Environmentalist / Corporate Rapprochement around Immigration", Council of European Canadians (July 14, 2014), http://www. Euro-Canadian.ca/2014/07/environmentalist-corporate-rapprochement-around-immigration.html

29   "Human Capital Flight", Wikipedia, (https://en.wikipedia.org/wiki/Human_capital_flight#Sub-Saharan_Africa). A study on "Skilled Labor Migration from Developing Countries: Study on India" in International Migration Papers 49, by Binod Khadria, (http://www.fudepa.org/Biblioteca/recursos/ficheros/BMI20060000455/imp49e.pdf) concludes, after a very detailed compilation of data, that "a large outflow of skilled persons poses a threat of a brain drain, which can adversely impact growth and development [...] The scale and magnitude of the brain drain from India continues to be substantial". The argument that remittances from international migrants helps poor nations is very weak. Remittance money is hardly used for productive purposes but mostly for immediate consumption, which actually encourages consumption of imports, which creates dependency. See, Kathleen Newland, "Migration as a Factor in Development and Poverty Reduction" MPI, Migration Policy Institute (June 1, 2003).

Xenophobia

What about evidence regarding the integration of Canadians of European ancestry to multiculturalism? Kymlicka's handling of this issue is best categorized under "xenophobic fears among natives". While positive feelings by immigrants towards Canada are deemed to be evidence of successful integration, negative feelings by members of the host culture are deemed to be "xenophobic" and thus automatically disqualified as evidence. Kymlicka does not consider how the founding European peoples of Canada have been affected by the influx of millions of immigrants since Canada's borders were opened to an average of 250,000 immigrants every year since 1990.

Here the only evidence that counts is of Canadians who have "progressively" come to accept a polyethnic Canada.[30] Native citizens with a strong sense of European identity are automatically categorized as "intolerant" and consequently ostracized as individuals whose sensitivities and opinions cannot be used as evidence against the multicultural experiment. Kymlicka uses as evidence the observation that "Canadians have become progressively more supportive of existing immigration levels over the last two decades". [31] He notes that over 60% of Canadians in 1988 wanted fewer immigrants, whereas in 2006 just over 20% wanted fewer immigrants. The fact that a majority of Canadians in 1988 wanted lower immigration, or that 20 to 25% percent wanted fewer immigrants in 2006, is not seriously addressed.

He never ponders whether Canadians have been drilled into compliance rather than persuaded through open debates, though he admits, amazingly so, that multiculturalism has been "barely explained at all to the Canadian public". [32] Even supporters of this policy agree that immigrant multiculturalism has proceeded for the most part by way of non-transparent regulations, executive directives, and administrative

---

30   Kymlicka considers any statistical assessment of Caribbean criminality as "old-fashioned racism" (2005:74). It does not matter, as journalist Peter Worthington among others has noted, that "in Toronto, the ones using guns — and the victims of shootings — mostly tend to be of Jamaican origin. Police know this, even if they can't say so publicly". Huffington Post (July 18, 2012), http://www.huffingtonpost.ca/peter-worthington/toronto-shooting_b_1683102.html

31   Banting and Kymlicka, p. 57

32   Hawkins, Freda. *Critical Years in Immigration: Canada and Australia Compared* (McGill-Queens University Press, 1991), p. 221.

discretion rather than by legislative action and popular demand. We already mentioned Gallup polls in the 1960s showing that only about one third of Canadians thought that Canada should bring in more immigrants, and over 60 percent thought that the fairly low levels of Asian immigration (at the time) were already too high.[33] The Canadian public in the 1960s, and even the 1970s, as we shall see in Part IV, still agreed with Prime Minister Mackenzie King's words in 1947:

> The people of Canada do not wish, as a result of mass immigration, to make a fundamental alteration in the character of our population.[34]

But liberal elites were determined to re-engineer the souls of average Canadians. Accordingly, numerous programs were implemented right after multiculturalism became official policy in 1971, with the result that today diversity has been institutionally implanted in every federal government department and public institution, written into the programming and advertisement directives of the media, and mandated in every public school, museum, and university curriculum. There is no denying that, in this respect, multiculturalism has been a resounding success.

Kymlicka refers to this imposition of multiculturalism as "a long march through the institutions at all levels of Canadian society".[35]

---

33   The same Kymlicka who says that multiculturalism is supported by the majority of Canadians, and that it was enacted democratically, and that it is all about making Canada live up to its democratic principles, admits in a chapter published in 2007, in which he cites the words of Freda Hawkins, that "virtually every study of multiculturalism in Canada has concluded that the policy has been 'barely explained at all to the Canadian public,' that 'no serious effort has [been] made by any senior politician to define multiculturalism in a Canadian context,' and that this has seriously jeopardized public support for the policy". See "The Canadian Model of Multiculturalism", in Stephen Tierney, ed., *Multiculturalism and the Canadian Constitution* (UBC Press, 2007), p. 63. To those wondering — how could Kymlicka contradict himself this way? — my answer is that he wants to persuade government officials that they should give him more grants so that he can keep accumulating wealth explaining multiculturalism.

34   William Lyon Mackenzie, "Statement of...Canada's Immigration Policy", 1947, in Howard Palmer, ed., *Immigration and the Rise of Multiculturalism* (Copp Clark Publishing, 1975). It is worth mentioning that these words by Mackenzie are not readily available in the internet, and rarely cited; Makenzie was once identified by Canadian historians as the most successful Prime Minister, but these words, and more will be brought up later, don't square well with an agenda that would have us believe, as we saw in earlier chapters, that Canada was always striving to be a nation of diverse immigrants.

35   Banting and Kymlicka, p. 52

This phrase, which regularly recurs in Kymlicka's writings, as observed in the last chapter, points to a successful strategy whereby leftists in the 1960s, instead of calling for a communist takeover of the state, as in Russia and China, called for the gradual infiltration of all the pivotal opinion forming institutions of Western society. Opposition to this march is seen by Kymlicka as an impediment to be suppressed. Indeed, the same Kymlicka who demands "respect" for newly arrived immigrants, never fails to designate those natives who show loyalty and affection for Canada's European heritage as "neo-Nazis" or as members of a "far right backlash" – who must be persuaded to accept immigration in order thereby to produce evidence in favor of immigration![36] In his corporate-sponsored publication, "Multiculturalism: Success, Failure, and the Future", he mentions some of the problems critics of multiculturalism have brought up, but only to reply that these problems are signs of a xenophobic "backlash". This is exactly the same view he held in his book *Multicultural Citizenship* back in 1995:

> It is difficult to avoid the conclusion that much of the backlash against multiculturalism arises from a racist or xenophobic fear of these new immigrant groups.[37]

It is quite delusional to suppose that polls and discussions about the merits and demerits of Canada's multicultural model can be objective in this oppressive climate. Opposition is automatically viewed as intolerant, and not worthy of serious consideration. From the moment they are born, Canadians are brainwashed to think of multiculturalism as Canada's identity, compelled to think that their nation was created by immigrants and that Euro-Canadians with ancestries going back generations are no more Canadian than foreigners seeking citizenship.

As noted above, the entire research apparatus associated with the model has been structured to make this model work, all the institutions,

---

36   He much prefers to rely on the opinions of wealthy and powerful outsiders than on native Canadians, gushing over how Canada's international reputation "has grown steadily over the past fifteen years", and citing as supporting evidence the declaration of "his Highness the Aga Khan, spiritual head of the world's 15 million Muslims" that "Canada is today the most successful pluralist society on the face of the globe" (2005: 64). Apparently, this Muslim is not a conservative but a feminist who agrees with Canada's gay rights.

37   *Multicultural Citizenship*, p. 179.

media and businesses, are dedicated to making it successful. Therefore, all the reports, studies, dissertations, books, and articles produced about this model are biased in their determination to show that it is working and can be improved with further "increases in the resources directed toward the settlement of newcomers". Whenever problems are identified, such as the formation of ethnic enclaves, earning gaps between immigrants and whites, poor housing, these are framed as problems resulting from "failures" to implement the model properly. Multiculturalism is an industry that fuels lucrative salaries and perks for countless academics who are thus incentivized to portray the model in the best possible light. No graduate student or professor can get a grant if the proposal insinuates opposition to the very notion of immigrant multiculturalism.[38]

And yet, in the last few years Canadians are starting to show signs of discontent with immigration numbers and other related issues. But Tepperman is simply wrong in stating point blank that "polls have shown that two-thirds of them feel that immigration is one of Canada's key strengths, and the same proportion favors keeping it at its current level — or even increasing it".[39] Even if we were to accept polls as the only measurement of Canadian wishes, there is polling out there showing that Canadians would eagerly welcome significant aspects of Trump's immigration proposals relevant to the Canadian context.

In a poll reported in September 10, 2016,[40] they seem to agree with Trump that we should screen immigrants for anti-Canadian values: "Two-thirds of Canadians want prospective immigrants to be screened for 'anti-Canadian'". This preference for immigrants who are more

---

38 Kymlicka is now seen as the Don of this continuously expanding research agenda. Currently he is participating in the creation of a "Multiculturalism Policy Index" that will track down, and judge accordingly, whether Western nations are implementing properly such goals as dual citizenship for newcomers, funding of ethnic group activities, funding of bilingual education, affirmative action for immigrants, adoption of a pro-diversity school curricula, as well as ensuring full scale constitutional and legislative "affirmation of multiculturalism". See Erin Tolley, "Multiculturalism Policy Index, Immigrant Minority Policies", School of Policy Studies (Queen's University at Kingston, Canada, 2011), http://www.queensu.ca/mcp/sites/webpublish.queensu.ca.mcpwww/files/files/immigrantminorities/evidence/ImmigrantMinoritiesApr12.pdf

39 "How Canada Got Immigration Right" *Wall Street Journal* (September 16, 2016).

40 Bruce Campion-Smith, "Canadians favour screening would-be immigrants for anti-Canadian values" thestar.com (September 10, 2016).

inclined to accept Canadian values holds across the political spectrum: "Conservative supporters with 87 per cent backing the idea and just 8 per cent opposed compared to 57 per cent support among Liberals and 59 per cent for New Democrat voters". Canadians also seem to agree with Trump's concern about opening our borders to Syrian refugees. According to a new poll from the Angus Reid Institute:

> More than 70 per cent of Canadians don't support the federal government taking in more than 25,000 Syrian refugees, according to a new poll...Two in five respondents think Canada should stop taking in Syrian refugees immediately.[41] They also seem to agree with Trump that legal immigration should be cut in the future: In a survey conducted in 2013:

> When asked whether 'less immigration' or 'more immigration' would lead 'to a better future 25 years from now,' 61.7 per cent of Canadians said less immigration would be preferable, compared to 34.4 per cent who said more immigration would result in a better Canada.[42]

Enrichment

The third heading under which Kymlicka assesses multiculturalism concerns the assumed cultural "enrichment" millions of non-Europeans have brought to Canada. What is so disconcerting about this assessment is that "the intrinsic value of cultural diversity" is accepted *ab initio*.[43] Diversity, Kymlicka says without elaboration, will make "the larger anglophone culture...richer and more diverse".[44] One would think that someone so actively involved in defending multiculturalism would at the least devote a few paragraphs explaining why diversity is inherently good. What's so lacking about Euro-Canadian culture, and what's so amazing about African, Asian, and Islamic culture? In a section entitled "The Value of Cultural Diversity", he infers:

---

41   Kelly Hobson, "More than 70% of Canadians think that Liberals' refugee target is too high" (National Post, February 19, 2016).

42   Olesia Plokhii, "Canadians want less immigration", *iPolitics* (July 25, 2013).

43   This is repeated by countless politicians and academics as if it were a law from Moses.

44   *Multicultural Citizenship*, p. 79.

> ...liberals extol the virtue of having diversity of lifestyles within a culture, so presumably they also endorse the additional diversity which comes from having two or more cultures in the same country.

The implicit logic is that, since Europeans believe in freedom of choice, it follows that they prefer more cultures inside their nations to improve the "quality and richness" of their choices. I say "implicit" because Kymlicka does not debate whether choices will continuously improve as the culture is diversified. He does not differentiate the ever increasing diversity he wants (in which Europeans will be reduced, in his words, to "a constantly shrinking minority") and the diversity Canadians already enjoyed, say in 1971, when multiculturalism was announced as an official policy, when the ethnic distribution of the country was: British (44.6%), French (28.7%), German (6.1%), Italian (3.4%), Ukrainian (2.7%), Dutch (2.0%), Scandinavian (1.8%), Polish (1.5), Jewish (1.4%), Other Europe (4.2%), Asian (1.3%), and Aboriginal (1.3).[45] All Canadians in 1971, regardless of ethnicity and religious affiliation, enjoyed the same liberal rights. What was it about this diversity that was lacking in quality and choices? Kymlicka never asks this simple question in his many inflated and repetitive writings.

The vast majority of Canadians would never have endorsed policies that target them as oppressors to be dispossessed if the ultimate intentions of this ideology were presented to them with equal access to the public space and without fear of demonization and loss of livelihood. Kymlicka only offers idealized versions of an imagined future, but in between the lines one can detect the mind of someone intent on destroying Canada's Christian European heritage. In *Multicultural Citizenship*, he muses over the fact that "many state symbols such as flags, anthems, and mottoes reflect a particular ethnic or religious background" and that it would only be fair for other ethnic groups to demand "that their identity be given the same recognition as the original Anglo-Saxon settlers". [46] As a possible solution he proposes "redesigning" public holidays, uniforms, and state symbols. It is "easy", he says, to "replace religious oaths with secular ones, and so we should". It would be "more difficult but perhaps not impossible,

---

45   Leo Driedger, ed. *The Canadian Ethnic Mosaic, A Quest for Identity*. (McClelland and Stewart, 1978)

46   *Multicultural Citizenship*, p. 115.

to replace existing public holidays and work-weeks with more neutral schedules for schools and government offices". In other words, he is anticipating a point in Canada's history when the entire "societal culture" will be neutered and neutralized away from any Eurocentric characteristic. In this vein, he calls for a "multicultural education" to correspond to the emergence of multiple identities, a widening of the cultural perspectives that children are exposed to, as well the rewriting of Canada's history in order to give an equal voice to diverse ethnicities.

Destruction of Canada's Historic Identity

Ultimately the biggest problem is that projections are pointing to a future Canada in which "Caucasians" will be increasingly displaced by people who are "non-white in colour" — the term Statistic Canada uses. This fact is never seen as an issue by the mainstream political parties and the media. Instead, Euro-Canadians who lament their dwindling numbers are categorically denounced as "white supremacists", while "non-Caucasians in race" who call for a majority Asian Canada are celebrated as vibrant and liberal-minded — regardless of their otherwise intolerant customs, hyper-patriarchal dispositions, and unwillingness to marry outside their race. So, even if many are "aware" that they will become a minority, they are prohibited from discussing this issue.

"Never again", Kymlicka demands, should Canada be viewed as a "white country…as a British country".[47] Today, one in five Canadians is foreign-born, and Kymlicka is still encouraging more immigration and diversity. Major newspapers, academic and corporate elites alike, are calling for a doubling of Canada's intake of immigrants from 250,000 to 450,000, with the goal of raising the population from 35 to 100 million by the end of the century. Kymlicka and liberal elites generally believe that immigrant multiculturalism is the final stage in the march towards racial equality. This equality is obviously illusionary. White-created nations are the only ones experimenting with this ideology. What is not illusionary is that Canada is steadily becoming a nation overwhelmed by diverse cultures. A majority (70.2%) of the foreign-born population in 2006, more than 10 years ago, reported a mother tongue other than English or French. The

---

47 *Finding Our Way, Rethinking Ethnocultural Relations in Canada* (Oxford University Press, 1998), p. 57

Muslim, Hindu, Sikh and Buddhist faiths amounted to 33 per cent of those immigrants who arrived between 2001 and 2011. Canada's visible minority population is projected to make up one third of the population by the year 2031. Toronto and Vancouver are projected to become "majority-minority" cities in 2031, with the non-European ethnic population at 63 and 59 percent respectively. Similar massive increases are anticipated in Canada's major cities.[48]

The end of European Canada is now an impending reality. It is high time Kymlicka offered an explanation to native Canadians why they should accept policies that are fast reducing them to a minority within their own homelands. Given that humans by nature have a "very deep bond" to their ethnic and cultural identity, why should European Canadians be precluded from having a vital stake in retaining their culture, traditions and ethnic identity, the same stake Kymlicka attributes to non-Europeans?

---

48   Daniel Hiebert, "A new residential order?: The Social Geography of Visible Minority and Religious Groups in Montreal, Toronto, and Vancouver in 2031" Citizenship and Immigration Canada (July 2012), http://publications.gc.ca/collections/collection_2013/cic/Ci4-98-2012-eng.pdf

7

Recognizing Minorities While Suppressing Majorities

The Basic Difference Between Kymlicka and Taylor

Charles Taylor is possibly the most celebrated Canadian academic of the post WW II era. Best known for developing a liberal theory of multiculturalism that recognizes the collective cultural rights of minorities within the Canadian federation, he has a high international reputation as a major thinker in the social sciences and philosophy. His writings have brought him numerous eulogies, prizes, and honors, including the titles of "Companion of the Order of Canada" (1995), "Grand Officer of the National Order of Quebec" (2000), SSHRC Gold Medal ($100,000) for Achievement in Research (2003), the Kyoto Prize, Japan's highest private award for global achievement, the Templeton Prize (2007), awarded to an individual who "has made an exceptional contribution to affirming life's spiritual dimension", which included 1.5 million US dollars; and most recently (August 2015) the prestigious $1.5 million John W. Kluge Prize for Achievement in the Study of Humanity granted by the Library of Congress.[1]

His theory of "deep diversity" may appear to be similar to Kymlicka's in calling for a liberalism that is committed to the collectivist survival and enhancement of Aboriginals and Quebecois, as well as for cultural rights for minorities within Canada. Their arguments, to be sure, have been taken together by academics and media elites generally as ideological weapons in the promotion of diversification across the West. Both have been similarly committed, though Kymlicka more so, in selling Canadian multiculturalism abroad as a "successful model".

---

1   In addition to numerous articles and chapters, three books have been written exclusively on his intellectual contributions: Nicholas Smith, *Charles Taylor: Meaning, Morals and Modernity* (Polity Press, 2002), Ruth Abbey, *Charles Taylor* (Cambridge University Press, 2004), and Mark Redhead, *Charles Taylor: Thinking and Living Deep Diversity* (Rowman and Littlefield Publishers, 2002).

Critics of Taylor have said that his notion of "deep diversity" entails cultural demands by minorities inconsistent with the liberal principle that all citizens should enjoy the same rights as individuals – a criticism similarly directed against Kymlicka. But there is a key difference between these two: Taylor is more consistent in his adherence to the observation that all humans have a deep attachment to their ethno-cultural heritage. One should not expect cultural rights to be "temporary". Non-European groups may want to retain at least some key defining aspects of their cultural identity rather than integrate totally into a world of individual rights.

Taylor's explanation of the importance humans attach to their ethno-cultural identity goes deeper philosophically. He consistently shows that the theory of individual rights contains within its premises the idea that humans should have a right to have their ethno-cultural identities recognized, because such recognition is essential to the self-fulfillment of the individual. It is not that Kymlicka does not make similar statements. Both argue that individuals can only fulfill themselves as individuals within a community, and both correctly criticize mainstream liberalism for advocating an incoherent conception of the individual existing outside and apart from a particular society. The difference, simply stated, is that Taylor goes deeper into the Western philosophical tradition in showing that individual fulfillment can only be obtained when individuals from different cultural groups "mutually recognize" the importance each attaches to their cultural life world.

Taylor's profounder emphasis on the importance of ethno-cultural identity makes the contradictions we saw in Kymlicka all the more stark, in the way he applies the theory of communitarian rights only to Aboriginals, Quebecois, and immigrants in complete disregard for the cultural rights of the majority Euro-Canadians. He never addresses the way Canadian identity was constructed primarily within a particular Anglo community, but views this community as a place in need of alteration to accommodate the cultural expectations of minorities. His communitarianism recognizes the group rights of minorities with the expectation that different cultural groups may redefine the meaning of individual rights in ways that reflect their collective cultural norms. At the same time, his communitarianism recognizes only the individual rights of European Canadians without recognizing their collective cultural rights. The only collective identity he acknowledges among Euro-Canadians is a multiculturalism imposed from above by cosmopolitan elites intended to celebrate the group rights of others. Accordingly, in the same breath as Taylor argues that liberalism is consistent with the recognition of the communitarian rights of minorities, he warns against any communitarian politics associated with European majorities. European ethnic identification as such is targeted as inherently illiberal and discriminatory in nature.

Taylor's communitarianism, rather than being rooted in the longings and historical identities of Europeans, is yet another theory concocted by a privileged academic devoid of loyalty and affection for his community of birth. Taylor regularly uses the word "embedded" — dutifully abiding by the academic lexicon — to accentuate the way human behavior needs to be understood within the context of historically concrete social settings. But he is completely oblivious to the distinctive, historically based character of Canada as a nation with a dominant British core that in the BNA Act, 1867, willingly acknowledged certain collective rights of the national Francophone minority in Quebec. The communitarian sensitivity that he calls upon Canadians to extend to minorities, he does not demand upon other minorities to extend to Anglo Canadians, but instead takes for granted the standard image of British Canada as a colonial hangover, an "imagined community" imposed by WASPS upon the rest of Canadians, a conservative, reactionary, and imperialist heritage that should be discarded altogether.[2]

The Relevance of Taylor to Euro-Canadians

Why should European nationalists take seriously Taylor's

---

2   The "Britishness" of Canada has been the subject of attacks for a long time, to the point that now historians, and the entire academic world, think that this identity was "imposed presumptuously upon others by Wasps", an identity without historical basis, "inflicted on non-British immigrants, reserving for Wasps a dominant, masculinist, exclusive universalism presented as nature, true, authentic". While it is easy to recognize that identities always contain constructed elements, in varying degrees, expressing the ways humans give meaning to their ancestry, memories, and sense of place, the idea that Canada's Britishness was a pure fiction is an extremist position only an academic world lacking any sense of historical accuracy, the statistical analysis presented in Part 1, would endorse. Taylor endorses this extremist view. The just cited words are taken from C.P. Champion, *The Strange Demise of British Canada. The Liberal and Canadian Nationalism, 1964-1968* (McGill-Queens Press, 2010), pp. 7-8. Champion tries timidly to challenge this extremist view.

communitarianism if it is so inconsistently against the collective rights of Europeans? Because Taylor is the one communitarian who recognizes that humans have a strong need to have their ethno-cultural collective identity acknowledged by the state. Taylor's concept of deep diversity goes beyond the standard communitarianism of Michael Walzer,[3] Michael Sandel,[4] and Alasdair MacIntyre,[5] who tend to be preoccupied with socialistic policies, face to face sentiments of trust, family life, or the way individual values cannot be understood outside the living tradition of a particular community, without making references to the importance of in-group ethnic identity. It also goes beyond Kymlicka's temporary recognition of minority group rights.

Paradoxically as it may seem to those who think assimilation is the key to solving the problems of mass immigration, Taylor's stronger emphasis on group cultural identities makes his arguments all the more valuable for those who care about the cultural identity of Euro-Canadians. Indeed, at a time when European ethno-nationalists are in need of developing multiple strategies to counter the dominant discourse of cultural Marxism it might be worthwhile to bring out the ways in which Taylor's justification and worldwide promotion of Canadian multiculturalism contains within itself the seeds for a strong political argument in favor of European ethnic identity. The critical assessment I am proposing against Taylor may be defined as an "immanent critique" in which the objective is to detect contradictions in his thinking which point to determinate possibilities for European nationalism within the current multicultural establishment.[6]

There is no reason to reject the substantive premises and truth-claims of Taylor's communitarianism. We can instead enter his theory, so to speak, register key contradictions, as we outlined above, develop these contradictions according to their own logic, and, in this way, bring out support for European ethnic nationalism from within his

3   Michael Walzer, "The Communitarian Critique of Liberalism". *Political Theory*, Vol. 18, No. 1. (Feb., 1990), pp. 6-23.

4   Michael Sandel, *Liberalism and the Limits of Justice*. (Cambridge, UK New York: Cambridge University Press, 1998).

5   Alasdair MacIntyre, *After Virtue: A Study in Moral Theory* (University of Notre Dame Press, 1984).

6   Robert J. Antonio, "Immanent Critique as the Core of Critical Theory: Its Origins and Developments in Hegel, Marx and Contemporary Thought". *British Journal of Sociology*, Vol. 32, No. 3 (Sep., 1981).

communitarian premises. We can show, in fact, that ethnic European nationalism is already implied in the theory of liberalism and in the current rationale for multiculturalism. The right of European Canadians to fulfill their potential as individuals is being constrained by their inability to express themselves as members of a cultural community rooted in deep historical experiences to which they belong collectively and which is intrinsically valuable to them as human beings.

Recognition and Dialogue

Taylor's theory of "deep diversity" contains three key concepts: "mutual recognition", "dialogue", and "fusion of horizons". This theory is clearly expressed in a widely popular essay entitled, "The Politics of Recognition". Since 1992, this essay has appeared in many languages, discussed numerous times in conferences, books, articles, and PhD Dissertations. According to a Google Scholar search I did some months ago, it has been cited by close to 7000 sources. The book version, which appeared in *Multiculturalism: Examining the Politics of Recognition* (1994), edited by Amy Gutmann, with commentaries on this essay by established academics, has been cited close to 12,000 times![7]

The first point Taylor makes in this essay is that the driving motivation behind current movements for gender parity, national self-determination, "subaltern" identities, black civil rights, aboriginal rights is a deeply-felt human need for recognition. The need to be respected and acknowledged by others is a defining trait of our human nature. He writes:

Nonrecognition or misrecognition can inflict harm, can be a

---

7   James Tully, "Distinguished Professor of Political Science" at the University of Victoria, believes that Taylor's way of thinking about Canadian diversity has had a "revolutionary" role in the way Canadians have come to understand multiculturalism. Tully taught together with Taylor at McGill University for about 17 years. I took two undergraduate courses with him, assiduously attending all the lectures and doing the readings, but never completing the essays on time, obtaining a "J" in one course, and a "KF" in another. At a lecture Tully gave in 2012, as part of a conference under the theme "Charles Taylor at 80", he effectively explains Taylor's theory. This lecture is available online (https://www.youtube.com/watch?v=-raJWEplmxg) as part of a conference of the Groupe de Recherche Interuniversitaire en Philosophie Politique (GRIPP) de Montréal, the Centre de Recherche en Éthique de l'Université de Montréal (CRÉUM) and McGill University' Research Group on Constitutional Studies (RGCS). The influence of Taylor on Tully's book, *Strange Multiplicity, Constitutionalism in an Age of Diversity* (Cambridge University Press, 1995).

form of oppression, imprisoning someone in a false, distorted, and reduced mode of being.[8]

It was only in the modern era and in Europe, he explains, that humans came to develop a liberal way of thinking that eventually led to our current preoccupation with struggles for recognition. The liberal concern with the dignity of the individual, the right of every individual to be recognized as a citizen with equal rights, was itself a form of thinking calling for the equal recognition of humans as public citizens regardless of station, which was the basis for the rise of democratic culture in the West and the institutionalization of equal rights for all.

According to Taylor, another intellectual current was added at the end of the eighteenth century to this concern with individual rights and recognition, a current best articulated by J-J Rousseau, which had to do with recovering one's inner authentic voice in the face of social conformity. Each human has a unique inner nature, insisted Rousseau, to which they should be true if they are to develop as original personalities. Then Johann Gottfried Herder (1744-1803) came along expressing this ideal "at two levels", not only in terms of individual self-fulfillment but also in terms of the fulfillment of national peoples to their own sense of identity. According to Herder, writes Taylor, "just like individuals, a Volk should be true to itself, that is, its own culture". [9] This concern with individual and national/cultural authenticity was behind the Romantic concern for the inner depths of individuals and the nationalist movements for self-determination in the nineteenth century.

Taylor then writes about how Europeans later came to realize that the ideal of authenticity cannot be developed and fulfilled "monologically" but presupposes a "crucial feature of the human condition", which is that we can only develop as human beings through interaction with others, "dialogically". Discovering our personal and our national/ cultural identities doesn't mean separating ourselves from others and finding out who we are in isolation; only by interacting with others do we form our identities and get to be recognized in varying degrees and ways. Taylor refers to the writings of George Herbert Mead and

---

8   The version of "The Politics of Recognition" I am using here is the one in Gutmann, ed., *Multiculturalism: Examining the Politics of Recognition* (1994), p. 25.

9   *Ibid*, 31.

M. M. Bakhtin for this argument. It is now widely accepted in the Western world, he says, that our identities and sense of self-worth are formed in open dialogue:

> Not only contemporary feminism but also race relations and discussions of multiculturalism are undergirded by the premise that the withholding of recognition can be a form of oppression.[10]

Politics of Difference

Taylor tries to make a contribution to this accepted idea by working out a new theory of liberalism based on the principle of cultural recognition. He says that the principle of recognition is already implied by the standard theory of liberalism, since this theory proclaims that all humans want to be recognized as equal beings with the same public dignity, rather than divided into first and second class citizens. However, while this liberalism of individual rights speaks about the equal dignity of all, and promotes rights meant to be universally the same, the cultural liberalism Taylor writes about recognizes the right of all humans to have their own cultural identities; it emphasizes the right to collective difference and authenticity. This liberalism is about the "politics of difference". It is not about Aboriginals enjoying the same civic rights as whites, but about Aboriginals having the right to be culturally different, about living in a society in which they are not seen as an inferior cultural group expected to assimilate to a superior majority modern culture based on individual rights.

While Taylor is clearly aware of the tensions that exist between a liberalism based on individual rights and a liberalism that grants minorities certain cultural rights and powers not enjoyed by other Canadians, he insists that "the politics of difference grows organically out of the politics of universal dignity", that is, the politics of cultural rights grows organically out of the politics of individual rights.[11] If the politics of individual rights says that all humans by birth are worthy of equal respect, the politics of cultural differences says that the identities of all humans as members of different culture groups should be accorded equal respect.

---

10   *Ibid,* 36.

11   *Ibid,* 39.

Taylor distances himself from the notion that all products of all cultures should be accorded equal respect, adding that the recognition that is expected here is that we grant members of all cultures "the presumption" that their culture has worth or value. He criticizes postmodernists who argue that there are no universal standards by which to judge different cultures and that standards of worth are based on "power structures", but also criticizes multiculturalists who believe that all cultures are of equal worth in their unique ways and that it is "Eurocentric" to judge them, arguing that it is patronizing for Westerners to voice equal love for all cultures. Yet, in the end, Taylor insists that we should recognize the equal (potential) worth of different cultures.

Recognition of Quebecois and Aboriginals as Nationalities

He finds limiting the liberalism of individual rights (endorsed by John Rawls, Ronald Dworkin and Jürgen Habermas) and its claim that a liberal government should not endorse any culture but should remain neutral and simply afford all citizens the right to choose their own cultural ends.[12] He defends the cultural right of the Quebec government to take a stand on the importance of preserving the culture of Quebec's ancestors. The Quebecois nationalists are correct to endorse a view of the "good life" rather than remaining neutral. It is "good" for the well-being of the Quebecois to feel that their cultural traditions are respected by the Canadian federal government. Quebec can be "a society with strong collective goals" and still "be liberal...provided it is also capable of respecting diversity, especially when dealing with those who do not share its common goals". [13] Quebec can guarantee the survival of its ancestors while endorsing the rights to life, liberty, due process, free speech, free practice of religion of its citizens, including immigrants who wish to maintain their own cultural identity.

Taylor thus endorses the collective right of Quebeckers and aboriginal peoples to a "distinct society" status within the Canadian federation, a form of national self-government with the constitutional "ability to

---

12   John Rawls, *A Theory of Justice* (Harvard University Press, 1971), Ronald Dworkin, *Taking Rights Seriously* (London: Duckworth, 1977), and Jurgen Habermas, *Theory of Communicative Action* (Boston: Beacon Press, 1984).

13   Gutmann, ed., *Multiculturalism: Examining the Politics of Recognition, p. 59.*

adopt certain kinds of legislation deemed necessary for [their] survival". Quebecois and Aboriginals should have their own communal culture with their own territories with their own institutional arrangements, holidays and languages. Quebecois and Aboriginals are national peoples that may wish to remain distinctive "through indefinite future generations". [14]

Recognition of Cultural Rights of Non-European Immigrants

While he does not think that immigrant groups should be creating semi-autonomous territories and provinces in Canada such as Nunavut and Quebec, he thinks that immigrants need more than "external protections" against majority decisions and affirmative programs that provide them with opportunities for individual success within the Canadian communal culture. The differences between Taylor and Kymlicka are not obvious at first reading, since Kymlicka also calls for national self-determination within Canada's federation for Aboriginals and Quebecois, and for group rights for immigrant minorities. Both are very enthusiastic about the constitutional affirmation of multiculturalism in Canada at all levels of government, adoption of multiculturalism in the school curriculum, ethnic minority representation in the media and public institutions, exemptions from dress codes, such as allowing Sikhs to wear head turbans, dual citizenship, government funding of ethnic organizations, and affirmative action for "disadvantaged groups".

There is an important difference, however, and it is that Kymlicka conceives group rights as temporarily intended to facilitate immigrant integration into a multicultural Canada, whereas Taylor thinks immigrants deserve cultural rights for the sake of protecting a cultural identity that, in his view, may be "intrinsically valuable" to them, and not just a matter of facilitating their integration into Canada.[15] Taylor pushes for a stronger communitarian liberalism that recognizes the wish of immigrant groups to retain their traditions, survive as different communities, and enhance themselves as members of particular cultures, even if this entails collectivist demands by minorities that are

---

14   *Ibid*, p. 49.

15   Charles Taylor, "Can Liberalism be Communitarian". *Critical Review: A Journal of Politics and Society* (Volume 8, Issue 2, 1994).

inconsistent, or in tension with, the principle of equal individual rights.

It is not that Taylor does not say that the endorsement of cultural differences should not be balanced with the principle of individual rights; he admits that there are limits to the cultural differences that the principle of individual rights can tolerate, and Taylor does raise the problems liberal societies have with accommodating the Islamic predilection for keeping politics and religion together. But he insists that this is not a self-refuting contradiction to the liberal politics of difference; it is a "challenge" that Western societies have to deal with.

Taylor's call for diversity is said to be "deep" because it grants extensive powers for territorial self-determination to Quebecois and Aboriginals, and because it goes beyond a merely legalistic understanding, affirmative action and anti-discrimination laws, and because it calls as well for a new concept of self-hood and identity among Canadians generally in which diversity becomes intrinsic to their sense of well-being, something they practice, feel, and internalize within as part of their psychological make-up and everyday life-experiences within their families, schools, friends, churches, and careers. Taylor offers philosophical arguments calling for a totally new identity for Canadians separate from any notion of Europeanness[16] and intrinsically multicultural.

No Cultural Rights for Euro-Canadians

I agree with Taylor that Quebecois and Aboriginals have a right to their own forms of national self-determination. Humans have a deep need to have their culture and ethnic identity recognized. I also agree that cultural identities are not easily reconcilable with the mainstream principle of individual rights and that the demand for cultural recognition may entail a demand for cultural survival requiring individuals to exercise their choices and autonomy as members of a community. Taylor is realistic in understanding that millions of immigrants arriving from cultures lacking a liberal tradition may not want to relinquish their cultural and ethnic identities and dissolve themselves within an Anglo communal culture characterized by a strong sense of individualism.

---

16   My use of this term draws on Dominique Venner's, "Europe & Europeanness". *Counter Currents* (June 29, 2010).

But it never enters Taylor's mind to consider the possibility that Europeans have their own collective customs, religious ways, and historical memories, including a strong belief in individual rights, which they may want to protect in the face of immigrants from illiberal cultures. The only communal identity Taylor seems to acknowledge among European Canadians is that they inhabit a country with a set of procedural laws that are intended for all human beings, equality under the law, democratic templates, and a market economy, deemed to be culturally neutral, and therefore equally available to others. Everyone else except European Canadians bespeaks of authentic traditions, particular customs and historical experiences. Cultural survival and recognition are words reserved for minorities. The culture of Euro-Canadians is somehow inherently other-oriented, for the benefit of others. Euro-Canadians are the host nation, responsible for creating a framework within which Europeans engage in dialogue with others for the purpose of including their voices and allowing them to have their spaces for cultural affirmation. It is not fair, Taylor insists, to expect immigrants to give up their cultural ancestries and assimilate to a majority culture. Claiming that immigrants endanger European culture only intensifies discrimination against them. Western culture belongs to everyone, and so it should be shared with all other cultures. It is racist for Euro-Canadians to insist that they have a Western identity that is uniquely theirs.

Anglos are perennially portrayed by Taylor as the dominant group in need of recognizing others the same way a master needs to recognize the equal worth of a slave: "since 1492", he writes, they "have projected an image" of minorities "as somehow inferior, uncivilized, and through the force of conquest have often been able to impose this image on the conquered". [17] Europeans were colonial masters of many peoples around the world, and so it would be "crude and insensitive" for them (the Europeans of today who never colonized anyone) to expect the immigrants (who were never colonized by current generations) to be satisfied with a mere politics of individual rights. They must be granted communal rights inside the very nation Europeans created. Euro-Canadians must stop teaching about the history of this nation as if it were a history of European settlers and nation builders. They must desist from lecturing students about the "great books" of

17   Gutmann, ed., *Multiculturalism: Examining the Politics of Recognition*, p. 26.

Europe; instead, they must implement a "multicultural curricula" in which "non-European races and cultures" are given equal worth. He writes:

> Enlarging and changing the curriculum is therefore essential not so much in the name of a broader culture for everyone as in order to give due recognition to the hitherto excluded.[18]

No consideration is offered as to what this change in curricula will entail other than vaporous statements about how Canadians will benefit from learning about many cultures. Why would it be broadminded for students to know a little bit about Aztecs, Bantus, and Mongolians, but narrowly parochial to have a solid background in the philosophical accomplishments of ancient Greece, Rome's development of a formal-rational type of legal order, the Catholic scholastic method and invention of universities, the humanistic and artistic tradition of the Renaissance, the Cartographic revolution of the sixteenth century, the Reformation, the Scientific Revolution from Copernicus to Newton, the Enlightenment, the Romantic era, the rise of representative institutions, and the permanent German philosophical revolution from Leibniz to Kant to Hegel to Nietzsche to Heidegger?

Charles Murray's book, *Human Accomplishment, Pursuit of Excellence in the Arts and Sciences, 800 BC to 1950,* informs us that ninety-seven percent of accomplishment in the sciences occurred in Europe and North America from 800 BC to 1950.[19] Would it not be reasonable, then, for students interested in an education in the history of science to concentrate on the accomplishments of Europeans? The fact is that Taylor relies *solely* on European thinkers to make his arguments about the politics of recognition. Efforts to acknowledge the viewpoint of others, or understand different cultural ways in their own terms, are a uniquely European attribute. Taylor's academic career has been centered on the Western intellectual tradition. His book, *Sources of the Self: The Making of Modern Identity,* is all about the making of the *Western* modern self, and should have been titled accordingly.[20]

---

18   *Ibid,* p. 66.

19   Charles Murray, *Human Accomplishment, Pursuit of Excellence in the Arts and Sciences, 800 BC to 1950.* (HarperCollins, 2003).

20   Charles Taylor, *Sources of the Self: The Making of Modern* Identity (Harvard University

Herder Was a German Ethnic Nationalist

The fundamental flaw in Taylor's argument is tied to many other inadequacies, misapplications of classical thinkers, and projections onto the past of contemporary agendas. Taylor relies on the ideas of Johan Gottfried Herder and Hans-Georg Gadamer in support of his argument about the human need for cultural recognition. Yet, an accurate rendition of Herder and Gadamer would have entailed recognition of the majority culture of Europeans in Canada. This misuse of the ideas of past Europeans thinkers, two German conservatives, is typical among leftist academics. They like to create the impression that the efforts we have been witnessing in the last few decades to transform European nations into diverse societies are somehow supported by the great minds of the past.[21] But immigrant multiculturalism is only a decades-old policy without precedent in human history. Taylor misinterprets Herder›s idea about how all the "variety of culture" in the world produced by a divine providence "was meant to bring about a greater harmony", as if Herder was speaking about the promotion of diversity inside nations.[22] Herder cherished the variety of races and cultures he saw in different regions of the earth, in time and space.[23] He rejected a universal history for humanity in which the unique national and ethnic character of peoples would disappear as every nation came to adopt the same values. He proposed a different universalism based on the unique historical experiences and trajectories of each people (Volk). Every people had their own particular language, religion, songs, gestures, legends and customs. There was no common humanity but a division of peoples into language and ethnic groups. He was a German nationalist who defended the maintenance of German particularity in the face of universal pronouncements about the "rights of man" coming from revolutionary France. In fact, Herder was a racialist who

---

Press, 1989). This is true of all his earlier publications, such as *Hegel* (Cambridge University Press, 1975), and his most recent books, such as *Modern Social Imaginaries* (Duke University Press, 2004); all of which are entirely about the Western intellectual tradition. In *The Uniqueness of Western Civilization* (Brill, 2011), I write in agreement about Taylor's Eurocentric books.

21   See, for example, Fred Dallmayr, "Self and Other: Gadamer and the Hermeneutics of the Other". *Yale Journal of Law and the Humanities* (Vol. 5, 2013). Also the online article, https://www.bu.edu/wcp/Papers/Educ/EducSund.htm.

22   Gutmann, ed., *Multiculturalism: Examining the Politics of Recognition, p. 72.*

23   Hans Adler and Ernest Menze, eds., *On World History, Johan Gottfried Herder: An Anthology* (Sharpe: New York, 1997).

viewed the races of the world in clearly demarcated ways with their own genetic predispositions, and would have dismissed Taylor's effort to "fuse" all the races and cultures in Canada as a transgression of the way providence had created the varieties of peoples.

Gadamer Never Called for a "Fusion" of Races and Cultures

Similarly, Taylor misuses the intended purpose of what Gadamer meant by the "fusion of horizons" in making the argument that Canadians should learn to "move in a broader horizon" by fusing together many cultural outlooks inside their heads and in this way overcome their "narrow" Eurocentric perspective in a new direction in which "real judgments of worth suppose a fused horizon of standards". [24] For Gadamer, however, a "horizon" was a standpoint that limited the possibility of having an impartial, objective vision. It was an inescapable reality of the human situation that we cannot but find ourselves situated within a horizon however much we may try to stand above it in the name of impartiality.[25] While Gadamer says that such horizons are not fixed or closed to other perspectives, for otherwise there would have been no changes in the outlooks of the peoples of the world, he does say that all humans inevitably inhabit a horizon which conditions their interpretations, which are necessarily prejudicial, but not in the sense that they result in blanket distortions of our understanding of other outlooks, but in the sense that human beings are creatures who can only interpret the world within the horizons they inhabit, they can't be "neutral" observers outside a context which exists nowhere else.

Gadamer is known for developing the art or technique of interpretation, hermeneutics, which teaches how to "interpret", "explicate", or "translate" texts from a horizon different from one's own. It teaches one to be aware of one's limitedness, how one is always surrounded by a historical context and a tradition. By teaching that one can never overcome one's finitude, one learns about how one is situated in a horizon, and, in so learning, one learns how others are situated

---

24   Gutmann, ed., *Multiculturalism: Examining the Politics of Recognition*, p. 70

25   In addition to relying on Gadamer's central text, *Truth and Method* (Crossroad, 1989 [1960]). For those interested in Gadamer's intellectual lineage, I recommend the well-crafted biography by Jean Grondin, *Hans-Georg Gadamer, A Biography*. Translated by Joel Weinsheimer (New Haven: Yale University Press, 2003).

in different horizons and, in this way, one may learn how to become more open to other experiences, since one becomes aware that we are all operating within horizons, affected by our own traditions, and that the perspectives of others are as legitimate to them as our perspective is to us.

Taylor is very knowledgeable about the intellectual history of this technique of interpretation, as evident from his two volume *Philosophical Papers*.[26] The problem is that Taylor does not reflect upon his own situation, living in a Canada dedicated to the promotion of multiculturalism, and, therefore, does not realize that he is misusing Gadamer's fusion of horizons for a purpose it was never intended. Gadamer never said anything about radically transforming the perspective of European nationals by fusing their cultures with the cultures of the world through mass immigration. His philosophy welcomes the variety of perspectives in the world and does not seek to create a culture that pretends to be universal in its ability to fuse every other horizon within its own horizon. Gadamer was a strong traditionalist who insisted on the unavoidable reality of human "prejudices", not as a negative attribute, but as the very condition of human understanding, since one's horizon is what allows one to have "fore-sight". But what Taylor is saying is that European Canadians, Anglo Canadians in particular, should overcome their own attachments to Canada's Britishness by "recognizing" and "respecting" the cultures of others while suppressing their own heritage and affirming only their individual rights and the state-imposed ideology of multiculturalism.

A truly hermeneutic thinking would acknowledge the importance of the Anglo and European traditions and prejudices, and thus show respect and sympathy for Canadians who are extremely apprehensive and worried about how Canada is undergoing a radical alteration through mass immigration. Gadamer was particularly concerned about our ability to "transpose ourselves into the historical horizon from which the traditionary text speaks", otherwise "we will misunderstand the significance of what it has to say to us". He says that it is "constantly necessary to guard against overhastily assimilating the past to our own expectations of meaning". We must "listen to tradition in a way that permits it to make its own meaning

---

26   *Philosophical Papers: Volume 1, Human Agency and Language* (Cambridge Press, 1985), and *Philosophical Papers: Volume 2, Philosophy and the Human Sciences* (Cambridge Press, 1985).

heard". [27] But Taylor, a Canadian, can be said to have read Gadamer's German text, the product of a cultural setting in 1920/30/40s Germany, in a rather overhasty manner by imposing on it meanings and ideas best understood within Canada's mandated multicultural horizon.

Mass Immigration Without Dialogue

Why should Canadians have to deal with the challenge of increasing diversity through mass immigration beyond Aboriginal and Quebecois self-determination? Taylor does not pose this question but assumes immigration and inclusion of millions of non-Western individuals is part of the natural course of things: "All societies are becoming increasingly multicultural, while at the same time becoming more porous". [28] It is worth citing a few more words about this:

> This porousness means that they are more open to multinational migration; more of their members live the life of diaspora, whose center is elsewhere. In these circumstances, there is something awkward about replying simply, 'This is how we do things here'. [29]

What is awkward is demanding that Euro-Canadians promote the way others do things while prohibiting their own majoritarian way of doing things. Taylor is willfully misleading Canadians into thinking that mass immigration is happening everywhere when in truth globalization in most of the world is not associated with immigration. Immobility, as indicated in our refutation of Kymlicka, is typical for the vast majority of the world's population: Over 98 percent of the people in less developed countries in 2005 were born in the country where they reside. Immigrants, if I may cite this fact again, have accounted for a mere 1.4 - 1.6% of Asia's population over the past twenty years — despite fertility rates well below replacement levels in Japan, Singapore, South Korea, Taiwan, and other Asian countries. [30]

---

27 Hans Gadamer, *Truth and Method* (London: Continuum Publishing Book, 1975), pp. 300-07.

28 Gutmann, ed., *Multiculturalism: Examining the Politics of Recognition*, p. 63.

29 *Ibid.*

30 Alan Simmons, *Immigration and Canada: Global and Transnational Perspectives* (Canadian Scholar's Press, 2010). See also: Asia Century Institute, http://www.asiancenturyinstitute.com/migration/188-asia-s-wasted-migration-opportunities

How could someone with Taylor's intellectual stature misinterpret Gadamer's text in this manner? A short answer is that he wants philosophically sophisticated concepts to justify mass immigration, but since the idea of mass immigration is unprecedented in history, and is therefore devoid of any intellectual justifications in the past, he has no option but to interpret past thinkers as if they were calling for immigrant diversity. A longer answer would require a deep investigation of the liberal communitarianism Taylor advocates, which is part of a wider movement critical of the excessive individualism of classical liberalism, which sounds very appealing in its endearing concerns with the erosion of communal life in an "increasingly fragmented society", but is ultimately a phony form of communitarianism fabricated by Western academics dedicated to the destruction of the organic communitarianism of their own people. One can actually argue that Taylor has accepted the rational transnationalism of the Enlightenment he pretends to be criticizing, in the way he treats Anglo Canadian culture, and European culture generally, of which he is a member, as a culture that should be committed to the generation of universal human values that aim at respecting and acknowledging every other horizon while insisting that Euro-Canadians must detach themselves from their own horizon, from their ancestral roots and community norms. He wants Westerners to take an impartial stand in relation to their own culture, a purely rationalist stand, in order that they may be open to other horizons, and then to take an academic communitarian stand in order that they may be able to appreciate the communitarian impulses of non-Western peoples. This way of being, which pretends to be self-reflective, is actually lacking in awareness of its own Western-centric dispositions, its Enlightenment roots and its unique European hermeneutic preoccupations.

It was not long ago that in Canada communitarian thinking, prior to the post-60s, was heavily conservative in nature rather than based on theoretical postulations by academics willfully seeking to create new communities through government intervention. We will have a few words to say about Canada's Tory communitarian conservatism in later chapters. Suffice it to say now that communitarian feelings have come from actually existing communities populated by inhabitants with a deep sense of belonging and kinship attachment.[31] But for decades

---

31   Ferdinand Tönnies, *Community and Society* (Cambridge University Press, 2001[orig. in German 1887]. Many may be surprised to learn that sociology began as a conservative

cultural Marxists, like Charles Taylor, have been assiduously trying to break down traditional relations, patriarchal families and kinship ties, designating them as racist and oppressive without a clear grasp of the unique ways in which European peoples had long been, up until the 60s, balancing individual rights and traditions in relatively peaceful ways with immigration policies committed to protecting their ethno communal feelings.

Taylor's career has been driven by a rejection of this uniquely European sense of community, in the name of a new communitarianism aimed at serving Third World peoples, while offering Euro-Canadians a multicultural communitarianism lacking any historical basis and philosophical tradition, but which aims at creating a totally new form of identity. While Taylor has become rich working against Euro-Canadian communitarianism, we can safely show that we are the true communitarians by working from within his critique of mainstream liberalism, reminding Euro-Canadians that it is natural and intrinsic for them to affirm themselves collectively as the people who created Canada. We need to hold Taylor, and his many uncritical followers, morally accountable as to why they think that European individuals should be disallowed from having a sense of ethnic identity in the same breath as non-Europeans and immigrants are said to have this collective right.

Multiculturalists to the Left of Kymlicka and Taylor

What could some leftists find missing in Kymlicka and Taylor? The radical leftist view on immigration is extremely important; its exponents have enormous control over Canadian universities and colleges, editorships over key journals,[32] including multiple publishing

---

concern over the breakdown of communities and traditional forms of identity with the onset of industrialization, and that the sociology taught today has broken altogether from this concern and is now dedicated to the imposition of totally new communities across the West by means of government totalitarian measures and the deception of the public. For the conservative orientation of sociology, see the work of the greatest American sociologist of the twentieth century, Robert Nisbet; for example, *The Sociological Tradition* (New York: Basic Books, 1966), and his best known, *The Quest for Community: A Study in the Ethics of Order and Freedom* (ISI Books, 2010 [1953]).

32 For example: *Canadian Ethnic Studies, Journal of Canadian Studies, International Journal of Canadian Studies, Journal of Critical Race Inquiry*, and numerous other journals across the West offering "refereed" guarantees for minority scholars and leftists to maintain a firm control over hundreds of academic sinecures.

houses.[33] They are the authors of the books written about Canadian racism, multiculturalism, and immigration. Seen as the driving "moral conscience" sustaining the fight against white racism, they have kept all the arguments tilting leftward, eliciting continuous apologies from conservatives and keeping academics in a state of anxiety about their potential "racist" attitudes. I need hardly say that this left-wing professoriate faces next to zero opposition in academia. Writing a proper assessment of the radical left would require a book onto itself. Here I only want to acknowledge this side and bring up their essential arguments. Part IV, however, will implicitly have this side in mind, sometimes explicitly, as we explain the radicalizing dynamic that has been driving Canada "out of control" since WWII.

Essentially, the radical left diverges from Kymlicka and Taylor in believing that Canadian multiculturalism is still ethnocentric, conceived by a European majority within the framework of "Western" liberalism and "Western" multiculturalism. A true egalitarian multiculturalism, this side claims, will blossom only when Canada ceases to be a "nation-state" populated by a European majority, and only when such symbols as the English maple leaf, the Quebec *fleurs-de-lis*, the RCMP uniform, and Christian religious oaths and holidays are fully displaced and "provincialized" from their "supremacy" by the symbols of other cultures. The very notion of minority rights is unfair, according to this side; ethnic groups must be allowed to establish and maintain their own traditions, beliefs, and institutions without any subservience to a liberalism that is still imbued with Western prejudices and formulas. Euro-Canadians should not stand in the way of demands by minorities to create institutions of their own, justice systems, schools, health services, and more.

The best way to illustrate the rabidly anti-European mindset of this leftist critique is to examine the sayings of some of its major exponents, starting with Professor Sunera Thobani, currently Associate Professor

---

33 The list is long; I will mention Fernwood Publishing, Critical Books for Critical Thinkers, and Canadian Scholar's Press. These publishing houses release new titles every month, a veritable industry that is destroying the minds of millions of students while ensuring permanent tenure for mediocre academics. Forthcoming titles at Fernwood include *The Medicine of Peace: Indigenous Youth Decolonizing Healing and Resisting Violence*; *Working for the Common Good: Canadian Women Politicians*; *One-Dimensional Man 50 Years On: The Struggle Continues*; *Power and Resistance: Critical Thinking about Canadian Social Issues*; *Doing Anti-Oppressive Practice*; *Canadian Crime Films, Culture and Society*; *Blood of Extraction: Canadian Imperialism in Latin America*; *Did You Just Call Me Old Lady? A Ninety-Year-Old Tells Why Aging Is Positive*; *A Propaganda System: How Canada's Government, Corporations, Media and Academia Sell War*; *Paying for Masculinity: Boys, Men and the Patriarchal Dividend*.

at the Centre for Women's and Gender Studies at the University of British Columbia. She has held similar prestigious titles at other Canadian universities, including president in 1993-1996, a mere few years after she arrived in Canada, of the National Action Committee on the Status of Women, Canada's largest feminist organization. Her ideas on multiculturalism are expressed in her 2007 book, *Exalted Subjects: Studies in the Making of Race and Nation in Canada*. The adoption of multiculturalism, according to Thobani, was essentially a way to "stabilize white supremacy" in Canada in an age of civil rights for minorities and decolonization, when whites could no longer hold their power openly. The small population base of Canada, declining birth rates among whites and in Europe, coupled with the need for labor to sustain a growing capitalist economy, created a situation in which the "outright exclusion of people of colour [...] was no longer tenable".[34] There is no denying that Thobani captures well the motivations of the right in their adoption of immigration and assimilation, and that if we replace "whites" with "corporate sell outs" we have a pretty good argument.

According to her, multiculturalism allowed whites to reconstitute themselves "as tolerant and respectful of difference and diversity" at the same time as non-white immigrants were expected to assimilate to this "tolerant" culture. Non-whites were from the beginning, Thobani charges, defined as "visible minorities", not quite as Canadians, and expected to forego "their primitive and backward cultural practices, their corruptions, misogyny, cronyism and violence".[35] In exchange for Canada's recognition of certain "harmless" aspects of immigrant cultures, such as foods, exotic dresses, and songs, the immigrant was expected to join the world of "cosmopolitan sensibility" graciously offered to them by whites. This was a wonderful arrangement for whites, Thobani sneers, allowing them to celebrate the superficial differences of others while gaining an "exalted" status as they paraded their tolerance and openness to the world. Whites stood for individual rights and "progress" against such backward immigrant customs as arranged marriages or the wearing of the hijab or chador. Even the "loud voice and excitable speech of the ethnic", "the 'smelly' odors and 'gaudy' colors of the Chinatowns and Little Indias" were best kept in private, or subdued and reformed in public — lest its practitioners remain outside the normal world of white urbanity, reasonableness, and liberality.

---

34   Sunera Thobani, *Exalted Subjects: Studies in the Making of Race and Nation in Canada* (University of Toronto, 2007), p. 146.

35   *Ibid*, p. 155.

Most significantly, she explains how the Western multicultural discourse still draws an Us versus Them dichotomy in separating "good Muslims" who are "moderate" or more Westernized, and "bad Muslims" who follow Islam more strictly. This is a form of discrimination that violates the universal principle of equal rights, since this dichotomy divides immigrants into those who are fully "human" and can be afforded human rights of citizenship, and those who cannot be afforded such rights. Thobani believes that it is not for Europeans to dictate the terms under which non-Europeans should participate as Canadians. Whites have their own intolerant ways, she argues, starting with the expectation that everyone must become a liberal to be tolerated. In her own ethnocentric way, she is right that immigrant communities do exhibit a preference for their own cultural ways, and that to expect them to forego these ways is either a cultural Marxist illusion or a form of intolerance. Why should Hindu parents not be worried about their children assimilating into leftist pop culture and gay-marriage education in elementary schools? But Thobani never allows for the possibility that Europeans too have their own collective customs, political institutions, religious ways, and historical memories, including a strong belief in individual rights, which it may be natural and right for them to want to protect. For her, unless whites accept the arguments she makes and thus hand over their country to immigrant non-whites, they are racist defenders of corporate capitalism.

Thobani is quite typical among immigrant intellectuals in European countries who exploit ideas produced by leftist whites to advance their own ethnic interests. She believes Canada should become a place filled with autonomous cultures coexisting with a deracinated white population stripped of any group rights. But it is not only immigrants who want this; white leftists may be even more determined as it is amply clear in Richard Day's call for the abolition of the Canadian nation state. Professor of Global Development Studies at Queen's University, Day's ideas are fully articulated in his book *Multiculturalism and the History of Canadian Diversity*.[36] Using ideas derived from postmodernist Marxists, Day employs many pretentiously empty words in order to claim, in essence, that Kymlicka's theory of minority rights, as well as Taylor's "deep diversity", are unfair because they allow the European "colonizers" to maintain a majority culture while disallowing immigrants to develop their "own societal cultures" or their own fully

---

36   Richard Day, *Multiculturalism and the History of Canadian Diversity* (University of Toronto Press, 2000).

developed political and social institutions. He questions Taylor's theory of mutual recognition on the grounds that the recognition is conditional on the acceptance of Western liberalism. How can the "equal worth of others" be truly recognized unless other cultures are "unconditionally" given the same right to maintain and develop their cultures within Canada?[37] Why are majority Canadians imposing an "Immigration Points System" that excludes certain categories of individuals from entering Canada? Everyone and anyone who wants to come should be given the same right to immigrate. The current Canadian nation state is inextricably associated with the "capitalist European male"; accordingly, the only way to achieve racial equality is to abolish Canada and create a de-territorialized culture with porous borders characterized by "deep diversity" and the acceptance of "the necessity of an ongoing negotiation of all universal horizons".[38]

Day's ideas are self-evidently ludicrous to those not inhabiting an academic world where careless thinking is the prevailing ethos. Alan Simmons's book *Immigration and Canada: Global and Transnational Perspectives* offers a more empirically based argument, according to which the transformation of Canada into an immigrant place should be seen as part of a "global-transnational" process that is bringing multiple ethnicities and cultures from all over the world closer together within Canada, making this nation no longer a state onto itself but a component part of an interdependent network of global relations.[39] A Senior Scholar in the Department of Sociology at York University, Simmons claims that Canada is a more advanced model of what is happening among other nations in the world. With globalization, expanding trade, travel telecommunications, we are witnessing "more frequent and intense" economic, social, and political links amongst the peoples of the world. We are also witnessing the emergence of hybrid and transnational identities distinct from the more fixed national ethnicities of the past, which were deeply grounded in culture, kinship, and custom. He is enthusiastic that Canada is at the forefront of this new "postmodern" ethnic identity, with immigrants retaining links to their original homelands and establishing new links within

---

37   *Ibid*, pp. 216-228.

38   *Ibid*, pp 227.

39   Alan Simmons, *Immigration and Canada: global and Transnational Perspectives* (Canadian Scholar's Press, 2010).

Canada, and native Canadians participating within global economic and cultural networks de-linked from "home". Canada is now truly a mosaic expressed in hyphenated identities with Canadians having multiple ethnic roots that "specify different ways of belonging".[40] Just as Canada was once "imagined" as a white nation, he says that we can now imagine its future as a utopian global village "in which sophisticated technology, communications, and knowledge industries and services create the desired efficiencies and affluence", and in which "immigrants are to be welcomed in relatively large numbers as important contributors to this imagined future.[41]

Empirically oriented as Simmons is, it is worth noting that his own facts, when read properly, do not corroborate his thesis. First, as we saw in our criticism of Kymlicka's and Taylor's false claim that immigration is happening across the world, globalization and immigration are not necessarily connected. We already cited some words from Simmons, and we can now cite a few more, to the effect that "only a tiny proportion of the world's population is mobile across international borders...about 97 percent of the world's population are living in the country in which they were born...More than 98 percent of the people in less developed countries were born in the country where they reside".[42] Simmons is fundamentally wrong, therefore, in framing immigration in Canada as part of a "global-transnational" process. Huge areas of Asia have long been part of a global transnational process, and so have Brazil, Mexico, and now most countries, and yet the glorification of diversity is taking place only in the West. Simmons makes a profound error in presuming, without even reflecting about it, that the diversification of Canada, the arrival every year of at least 250,000 immigrants since the early 1990s, with numbers currently at over 300,000, is a natural consequence of globalization. Immigration before the 1970s did not come with the celebration of diversity and the utopian illusion that creating a multiracial Canada would solve antagonisms in Canada. Simmons should have framed his book in terms of the ideology of "globalism". As Robert Locke very aptly explains in "Nation Busting", globalization and globalism

---

40   *Ibid*, pp. 173-180.

41   *Ibid*, pp. 13-24.

42   *Ibid*, p, 121.

are fundamentally different: globalization is an historical process, a fact of how things are, but globalism is an ideology, a set of opinions about how things ought to be. Globalism is the ideology that advocates the liquidation of nations. Its opposite is nationalism. Globalization, on the other hand, is not an ideology at all. Ultimately, it is just the growth of communications and trade, and it has been happening since 1492....Globalism is a deliberate political choice, no more inevitable than socialism... Globalization can exist without globalism...Japan has based her economy on exports for 50 years without ceasing to be one of the most nationalistic and culturally distinctive nations on earth.[43]

Mass immigration is a "deliberate choice" to create a Canada, in the words of Kymlicka, which is "never again white or British". Both the cultural Marxist left and the corporate right, which are well balanced in Simmons's celebration, masquerade globalism as if it were an intrinsic component of globalization in order to create an impression of inevitability about the diversification of Western nations. Republican conservatives in the United States have long been pushing the ideology that American values are universal, insisting that American institutions and corporate culture must be exported to the rest of the world by force if necessary. They have done so in the name of capitalist globalization, open markets, rule of law, and a peaceful world order, against Islamic extremism and populist nationalism in Europe. But the presence of many "authoritarian" nations with pseudo liberal institutions, India, South Korea, Taiwan, even China, demonstrates that capitalist globalization does not require the spread of American values.

Simmons is also wrong in saying that ethnicity is not a biological but a socially constructed fact.[44] He really goes out of his way calling upon Canadians to "imagine a future" Canada as a utopian paradise filled by hybrids in a state of harmonious affluence.[45] Why should Canadians accept such an "imagined future"? The use of the term "imagined", quite common among academics nowadays, should be seen as a clever discursive strategy to downgrade the empirically founded claims of past Western historians as mere "imaginations". In the case of Canadian

---

43 Robert Locke, "Nation Busting" *The American Conservative* (June 2003).

44 Alan Simmons, *Immigration and Canada: Global and Transnational Perspectives*, pp. 196-201.

45 *Ibid*, pp. 14-19.

history, as we saw in Part I, this has entailed the claim that "White Canada" is an "imaginary past" concocted to suit the racist interests of Anglos, and at the same time it has entailed the claim that we can imagine Canada as diverse from the beginning in order to imagine a future Canada populated by diverse races.[46]

---

46   As Christopher Armstrong says: "Cultural imaginary refers to a matrix of images and ideas, symbols, and stories whose shape is codified in relatively distinct discursive form at specific historical moments to suit specific historical needs". See "Migrant Imaginings and Atlantic Canadian Regionalisms", in Barbara Messamore, ed., *Canadian Immigration Patterns From Britain and North America* (University of Ottawa Press (2004), p. 246. Charles Taylor, in *Modern Social Imaginaries* (Duke University Press, 2004), claims that Westerners have imagined themselves as the progenitors of the modern world, market economies, science, and technology, which he condemns as arrogantly out of tune with a future world in which multiple cultures should be imagined as carving out their own path to modernity, which he does by projecting onto the Western past a different "social imaginary" about its own modern path, one leading to a future socialistic world with multiple modernities. He, apparently, does not mind imagining a future without a white race having its own homeland, while the other races follow their own modern path retaining their racial integrity!

Part Three

Refuting the Assimilationist Argument

All assimilation is equivalent to cultural genocide, for the assimilator or the assimilated. — Guillaume Faye

A cuckservative is a self-styled "conservative" who will cravenly sell out and undermine his home country's people, culture, and national interest in order to win approval with parties hostile or indifferent to them. – Urban Dictionary

8

The Cuckservative Critique of Multiculturalism

The main question of this chapter is why the right wing or "conservative" critique of multiculturalism is still trapped to certain cultural Marxist precepts in its endorsement of mass immigration, rejection of identity politics, and denial of the right of Euro-Canadians to affirm their ethnic group interests. In the next chapters I will examine some key proponents of the right wing "assimilationist" view, mainly, Neil Bissoondath, Salim Mansur, and Janet Ajzenstat. In this chapter I will criticize the assimilationist view generally while advancing my own view that a proper, long term assessment of immigrant multiculturalism requires a conscious acknowledgement of the reality of ethnic identity. Only by speaking up front about the ethnic interests of Euro-Canadians can we mount a proper challenge to the otherwise impending reduction of Euro-Canadians to minority status in Canada.

The right wing position on multiculturalism in Canada is mainly expressed in the *National Post*, *Financial Post*, and the Conservative Party. There are significant variations within these venues and among current leaders of the Conservative Party, particularly now that Trump has given some Canadian conservatives the courage to express their views without feeling so guilty and afraid. Canadian conservatives have learned a few lessons from the Trump movement on the flaws of globalism, the stupidity of interventionism in the Middle East, and the importance of putting your nation's peoples first. Certain differences among conservatives have been indeed accentuated by the candidacy and election of Trump. Some conservatives, better known as "cuckservatives", now sound like "moderate" liberals in their attacks on Trump's "racist" policies. But there are other pro-Trump conservatives, located in such venues as Rebel News, who are increasingly more critical of immigration even if they still voice the assimilationist view.[1]

---

1   Particularly some journalists at the *National Post* have used standard leftist arguments against Trump. Andrew Coyne, who plays the conservative good guy at CBC, thinks that Trump's populist politics pose a greater threat to liberal democracy and the West than the ideas espoused by academic leftists, with whom he gets along quite well at

Basically conservatives criticize the way multiculturalism discourages immigrants from integrating into the culture of liberal individual rights. They adhere in a stronger way to the classical liberal values of smaller government, free speech (and thus less political correctness), and civic national pride in Western values.[2] They reject "communitarian" liberalism and "identity politics". What makes them part of the mainstream, in Canada where Trump's political views have yet to make it nationally, is that they are critics of multiculturalism but not of mass immigration. They reject any form of politics that speaks about the ethnic interests of whites or Euro-Canadians, and they refuse to consider the impending reduction of Euro-Canadians to a minority in Canada. They are under the illusion that race is not real and that a Canada with a majority of non-Europeans can be just as "Western".

Another criticism conservatives have is that they want greater assurances against the arrival of "radical Islamists". They worry about lack of Muslim integration. We also find some conservatives endorsing "populist" concerns about rising house prices in cities like Vancouver due to mass buyouts by absentee Chinese millionaires. Some conservatives will raise concerns about the costs to taxpayers incurred by multicultural programs and arrival of immigrants without the required skills.

All in all, however, the Conservative Party of Canada, in the last few decades, has been no less enamored with mass immigration than the Liberal Party, even going beyond them in their effort to displace the Liberals as the "Party of Immigrants" in order to get a greater proportion of the "ethnic vote". Let us not forget that it was Brian Mulroney's conservative government, as we will examine in Part IV, which committed Canada to an annual immigration intake of 250,000 immigrants per year regardless of fluctuations in the unemployment

---

CBC. See "Trump has proven that nothing really matters — at least for the purpose of getting elected" (*National Post*, November 9, 2016). The worst reaction came from legendary, wannabe man-of-letters Robert Fulford, who called Trump an ignorant misogynist racist (*National Post*, October 16, 2016).This is the same guy who has never apologized for his rabidly aggressive support of the invasion of Iraq in 2003. Conrad Black is one of a few conservatives in Canada sympathetic to Trump, writing that Trump "promised to drain the swamp, and will do it; it will be a changed America in six months" (*National Post*, December 16, 2016).

2 Donald Trump, despite his endorsement of civic nationalism, is far from a "cuckservative" for the simple reason that he is a tough white male unafraid to take on the DC establishment.

rate. And it was during Stephen Harper's reign (2006-2015) that the Canadian state made a habit of boasting about how it sustained immigration levels that made "Canada the largest per capita receiver of new immigrants in the entire world".

Assimilation is Fundamentally Flawed

The fundamental flaw with the conservative critique is that it is oblivious to the central question at hand, which is that current mass immigration trends, and the birth rates of non-whites in Canada versus whites, are now pointing decisively to a situation in which Canada will cease to be a majority European nation.[3] Stats Canada has announced that by 2036 possibly as high as 40 percent of the working age population, defined as people between the ages of 15 and 64, will be visible minorities. Up to 30 per cent of Canadians could have a mother tongue that is neither English nor French, a potential jump of 10 points from 2011. Immigrants and second generation children of immigrants will make up nearly 50 percent of the population, up from 17.5 percent recorded in 2011.[4] Earlier projections by Statistics Canada (2010) suggest that "whites will become the minority in Toronto and Vancouver over the course of the next three decades".[5] In the city of Vancouver, according to Daniel Hierbert, white residents will be reduced to 2 out of 5 residents by 2031. In Toronto, Europeans will number only 37% of the population.[6]

---

3 Terrence Corcoran, editor of the *Financial Post*, joyfully anticipates the day when Canada's population will reach 100 million. "With 100 million Canadians, the dynamics of human interaction, economies of scale, larger numbers of entrepreneurs and creative talent, bigger cities and broader markets would turn Canada into an even greater country than it is today. One might even say that the 21st century could belong to Canada. We should try it". He does not give one thought to the impending demographic dispossession of whites; it is all about creating more consumers and shopping malls. He has no idea that the standard of living and innovative dynamic of the densely populated Asian nations he so admires pale in comparison to the richest white countries of Europe with their far smaller populations, Switzerland, Norway, and Denmark, assuming these nations don't self-destruct with the continuing arrival of immigrants banking on welfare benefits. This is how sickly Marxist free market extremists are. See "100 Million Canadians? We could only hope. *Financial Post* (October 27, 2016).

4 "Nearly A Third Of Canadians Will Be Immigrants By 2036", *The Huffington Post Canada* (January 31, 2017), http://www.huffingtonpost.ca/2017/01/25/nearly-a-third-of-canadia_n_14396226.html

5 "Projections of the Diversity of the Canadian Population, 2006 to 2031", by the Demosim Team. Report prepared by Éric Caron Malenfant, André Lebel and Laurent Martel, http://www.statcan.gc.ca/pub/91-551-x/91-551-x2010001-eng.htm

6 Douglas Todd, "Whites will decline to two out of five by 2036" *Vancouver Sun* (April 1,

It should be noted that Statistics Canada defines "visible minorities" as "persons, other than aboriginal peoples, who are non-Caucasian in race or non-white in colour". [7] If we take aboriginals into account, the projections are that "between 21% and 24% of the population of Saskatchewan and between 18% and 21% of the population of Manitoba" will have an Aboriginal identity in 2031.[8] Statistics Canada recognizes the existence of races in these projections, using regularly the terms "Caucasians" and "non-Caucasian in race" or "non-white in colour". As an obedient citizen, I will follow the terminology of Statistics Canada.

The fact that these projections are pointing to a future Canada in which "Caucasians" will be increasingly displaced by people who are "non-white in colour" is never seen as an issue by conservatives. Instead, the vast majority of leaders and media elites in both the left and the right will accuse those Caucasians who lament their dwindling numbers as racist. On the other hand, they don't think there is anything wrong with "non-Caucasians in race" who speak happily about a majority Asian Canada. Leftists, for sure, celebrate as vibrant and liberal-minded non-whites who eulogize about their rising numbers — regardless of their otherwise intolerant customs and hyper-patriarchal dispositions.

Conservative critics believe that immigration would "work" if only immigrants were encouraged to assimilate to "Canadian values". They want the government and the educational institutions to encourage a sense of Canadian citizenship, loyalty to Canada's liberal democratic culture. They firmly believe that any immigrant group (with the possible exception of radical Muslims) is capable of disaggregating itself into abstract individual units to become average Canadians. So long as ethnic group identification is discouraged, Canada can remain Canada, even if European Canadians are eventually reduced to a tiny minority and the country becomes populated by masses of Sikhs, Sri Lankans, Chinese, Indians, and Haitians. They criticize multiculturalists for encouraging race-based identities rather than individual rights.

2013), http://vancouversun.com/life/metro-vancouver-whites-will-decline-to-two-of-five-residents-by-2031

7   "Visible Minority of person". Statistics Canada, http://www.statcan.gc.ca/eng/concepts/definitions/minority01

8   "Population Projections by Aboriginal Identity, 2006-2031". Statistics Canada, http://www.statcan.gc.ca/pub/91-552-x/91-552-x2011001-eng.pdf

My view is quite different: if we are interested in preserving and advancing the ethnic interests of European Canadians, it is better to work within the existing framework of multiculturalism than to promote assimilation. Current conservatives are hyper-liberals in believing that all forms of group identity can be discarded, and that liberalism is all about "freeing" the individual from any historical and biological antecedents and making identities purely a matter of personal choice – except when they criticize leftists for ignoring biological differences between males and females. Yet, for all their talk about individualism, conservatives now agree with leftists that "Canadian values" include multiculturalism. While conservatives did not initiate multiculturalism, this ism has become deeply embedded in Canadian society, and conservatives have increasingly come to terms with it. Since the 1980s, no conservative government in power, at the federal or provincial level, has challenged the institutional framework of multiculturalism in Canada, or sought to carry major reforms against the sweeping structures, power networks, and programs now in place across Canada pushing multiculturalism. At most, they have cut funding to a few programs.

Then again, even if multiculturalism was not the official policy, or the accepted norm in Canada, the issue that matters in the long run is the ethnic origins of the immigrants and their proportion relative to Euro-Canadians. If the immigrants coming to Canada were "Caucasian" we would not be having this debate. History shows that assimilation works when the immigrants are primarily "Caucasian". Assimilation does not work with masses of immigrants from regions that are "non-white in colour". The much talked about contrast between the American "melting pot" and the Canadian "mosaic" has lost any substantial meaning. Before the 1970s, Canada was a mosaic in the relative separation of the English and the French within Confederation, and in the presence of "other Europeans" and a few Amerindians. Conversely, America was a melting pot in the assimilation of European peoples to the "American dream". But to this day, in America, Blacks and Amerindians have not assimilated well to the culture created by the majority European peoples, despite large scale affirmative action and propaganda. The assimilation now seems to be going the other way: white assimilation to African-American norms, or integration of everyone into some generic mass consumer culture.

The melting pot worked — after major difficulties and persisting divisions — only in regards to European immigrants. In recent decades, with the mass entry of Mexicans, there is little melting going on in many areas of the United States. While the United States does not have an official policy of multiculturalism at the federal level, one finds, under the pressure of relentless immigration and political correctness, a multiplicity of pro-diversity policies and programs at the state and municipal levels on matters related to school curricula, policing, hiring practices, and race relations generally. As Nathan Glazer already observed in the late 1990s, under the title, *We Are All Multiculturalists Now*:

> America's melting pot is no more. Where not very long ago we sought assimilation, we now pursue multiculturalism. Nowhere has this transformation been more evident than in the public schools, where a traditional Eurocentric curriculum has yielded to diversity — and, often, to confrontation and confusion.[9]

Humans are Naturally Ethnocentric

The weakest aspect of the assimilationist view, which lies at the bottom of all its flaws, is its purely cultural approach to immigration in overt opposition to any reference to race. The argument that a Canada without whites can still be "Canadian" is cultural Marxist in denying the reality of race. Can China be China with a majority population of Europeans? Culture does matter, and this is why I prefer the term "ethnicity" rather than race, because "ethnicity" refers to culture and race combined. The point is not that Canada has to be purely European. Non-whites in race have been historically present throughout Canada's history and their equal rights were recognized in full by the 1960s, before the imposition of mass immigration and the artificial creation of diversity. Canada was created by Euro-Canadians, and for most of her history, "Caucasians" have been the overwhelming majority. What conservatives refuse to accept is not only the extensive scientific evidence pointing towards some very important behavioral and general intelligence differences between racial groupings, but also, and this is the point I wish to emphasize, the fact that all humans have a natural disposition to view other ethnic groups from within the

---

9   Nathan Glazer, *We Are All Multiculturalists Now*. Harvard University Press, 1998, p.184.

standpoint of their own in-group. As I argued in my book, *Faustian Man in a Multicultural Age*, relying on the scientific literature, "ethnic and racial sentiments are an extension of kinship sentiment". [10] Preference for individuals of the same ethnicity (Irish, German, Chinese, Mexican), or of the same race (White, Black, Asian) is part of our human nature. Ethnocentrism is simply a "propensity" to favor kin, and this propensity, as actualized in politics, is a form of nepotism. Secondly, ethnic groups are extended families sharing distinctive genes. [11]

Conservative assimilationists are simply abiding to the dictates of cultural Marxist social scientists who decided, first, to portray ethnocentrism as a "purely cultural product peculiar to certain types of society", and, second, to portray it as a dysfunctional malady that needed to be removed from human behavior. But if these ideas carried greater persuasion before the age of genetics, there is now a massive literature, and an entire new field of research known as Evolutionary Psychology, which studies the ways in which humans have evolved psychological dispositions and behaviors as adaptations to recurring survival problems in the environment. Numerous "sociobiological" books have been published on how humans discern kin from non-kin, identify and prefer healthier mates, cooperate with others and follow leaders, infanticide, marriage patterns, promiscuity, and the perception of beauty, parental investment, and cross-cultural differences. [12]

There are now also a number of important studies on the genetic interests of humans and the need of Europeans to affirm their own ethnic identity as a rightful disposition that is currently suppressed at the same time as the ethnic identity of non-Europeans is celebrated. Frank

---

10   Ricardo Duchesne, *Faustian Man in a Multicultural Age* (Arktos, 2017). The following paragraphs draw on this book. The cited words come from Pierre L. van den Berghe, *The Ethnic Phenomenon* (New York: Elsevier North- Holland, 1981),p. 18.

11   Pierre L. van den Berghe, *The Ethnic Phenomenon*.

12   The literature favoring sociobiology or evolutionary psychology is both abundant and populated by major figures. Following are some key authors and texts: Steven Pinker, *The Blank Slate: The Modern Denial of Human Nature* (New York: Viking, 2002); Robert Wright, *The Moral Animal: Evolutionary Psychology and Everyday Life* (1995); Jerome Barkow, ed., *Missing the Revolution: Darwinism for Social Scientists* (Oxford University Press, 2005); Jerome Barkow, Leda Cosmides, and John Tooby, eds., *The Adapted Mind: Evolutionary Psychology and the Generation of Culture* (Oxford University Press, 1992); David M Buss, *Evolutionary Psychology: the New Science of the Mind* (Boston, MA: Pearson Education; 2004); Richard Joyce, *The Evolution of Morality* (Cambridge, Mass: The MIT Press, 2006); Geoffrey P. Miller, *The Mating Mind: How Sexual Choice Shaped the Evolution of Human Nature* (Garden City, N.Y: Doubleday, 2000); Azar Gat, War in Human Civilization (Oxford University Press, 2006).

Salter's ideas in this respect are particularly relevant because of the way he has framed them in opposition to the policies of mass immigration across the West.[13] Salter explains that to speak of the European 'ethny' in general, not of an actual group of Europeans organized in an ethnically conscious way as an in-group, but of Europeans generally as a geographic race, is to speak of a people with both a common cultural ancestry and a common constellation of genetic traits. Favoring your own ethnic group is adaptive for the simple reason that it improves the standing of your ethny in competition with other groups. This applies as well to races, for members of a race share more genetic information with each other than with people from other races. The best strategy for the preservation and advancement of the genetic interests of an ethny is a well-defined territorial state. Immigration is not merely about the risk that alien cultures pose to the West and the inability of Muslims to assimilate. Mass immigration by non-Europeans involves ethnic displacement by people with different genetic interests. The greater the genetic distance between the native Europeans and the immigrants, the greater the genetic loss to the nation.

Now, we all know that Europeans tend to be more individualistic, less collective in their ethnic awareness, for complex historical reasons.[14] On the other hand, non-Europeans are more collective and racially aware,[15] more inclined to practice ethnic nepotism[16] and to engage in the highly threatening practice of free-riding ethnic behavior by utilizing welfare services, schools and national infrastructure created and sustained by Europeans, at the same time that they are cheered on by a cultural Marxist establishment that prohibits whites from engaging in the same behaviors. Salter thus calls for genetic interests to be "explicitly incorporated" into Western political theory and for strong constitutional guarantees favoring the ethnic interests of European peoples.

What we have now is exactly the opposite, as we have seen in

---

13   Frank Salter, *On Genetic Interests. Family, Ethnicity, and Humanity in an Age of Mass Migration* (Transaction Publishers, 2007).

14   Ricardo Duchesne, *The Uniqueness of Western Civilization* (Brill, 2011).

15   Hbd chick, "national individualism-collectivism scores" (2013), https://hbdchick. wordpress.com/2013/09/07/national-individualism-collectivism-scores/

16   Tatu Vanhanen, "Ethnic Nepotism as a Cross-Cultural Background Factor of Ethnic Conflicts" OJPS Vol.4 No.3, July 2014, http://www.scirp.org/journal/ PaperInformation.aspx?PaperID=48450

our assessment of Kymlicka and Taylor. Multiculturalism is an asymmetrical system in which Europeans, and only Europeans, are expected to celebrate other cultures and behave as universal altruists, at the same time that non-Europeans are encouraged to practice in-group ethnic interests inside the homelands of Europeans. It was with this idea in mind that I decided to create a blog, Council of European Canadians, in the summer of 2014 "dedicated to the promotion and defense of the ethnic interests of European Canadians". I called for a strategy in which European Canadians would unify their economic, environmental, and cultural concerns about immigration under a pro-European ethnic group strategy that is operational within, but recognizes the limitations of, multiculturalism in Canada. As part of the 'Beliefs and Goals' of the Council,[17] I stated:

Canada is a nation founded by Anglo and French Europeans. In 1971, over one century after Confederation, the Anglo and French composition of the Canadian population stood at 44.6 percent and 28.7 percent respectively. Over 96 percent of the population was European in origin. We therefore oppose all efforts to deny or weaken the European character of Canada. We believe that the pioneers and settlers who built the Canadian nation are part of the European people. Therefore we believe that Canada derives from and is an integral part of European civilization and that Canada should remain majority, not exclusively, European in its thnic composition and cultural character.

We believe that existing strategies for immigration reform have not been successful and must be abandoned. We believe that assimilation (of non-Europeans in the current state of mass immigration) would be fatal to our European heritage, and that if we aim to enhance European Canada we must rely upon the current principles afforded by multiculturalism. Section 27 of the Charter of Rights and Freedom (1982), as well as the "Canadian Multiculturalism Act", otherwise known as Bill C-93, which was passed into law on July 21, 1988, recognize the freedom of all members of Canadian society to preserve and enhance their cultural heritage.

---

17   Council of European Canadians, Promoting Canada's European Heritage, "Our Goals and Beliefs", http://www.Euro-Canadian.ca/2014/05/our-beliefs-and-goals.html

Some may find it difficult to understand why this Council would encourage Euro-Canadians to employ multicultural principles considering that this ideology was implemented to encourage minority groups to foster their ethnic and religious identities. The answer is twofold. Firstly, multiculturalism uses the language of collective rights designed to guarantee the cultural survival of ethnic and religious groups. It seeks to help minorities express their collective identities and pride without discrimination. Secondly, multiculturalism affirms the right of all individuals to preserve and enhance their ethnic and cultural heritage. The idea that collective rights should apply as well to the culture of the majority of Europeans follows logically from multiculturalism. Why should members of the majority culture be excluded from affirming their right to collective survival in the face of immigration patterns that are threatening to reduce them to a minority while destroying their heritage in Canada? Why should the majority culture be viewed as the only group that is capable of engaging in discrimination rather than as the one culture that has been singled out to be excluded from affirming its identity?

As Euro-Canadians, we will not be arguing in favour of multiculturalism as a minority to advance our group rights, but will be arguing within multiculturalism in order to make Europeans aware that they are the founding peoples and that Canada is their homeland and that we intend to keep the country majority European.

We agree with the Multiculturalism Act of 1988 that all citizens should "receive equal treatment and equal protection under the law". However, we believe that this Act makes an egregious historical error in stating that "multiculturalism is a fundamental characteristic of the Canadian heritage and identity". This is a cultural Marxist claim inconsistent with the fact that Canada was created by French families mostly born in the soil of "New France" and by Anglo families also born in Canada, as well as by hard working settlers from France and England, and then from Europe generally.

Canada is a nation created by individuals with an Anglo/French/

European heritage, not by individuals from diverse races and cultures. The cultural Marxists currently controlling Canada want to legitimize their imposition of diversity on Canadians since 1971 by falsely claiming that Canada was diverse from the beginning. But this is a historical fabrication we Euro-Canadians are exposing, and will continue to expose. The political record shows that the racial diversification of Canada has entailed the illiberal imposition of political correctness against Canadians who wish to preserve Canada's European identity [...]

9

Multiculturalism Is Not the Problem

Bissoondath's *Selling Illusions*

As the subtitle of Neil Bissoondath's book says, multiculturalism is a "cult" in Canada, not a typical cult in which a small group of very devoted supporters worship something or someone, but a cult officially endorsed by the elites across the nation, seemingly accepted by the majority, inscribed in the legal system, the media, schools, textbooks, historical narratives, and endorsed by all the political parties. Published in 1994, *Selling Illusions* became one of the most controversial books in the 1990s. In the revised edition published in 2002, Bissoondath recounts the "roller-coaster ride" he experienced upon publication, the many reviews, promotion circuit across the country, rounds of media interviews and talks at universities and community colleges, phone-in shows on local television, and addresses to "audiences in one packed hall after another".[1]

But he soon noticed that the "unduly critical" responses were coming not from the general public, but the established media, political parties, and university professors. The many Canadians he encountered in his talks were either sympathetic or quite willing to discuss the arguments of the book. The "cult" of multiculturalism has been, indeed, a state-sanctioned ideology imposed from above without democratic consent.

Bissoondath refers to a survey conducted in 1993 in which about 72 percent of the respondents stated that Canadian multiculturalism was not working and should be replaced by the cultural melting pot policy of the United States. The argument of *Selling Illusions* is in line with the feelings of these respondents: multiculturalism encourages immigrants to hold on to the habits, values, and ethnic identities of their former homelands rather than assimilate into the culture of Canada.

The general public senses that something is amiss in Canada but misses the target in believing that the problem is multiculturalism

---

1   *Selling Illusions. The Cult of Multiculturalism in Canada* (Penguin, 2002).

as such. The problem is the policy of mass immigration from non-European cultures. Will Kymlicka and Charles Taylor are right: individual fulfillment is not something that can be achieved in isolation but only as a member of a community; a constituent component of a community is the cultural and ethnic identity of the members belonging to it. One of the key goals of multiculturalism is for "mainstream" Canadians to acknowledge the ethno-cultural attachments of minorities; hundreds of thousands of immigrants arriving from non-European lands every year cannot be expected to brush aside their customs and ethnic identities.

The policy of multiculturalism, of course, does not call upon immigrants to create a new political order with illiberal institutions but expects them to accept freedom of speech, representative government, and cultural pluralism. In many ways, what makes Canada the most interesting example of multiculturalism in the world is that it was the first country to come to the political (and theoretical) realization that you can't have mass immigration from non-European lands without multiculturalism. Mass immigration from non-European lands calls for multiculturalism — whether this is recognized officially or not by the central authorities. The American melting pot model is anachronistic; it made sense when the vast majority of immigrants into the U.S. were from Europe. This is not because there is something wrong with Mexicans; they are all too human. It is because Mexicans are very different from European Americans; they have a strong attachment to their mestizo identity, pride in their history, and Spanish language; they don't want to sit in classrooms hearing about how the Americans modernized the former Aztlan territories, the Battle of the Alamo, or how many inventions white Americans were responsible for as compared to Mexicans. Multiculturalists are correct in realizing that there is a form of cultural supremacism in the expectation that they should obediently assimilate to the history, habits, and folkways of Europeans. Bissoondath inadvertently recognizes that the American melting pot has dissolved in the face of mass immigration from non-Europe when he cites the following words from the American historian Arthur Schlesinger:

> The cult of ethnicity exaggerates differences, intensifies resentments and antagonisms...between races and nationalities.[2]

---

2   As cited in *Selling Illusions*, p. 90.

These words come from *The Disuniting of America: Reflections on a Multicultural Society*, in which the author shows that America is just as multicultural as Canada (despite the endless pageants among Canadian assimilationists about its melting pot culture).[3] What Schlesinger failed to understand is that the blame he otherwise attributed to the spread of political correctness, with its promotion of bilingual education, Afrocentrism, and minority pride in schools, was developed not in a vacuum but in direct response to the new racial realities of the United States brought on by immigration and the presence of blacks. Non-Europeans in America were both growing in numbers and in awareness of their identity, and they did not want to join a so-called "common American identity" which came from European whites. Minority histories were first introduced in the curriculum in recognition of the fact that, to this day, Blacks and Indians have not assimilated well to the culture created by the majority European peoples of America.

Therefore I recognize the inescapable multicultural reality of a culture with diverse ethnicities and open borders. Assimilation is the illusion. Given this racial reality, we Europeans need to make use of the levers of multiculturalism for the protection and enhancement of our ethnic and cultural heritage. To demand assimilation is suicidal.

Bissoondath Is for Assimilation

His book was popular in large measure because he was an immigrant from Trinidad calling upon other immigrants to let go of their ethnic ancestries, not play multicultural politics, but join the "common Canadian culture". Nevertheless, in the end, the Canada Bissoondath envisions and cherishes is not of immigrants assimilating to the Canada created by Europeans, but of immigrants joining him in celebrating the making of a radically new Canada characterized by a fusion of cultures, a potpourri of mixed ethnicities constructed out of the "free" choices of deracinated individuals.

Bissoondath's sense of assimilation is akin to that of some of the most ardent and eloquent defenders of "Western values" — from Amartya

---

3   Arthur Schlesinger, *The Disuniting of America: Reflections on a Multicultural Society* (W.W. Norton, 1991).

169

Sen to Liu Xiaobo, from Ayaan Hirsi Ali to Bissoondath's own uncle, Nobel prize writer V.S. Naipaul, who also left his country of origin to become a British citizen, and believes in assimilation to the "universal" values of freedom and democracy. Bissoondath came from a family of relatively well educated Trinidadians fond of European lands. He mentions a letter he received "from a relative long living in England" soon after he departed for Canada, saying:

> Trinidad is behind you, and you have to forget Trinidad and Trinidad attitudes. You have to understand the larger world you are now in...try to understand the country and the people and don't fall into the trap of thinking about race all the time.[4]

Bissoondath's childhood memories of Trinidad are both boring and few; before coming to Canada he was already seeking to escape the "confines" of his heritage; and when he visited Trinidad a mere year after departing, he was "impatient to get back to Toronto". This utter lack of attachment to his homeland is unusual, but understandable in light of the culture of violence and racial tensions in Trinidad. It is also the case that non-whites are attracted to the more successful *and* increasingly diverse world of the West. This is likely why he takes it for granted that everyone can and should escape from the confining atmosphere of their heritage. He arrived in Toronto in 1973, and was immediately drawn to its diversity and the multiple choices it afforded individuals.

While about 95 percent of the Canadian population was ethnically European in 1973, non-Europeans had started arriving in larger numbers in the 1960s, so that, by 1970, half of all immigrants were coming from Caribbean nations, Asia and South America. It was this reality that Bissoondath encountered in Toronto where many of these immigrants were taking residence, not to mention the diversity among Europeans themselves. From his arrival until the writing of his book in 1994, or the publication of the revised edition in 2001, the number of immigrants from non-European lands kept increasing. From 1981 to 2001, the number of visible minorities — excluding Aboriginals — increased more than threefold from 1.1 million people, or nearly 5% of the population, to 4.0 million people, or 13% of the population.

This rapidly changing ethnic reality is what Bissoondath identifies

---

4   *Selling Illusions*, p. 222.

with Canada. He is calling for assimilation to this newly emerging racially and culturally mixed Canada. He is not calling for assimilation to European Canada.

Bissoondath is just as critical of Euro-Canadians attached to their heritage in Canada as he is of immigrants attached to the recognition multiculturalism affords them. Actually, he is more critical, designating as "racist" members of the "political right" who oppose our current immigration levels. He is right on target about the way the left brands as racist "anyone critical of multiculturalism policy", and the way minorities manipulate multiculturalism both as victims in need of special treatment and as proud members of their ethnic groups, while accusing Europeans of being racist if they show pride in their own heritage. Bissoondath would like all individuals to stop thinking in terms of their collective identities and view their identities as social constructs shaped by the free play of their own choices in a changing environment. But why does he presume that preferring one's race and historical culture is wrong and somehow not a real individual choice? He knows that the charge of racism has "particularly virulent" consequences in Canada, and yet he says that to define oneself by one's ethnicity or race is racist.[5]

Are all Canadians then obligated to feel the way Bissoondath feels about his identity? This is what has happened to Euro-Canadians; they are the only ethnic groups disallowed from showing any pride and attachment to their heritage — despite, or, I should say, because of the way multiculturalism has been understood as a call only to minorities to protect and enhance their ethnic identity.

Anyone who endorses the radical transformation of Canada's culture from an overwhelmingly European nation into a thoroughly immigrant and ethnically mixed culture is a cultural Marxist. He says that multiculturalism "is in many ways a statement of activism" directing the government to play a role in shaping the cultural evolution of Canada.[6] But the real force of activism is mass immigration from the non-European lands. Multiculturalism in a Canada that was still 96% percent European in 1971 would have amounted to the reinforcement of Canada's already existing identity. By contrast, advocating

---

5 *Ibid*, p. 163.

6 *Ibid*, p. 39.

assimilation in the context of mass immigration from non-European lands is a form of activism that is radically transforming the nation forever at a pace never witnessed in human history.

He brushes the political right as "mostly driven by its fears" and "fantasies" about Canada's past.[7] But the views I am defending are actually based on how things were in Canada for centuries, whereas Bissoondath's party is endorsing an experiment without precedent and based on a willful misinterpretation of Canada's history. He writes:

> Homogeneous Canada, a reality only so long as its minorities could be ignored, is no more. If Canada was never exclusively a 'White Christian country', it is even less so now.[8]

Which is it? Did European Canadians exclude minorities and inhabit an exclusively white country, or were they wrong to pretend that Canada was exclusively white and Christian? The historical record, as we saw in considerable detail in Part I, shows that 90 per cent of all immigrants who came to Canada before 1961 were from Britain. At the time of Confederation in 1867, despite the large numbers of immigrants in the preceding decades, 79 percent of the population had been born in Canada. The French-speaking population numbered about 70,000 in the 1760s, and thereafter, until the 1950s, the population expanded rapidly, not through immigration, which had essentially ceased after the British assumed control, but through the high fertility rates of the French native mothers. Therefore, Canada was a nation created — all its institutions, culture, education, parliamentary government, common and civil law, modern infrastructure — by Anglo and French natives and settlers. I repeat, when Bissoondath arrived in 1973, Canada was still overwhelmingly European in ethnicity.

The claim that Canada was never a "White Christian country" is a historical fabrication intended to justify the current cultural Marxist agenda. Bissoondath says mainstream Canadians should not fear that an "ill-defined Canadian way of life is disappearing", accepting mass immigration is just "part of growing up".[9] He implies that before

---

7   *Ibid*, p. 57.

8   *Ibid*, p. 54.

9   *Ibid*, p. 69.

diversity arrived, Canada had no identity other than being racist in excluding minorities; for all his emphasis on assimilation to Canada, he never says anything positive about the history of Canada; it is all about the world he encountered in Toronto and how he felt about his own identity; the Canadians who created the country are portrayed as closed minded, even though most of Canada's cultural heritage was already in place in the 1970s, and many of the contributions made thereafter have been in pop culture and cultural Marxist thinking.

He notes that the language used by proponents of multiculturalism consists mostly of "comforting and soothing" words, but his book is suffused with equally insubstantial words about the wonderful cultural complexity and vibrancy of diversity. How does one explain the incredible cultural accomplishments of ethnically homogeneous ancient Greece, Elizabethan England, and golden age Spain? How many truly great artists, philosophers, and scientists has Canada produced since diversity began in earnest? Bissoondath rightfully criticizes multiculturalists for never addressing the question of limits:

> How far do we go as far as a country in encouraging and promoting cultural difference? How far is far enough, how far too far? Is there a point at which diversity begins to threaten social cohesion?[10]

Bissoondath presumes throughout that multiculturalism on its own nurtures a strong sense of ethnic identity. But multiculturalism is best seen as an official acknowledgement of the growing and planned diversification of Canada and the strong bonds humans have naturally to their ethnic heritage. In this light, the question that needs addressing is how far should Canada go in promoting mass immigration; is there a point at which the actual diversity of races begins to threaten the "Western" cohesion of Canada? There are no known cases in human history of liberal democratic cultures outside Europe. There are no known cases of racially mixed liberal democracies in the world. We are currently in a state of experimentation.

Bissoondath chastises the former Reform Party's policy of reducing our immigration intake from 250,000 to 150,000. He wants more diversification. He prefers his city of residence, Quebec City, above

---

10   *Ibid*, p. 40.

all other cities, but feels uncomfortable with the "old, racially minded nationalists" in Quebec. Race is "simply like the shape of one's ears", why should it matter to the native Quebecois if millions upon millions of immigrants keep pouring in, so long as there are no multicultural policies? Well, for one, the PQ party, which is a party that emphasizes civic, not ethnic, nationalism, has been unable to advance its drive for independence due to the "ethnic vote", the mistrust immigrants have of civic-linguistic nationalism. For another, the Quebecois are a racial people with different looks, temperaments, histories, and so allowing their lands to be populated by other races constitutes an acceptance of racial displacement and eventual genocide.

Bissoondath categorizes any policy or idea about setting limits to immigration as if it were a call for a racially homogeneous Canada. How many more years of mass immigration does Canada need before it ceases to be homogeneous and can be identified as diverse? Why is he assuming that a Canada that is minority European is bound to be richer culturally than a Canada that is 90 percent European? None of these questions are ever asked in Canada because, when all is said, the cult of immigration from non-European lands is the true religion accepted by all parties and elites without debate and democratic input — unlike Bissoondath's critique of multiculturalism which was the subject of open debate across the nation and did not preclude him from achieving honorary doctorates and being named "a Chevalier of the Ordre national du Quebec".[11]

Salim Mansur and the Small-l Liberal Critique of Multiculturalism

Salim Mansur, an associate professor at the University of Western Ontario in the department of political science, is a prominent public intellectual in Canada,[12] a frequent commentator on radio and television, a regular writer for *Toronto Sun*, and occasional columnist for *FrontPage Magazine*, *National Review Online* and *PajamasMedia*. His book, *Delectable Lie: A Liberal Repudiation of Multiculturalism*, synthesizes arguments he has made over the last decade about the threat Islamic fundamentalism poses for liberal democratic societies

---

11   https://en.wikipedia.org/wiki/Neil_Bissoondath#Awards

12   https://en.wikipedia.org/wiki/Salim_Mansur

captivated by the notion that all cultures deserve equal respect.[13] The thesis of this book was already articulated in his essay "The Muddle of Multiculturalism", which I will use as the main point of reference.[14]

Mansur says that his critique of multiculturalism is "from a small-l liberal perspective distinct from the animating spirit of the contemporary Liberalism with a big-L of the Liberal Party in Canada". [15] The cardinal principle to which Mansur adheres is that of the "freedom of the individual from any untoward coercion by the collective in society". For him all forms of collective identity — religious, ethnic, and sexual (including the pursuit of economic equality by the collective authority of the government) — impede the liberty of the individuals to achieve their potential as human beings. As a small-l liberal, Mansur prefers the policies of the Conservative Party of Canada, and is thus known as a conservative. I will classify him as a right wing cultural Marxist. I may be stretching the term "cultural Marxist", but it seems to me that any position uncritical of the current policy of mass immigration in Canada, and European countries generally, must be so designated since it amounts to a denial to European peoples of the right to a homeland where they can freely express and protect their ethnic identities.

I also designated Bissoondath as a right wing assimilationist (notwithstanding his leftist economic views), but Mansur may be said to be further to the right in his keener focus on the "uniquely Western" values of the Enlightenment coupled with his lack of emphasis on the supposed "richness" of mixed identities, which Bissoondath enjoys writing about. Will Kymlicka (and Charles Taylor) are also against the acceptance of Islamic fundamentalists with illiberal values, although they favor, in varying degrees, multiculturalism or group rights for minorities. The difference with Mansur is that he not only opposes multiculturalism, like Bissoondath, but focuses directly on the dangers of Islamic culture to Canada and calls for a strong patriotic endorsement of Canadian values against "enemies" who want to destroy the freedoms of the West. Still, Mansur's strongly-worded objections to Islamic radicalism, to the opportunism of politicians who play up the immigrant vote, all fall within the acceptable cultural Marxist discourse

---

13   *Delectable Lie: A Liberal Repudiation of Multiculturalism* (Mantua Books, 2011).

14   "The Muddle of Multiculturalism: A Liberal Critique" *Frontier Centre for Policy* (No. 100, February 2011), https://fcpp.org/files/1/PS100_MMulticulturalism_F2.pdf

15   *Ibid.*

of multiracialism inside all European nations. All these intellectuals I have been writing about agree that liberal democratic societies should not accommodate illiberal values, and by illiberal values they mean not only Islamic fundamentalism but ethno-nationalist European ideas.

Some years ago I was satisfied with Mansur's line of reasoning. But having come to the realization that European ethnicity is an intrinsic foundational component of Western civilization, I now see a clear difference between our views. I disagree that his position is consistent with classical liberalism, but believe instead that my emphasis on ethnic identity is consistent with classical liberalism. The freedom of the individual can only be sustained and actualized if this freedom is part of a larger community, and there can be no communitarian fellow-feeling without families, traditional marriages, and without ethnic cohesion. The bureaucratic communitarianism advocated by Kymlicka and Taylor can never be a substitute for the age-old historical ancestries and evolutionary-driven associations of ethnic groups. Science has now confirmed that ethnocentrism, that is, in-group preference for one's ethnic and cultural group, is an evolutionary selected behavior very closely associated with cooperation and altruism, in tandem with a sense of derogation for out-group members. All modern liberal states were created by ethnically unified Europeans. The liberal-democratic nation of Canada (where all Canadians gradually came to enjoy individual rights regardless of ethnicity) was created under racially discriminatory immigration policies. This is not a paradox; it is a reflection of the way liberal cultures came to terms with long existing minorities. The deception comes when liberals extrapolate this recognition of native minorities with an endorsement of mass immigration.

I have met Mansur a few times; he is a decent human being, sincere in his personal attachment to Canada and his loyalty to Canada's values and institutions, as he defines them. He arrived in Toronto in 1974 from the "ethnically driven politics", the "terror and savage killings" of Pakistan/Bangladesh. In Canada he saw a Western society based on the Kantian idea that "man as a free agent and a rational creature is an end in himself and must never be treated as a means" trapped within the ends of collective groups and identities.[16] He criticizes both the left and the traditional right for their emphasis on group identity over the right

---

16   *Ibid.*

of the individuals. He attributes Canada's peacefulness and prosperity to its individual freedom and thinks that group identities create divisions that sooner or later will result in violence and societal breakdown.

On the question of the individual's relation to society, I have more in common with multicultural communitarians than with assimilationists who view humans as atomized creatures. Wikipedia neatly summarizes the views of communitarians such as Charles Taylor and Kymlicka, among others:

> They argued that contemporary liberalism and libertarianism presuppose an incoherent notion of the individual as existing outside and apart from society, rather than embedded within it. To the contrary, they argued, there are no generic individuals but rather only Germans or Russians, Berliners or Muscovites — or members of some other particularistic community. Because individual identity is partly constructed by culture and social relations, there is no coherent way of formulating individual rights or interests in abstraction from social contexts.[17]

But I disagree with the "academic communitarianism" of multiculturalists in that they recognize the group rights of minorities but not the group rights of majorities, in relation to which they emphasize the principle of individual rights, and view any communitarian politics associated with majorities as illiberal in nature. Again, Wikipedia sums up well the misgivings academic communitarians have with "early" or traditional communitarianism:

> Early communitarians were charged with being, in effect, social conservatives. However, many contemporary communitarians, especially those who define themselves as responsive [leftist] communitarians, fully realize and often stress that they do not seek to return to traditional communities, with their authoritarian power structure, rigid stratification, and discriminatory practices against minorities and women. Responsive communitarians seek to build communities based on open participation, dialogue, and truly shared values.[18]

---

17   Slight revisions in Wikipedia entries are normal and the wording may have changed by the time this book makes it to press: https://en.wikipedia.org/wiki/Communitarianism#Communitarian_philosophy

18   The apt term "academic communitarianism" comes from Wikipedia: https://

I endorse a form of communitarianism that may be labelled as Traditionalist, Darwinian and Western-white simultaneously. The term "academic communitarianism" used by Wikipedia is quite appropriate in pointing to the artificial character of leftist communitarianism: it is, on the one hand, radically individualist in seeking to dismantle all traditional associations including the family, and, on the other, extremely statist in seeking to create new associations by administrative fiat, by a nanny state using manipulative child-rearing practices and "educational" brainwashing techniques against the natural ends of humans. I will try to convey what I mean by a "traditionalist-evolutionary-Western" communitarianism by citing key passages from Mansur and then offering brief counter-arguments. Rather than indenting cited passages, I will organize this as a brief dialogue using our names.

Dialogue with Mansur

Salim Mansur: [T]he West represents the idea of a civilization nurtured by the values of the Enlightenment that Kant famously defined as "dare to know", its genealogy traced back to ancient Greece, its faith tradition anchored in Judeo-Christian ethics, its politics shaped by the democratic impulse of revolutions against hereditary rule, its philosophy influenced by the development of the scientific method of controlled experiments and tests, its culture open and embracing of new ideas. The sum total of these values uniquely defines the West in terms of liberal democracy...My own journey from the East to the West has been an education that encourages putting aside those ideas and values that confine an individual to the requirements of collective identity and group solidarity.

Reply: I agree with Hegel's communitarian argument[19] that Kant's "dare to know" was a product of a particular modern European culture; the willingness to employ one's reason against the political dogmas of the eighteenth century was nurtured after a long struggle inside a Europe that had already experienced the Greek discovery

---

en.wikipedia.org/wiki/Communitarianism#Academic_communitarianism

19 Timothy C. Luther, *Hegel's Critique of Modernity: Reconciling Individual Freedom and the Community* (Lexington Books, 2009). Luther explains how "Hegel's conception of freedom enable us to reconcile many of the differences that divide liberalism and communitarianism" (p. 10).

of reason, the Roman discovery of the legal persona, the Christian invention of universities and open inquiry, the Renaissance invention of perspective painting through the employment of mathematics, the Protestant emphasis on the inner conscience of believers. Kant's principle of moral self-legislation is purely formal and subjective in its presupposition that the determination of what is right and good is a pure act of cognitive willing by an abstract agent rather than the achievement of a concrete European culture. The self-legislating individual is not natural but constructed out of a historically specific community, a European community that includes certain ethnic traits, religious background, and historical memories.

Salim Mansur: [T]he collectivist demands of jihad are pushing hard against the values of liberalism. This is the return of the primitive and the denial of the view that progress in history results from the daring of the few to question the consensus of the many; it is bending to the wishes of the crowd and its unwillingness to protect the minority from the tyranny of the majority; it is the jihad of the tribe, of the class-based or ethnic-based or religiously-organized party against the ultimate minority, the solitary individual, standing alone against the weight of the many.

Reply: Aside from the fact that no individual has ever existed outside a community, and that Western individualism is "Western" because it was produced only by Western communities, why do cultural Marxists always identify any form of collectivity with coercion, tyranny, and violence? The United States, Australia, and Canada were all liberal democratic societies with strong communitarian identities before the policies restricting immigration were dismantled. The opening of European borders was imposed from above without democratic consent, and today no free criticism of the supposed merits of diversification is allowed. The more traditional community of Canada before the 1970s was more open to critical reflection.

Salim Mansur: Multiculturalism promotes the notion of cultural relativism, which states that since each culture is by definition unique, any independent standard to distinguish among cultures would itself represent cultural bias nullifying the objectivity of any test applied.

Reply: Mansur is saying that Western culture should be seen as the standard by which to judge every other culture. He does not explain but implies that the Western idea of the rational individual can be used as an objective test to judge other cultures. But if most cultures in the world, as Mansur observes, are still tribal, collectivist, ethnocentric, and authoritarian, how can one argue that one particular culture, the West, can serve as a neutral test for every other culture? In what ways are the values of the West universally true for humanity if these values were not nurtured by most of humanity?

Salim Mansur: Allan Bloom discusses this paradox as follows: "Men cannot remain content with what is given them by their culture if they are to be fully human...Nature should be the standard by which we judge our own lives and the lives of people. This is why philosophy, not history or anthropology, is the most important human science...What is most characteristic of the West is science, particularly understood as the quest to know nature and the consequent denigration of convention — i.e., culture or the West understood as a culture — in favour of what is accessible to all men as men through their common and distinctive faculty, reason".

Reply: In the next chapter I will be discussing Leo Strauss, the intellectual behind Allan Bloom's popular book, *The Closing of the American Mind*.[20] Mansur does not explain, but Straussians believe that the West can be identified with Nature as the standard by which to judge all other cultures on the grounds that this was the first culture to employ human reason and, in so doing, transcend the biases and distorting lenses of its culture and thereby apprehend the highest ends of Nature. Westerners were able to see what is best for men as men by apprehending, through the employment of reason, what is most admirable about human nature. Westerners were the first to "liberate" themselves "from culture" and see what is universally best for all human beings. Multiculturalism brings back the blind lenses of cultural particularism rather than allowing immigrants to free themselves from their cultural background. But why is Mansur (or Bloom) assuming (dogmatically) that if we employ our reason in an open manner without authoritarian restrictions we will come to the conclusion that humans can rise above their cultural prejudices,

---

20   *The Closing of the American Mind* (Simon and Schuster, 1987). This readable book influenced many conservatives to believe that the West is all about natural rights for the human race.

overcome their emotional attachments to their culture, and develop a universal concept of "we" freed of any ethnocentric longings?

Assuming that the Enlightenment was the end of history, Mansur ignores major intellectual developments after the eighteenth century emphasizing the importance of human emotions, irrational impulses, and diverse ways of life and thinking around the world. Even in Kant's own time, Johann Gottfried Herder, as we saw earlier, questioned the notion of a cosmopolitan world based on generic human values. He believed it was illusory to postulate a universal philosophy for humanity in which the national character of peoples would disappear and each human on earth would "love each other and every one...being all equally polite, well-mannered and even-tempered...all philanthropic citizens of the world".[21] In fact, Enlightenment philosophers themselves, including Kant, argued "in text after text...in the works of Hume, Diderot, Montesquieu, Kant, and many lesser lights" that men "are not uniform but are divided up into sexes, races, national characters... and many other categories". This is the argument Aaron Garrett makes in a chapter titled "Human Nature" in *The Cambridge History of Eighteenth-Century Philosophy*.[22] But because we have been approaching the study of races under the tutelage of our current belief that race is purely "a social construct" and that any division of mankind into races is based on malevolent "presumptions unsupported by available evidence", as Wikipedia would have us believe,[23] we have failed to appreciate that this subject was part and parcel of what the philosophes meant by "enlightenment". Contrary to the philosophical gibberish of the Straussians, the study of Nature is showing that there are significant varieties in the mental states of peoples,[24] and that ethnocentrism, rather than Western liberalism, is a universal feature of human nature which only Europeans have managed to reflect upon and accommodate with their liberal values.[25] Western people are different only in

---

21   Cited in Gurutz Jáuregui Bereciartu, *Decline of the Nation State* (University of Nevada Press, 1984), p. 26.

22   Aaron Garrett, "Nature" in *The Cambridge History of Eighteenth Century Philosophy*, Vol One. Edited by Knud Haakonssen (Cambridge University Press, 2008).

23   "Scientific Racism", https://en.wikipedia.org/wiki/Scientific_racism

24   Sherry Ortner, "East Brain, West Brain" *New York Times* (April 20, 2003).

25   I will be returning to this issue in the next chapter.

being less ethnocentric due to their individualistic temperament, which is a product of their unique historical origins.[26]

Salim Mansur: Since the immigration tap, once opened, creates its own pressures that will not allow for it to be closed easily, making the West more multi-ethnic and multi-faith likely will remain irreversible. This fact should not necessarily be a cause for alarm, except for the reality of the post-9/11 situation.

Reply: This passage contains the crucial flaw in the "conservative" critique of immigration. For all the alarms this critique raises about radical Muslims, it dares not talk, or simply does not care, about the projected reduction of white Canadians to a shrinking minority in the coming decades. It presumes that Canadian identity is all a matter of inculcating "new Canadians" with liberal democratic values. It blames multiculturalism for discouraging immigrants, in the words of Mansur, "to make the passage from their traditional cultures and embrace modernity with its liberal values". It thinks that multicultural programs are at the source of the formation of ethnic enclaves in Canada and never asks why Blacks and Aboriginals in the United States are still separated in residential locations,[27] in voting patterns,[28] and in educational attainments, even though there is no official multiculturalism. It does not ask why Mexicans, and Hispanics generally, once they started arriving in large numbers, have refused to adopt English as their public language, while attaining academic standards barely above black levels.[29] History shows that assimilation

---

26 Ricardo Duchesne, *Faustian Man in a Multicultural Age* (Arktos, 2017).

27 Charles M. Lamb, *Housing Segregation in Suburban America since 1960* (Cambridge University Press, 2005). Patrick Sharkey, *Stuck in Place: Urban Neighborhoods and the End of Progress Toward Racial Equality*. The University of Chicago Press, 2013).

28 Alec Tyson and Shiva Maniam, "Behind Trump's victory: Divisions by race, gender, education" Pew Research Center, (November 9, 2017), http://www.pewresearch.org/fact-tank/2016/11/09/behind-trumps-victory-divisions-by-race-gender-education/

29 Danyel A. V. Moosmann, Mark W. Roosa, and George P. Knight, "Generational Patterns in Mexican Americans' Academic Performance in an Unwelcoming Political Context" J Appl Dev Psychol, vol. 35, no. 2 (2014 March-April). Of course, the standard explanations for these educational differences are that Blacks and Hispanics are discriminated against; as one of hundreds of similar studies puts it: "For Hispanics in the United States, the educational experience is one of accumulated disadvantage". See Marta Tienda and Faith Mitchell, eds. *Hispanics and the Future of America. National Research Council of the National Academies* (Washington, D.C., 2006), https://www.ncbi.nlm.nih.gov/books/NBK19909/   If only they would ask why East Asian immigrants have higher attainments than whites; a difference the assimilationist would use, and uses, to show that, yes, immigrants can integrate

of large populations only worked, through many conflicts and divisions, with European immigrants. It is not that non-Europeans in small numbers are incapable of assimilating, or that there is something wrong with them as human beings. It is that they cannot assimilate in large numbers because the differences between them and Europeans are more substantial. In a later chapter we will be addressing some additional scientific evidence about the human tendency to form in-groups in derogation of out-groups.

Salim Mansur: [Quotes Pascal Bruckner's words about those who weaken the "self-confidence" of the West]: "Europe against itself: anti-Occidentalism, as we know is a European tradition that stretches from Montaigne to Sartre and instills relativism and doubt".

Reply: Bruckner is the author of *The Tyranny of Guilt: An Essay on Western Masochism* where he laments the lack of confidence Europeans have in their liberal values and the history that produced these values; meanwhile, however, Bruckner is very pleased that France, the country of his birth, is no longer ethnically Gallic. In his book, which I used once for a course when I was looking for alternatives to the multicultural narrative, he sprays countless words about how multiculturalism weakens our resolve to fight radical Islam, while defending a thoroughly multiracial Western universalism against those who were "hostile to the diversity of physiognomies and the plurality of ways of life...the great mixtures of [Western] cities". [30] Muslims and Africans need not fear the West, Bruckner enlightens us: "monochrome Europe, which was mostly white, is gone". Bruckner is another trickster pretending to be for the West while celebrating the destruction of white Gallic France.

---

if only they try and have good family support. This type of argument is implicitly disputed here throughout this book for its complete reduction of Western identity to a modern identity, ignoring the deep cultural differences, historical characteristics and interesting biological physiognomies of the races; see also Ricardo Duchesne, *Faustian Man in a Multicultural Age* (Arktos 2017), for a detailed account of why race is an inescapable trait in the identification of Western culture.

30   Pascal Bruckner, *The Tyranny of Guilt: An Essay on Western Masochism* (Princeton University Press, 2010), p. 154.

10

The Straussian Assault on the West

A major weakness in the critiques of multiculturalism we have examined thus far is their lack of philosophical depth, which partly explains why this critique has been unable to mount a sustained challenge against the far better developed ideas of multiculturalists. There are, however, a number of lesser known Canadian critics of multiculturalism who have provided substantive philosophical arguments by drawing on the arguments of the American Leo Strauss and his pupils against the "relativism" of multiculturalism and in favor of Western civilization. I am not an expert in the Straussian school. My aim in this chapter is to focus, firstly, on a recent book by Grant Havers, a Canadian Tory conservative teaching at Trinity Western University, with the title, *Leo Strauss and Anglo-American Democracy: A Conservative Critique.*[1] This heavily researched book covers key debates in the development of the Straussian school, with illuminating references to Canadians who came under the influence of this school, such as George Grant. The importance of Havers's book lies in its affiliation to the Tory conservative tradition currently rejected by the small-l liberals Mansur endorses. Secondly, in this chapter I will examine the writings of Janet Ajzenstat, who proposes a new interpretation of Canada's founding principles against both the old Tory interpretation and the dominant multicultural view of Canada's identity. She is a true Straussian, unlike the traditionalist George Grant, who sympathized with Strauss under the erroneous belief that he was a like-minded traditionalist.

Notwithstanding Shadia Drury's leftist polemic in *Leo Strauss and the American Right* (1997), Havers shows in a calm but very effective way that Strauss was not the traditional conservative defender of the West leftists have made him out to be. He was, rather, a firm believer in the principles of liberal equality and an unswerving opponent of any form of Western citizenship anchored in Christianity and

---

1   Grant Havers, *Leo Strauss and Anglo-American Democracy: A Conservative Critique* (DeKalb, IL: Northern Illinois University Press, 2013).

European ethnic identity. A main pillar sustaining most of what passes today as the "conservative" critique of multiculturalism is their view that Western nations are inherently characterized by a "civic" form of national membership without any ethnic foundations. Western nations, they believe, express the "natural" wishes of "man as man" for equal rights, rule of law, freedom of expression, and private property. Mainstream leftists and current conservatives alike insist on the historical genuineness of this civic definition. This civic identity, they tell us, is what identifies the nations of Western civilization as unique and universal all at once. Unique because they are the only nations in which the idea of citizenship has been radically separated from any ethnic and religious background; and universal because these civic values are self-evident truths all humans want whenever they are given the opportunity to choose.

Where do these ideas come from? Recall in the last chapter Mansur's reference to Allan Bloom's bestseller, *The Closing of the American Mind*? Leo Strauss was the teacher of Bloom, possibly the most influential philosopher in persuading countless academics and journalists that conservatism should be about defending Western classical liberal values. Strauss articulated a strong defense of liberal values as the best values in our modern world, with roots in ancient Greek times. He did so against the otherwise relativistic tendencies that he also detected within modern liberalism, which misguided Westerners into the endorsement of multiculturalism and its claim that all cultures are equally valid in their own terms, with a right of recognition inside the West, as Taylor would argue. Straussians called for a firm defense of "superior" Western values against both the liberal collectivism of multiculturalists and the traditional collectivism of non-Western and old conservative or "fascistic" Western ideologies. In this vein, the Straussians insisted that to include the criteria of ethnicity or religious ancestry in the concept of Western citizenship was manifestly illiberal. Even more, they argued that if Western nations were to live up to their idea of civic citizenship they would have to relinquish any sense of European peoplehood and Christian ancestry. Welcoming immigrants from multiple ethnic and religious backgrounds was not a problem as long as immigrants were assimilated to the universal values of the West.

The reality that the liberal constitutions of Western nations were conceived and understood in ethnic and Christian terms (if only implicitly since the builders and founders of European nations never envisioned an age of mass migrations) was conveniently overlooked by the followers of Strauss and the new conservatives who agreed with these ideas.

Current conservatives, just like leftists, then, have been pushing for a purely civic interpretation of Western nationhood, in trying to root out Christianity and ethnicity from the historical experiences and founding principles of European nations. Their discursive strategy has not been one of dishonoring the past but of projecting backwards into European history a universal notion of Western citizenship that includes the human race. Grant Havers carefully demonstrates that the most prominent school in the formulation of this view has come out of the writings of Leo Strauss. Strauss's vehement opposition to communism coupled with his enthusiastic defense of American democracy, as it stood in the 1950s, created the erroneous impression that he was a "right wing conservative". But, as Havers explains, Strauss was no less critical of "right wing extremists" (who valued forms of citizenship tied to the nationalist customs and historical memories of a particular people) than of the New Left.

Strauss believed that America was a universal nation in being founded on principles that reflected the "natural" disposition of all humans for life, liberty and happiness. These principles were discovered first by the ancient Greeks in a philosophical and rational manner, but they were not particular to the Greeks; rather, they were "eternal truths" apprehended by Greek philosophers in their writings against tyrannical regimes. While these principles were accessible to all humans as humans, only a few great philosophers and statesmen exhibited the intellectual and personal fortitude to fully grasp and actualize these principles. Nevertheless, most humans possessed enough mental equipment as reasoning beings to recognize these principles as "rights" intrinsic to their nature, so long as they were given the chance to deliberate on "the good" life.

Havers's "conservative critique" of Strauss consists essentially in emphasizing the uniquely Western and Christian origins of the foundational principles of Anglo-American democracy. While

Havers's traditional conservatism includes admiration for such classical liberal principles as the rule of law, constitutional government, and separation of church and state, his argument is that these liberal principles are rooted primarily in Christianity, particularly its ideal of charity. He takes for granted the reader's familiarity with this ideal, which is unfortunate, since it is not well understood, but is generally taken to mean that Christianity encourages charitable activities, relief of poverty and advancement of education. Havers has something more profound in mind. Christian charity from a political perspective is a state of being wherein one seeks a sympathetic understanding of ideas and beliefs that are different to one's own. Charitable Christians seek to understand other viewpoints and are willing to engage alternative ideas and political proposals rather than oppose them without open dialogue. Havers argues that the principles of natural rights embodied in America's founding cannot be separated from this charitable disposition; not only were the founders of America, the men who wrote the Federalist Papers, quite definite in voicing the view that they were acting as Christian believers in formulating America's founding, they were also very critical of Greek slavery, militarism, and aristocratic license against the will of the people.

Throughout the book Havers debates the rather ahistorical way Strauss and his followers have gone about "downplaying or ignoring the role of Christianity in shaping the Anglo-American tradition" — when the historical record copiously shows that Christianity played a central role nurturing the ideals of individualism and tolerance, abolition of slavery and respect for the dignity of all humans. Havers debates and refutes the similarly perplexing ways in which Straussians have gone about highlighting the role of Greek philosophy in shaping the Anglo-American tradition — when the historical record amply shows that Greek philosophers were opponents of the natural equality of humans, defenders of slavery, proponents of a tragic view of history, the inevitability of war and the rule of the mighty.

Havers also challenges the Straussian elevation of such figures as Lincoln, Churchill, Roosevelt, Hobbes and Locke as proponents of an Anglo-American tradition founded on "timeless" Greek ideas. He shows that Christianity was the prevailing influence in the intellectual development and actions of all these men. Havers imparts on the readers a sense of disbelief as to how the Straussians ever managed to exert so much influence on American conservatism (to the point of transforming its original emphasis on traditions and communities into a call for the spread of universal values across the world), despite proposing views that were so blissfully indifferent to "readily available facts".

Basically, the Straussians were not worried about historical veracity as much as they were determined to argue that Western civilization (which they identified with the Anglo-American tradition) was philosophically conceived from its beginnings as a universal civilization. In this effort, Strauss and his followers genuinely believed that American liberalism had fallen prey to the "yoke" of German historicism and relativism, infusing the American principles of natural rights with the notion that these were merely valid for a particular people rather than based on Human Reason. German historicism — the idea that each culture exhibits a particular world view and that there is no such thing as a rational faculty standing above history — led to the belittlement of the principles of natural rights by limiting them to a particular time and place. Worse than this — and the modern philosophers, Hobbes and Locke, were to be blamed as well — the principles of natural rights came to be separated from the ancient Greek idea that we can rank ways of life according to their degree of excellence and elevation of the human soul. The modern philosophy of natural rights merely afforded individuals the right to choose their own lifestyle without any guidance as to what is "the good life".

Strauss believed that this relativist liberalism would not be able to withstand challenges from other philosophical outlooks and illiberal ways of life, from Communism and Fascism, for example, unless it was rationally grounded on eternal principles. He thought the ancient Greeks had understood better than anyone else that some truths are deeply grounded in the actual nature of men, not relative to a particular time and culture, but essential to what is best for "man as man". These truths were summoned up in the modern philosophy of natural rights, though in a flawed manner. The moderns tended to appeal to the lower instincts of humans, to a society that would merely ensure security and the pursuit of pleasure, in defending their ideals of liberty and happiness. But with a proper reading of the ancient texts, and a curriculum based on the "Great Books", the soul of contemporaneous students could be elevated above a life of trivial pursuits.

This emphasis on absolute, universal, and "natural" standards attracted a number of prominent Christians to Strauss. The Canadian George Grant (1918-1988) for one, was drawn to the potential uses Strauss's emphasis on eternal values might have to fight off the erosion of Christian conviction in the ever more secular, liberal, and consumerist Canada of his day. However, as Havers explains, Grant did not quite realize that Strauss was not really a traditional conservative, but a staunch proponent of a philosophically based liberalism bereft of any Christian identity. Grant was indeed puzzled by Strauss's marginalization of the influence of Christianity in Western political philosophy. Grant relished the British and Protestant roots of the Anglo-American tradition, though there were certain affinities between him and Strauss; Grant was a firm believer in the superiority of Anglo-Saxon civilization and its rightful responsibility in bringing humanity to a higher cultural level. The difference is that Grant affirmed the religious and ethnic particularities of Anglo-Saxon civilization, whereas Strauss, though a Zionist who believed in a Jewish nation state, sought to portray Anglo-American civilization in a philosophical language cleansed of any Christian particularities and European ethnicity.

Strauss wanted a revised interpretation of Anglo-American citizenship standing above tribal identities and historical particularities. Strauss's objective was to provide Anglo-American government with a political philosophy that would stand as a bulwark against "intolerable" challenges from the left and the right, which endangered liberalism itself. The West had to affirm the universal truthfulness of its way of life and be guarded against the tolerance of forms of expression that threaten this way of life. Havers observes that Strauss was particularly worried about the inability of liberal regimes, as was the case with the Weimar republic, to face up to illiberal challenges. He wanted a liberal order that would ensure the survival of the Jews, and the best assurance for this was a liberal order that spoke in a neutral and purely philosophical idiom without giving any preference to any religious faith and any historical and ethnic ancestries. He wanted a liberalism that would work to undermine any ancestral or traditionally conservative norms that gave preference to a particular people in the heritage of America's founding, and thereby may discriminate against Jews. Only in a strictly universal civilization would Jews feel safe while retaining their identity.

Havers brings up another old conservative, Willmore Kendall (1909-67), who was drawn to Straussian thought even though substantial aspects of his thought were incompatible with Strauss's. Among these differences was the "majoritarian populism" of Kendall versus the aristocratic elitism of Strauss. The aristocrats Strauss had in mind were philosophers and statesmen who understood the eternal values of the West whereas the majoritarian people Kendall had in mind were Americans who were conservative by tradition and deeply attached to their ancestral roots in America, rather than believers in universal rights concocted by philosophers. While Kendall was drawn to Strauss's scepticism over unlimited speech, what he feared was not the ways in which particular ethnic/religious groups might use free speech to protect their ancestral rights and thereby violate — from Strauss's perspective — the universality of liberalism, but "the opposite of what Strauss fear[ed]": that an open society unmindful of its actual historical roots, allowing unlimited questioning of its ancestral identities, against the natural wishes of the majority for their roots and traditions, would eventually destroy the Anglo-American tradition.[2]

Havers brings up as well Kendall's call for a restricted immigration policy consistent with majoritarian wishes. While Havers is primarily concerned with the Christian roots of Anglo-American democracy, he identifies this view by Kendall with conservatism proper. The Straussian view that America is an exceptional nation by virtue of being founded on the basis of philosophical propositions, which somehow have elevated this nation to be a model to the world, is, in Havers view, closer to the leftist dismissal of religious identities and traditions than it is to any true conservatism. Conservatives, or Paleo-Conservatives, believe that human identities are not mere private choices arbitrarily decided by abstract individuals in complete disregard of history and the natural dispositions of humans for social groupings with similar ethnic and religious identities.

---

2   *Ibid*, pp. 47-52.

These differences between the Straussians and old conservatives are all the more peculiar since, as Havers notes, Strauss was very mindful of the particular identities of Jewish people, criticizing those who called for a liberalized form of Jewish identity based on values alone. Jews, Strauss insisted, must maintain fidelity to their own nationality rather than to a "liberal theology", otherwise they would end up destroying their particular historical identity.

Now, Straussians could well respond that the Anglo-American identity is different, consciously dedicated to universal values, but, as Havers carefully shows, this emphasis on the philosophy of natural rights cannot be properly understood outside the religious ancestry of the founders, and (although Havers is less emphatic about this) outside the customs, institutions and ethnicity of the founders. As the Australian Frank Salter has written:

> The United States began as an implicit ethnic state, whose Protestant European identity was taken for granted. As a result, the founding fathers made few remarks about ethnicity, but John Jay famously stated in 1787 that America was 'one united people, a people descended from the same ancestors', a prominent statement in one of the republic's founding philosophical documents that attracted no disagreement.[3]

This idea that Western nations are all propositional nations is not restricted to the United States, but has been applied to the settler nations of Canada and Australia. Mainstream liberals and conservatives alike regularly insist today that Europe along with the settler nations of the West are each a "community of values" that belong to humanity and that anyone can, in principle, assimilate to.

Janet Ajzenstat on Canada's "Political Nationality"

The most prominent exponent of a Straussian interpretation of Canada's identity is Janet Ajzenstat. She has gone right back to the arguments of the "Fathers of Confederation" to counter the long

---

3   Frank Salter, *On Genetic Interests: Family, Ethnicity, and Humanity in an Age of Mass Migration* (Transaction Publishers, 2007), p. 230.

prevailing "Tory" argument that Canada was envisioned as a nation founded by two cultural groups who view the government as not only a paternalistic protector of the liberties of citizens but of the cultural identities of the British and French-Catholics. Ajzenstat fully expresses this new thesis in *The Canadian Founding: John Locke and Parliament*, published in 2007. I will focus first on her carefully constructed arguments, which are categorized within the field of political philosophy, before moving on to examine two books by two historians who may be said to be Straussians in their assessment of Canada's identity without prioritizing any culture except the universal principles of liberalism. These two historians are Roger Riendeau and J.L. Granatstein. Ajzenstat and Granatstein are both known "conservatives", while Riendeau appears to be a middle of the road liberal.

Janet Ajzenstat's *The Canadian Founding: John Locke and Parliament*, winner of the John T. Saywell Prize for Canadian Constitutional Legal History, seeks out to determine what Canadian identity is by digging into lesser known writings associated with the making of the BNA Act, as well as re-interpreting, or finding new meanings in the classical writings of the Fathers of Confederation. She questions both i) the economic nationalist leftist idea that Canada's identity has been characterized by its anti-Americanism and its socialistic commitment to government funded programs such as public health care, and a top-down enactment of what is deemed to be good for the citizens, and ii) the old Tory idea that the BNA Act was all about a Canada with "peace, order and good Government", as contrasted to America's Declaration of Independence, which was about "life, liberty, and the pursuit of happiness". It is really this second "old" conservative idea that Ajzenstat goes after in her effort to propose a new interpretation of Canada's founding principles, whereas it is the leftist interpretation she challenges in her assessment of the way Canada is governed today by a leftist political ideology that relies on the courts, an activist Supreme Court, even international tribunals, that disregard the traditional principle of legislative supremacy.

Since my concern is with Ajzenstat's re-interpretation of Canada's past, I will focus on her criticisms of the Tory interpretation of Canada's foundation. Ajzenstat is known as a conservative who emphasizes individual rights rather than any form of collective identity, and therefore as a "Neoconservative" in her rejection of the old Tory conservatism of Canada. The Tory interpretation of Canada's founding values has been quite influential, and Ajzenstat is determined to show that it is based on an incorrect reading of writings and documents associated with Confederation. The Tory argument is that the Loyalists who fled to Canada during the Revolutionary Era were very attached to their Anglo-Saxon heritage and that their descendants, who formed the ruling elite of Upper Canada, conceived Canada as a nation "founded on a resistance to the American way of life". [4] The dominant Tory group, the argument goes, formed an alliance with certain French Canadian leaders, to create a new federal union in 1867 in which the Tory view would come to prevail in English Canada, while French Canadians would gain control of a provincial government with its own legislature, Civil Code, French as the official language in Quebec, and religious minorities enjoying the right to separate schools in all provinces. English Canada would be British in its collective cultural traditions, and French Canada would be French in its collective culture. [5] Overall, this would be a Canada committed to the wisdom of tradition and respect for the order provided by the elected government representatives, both in Quebec and English Canada. The common good would be assured by a federal government concerned with the collective wellbeing of Canada as a culture rather than as a mere aggregation of competing individuals with abstract rights. English Canada would be a collective of citizens with a strong British identity and a strong Anglican Christian identity.

Claiming to base her ideas on an in-depth textual examination of the writings of the founders, the transcripts of the provincial legislatures' debates, Ajzenstat argues that the founders were just as influenced by John Locke as the American founders. The founders agreed with the Lockean doctrine of popular sovereignty, the notion that the government does not have a predetermined set of "common"

---

4   See Grant Havers, "Canada as a Cradle of Conservatism?" *The University Bookman* (Winter 2017).

5   I am aware that the "Tory" interpretation comes with variations, and that the celebrated historian Donald Creighton was adamant in his view that in 1867 Canada was "not declared to be a bilingual or a bicultural nation". "The rule of the Civil Code and the use of the French language were confirmed in those parts of Canada in which they had already been confirmed by law or convention. But that was all". See Donald Creighton, "The Use and Abuse of History" in *Towards the Discovery of Canada, Selected Essays* (Macmillan, 1972), pp. 72-73.

concerns for the wellbeing of the populous and cultural affiliations of the majority, other than to ensure the rights to liberty and security of citizens. She writes that "the Fathers of Confederation… intended to give the new country what we call today a 'civic identity,'" that is, "inculcate a sense of nationhood" that is "inclusive" of all cultures and races, rather than have a country ensuring British/French cultural values. She says that what "today's social scientists" call "civic identity" is what the Fathers called "the political nationality". [6] She means that Canada was envisioned as a nation based on political values, popular sovereignty and the parliamentary tradition of "responsible" (representative) government, liberty, equality, nondiscrimination, and the rule of law. This argument is akin to the American idea that the United States was founded as a "propositional nation", an idea promoted by libertarian and Neoconservative circles in the 1980s and 1990s. Neoconservatives were heavily influenced by Strauss. Ajzenstat is an admitted Straussian who happily acknowledges the influence of Allan Bloom in her intellectual development and method of research.[7] According to Ajzenstat, the Fathers of Confederation were deliberate in their rejection of the idea that Canada was founded on a common cultural identity.

The Canadian founders rejected the idea of a national cultural identity not only because those meeting at Quebec in 1864 represented different political constituencies and not only because they required the agreement of Liberals and provincial rights advocates as well as dyed-in-the-wool Conservatives. They also rejected it because a substantive identity is inevitably exclusive, favouring the founding peoples over late-comers, the majority over minorities. The founders' rejection of the collective national identity was considered and deliberate. They expected the population of the new nation to take pride in their "identity" not because it was distinctive, not because it encapsulated a social vision, not because it incorporated a

---

6   Janet Ajzenstat, *The Canadian Founding: John Locke and Parliament* (McGill-Queen's Press), pp. 67-87.

7   See her more recent book, *Discovering Confederation: A Canadian's Story* (McGill-Queen's Press, 2014), pp. 129-30, where she also writes about her "rabbinical studies". She took a seminar with Bloom and acted as teaching assistant for him while she was completing her dissertation, and once noted that "Mr. Bloom gave me the instruction that guides my research to this day". See "Historians in Search of a Framework" *The Underhill Review* (Fall 2009), http://www3.carleton.ca/underhillreview/09/fall/reviews/ajzenstat.htm

particular history or expressed particular social and economic values. Rather, they expected the population to be proud that the country's Constitution and laws would allow it to do well the things that all countries should do: promote equality, non-discrimination, the rule of law, justice, civil peace, and prosperity.[8]

Despite the appearance of textual support for these claims, the citation of many quotes from pre-Confederation transcripts seemingly imbued with Lockean ideas about religious tolerance and against the imposition of values by a strong government, this argument is fundamentally wrong in ascribing "what we call *today* a 'civic identity'" and "inclusiveness" to the Fathers of Confederation. If this argument carries little credibility in the case of America's founding principles, as we saw above, it carriers zero credibility in the case of Canada's founding. Ajzenstat is correct that the BNA Act was a rejection of the subordination of French Canadians to the majority British culture, and an endorsement of the central liberal principle that the laws of the lands must apply equally to all citizens against discrimination on the basis of race, origin, or creed. But she is wrong in extrapolating this rejection and prohibition as evidence that the Fathers were *not* concerned with the cultural identity of Canada as a nation founded by two dominant races and cultures. At the time of Confederation about 70 percent of the population spoke English and 30 percent French. The Fathers took it for granted that with language came culture. The Fathers, both English and French, understood that Francophones saw themselves as a distinct nation, a distinct collectivity of people, within Canada. While the Anglophones did not see themselves as a distinct cultural nation within Canada, they did see themselves as a people of British nationality who were creating a majority British nation that would acknowledge the French majority in Quebec but would see itself as an integral part of the British Empire. Ajzenstat fails to refute John A. Macdonald's famous conviction that the new Canada was to be "a British nation, under the British flag and under British institutions". [9]

She is correct that the Fathers of Confederation envisioned Canada as a "Lockean" nation insofar as they did not impose an official

---

8   *The Canadian Founding: John Locke and Parliament*, pp. 108-109.

9   Cited in P.B. Waite, *The Life and Times of Confederation, 1864-1867* (Toronto: University of Toronto Press, 1962), p. 22.

religion on all Canadians, a High Church, and a hierarchical order with the British at the top of the legal system with exclusive rights. The Fathers "were not designing a constitution for English speakers alone". [10] But she errs in the imposition of contemporaneous notions of "inclusiveness" and "civic identity" onto the Fathers. How can the same Straussians who insist on paying delicate attention to the meaning of words, calling for exacting readings of original texts, project onto the writings of the Fathers of Confederation our current obsession with "inclusiveness"?

She misreads George-Etienne Cartier's statement that "we would form a political nationality with which neither the national origin, nor the religion of any individual, would interfere". When Cartier wrote, "we could not do away with the distinctions of race", he meant what was obvious to everyone then and should still be obvious to us now, that "we could not legislate for the disappearance of the French Canadians from American soil". He did say that in Canada "we should have Catholic and Protestant, English, French, Irish and Scotch, and each by his efforts and his success would increase the prosperity and glory of the new Confederacy ... we were of different races, not for the purpose of warring against each other, but in order to compete and emulate for the general welfare". [11] But why should we be surprised by these words, or engage in pompous claims that these words contain hidden meanings that Canadian scholars have underestimated because they make them uncomfortable? On the contrary, Ajzenstat is imposing this reading onto the Fathers as a way of framing Canada's identity in a way that suits the politically correct expectations of mass immigration. The BNA Act, after all, was a document consistent with British principles of individual liberty, religious freedom, and equality under the law. Canadian Loyalists, and the conservative Cartier, were likewise liberals as that term was understood at the time. Cartier was not envisioning a Canada that would be for the races of the world, otherwise immigration would not have been restricted to whites until as late as 1962/67. We will see in Part IV how Canada's liberalism before WWII/1960s was heavily Anglocentric in English Canada and heavily Quebecois and Catholic in Quebec.

---

10   *Discovering Confederation: A Canadian's Story* (McGill-Queen's Press, 2014). P. 133.

11   Thomas Thorner, Thor Frohn-Nielsen, eds. *A Few Acres of Snow: Documents in Pre-Confederation Canadian History* (University of Toronto Press, 2009), p. 299.

Nevertheless, we will also see, in the first chapter of Part IV, which deals with Carl Schmitt's critique of liberalism, that liberalism does have an internal tendency to underestimate its own communitarian sources in British/European culture, because of its imaginary starting premise about the "natural rights" of individuals. We need to interpret Ajzenstat as someone who has effectively employed the current derogation of any form of collective identity to play up those passages in the writings of the Fathers of Confederation that give credence to this derogation and bespeak of abstract individual rights, which is not that difficult since the Fathers did tend to imagine themselves as individuals with liberties, notwithstanding their British (and French) communitarian identities.

While the idea that Canada was based on political values designed for "man as man" is the prevailing conservative view today, as we saw in the case of Salim Mansur, and even of Bissoondath, strictly speaking the number of Straussians in Canada is small, if only because this is a highly intellectualized movement.[12] Nonetheless, in a loosely speaking way, the Straussian perspective is quite dominant among Canadian conservatives. Ajzenstat's ideas have been welcomed in official conservative circles, praised by scholars such as Barry Cooper and former Prime Minister Stephen Harper's one time chief of staff, Ian Brodie. They like her rejection of multiculturalism,[13] her opposition to the idea of granting special status for Quebec and Aboriginals, her emphasis on assimilation and her objections to leftist judicial activism. As it is, the notion that Canada's identity is limited to the British or any people identified culturally, is rejected almost *ab initio* by the entire establishment, and is indeed an idea that has made its way into the writing of Canadian history. This is quite apparent in a recent book by the middle of the road liberal Roger Riendeau, *A Brief History of Canada*. Riendeau, who is Vice Principal of Canada's historic Innis College at the University of Toronto, opens his not so short book of 444 pages asking "What is Canada? What is a Canadian?" In response, he refers to words

---

12 Clifford Orwin, former professor at the University of Toronto, has been identified as a Straussian, though he is an American who supports the Democratic Party and questioned the Neoconservative position on Iraq. Kenneth Green, also at Toronto, has written favorable works on Strauss, and is editor of a SUNY Press series on "The Thought and Legacy of Leo Strauss".

13 Though only in theory, since no conservative politician has ever dared to take on multiculturalism other than cutting a few programs.

from George-Étienne Cartier expressed in 1865, which I already cited, in which Cartier, apparently, envisioned Canada as a "political nationality" open to peoples from all religious backgrounds, races, and nations in the world. He references as well Cartier's statement that with Confederation Canada "would form a political community with which neither the national origin, nor religion of any individual, would interfere". [14]

Riendeau and Granatstein

From these statements we are supposed to believe that Canada was always meant to be a political community without an ethno-cultural identity, that the meaning of "Canadian" is historically tied to a supposed original founding decision to be a nation of diverse immigrants. But what Cartier really meant was that Canada would be a confederation of provinces with their own local institutions, rather than a single legislative union like Britain or a British Dominion, in which French Canadians would be compelled to assimilate. It is very anachronistic for Riendeau to say that "since 1867" Canada's inhabitants, "whether they are descended from the Aboriginal, French, Anglo-Saxon, other European, Asian, African, or Latin American cultures" have shown an inclination to see themselves as members of a common "political nationality", or have "survived as a distinct national community", a nation based solely on political values regardless of race and culture. It is also quite fictional to describe the native landscape before Europeans arrived as "multicultural and multilingual", as well as to say that the peoples of Canada have always felt that what made them Canadian was not their ethnicity or culture but the mere fact that they were "bound by a common experience" as inhabitants of the same country.[15]

By "common" he means that all the inhabitants were somehow forging a sense of political identity that transcended their ethnicity and culture.[16] Yet, as is evident from his own narrative, the entire history

---

14   Roger Riendeau, *A Brief History of Canada* (Infobase Publishing, 2007), p. xv.

15   *Ibid,* p. 385

16   Desmond Morton states in *A Short History of Canada* (McClelland & Stewart, 1994) that Canada's history is not about a people with a "common *culture*" but simply a "shared experience". "History is what Canadians" have experienced "in *common*" (p. 9). Then he wonders why Canadians have no interest in their history!

of Canada prior to the 1970s goes against this notion of a common political nationality. Not only were the British well aware of their Britishness, and for this reason preferred Anglo-Saxon immigrants, which Riendeau otherwise knows, but the actual "common" experience of the nation was overwhelmingly British/European outside Quebec. This is what the statistics say. Riendeau's own demographic stats on ethnic proportions cannot hide this reality. He observes, for example, that prior to the late 1960s "almost 90 percent of immigrants were of European origins", and only during the 1970s did immigrants start to come in large numbers "from other regions including the West Indies, Africa, South America, and Asia".[17] This is not a historian who invents facts and alters photographs. He is more "subtle". He wants students to believe that Canada's past already contained the seeds of its current multiracial trends. "Canada has always been a multicultural society", he writes[18] However, while he enjoys writing about the "changing racial composition of Canada" in relation to the influx of non-French and non-British *European* immigrants,[19] he does not enjoy saying that Canada was still 96 percent racially white as late as 1971, when multiculturalism was officially announced. He would rather blame the government in the early 20th century for "inculcating British-Canadian beliefs in citizenship, democracy, and the Protestant ethic". He thinks they should have started promoting multiculturalism as a government policy from the beginning. Canada was "universally racist, inasmuch as the concept of a multicultural society still lay...in the future".[20] Canada became what it was always meant to be inasmuch as immigration restrictions against non-Europeans were abolished in the 1960s, the Multiculturalism Act of 1988 was legislated, and the ceiling on immigration was raised from 100,000 to 250,000 in the late 1980s.

A very popular book, also called "a classic", that is highly critical of multiculturalism in the name of a "common" history that speaks to all Canadians irrespective of race and culture, is Granatstein's *Who Killed Canadian History?* Granatstein laments the way multiculturalists have broken up Canada's historical narrative into separate compartments according to ethnic, gender, and class

---

17   Riendeau, *A Brief History of Canada*, p. 332

18   *Ibid.*

19   *Ibid,* p. 331.

20   *Ibid,* p. 229.

identities at the cost of a "uniting" national story that emphasizes the liberalizing character of a nation committed to the equal rights of all humans open to immigrants from every region of the world. He takes pains trying to persuade multiculturalists and feminists that he is not anti-immigrant but "a child of immigrants" who believes "the glory of this nation is that its people, including even its Native people, came from somewhere else". [21] This simple-minded book is suffused with similar bromides, which are effective, nevertheless, in puffing up the righteous chests of conservatives desperately seeking acceptance while questioning Canada's multicultic state. So caught up is Granatstein with fatuous phrases about "our history, our belief that we have done great things together in the past",[22] he can't see how absurd it is to identify the "glory" of Canada with the observation that everyone "came from somewhere else" – which can be said about every nation in the world!

What makes this all the more absurd is that the central question of this book is "what is uniquely Canadian?" "What is Canadian identity?" The answer he offers shows what happens when one takes pretentiously lofty thoughts such as "we are a nation of immigrants committed to equal rights", as mottoes for the understanding of Canada's history. For all the talk about a "national" narrative against multicultural divisiveness what we are left with is that "the key to Canadian identity" is a history commonly made by "both the native-born and immigrants". The way to nurture this common identity is to make all immigrants, all cultures, and all religions, feel as much a part of Canada's history as the British and Quebecois. We can then feel that it is "our history", "Protestants or Muslims, ethnics or Anglos".[23] Since Canada is inherently committed to equality under the law against racial discrimination, Muslims are no less important to the making of Confederation than Protestants. We can make them feel attached to the history of the Loyalists by teaching this history as "our" common history. This argument was hailed "a literary hand grenade". It tells you how silly the Canadian mind has become.

---

21   J.L. Granatstein, *Who Killed Canadian History?* (Harper Perennial, 2007), p.88.

22   *Ibid*, p. 164.

23   *Ibid*, pp. 164-65.

Natural In-Group Behaviors Rather Than "Natural Rights" and "Political Nationality"

Granatstein's argument, like Ajzenstat's, has no basis in history. It has no basis in what we are learning about the science of human nature. The proponents of the claim that the identity of all European nationalities have always been about political values held in "common", rather than "romantic" notions of race and national collectivism, forget that the liberals who produced the Enlightenment and Confederation were themselves the progenitors of a science of race differences which laid the foundations for what we are learning today about the way in which humans organize themselves into ethnic in-groups versus out-groups, which is refuting the pretension, based on literary bromides, that we are members of a universal humanity with a common history.[24] As Salter points out,

> This is hardly a complete reading of Enlightenment ideas, which include the birth of modern nationalism, the democratic privileging of majority ethnicity, and the linking of minority emancipation to assimilation. The Enlightenment also celebrates empirical science including biology, which culminated in man's fuller understanding of himself as part of nature.[25]

Beyond the now extensive literature on race I mentioned earlier, numerous papers are continuously coming out supporting the view that humans are ethnocentric and that such altruistic dispositions as sharing, loyalty, caring, and even motherly love, are exhibited primarily and intensively within in-groups rather than toward a universal "we" in disregard for one's community. I will start with a recently published, but heavily cited article, "Oxytocin Promotes Human Ethnocentrism" by Carsten K. W. De Dreu and his associates.[26] Be it noted that the arguments of this article have been backed by a continuous line of subsequent articles, and other researchers, which

---

24 Paul J. Zak, Angela A. Stanton, Sheila Ahmadi, "Oxytocin Increases Generosity in Humans", *PLOS One Journal* (November 7, 2007), http://journals.plos.org/plosone/article?id=10.1371/journal.pone.0001128

25 *Ibid*, p. 213.

26 Carsten K. W. De Dreu, Lindred L. Greer, Gerben A. Van Kleef, Shaul Shalvi, and Michael J. J. Handgraaf, "Oxytocin Promotes Human Ethnocentrism", *PNAS: Proceedings of the National Academy of Sciences* 108, no. 4 (January 25, 2011).

I will be citing below, notwithstanding the usual debates in the scientific community. Written by a research team at the University of Amsterdam, this article shows that oxytocin is a molecule associated with in-group favoritism and out-group derogation. Through a series of experiments in which participants were administered doses of oxytocin, the researchers learned that "a key mechanism facilitating in-group cooperation is ethnocentrism, the tendency to view one's group as centrally important and as superior to other groups" at the expense of an out-group.

What makes this finding all the more revealing is that oxytocin had long been identified as a hormone made in the brain during sexual reproduction, particularly during childbirth and breastfeeding, in association with motherly bonding and affection. A mere few years ago, many were even calling it the "love hormone" after researchers observed that the human body released the highest doses of oxytocin (into the bloodstream) during intimate situations, caressing, and sexual climax. The pop psychology establishment and the liberal press could not contain their enthusiasm for what appeared to be a "moral molecule" which could be studied, nurtured, and then administered medically to enhance love across the world. Here is part of an abstract to a 2007 article "Oxytocin Increases Generosity in Humans",

> In this study, participants were infused with 40 IU oxytocin (OT) or placebo and engaged in a blinded, one-shot decision on how to split a sum of money with a stranger that could be rejected [in which case, no one got any money]. Those on OT were 80% more generous than those given a placebo. ... OT and altruism together predicted almost half the interpersonal variation in generosity. Notably, OT had twofold larger impact on generosity compared to altruism. This indicates that generosity is associated with both altruism as well as an emotional identification with another person.[27]

It was not long before the pro-diversity media establishment picked up the good news. With an endearing title, "A Dose of Oxytocin Increases the Cuddles", Jeffrey Kluger from *Time* reported (May 02, 2010) on the efforts of Psychiatrist Rene Hurlemann of Bonn University and neuroscientist Keith Kendrick of the Cambridge Babraham Institute

---

27   Paul J. Zak, Angela A. Stanton, Sheila Ahmadi, "Oxytocin Increases Generosity in Humans", *PLOS One Journal* (November 7, 2007), http://journals.plos.org/plosone/article?id=10.1371/journal.pone.0001128

to determine if oxytocin "could be artificially administered to a person to manipulate feelings of empathy and perhaps even learning". Kluger described their experiment as follows:

> To test how oxytocin might affect those capabilities, Hurlemann and Kendrick ran a two-part experiment. In the first, 48 males were divided into two groups — half received an aerosol shot of oxytocin and half got a placebo — and then shown evocative pictures of things like a crying child, a grieving man and a girl hugging a cat. They were then asked to describe how deeply they were feeling the emotions associated with the pictures. On the whole, the men in the oxytocin group exhibited "significantly higher emotional empathy levels" than those in the placebo group.[28]

But the "ethnocentric" paper I cited above soon came upon the scene. This article's conclusion was clear: the "widespread view" of oxytocin as a 'cuddle chemical' or 'love drug' was simple minded; oxytocin was a peptide shown to promote "intergroup bias: the unfair response toward another group that devalues or disadvantages the other group and its members by valuing or privileging members of one's in-group". These findings were framed in evolutionary terms; humans favor their own ethnic group because this attitude enhances their adaptive capacity.

This evolutionary perspective was emphasized in an earlier paper by the same author, Carsten de Dreu, and his associates, published in *Science* (11 June 2010), "The Neuropeptide Oxytocin Regulates Parochial Altruism in Intergroup Conflict among Humans". Oxytocin is a "bonding hormone», but one which functions for group unity (and not only for motherly love) in the face of out-groups. The point is not that in-groups needlessly seek to attack any out-group; it is neither that in-groups have an inborn disposition to hate others. In-group members concentrate on the performance of altruism within the group rather than aggression towards outsiders unless the competing out-group comes to be seen as a threat. Conflict escalation between ethnic groups is lower when physical barriers exist between them. The role of oxytocin is thus to promote altruism within in-groups and aggression towards out-groups that are threatening the interests of the in-group.[29]

---

28 Jeffrey Kluger, "A Dose of Oxytocin Increases the Cuddles", *Time* (May 02, 2010).

29 Carsten de Dreu, et al., "The Neuropeptide Oxytocin Regulates Parochial Altruism

For the pro-diversity establishment these findings have been a major blow in that they challenge the notion that we can create in the West a universal brotherhood in which in-group identities are eradicated and all races and religions happily join one universal in-group. Many have just ignored this research. The popular pseudo-psychologist Paul J. Zak, for example, a public speaker and featured writer in *The New York Times*, *Wall Street Journal*, and *USA Today*, pushed ahead with a book entitled *The Moral Molecule: The Source of Love and Prosperity* (2012), claiming he had discovered and explored the biochemistry of sympathy, love, and trust – never mind that he paid no attention to any contrary argumentation. Other liberals were not as oblivious, but instead switched gears and went on to condemn the molecule oxytocin as if it were a right wing political party spoiling the ennobling ideals of cultural Marxism: David Mosher from *Wired Magazine* (January 12, 2011) announced "'Cuddle Chemical' Also Fuels Favoritism, Bigotry". Lindsay Abrams from *The Atlantic* (September 21, 2012) declared: "Study: Oxytocin ('The Hormone of Love') Also Makes Us Conformists". The *Social Capital Blog*, dedicated to human interaction and community, spoke of "Oxytocin's Dark Side" (August 2012). *Slate* magazine warned us "why the hype about oxytocin is dumb and dangerous" (July 2012). *Psychological Science* printed an article (September 2012) ratified as "The Herding Hormone: Oxytocin Stimulates In-Group Conformity". Only Nicholas Wade, author of the controversial book, *A Troublesome Inheritance: Genes, Race and Human History* (2014), which dissects all the latest research to argue that human races can be differentiated genetically, reported Carsten de Dreu's findings in a matter of fact tone, writing that "the love and trust it [oxytocin] promotes are not toward the world in general, just toward a person's in-group. Oxytocin turns out to be the hormone of the clan, not of universal brotherhood". [30]

---

in Intergroup Conflict among Humans" *Science* (11 June 2010). As Carsten de Dreu et al., observe in "Oxytocin Promotes Human Ethnocentrism", the tendency for in-group members is to favour their own rather than to hate outsiders: "[T]here is good reason to believe that the in-group prejudice effect is far more basic to human life than is the out-group hate prejudice effect, and research on human ethnocentrism supported this positive-negative asymmetry of social discrimination…showing that oxytocin creates intergroup bias primarily because it motivates in-group favoritism and not because it motivates out-group derogation".

30   Nicholas Wade, "Depth of the Kindness Hormone Appears to Know Some Bounds" *New York Times* (January 10, 2011). I should mention the "Silvio O Conte Center for Oxytocin and Social Cognition" at Emory University, which studies oxytocin, "a brain chemical known for forming bonds between mother and baby". One member

But here's a dilemma Carsten de Dreu and his group seemed unable to handle, including every researcher I have read in regards to oxytocin: despite their realization that ethnocentrism is not an irrational fear but a natural reaction, how is it that a hormone associated with breastfeeding and love, promotes "tribal" behavior, aggression and conflict? How can the same "cuddle chemical" be associated with ostensibly opposite behaviors such as out-group derogation and violence? It is not that these scientists view this molecule naively in either-or, good-bad terms; de Dreu uses affirmative words —"loyalty", "reliable and trustworthy", "cooperation" — to describe in-group favoritism. But the use of these words, by de Dreu and his associates, are minimal and pretty much restricted to these examples. This compares to the many occasions in which they write of such "unfortunate" behaviors as "in-group bias", "unfair treatment, negative emotions", "violent protest, and aggression among disfavored and excluded individuals". These traits are abhorrent to a liberal psyche seeking to equalize results — within a cultural landscape in which every institution operates in the name of a projected universal community.

In the face of these findings, liberals have thus reacted in two closely related ways: 1) reject the experiments as "abstractions" which do not take into consideration the way in which "proper" socialization may encourage other dispositions and eventually break the "irrationality" of tribalism, or 2) find ways to medicate this disposition through experimental, psychological intervention; that is, attempt to find ways to re-engineer other attributes within human nature in order that these may grow to colonize the rather

---

of the research team at this center, Larry Young, "investigates the nature of social bonding in highly affiliative and socially monogamous prairie voles". Dr. Young is now collaborating with several other members of the Center for Translational Social Neuroscience "to extend his finding in rodent models to non-human primates, including rhesus macaques and chimpanzees". In a recent interview in CBC radio, Young admitted that the so-called "cuddle hormone", "the love drug", identified as "the moral molecule" that would usher in a new era of cooperation across the world, has now been revealed by scientists as having a "dark side". Young noted that when it comes to human behavior, the latest science suggests oxytocin plays a similar role, as in his study of primates, in creating an "us versus them" dynamic. Dr. Catherine Crockford, from the Max Planck Institute for Evolutionary Anthropology, was cited in this interview, her discovery that chimpanzees' oxytocin levels surge in anticipation of and when they go to war. These findings have troubled these scientists made to believe as students that aggression, in-group behaviors, are "imagined" realities constructed by white male biological determinists. See CBC Radio, Quirks and Quarks with Bob MacDonald, "Chimps, war, and the 'cuddle hormone'" (January 28, 2017).

"irrational" and "archaic" trait of ethnocentrism. Liberals recoil from the possibility that an ethnocentric chemical is likewise a source of motherly affection. Scientists, too, can't help interpreting ethnic identification as a form of prejudice leading to conflict, for the reason that they are working for a multicultural state dedicated to "conflict resolution". This is why Carsten de Dreu tends to set up his findings as if they negated the "widespread view of oxytocin as a 'cuddle chemical' or a 'love drug'". Instead of thinking of ethnocentrism in positive terms as involving loyalty and commitment (hence love) for one's group, he tends to draw a sharp dichotomy between these two emotions. They operate under the illusion that it is possible to speak of a universal humanity, the natural rights of man as man, without outside-ness and automatically assume that the other, the enemy, can only be seen in a hateful way by in-group members.[31]

One debate worth watching is "The Great Debate – Xenophobia: why do we fear others?" This debate, which took place March 31, 2012 at Arizona State University, and is available online, was about the human instinct to form in-groups and out-groups particularly along ethnic lines. The scientists in this panel (primatologist Frans de Waal, economist Jeffrey Sachs, psychologist Steven Neuberg, neuroscientist Rebecca Saxe, and physicist and mathematician Freeman Dyson) all recognized in varying ways the powerful drive within all living beings, including bacteria, to organize themselves into in-groups and out-groups; and yet the tenor and objective of

---

31   After all, these scientists are all working for a multicultural state dedicated to "conflict resolution". The following papers all use words that portray in-group behavior negatively: Shaul Shalvi and Carsten K. W. De Dreu, "Oxytocin Promotes Group-Serving Dishonesty", *PNAS:* Proceedings of the National Academy of Sciences 111, no. 15 (April 15, 2014). Michael Gilead and Nira Liberman, "We Take Care of Our Own: Caregiving Salience Increases Out-Group Bias in Response to Out-Group Threat", *Psychological Science* 25, no. 7 (July 2014). Carsten K. W. De Dreu, Lindred L. Greer, Gerben A. Van Kleef, Shaul Shalvi, and Michael J. J. Handgraaf, "Reply to Chen et al.: Perhaps Goodwill is Unlimited but Oxytocin-Induced Goodwill is Not", *PNAS:* Proceedings of the National Academy of Sciences 108, no. 13 (March 29, 2011). Shaul Shalvi, and Carsten K. W. De Dreu, "Oxytocin promotes group-serving dishonesty", *PNAS*, vol. 111, no. 16 (January 2015). Maybe these scientists are unaware that research is also showing that the more ethnic diversity, the greater the potential for conflict, which requires greater enforcement of multicultural conformity against the naturally free dispositions of humans for their ethnic group. See Jayati Das-Munshi et al., "Ethnic Density as a Buffer for Psychotic Experiences: Findings from a National Survey (EMPIRIC)", *The British Journal of Psychiatry* 201, no. 4 (October 2012). According to this paper, "minority ethnic groups experience an increased risk of psychosis when living in neighborhoods of lower own-group density". For additional findings and debate, see "Related Articles" in the online version of this article, http:// bjp.rcpsych.org/content/201/4/282.full.

the conference, as evident from the title itself, was to view this as a challenge for Western, diversifying societies, to press on towards newer forms of community and human solidarity without outside-ness and without the irrational fear of xenophobia. Jeffrey Sachs openly acknowledged that societies with strong ethnic homogeneity (for which he mentioned the Nordic countries of Europe) were more peaceful and "happier" than diverse ones; and yet he did not even dare to ask why these societies and the European world generally are implementing mass immigration policies to "enrich" the nation with racial diversity! The underlying motif of the whole gathering was to call for a greater sense of the "we" across ethnic lines, and for more integration. Some walked over their own findings to emphasize the "plasticity" of human nature, its flexibility and ability to be changed in ways that will make humans (whites) become non-ethnocentric and willing participants in the creation of new, cosmopolitan identity. To top it all, the last panelist, *New York Times* editorialist Charles Blow, no scientist himself but a gratified Black man, reminded the audience how racist America still remains.

Concluding Thought

Strauss's concern for the identity of Jews is consistent with this science.[32] The Straussian language about "natural rights" belonging to "man as man" is mostly gibberish devoid of any historical veracity and scientific support. Already, from a philosophical historical position, Hegel presented powerful arguments against the notion that humans were born with natural rights which they never enjoyed until a few philosophers discovered them and then went on to create ex nihilo Western civilization. Man "in his immediate and natural way of existence" was never the possessor of natural rights. The natural rights the founders spoke about, which were also in varying ways announced in the creation of the nations of Canada and Australia, and prescribed in the modern constitutions of European nations, were acquired and won only through a long historical movement, the origins of which may be traced back to ancient Greece, but which also included, as Havers insists, the history of Christianity and, I would add, the entire history of the West up to the Enlightenment.

---

32 Ajzenstant's daughter, Oona Eisenstadt, is a professor of Jewish studies at Pomona College.

The Straussians believe that the way to overcome the tendency of liberal societies to relativism, or the celebration of pluralistic conceptions of life without any sense of ranking the lifestyle of citizens, is to impart reverence and patriotic attachment for the Anglo-American tradition by emphasizing not the heterogeneous identity of this tradition but its foundation in the ancient philosophical commitment to "the good" and the "perfection of humanity". But this effort to instill national commitment by teaching citizens about the classics of ancient Greece and the great statesmen of liberal freedom is doomed to failure and has been a failure. The problem of nihilism is nonexistent in societies with a strong sense of reverence for traditional practices, authoritative patriarchal figures, and a sense of peoplehood and healthy in-group instincts. The way out of the crisis of Western nihilism is to re-nationalize liberalism, throw away the cultural Marxist notion that freedom means liberation from all identities not chosen by the individual, and accentuate the historical and natural-ethnic basis of European identity.

11

Majority Rights for Europeans Are Not Enough

With the publication of *The Cultural Defense of Nations: A Liberal Theory of Majority Rights* in 2015 assimilationists may have finally contributed a major work that can be set up against the massive academic edifice multiculturalists have built in the last five decades on rights for minorities and immigrants.[1] The author is Liav Orgad, an Associate Professor of Law at the IDC Herzliya, Israel, Research Fellow at the Center for Ethics at Harvard University, and Marie Curie Fellow at Freie Universität Berlin. Hailed as one of the most significant books of the year, it has been extensively reviewed by rightist and leftist scholars alike, with the former generally welcoming his emphasis on the cultural rights of majorities and the latter objecting to the potential illiberal threats such rights may pose for minorities. The thesis of the book is incredibly simple in the self-evidential sense that anyone with the most minimal sense of cultural identity, justice, and fairness, would have wondered how can this thesis be expressed only now by liberals. The thesis is that the peoples of Europe have a legitimate right to evaluate mass immigration in light of the potential threats millions of immigrants with very different cultural values may pose upon the majority host cultures.

Have not the liberals who control our institutions ever considered the cultural rights of majorities after thousands of publications about rights? In the last four years, before I read Orgad's book, I have defended European majorities at my blog, Council of European Canadians, as a matter of course without ever encountering one argument about the rights of cultural majorities. Since WWII the only booming business in academia has been the rights of minorities and the "legitimate" cultural claims of immigrants. So why this book now? Because, or so I will argue, liberals are starting to realize that European nationalists are gaining popularity and that arguments for the ethno-cultural rights of

---

1   Liav Orgad, *The Cultural Defense of Nations: A Liberal Theory of Majority Rights* (Oxford University Press, 2015).

European peoples are gaining intellectual credibility. Therefore, the right wing side of the liberal establishment has dug deeper into the historical and philosophical roots of liberal theory to bring forth a theory about the cultural rights of majorities. Orgad's basic point is that majorities, as much as minorities, have a right to protect their cultural identity, and a right to be concerned about immigration levels and integration of immigrants to the liberal values of the majority culture. Just as minorities have a right to be concerned with the ways in which compulsion to assimilate may impact negatively on their cultural rights, so do majorities have a right to be concerned about the impact of constant high levels of immigration on their cultural national identity. Majority and minority rights can both be defended using the same liberal logic.

Yet, having said this, there is truth to Paul Blokker's assessment that Orgad's "argument might be less original than claimed". [2] Blokker thus cites Michael Walzer's defense of a communitarian liberalism, which "allows for a state committed to the survival and flourishing of a particular nation, culture, or religion, or of a (limited) set of nations, cultures, and religions — so long as the basic rights of citizens who have different commitments or no such commitments at all are protected". [3] Walzer, in other words, thinks there is nothing illiberal about taking "an interest in the cultural survival of the majority nation" so long as minority rights are protected.

Another way to put it is that Orgad expresses the assimilationist concerns of mainstream conservatives in the language of group cultural rights, not the language of individual rights, which is a distinction without a difference insomuch as individual rights are taken to be the foundational stone of the majority culture. Still, Orgad does go further than Walzer in challenging the standard assumption that the majority can still be "able to take care of itself"[4] in the context of mass immigration. He is seriously asking whether majority cultures have a right to call for lower immigration levels, or make decisions about which immigrants are more suited or friendlier to the preservation of the national culture. Orgad

---

2   Paul Blokker, "Cultural majorities, Constitutional essentials, and cosmopolitan citizenship" Verfasunsblogg (February 24, 2016), http://verfassungsblog.de/cultural-majorities-constitutional-essentials-and-cosmopolitan-citizenship/

3   *Ibid.*

4   Liav Orgad, *The Cultural Defense of Nations*, p. 196.

is also suggesting, though tenuously, that there is more to the majority culture of Europeans than rights for individuals.

Mainstream conservatives in the United States, much like Walzer, advocate strong supports for the national liberal culture without opposing mass immigration. But in Orgad's estimation, the West is currently facing a whole new reality never anticipated by the initial proponents of multiculturalism; the "scale, character, intensity" of immigration to Western nations, combined with the demographic decline of the majority culture, calls for a re-evaluation of multicultural liberalism, and compels us to ask "whether a culturally needy majority should be granted a right to defend its constitutional identity in the immigration context".[5] The continued emphasis on minority rights has lost its persuasiveness.

My criticism of Orgad, then, notwithstanding his correct estimation of the new realities facing the majority cultures of Europe and his sincere emphasis on majority cultural rights, is that he is simply re-asserting standard conservative arguments about the need for immigrants to assimilate and the need to protect the liberal values of the West. Leftist critics of Orgad, as we will see below, say that the implications of Orgad's theory is restriction of immigrants on the basis of ethnic/ religious criteria, which they claim is "illiberal" by definition; but, in my estimation, Orgad's theory is still too weak to defend the national cultures of Europe, in his refusal to challenge the very notion that liberalism cannot oppose mass immigration in principle and that the majority cultures of Europe are essentially defined by their liberal values alone rather than by deep cultural and bio-ethnic factors as well.

Orgad's theory has to be seen as yet another position carved inside a liberal establishment that has sought to make Europeans believe that mass immigration and diversification are somehow fundamentally connected to the liberal way of life. The entire liberal spectrum from left to right has come to accept the notion that Western nations, if they are to be true to their liberal principles, must welcome diversification. They have willfully misused the concept of minority rights developed by liberals for historical minorities to promote a program of mass

---

5   Liav Orgad, "The Law of Majorities: A Rejoinder", VerfBlog, 2016/3/12, http:// verfassungsblog.de/the-law-of-majorities-a-rejoinder/. This is a rejoinder Orgad wrote in reply to his critics organized by Verfassungsblog, about which I will say more below.

immigration and group rights for foreigners lacking citizenship. They claim to be defending the rights of minorities when in fact they are pushing a radical program of mass migration and miscegenation against the cultural rights of the majority indigenous Europeans.

Liav Orgad's Book

The Cultural Defense of Nations: A Liberal Theory of Majority Rights is an intelligently constructed book aimed at persuading a liberal audience that it is possible, and necessary, to talk in a liberal way about the cultural rights of Europeans, if liberals are not to become anachronistic. The goal is to frame immigration in ways that do not threaten the constitutional liberal culture of Europe and certain symbols such as the nation's flag, anthem, and official language, while sidestepping why mass immigration should be accepted as a liberal value in the first place. In the end, the goal is to persuade establishment liberals that majorities have a right to be concerned about their liberal heritage in order thereby to deflate a more powerful populist reaction against immigration itself. The editorial in the back cover of Orgad's book already reveals to us what the ulterior motive is:

> The book criticizes this state of affairs and proposes a new approach by which liberal democracies can welcome immigrants without fundamentally changing their cultural heritage, forsaking their liberal traditions, or slipping into extreme nationalism.

Will Kymlicka's argument (which he originated in the 1980s-1990s, and still advocates to this day) that we should not worry about immigrants demanding special group rights within Canada (or within European nations generally), seems obviously dated, as Orgad suggests, in light of demands by immigrants for sharia law, exemptions from many European cultural practices, including national standards of education, regular security threats from Muslims, excessive use of welfare, and impending reduction of Europeans in many nations to less than 50 percent of the population. Orgad brings up these problems, though in a subdued manner, and always on the supposition that these are "challenges" to the existing order rather than fundamental threats.

The liberalism Orgad is defending is "communitarian" in a way that may seem similar to Kymlicka's communitarian liberalism, or Charles Taylor's. But we know Kymlicka and Taylor only care about the communitarian needs of minorities and immigrants, while interpreting the majority European cultures as "societal cultures" consisting of modern amenities and liberal multicultural values, rather than traditions that identify Europeans as a particular people. It is true that in his later writings, Kymlicka, particularly in reaction to growing skepticism about the functionality of multiculturalism in Europe after 9/11, and other terrorist incidents, started insisting that his model of multiculturalism is not one in which immigrant groups are encouraged to remain "hermetically sealed and static",[6] but one in which they are guided by principles of equality, human rights, and individual freedoms; and which thus encourage immigrants to be open to other cultures, and renounce values and traditions within their heritage that run counter to these ideals.

In this respect, Orgad's entry into this debate should be seen as a recognition on his part that Kymlicka's expectation that immigrants would behave in the same way as Europeans, happily endorsing multiculturalism and human rights, has not transpired as expected but has instead resulted in a situation in which immigrants are reproducing their own cultures at the expense of the majority liberal culture of Europeans. However, the rationale Orgad employs in his justification of majority rights is the same communitarian rationale Kymlicka has employed in promoting minority group rights, except that for Orgad it is now the majority culture that is in need protection.

Orgad is quite open about recent projections about the demographic decline of European natives, including the impending fact that non-Hispanic whites in the United States are expected to become a minority by 2043, and that in the European union projections suggest that over a quarter of the population in many member states will have non-European ancestry by 2051. He wonders whether these demographic changes will adversely affect the secular constitutional culture of Western nations,[7] whether European peoples can "take care" of their

---

6   Will Kymlicka, "The rise and fall of multiculturalism? New debates on inclusion and accommodation in diverse societies" in Steven Vertovec and Suzanne Wessendorf, eds. *The Multiculturalism Backlash. European discourses, policies and practices* (Routledge 2010), p. 34.

7   *The Cultural Defense of Nations: A Liberal Theory of Majority Rights*, pp. 27-39.

culture, and whether it is fair to dismiss the anxieties of the majority about these changing demographics as unjustified fears or whether they have legitimate anxieties about national security, job prospects, community cohesion and the dissolution of their majority culture.[8]

Orgad is sympathetic to the enactment of policies aimed at preserving the majority culture, such as culture-based selection criteria, citizenship tests, language requirements, and policies aimed at encouraging immigrants to assimilate and identify with the nation's history, rather than shy away from celebrating the laws and institutions associated with constitutional liberalism. To be sure, these suggestions are to be welcomed in contrast to the constant propagation of policies intended to protect the "group rights of immigrants".

For Orgad these policies would be consistent with the cardinal liberal principle of individual rights. A state that protects the majority culture would be a state that "let citizens freely choose their way of life ... even when the individual's choice is incompatible with the mainstream, provided that it is lawful and fundamentally democratic".[9] Insofar as immigrants get to enjoy the same rights to benefits, resources and protection under the laws as members of the majority culture, they should be expected to accept the country's constitutionalism.[10] This is the only way to avoid liberal democracies from devolving into illiberal polities under the pressure of millions of immigrants arriving with their own political values without the expectation that they should assimilate.

It seems to me, nevertheless, that Orgad has a rather limited view of this majority culture, reducing it essentially to its political liberalism, construed in a way that resembles Leo Strauss's universalist interpretation of Western culture, as being about values that hold true for all humans, and in which European nations are no more than civic nations without ethnic origins and without strong customs, ancient Greek-Roman lineages, and Christian religious traditions. While Orgad argues that the majority should be afforded cultural rights to consider its "cultural interests and special circumstances when

---

8   *Ibid*, pp. 49-51.

9   *Ibid*, p. 151.

10   *Ibid*, p. 212-220.

determining the immigration capacity",[11] he fails to even ask why European nations need to have open borders to live up to their liberal traditions. Where in the foundational principles of liberalism does it say that nations must grant citizenship rights to foreigners?

In his reply to critics who see his majority rights argument as a threat to the rights of minorities, Orgad says openly that his notion of a majority culture is purely an "idea-based" form of constitutionalism without additional cultural attitudes, folkways by a people with millennial roots. In agreement, apparently, with Eric Hobsbawm's rejection of European ethnic national identity, he says that "majorities are largely imagined and socially constructed — majorities are made, not born". He adds, it is true, that the majority culture is defined not only by "a society's core constitutional identity" but also by "its language, holidays, symbols, values, and institutions".[12] He should be praised for saying this. But one cannot have it both ways; if the majority culture is essentially a construct and essentially based on "ideas", and not also on strong historical ancestries, strong kinship relations, then it is lacking in substance and in ability to address the key question at hand: why should European nations admit any immigrants in the first place and, just as important, why should Europeans simply sit back and watch themselves be reduced to a minority in light of current demographic trends? Don't Europeans have a cultural (*and a liberal*) right to repatriate the many thousands of immigrants who came under the deceptions of cultural Marxism?

The weakness of Orgad's cultural defense of European nations becomes evident in the sort of policies he proposes to safeguard this culture, starting with his equivalency between minority and majority rights. Why should the cultural rights of Muslims in Sweden, for example, be equivalent to the cultural rights of the native Swedish people? Orgad's policy suggestions resemble the weak calls by former British Prime Minister David Cameron for immigrants to take a little English language test. They also resemble the calls in Belgium, in the wake of the Brussels terrorist attack, for non-EU migrants to sign little integration contracts declaring their acceptance of Western values, which includes a little pledge by radical Muslims to report attempts

---

11   *Ibid*, p. 197.

12   Liav Orgad, "The Law of Majorities: A Rejoinder", VerfBlog, 2016/3/12, http:// verfassungsblog.de/the-law-of-majorities-a-rejoinder/

to commit acts of terrorism. Essentially, Orgad wants measures that encourage immigrants to pledge some sort of agreement with liberal principles upon admission. Big deal. The ones least interested in liberal values will be the first to make such pledges, particularly those who adhere to Islam, which allows believers to make false pledges to members of other religions.

He is not critical of the decades-old diversification of Europeans but is simply calling for "restrictions" or, really, assimilation of immigrants to a majority culture that is fundamentally defined not by its particularities but by its supposed universal principles. Why call the majority a socially constructed people when we know that European nationals have a long historical lineage behind them, institutionalized and practiced through generations, rather than a people produced by "ideas" articulated by academics? Obviously cultures are constructed by humans, not handed to them by nature, but, firstly, as Émile Durkheim argued, cultures have an objectivity which allows one to define cultural events as "social facts" that exert influences on the members of the culture as if they were externally existing facts.[13] The European institutions and norms of marriage, child rearing practices, folkways, etc., have an objective existence independently of Orgad's intellectual efforts to construct European identity in constitutional terms. This does not mean that they are fixed and can never be changed. It does mean that they cannot be interpreted any which way one wishes, because languages, ethnic appearances, customs do have a reality with generations behind them, attachments, and structures. Europeans, if given a free, and true liberal choice, as to whether they want mass immigration, would reject this policy, and embrace their ethno-cultural traditions.

Secondly, cultures don't exist above nature; humans are natural, biological beings, no less than social beings; and the cultural norms and institutions humans have created have been in ways that reflect their natural inclinations, sexual dispositions, differences between men and women, physical appearances, survival instincts, and so on, as physical anthropologists and sociobiologists have documented for numerous cultures. Orgad, however, accepts the standard doctrine of cultural Marxism, which says that everything is socially constructed,

---

13   In *The Rules of Sociological Method*, originally published in 1895, Durkheim defined
      sociology as "the science of social facts", by which he meant that social institutions such
      as kinship and marriage, language, religion, and political organization have a tangible,
      socially real, existence exhibited in the daily lives of the people.

and therefore changeable, and continuously changing, open for deconstruction and then reconstructed in new ways by immigrants, conforming to his definition of what liberalism entails in terms of rights. But now reality has struck back, Europeans are tired of having their majority culture demonized by minority right liberals, millions are endorsing nationalist parties, and so Orgad wants to reconstruct a new liberalism that co-opts this movement.

Refuting Left and Right Liberals

There are some 3,300 higher education establishments in the European Union, and these establishments are dominated by pro-immigration liberals from across the political spectrum. Almost all academics in Western Europe believe that liberalism demands diversification of all white-created nations and that increasing diversity equals democratization and liberation of Europeans from the oppressive and racist shackles of the past. Every conference, program, annual meeting on this issue takes a pro-immigration stand. Whenever a problem is discussed about immigration, be it Islamic radicalization, ethnic enclaves, or sexual assaults, it is always about "solving" them by emphasizing more diversification, less xenophobia, and a greater willingness on the part of whites to develop a "broader sense of cultural belonging". No one ever asks the most basic democratic and liberal questions one can ask: Did Europeans ever vote for a radical alteration of their ethnic and cultural identity? Why is the granting of citizenship to masses of foreign aliens a liberal principle? Why is no one allowed to oppose immigration?

Costica Dumbrava

Both the left and right liberal establishment believe that Orgad's idea-based conception is threatening to minorities and, indeed, to the very principles of liberalism. This is evident in a debate held by Verfassungsblog, "Cultural Majority Rights", to which they invited prominent academics, all liberal, to evaluate Orgad's book, with a "rejoinder" by Orgad. It is quite revealing how pervasive the notion that liberalism necessitates mass immigration is. The first reviewer, Costica Dumbrava, executive coordinator of the Maastricht Centre for Citizenship, Migration, and Development, says that a call by Europeans to protect their majority culture is illiberal because it would lead to "culturally exclusive immigration and citizenship policies", and that such attempts would run counter to the very idea-based, liberal constitutionalism Orgad advocates. He writes: "although liberal states can and should seek to ensure widespread respect for constitutional principles, they cannot do so by way of ethno-cultural engineering". [14]

I would agree that within the framework of Orgad's idea-based definition of majority cultures "there are liberal limits to selecting immigrants and future citizens on grounds of ethnic origin". But not if we reject this cultural Marxist definition of liberalism, and keep in mind that Europe's liberal traditions actually emerged in the 19th century within very ethnically homogeneous nations, and that up until the 1960s the settler nations of Australia, Canada, and the United States, the same ones that fought against Nazism, had "white only" immigration policies. We don't have to accept a one-sided idea-based conception of European culture. Liberalism can coexist with a strong form of ethnic nationalism. While liberalism has substantive flaws, these are remediable flaws, as will be argued in Part Four. The liberal emphasis on open inquiry has in fact taught us about the importance of ethnic kinship for the communal sense of belonging and wellbeing of peoples. There is nothing illiberal about a democratically elected government respecting the fundamental freedoms of its citizens while freely "discriminating among immigrants on ethno-cultural grounds" since immigrants are not citizens until they are given citizenship. This is what freedom and national self-determination are all about.

Dumbrava, safely working at Maastricht, which embodies both the right liberal advocacy of "cross-border labor mobility" and the left advocacy of radical diversification under the cover of humanitarian sensibilities, says that any effort to "preserve" a majority group within Europe is an effort to promote this "group's dominant position in the state beyond strict considerations of justice". This means, by implication, that majorities in Europe have no right to decide democratically what the cultural character of their nation should be, and instead must accept the mandates of elites, the claims of Dumbrava about what their culture

---

14   Costica Dumbrava, "Anticipatory minority rights for majorities turning into minorities" Verfassungsblog (2016), http://verfassungsblog.de/anticipatory-minority-rights-for-majorities-turning-into-minorities/

should be like. It means, actually, that they must accept what can only be called a program of genetic engineering through mass immigration leading to the genocide of European millennial ethnic identities.

One has to look at population projections in Africa, the ongoing migration patterns from this dark continent to Europe, and the Middle East, to get a sense of what is about to be unleashed upon Europeans unless they reject this perversion of liberalism. According to UNICEF, the population of Africa will increase from 1.033 billion in 2013 to a staggering 4.2 billion in 2100. In 1950, only 9 among 100 of the world's inhabitants were African; within 35 years, 1 in 4 will be African. Over a century ago, Europeans constituted 25 percent of the world's population; in 1950, the number of Europeans was double the number of Africans, but in 2010, the European population was only 11 percent. The population of Europe is shrinking fast with an average fertility rate of 1.5 per couple, with even lower rates in Greece, Spain, and Italy, to name some. In a few decades, the European old-age dependency ratio (the number of people age 65+ relative to those of productive age between 15 and 64), will be over 50 percent. In contrast, in Africa the average age today is only 18, and 40 percent of Africans are 14 years old or younger. Using these numbers and other startling estimations, Dan Roodt, founder of the Pro-Afrikaans Action Group, leaves us with this scenario:

> As the population grows, survival will mean only one thing: emigration. The bright lights of Europe and North America—and of South Africa for those who cannot manage to leave the continent — will exert a hypnotic attraction. Many Africans will buy plane tickets financed by their relatives already overseas, or by Western aid money, and those who cannot afford to fly will pile into rickety ships to cross the Mediterranean. The African avalanche is inevitable.

> The rush to Europe will be so massive and relentless that it will not be possible to stop it without direct military force. That would require a fundamental ideological change, and without such a change, at some point in the 21st century, Europe will accept African domination. This is not as preposterous as it sounds; most Europeans will be as resigned to black rule as white South Africans are today. Liberal Europeans will probably fight as hard

as Africans to implement the current South African system of race preferences, quotas and forced integration.

Africans are not good at engineering, science, management, maintenance of complex systems, and a host of other things, but they excel at politics. In fact, the entire African elite, as well as the Afro-American elite in the United States, is engaged in a form politics. Business, sport, culture, religion, education–in fact, all fields of human endeavor–become extensions of a racial politics designed to push forward the interests of one group at the expense of others.[15]

None of the academics debating the merits of Orgad's elegant argument are willing to contemplate the projections and scenarios Roodt writes about; instead, they call it "racist" to oppose the Africanization of Europe. It is indispensable to be aware that this is the state of insanity within liberal theory today before we proceed with the other debaters.[16]

David Abraham

David Abraham's stand against Orgad is simply that it is preferable to emphasize additional socialist spending as a way of integrating everyone within the nation's multicultural setting, rather than endorsing constitutional approaches to majority problems, centered "on normative principles, values, and institutions". [17] Abraham, professor at University of Miami - School of Law, and believer in the enrichment that mass immigration has brought to Florida, thinks that a more open, broader, and tolerant sense of "we" can be nurtured more

---

15   Dan Roodt, "An African Planet?" *American Renaissance* (July 10, 2015), https://www. amren.com/features/2015/07/an-african-planet/

16   Typically in our universities, all of them, white students are being told that i) European imperialism is responsible for the African migration, and that African migrants are adding a wonderful kaleidoscope of colors and ideas to European cultures. See the just released book, Jennifer Cole and Christian Groes, eds., *Affective Circuits, African Migrations to Europe and the Pursuit of Social Regeneration* (University of Chicago Press, 2016). The collection of essays examine "the many ways migrants sustain and rework" European culture for the better, while asking white students to show more sympathy for the plight of migrants by paying for their education and health and vibrant habits.

17   David Abraham, "Immigration, Majority Rights, and Welfare State Solidarity" Verfassungsblog (2016), http://verfassungsblog.de/immigration-majority-rights-and-welfare-state-solidarity/

effectively through "social equality" measures. In principle, therefore, he is in favor of keeping the borders open to hordes of Africans pushing their way into Europe for some decades now at ever higher numbers. Abraham, you see, has the best medicine: fight neoliberal economic policies and maximize spending on immigrants. This will help them integrate, and it will also make the Europeans feel "at home" in their diverse cities. He adds that Orgad's call for greater majority protections is "very slippery" and can quickly create a climate in which the supposedly illiberal views of a Viktor Orbán may become acceptable. But what's so unacceptable about Orbán, or the "AfD and similar populist parties that have grown enormously in Europe, including Donald Trump"?

Again, Abraham is operating within an unquestioned regime of cultural Marxist precepts, which takes it for granted that any form of ethnic demands by Europeans, any calls for strict limitations on immigration, are inherently illiberal, however democratic these calls may be.[18] Abraham reasons that the best way to treat a lack of assimilation (terrorist acts by Muslims, rape epidemics across Europe) is through additional "anti-discrimination policies, accelerated language instruction, job training programs, residential and school integration, the discouragement of enclaves". How is Sweden doing today in becoming the "humanitarian super power" of the world? braham has no clue.[19]

---

18 Any perusal of the party platforms of "anti-immigrant" parties shows that they occupy the full political range in their socialistic, libertarian, conservative, and/or ecologically oriented policies; see Ricardo Duchesne, "The Moderateness of the 'Far Right' and the Extremism of Immigration". www.Euro-Canadian.ca/2014/06/moderateness-of-the-far-right-and-extremism-of-immigration.html

19 You wonder how supposedly intelligent academics can't stop repeating decades on that the solution is more spending. As Daniel J. Mitchell, a Senior Fellow at the Cato Institute, writes, "Sweden has one of the world's biggest welfare states...the public sector consumes about 50 percent of economic output... Sweden has had an unusually open policy towards refugee and family immigrants. This openness is admirable, but is it successful? Are immigrants assimilating and contributing to Sweden's economy? Unfortunately, the answer in many cases is no". Mitchell, citing an expert: "The open attitude towards granting immigrants asylum is not matched by good opportunities on the labor market. An in-depth study by the daily paper Dagens Nyheter shows that many migrants struggle to find decent work even ten years after entering the country... The median income for the refugees in the group was found to be as low as £880 a month. The family immigrants of refugees earned even less. Ten years after arriving in the country, their median income was merely £360 a month. These very low figures suggest that a large segment of the group is still relying on welfare payments. Dagens Nyheter can show that at least four out of ten refugees ten years after arrival are supported by welfare. The paper acknowledges that this is likely an underestimation". *The Commentator* (March 20, 2015), http://www.thecommentator.com/article/5714/

David Owen

According to David Owen, Professor of Social and Political Philosophy at the University of Southampton, "Orgad is not offering a nationalist argument but rather proposes a narrow defense of majority culture... specified in terms of its legal acceptance of a constitutional identity". [20] Owen, in other words, recognizes that Orgad reduces European culture to its liberal-constitutional ideas; and yet Owen goes on to say that "granting privileges to the majority and imposing duties on others in order to secure those interests'...strikes me as rather worrying". Why should aboriginals in settler nations like Canada and Australia, Owens asks, be obligated to accept the liberal constitutional definition of the majority white inhabitants?

Yet, the same Owen who is willing to concede full national rights of self-determination for aboriginals, outside the framework of any constitutional liberalism, thinks that the white natives of Britain, and Europe generally, have a moral obligation to keep their borders open and not protect their national cultures. How about opening the borders of the self-governing territories of aboriginals in Canada to masses of immigrants? He says that "the history of previous immigration flows...of the late 19th and mid-20th century, do not suggest that, given appropriate state integration policies, there is a credible basis for the belief that immigration flows generally support the undermining of just constitutional essentials". He wants us to believe that current immigration flows are the same as the mostly intra-migration movements that happened over thousands of years within the continent of Europe. This is a very deceptive claim.

What is most striking is Owen's view that a majority culture has no right to restrict immigration even if such immigration reduces the majority

---

lessons_from_sweden_about_welfare_and_immigration According to another study, "Sweden's 16.5% foreign born population (massively overrepresented by Muslims) use 66.4% of the nation's government financial assistance. The cost of housing these foreign born is escalating out of control and in 2014 the 83.5% Swedish born population cost around 4,44 billion kroners while the foreign born population of 16.5% cost almost 8,88 billion kroners. The actual numbers may be even higher considering residence allowances, family allowances and old-age dependency support (ÄFS) is not included". Muslim Statistics (September 3, 2015), https://muslimstatistics.wordpress.com/2015/09/03/sweden-ten-times-higher-welfare-dependency-among-16-5-foreign-born-an-increase-of-82/

20   David Owen, "The Immigration Flow's Liability" Verfassungsblog (2016), http://verfassungsblog.de/the-immigration-flows-liability/

culture to a minority. He says there is "no moral basis" to any policies which restrict immigration on the grounds that such immigration is or will eventually reduce the original inhabitants of the nation to a minority. Owen never ponders why it is that only European elites, and only they, believe that it is moral for them to allow Europeans to be marginalized in their own homelands. Why is it that Japan, a liberal democratic culture, does not feel any moral obligation to open its borders to mass immigration despite its low fertility rates? Or South Korea? Or the rest of the non-white world?

Eric Kauffman

At first sight, Eric Kauffman, Professor of Politics at Birkbeck College, who has a keen grasp of the underlying reasons for the discontent that is fueling populism in Europe, the sense that Europeans, the white working classes in particular, are losing their nation, seems to be the one author in this debate who sympathizes with Orgad's theory, and even goes beyond in using the term "ethnic" to denote the majority group, mentioning an article he published back in 2000.[21] He even makes reference to David Coleman's politically incorrect "third demographic transition" and cites numbers to the effect that by the end of this century non-Europeans are expected to be the majority in many European nations.[22] But those of us who really care about the protection of European ethnics will not have a hard time detecting Kauffman's mainstream liberal position, which does not question the premises of mass immigration and diversification, does not ask why diversification became the central ideology of the West, and why liberals have been pushing this ideology for decades.

Kauffman says that "the idea of majority cultural rights is actually not seriously contested in academic political theory", and mentions two authors who support this idea. But in the next sentence he

---

21 Eric Kauffmann, "Why majority cultural preferences should shape but not determine immigration policy" Verfassungsblog (2016), http://verfassungsblog.de/why-majority-cultural-preferences-should-shape-but-not-determine-immigration-policy/

22 David Coleman, "Immigration and Ethnic Change in Low Fertility: A Third Demographic Transition" *Population and Development Review* (vol. 32, no. 3, 2006). Coleman is critical to this whole debate in predicting that Europe is currently experiencing a demographic revolution due to a combination of low fertility and mass immigration from the Third World. Most of the experts in population studies are ignoring his work.

says that academics, including the same ones who have initiated it, have felt "uncomfortable" with this idea and so "the message has not filtered through to political elites". Clearly, if this idea makes academics uncomfortable, to the point that few know about it, and it would be wrong to say that only politicians have failed to learn about it, since academia is where political correctness reigns supreme (and Kaufmann admits that liberals have directed almost all their efforts at developing theories of minority rights), how can one say that the theory of majority rights is "not seriously contested" in academia?

Kaufmann is a right wing liberal, or middle-of-the-road liberal, rather than a left liberal multiculturalist. This is obvious in his expression that ethnicity should be defined in liberal terms, which is to say that European ethnics, as he defines liberalism, have no right to oppose their eventual marginalization. He says that "discriminating against ethnic minorities within the state, is clearly illiberal". But what if it can be shown that the ethnic minorities (which are now reducing Europeans to majority-minority status, as he notices in the case of Vancouver and Toronto, among many other cities in the West), came to European lands through the undemocratic actions of elites employing deceptive arguments about cultural enrichment and the economic benefits of mass immigration, threatening the population with charges of "racism" for voicing dissenting views, loss of jobs, no promotions, and overall totalitarian-illiberal controls? Look for the headline: "Tony Blair betrayed Britain for his own political ends by overseeing a massive conspiracy to flood the country with millions of migrants, an explosive book has claimed".

Kaufmann, like every other author here, acts as if mass immigration just happened, as if the diversification of European lands, and only European lands, not Israel, which, as he acknowledges, is an Ethno-State, was itself a liberally initiated process blessed by theories of minority rights, rather than a undemocratic process initiated behind the backs of the population by elites that can only be identified as treacherous. He even says that since the ever growing ethnic minorities of Europe are now part of the nation, their wishes on issues of immigration must be taken into account, and the ethnic European majority "must not solely determine migration policy".

So, in the end, Kaufmann accepts the current illiberal regime of immigration. He says "young workers" should be allowed to meet economic needs, never mind that most of these workers have been a massive burden on the welfare states paid for and created by native Europeans, and never mind that Europe has high unemployment, and that robots are soon to perform many white collar jobs. "Refugee obligations" should also "weigh in the balance". I take it then that Germany was right and humanitarian in accepting over a 1 million in 2015, even though it has produced rape epidemics, hundreds of thousands of crimes, terrorist infiltration, and much more. The response to these crimes is that they should be asked to "weigh in the balance" about Europe's future!

He also says that even though the cultural majority has a right to show preference for immigrants closer to their cultural traditions, all ethnic groups should be presumed to be capable of assimilation "unless social scientific evidence from similar countries suggests otherwise". How about scientific evidence ignored by everyone in this debate that humans have a preference for their own ethnic groups, and evidence showing that non-Europeans are collectivist and engage in ethnic nepotism, whereas Europeans are uniquely a trust-oriented people, and liberalism is uniquely European and there is no evidence that large groups of non-Europeans endorse these values except insofar as these values can be exploited to advance their ethnic-group interests? Kaufmann indeed reveals his true cultural Marxist perspective when he writes: "Assimilation must be fully voluntary, not coerced, as minority groups have a right to remain apart if they so desire". Did you read that? Non-European groups have a right to remain apart and not assimilate, whereas whiteys have a moral obligation to open themselves to other ethnic groups, spend billions in assimilation programs, while never affirming their ethnic integrity.[23]

---

23 I had an email exchange with Kaufmann pressing him on his notion that liberalism requires acceptance of mass immigration, and as much as he equivocated showing concern for European anxieties about mass immigration, he stuck to this notion. The mainstream press establishment certainly welcomes his ideas as being consistent with mass immigration, some agreeing with him that governments should throw a few bones to the white workers to calm them down and persuade them away from nationalist parties. Kaufman is quite happy with the number of times the press cites his unthreatening words, http://www.sneps.net/

Randall Hansen

Randall Hansen, Director of the Centre for European, Russian, and Eurasian Studies, Munk School of Global Affairs, Canada, thinks that Orgad's argument is "conceptually rock solid", and is sympathetic to the concerns Orgad has for the problems immigration poses to the majority culture generally, security threats, excessive use of welfare spending by migrants, environmental threats, and direct threats to the cultural norms of the host nation, the language, symbols, manners, folklore.[24] But Hansen thinks that threats to liberal principles should be the main concern, not to the norms and customs of European nations. This emphasis on liberal values is consistent with Orgad's "idea-based" definition of the majority culture.

For Hansen, and for many Westerners, there is nothing unique or worthy of preservation in European cultures other than liberal values, which they actually view as values that can be assimilated by non-Europeans, and are not peculiarly European. Orgad is at least cognizant of the importance of everyday cultural norms, language differences, symbols, historical memories, to want to protect these, as cultural markers that distinguish European nations.

Hansen voices a common view among established conservatives, or right wing liberals, who think that Westerners should not compromise their political institutions. Nowadays it is common to hear leaders of Western nations identifying their national cultures mostly in terms of free speech, representative institutions, separation of church and state. English, Canadian, American, German, French leaders regularly tell their audiences that what makes their nations unique, "German", or "British", are their liberal values. They emphasize these values against those who threaten the security of these nations, act in ways that are not perceived to be liberal. They no longer emphasize cultural norms other than on private occasions. Hansen is following this standard line of argumentation.

He agrees with Orgad that "Muslim numbers will grow, but nowhere will they reach much more than 10% of the national population". It

---

24   Randall Hansen, "Does the majority have a right to have rights? On the Cultural Defence of Nations", Verfassungsblog (2016), http://verfassungsblog.de/does-the-majority-have-a-right-to-have-rights-on-the-cultural-defence-of-nations/

is absurd to say that they will not reach "much more than 10 percent" in other countries. As Pew Research Center's most recent population estimates have indicated, the Muslim share in Europe generally has been increasing steadily, "from mid-2010 to mid-2016 alone, the share increased more than 1 percentage point, from 3.8% to 4.9% (from 19.5 million to 25.8 million)." It is also very significant that in 2016, the median age of Muslims throughout Europe was 30.2, that is, 13 years younger than the median for other Europeans, which is 43.8. On top of this, the average Muslim woman in Europe is expected to have 2.6 children, "a full child more than the average non-Muslim woman (1.6 children). But why talk only about the Muslim share? Why not the immigrant share, the non-white share? Once we take these into account, what we are witnessing across Europe, in France, Sweden, Germany, Italy, and England is an actual population replacement. These establishment politicians (mainly from the right) believe that immigrants in principle can be expected to assimilate to these liberal values with proper measures to acculturate them. All humans in the world are the same, they all want the same things, security, affluence, a job. Culture should be relegated to the private sphere, should become another choice among others, rather than a collective responsibility of the state.

Right wing liberals are more realistic than leftist multiculturalists in realizing that radical Islam, and even Muslims generally, may not be compatible, or easily acculturated to Western values. Hansen brings out surveys showing that high percentages of Muslims hold "highly illiberal" views. But whereas Orgad is willing to write about immigration restriction, if in a subdued manner lest he rocks the politically correct expectations of academia, Hansen, as most right wing liberals, does not think that immigration should be restricted. Immigration merely "poses uncomfortable challenges", but liberals can fight off these challenges. Hansen does not care if Germany is half African and Turkish in a few decades, or Britain, or France — as long as everyone is acculturated to liberal values.[25]

---

25   Conrad Hackett, "Five Facts about the Muslim Population in Europe" *Pew Research Center* (November 29, 2017), http://www.pewresearch.org/fact-tank/2017/11/29/5-facts-about-the-muslim-population-in-europe/

Alexander Yakobson

Alexander Yakobson, an Israeli historian, professor of Ancient history at the Hebrew University of Jerusalem, asks a very simple yet rarely asked question: when are many immigrants too many?[26] And to his credit, he ponders about the effects that large numbers of immigrants may have on the culture regardless of whether they threaten or not its liberal values. He just asks whether there is a point at which large numbers will inevitably threaten the culture of the host nation. The issue for Yakobson, it would seem then, is not integration to liberal values per se, but at which point immigration threatens the cultural integrity of nations. More than this, Yakobson even suggests that a people desiring to protect its culture by limiting immigration would not necessarily be acting in illiberal or xenophobic ways.

Nevertheless, there is a key limitation in Yakobson, which I have observed in the other participants; he also assumes that if a European people were to speak of their culture "with some essentialist, inflexible and narrowly-ethnic meaning", then they would be "betraying" their liberalism. What makes this assertion all the more odd, but very revealing, is that Yakobson admits, though in passing, that the state of Israel is an ethnic state. He says this after lauding the acceptance by this state of millions of immigrants, "twice as large as its original population". Clearly, as he realizes, without really wanting to dwell on it, the immigrants accepted in the state of Israel are ethnically Jewish. It should be noted that Orgad includes Israel as a case of a liberal country also trying to protect its culture much like European nations and the United States; but as a reviewer notes, "Israel is not established as a country open to immigrants generally, but rather as one meant only for Jewish immigration". [27] There is a Law of Return, and while many Russians may have been accepted without firm confirmation of their Jewishness,[28] it cannot be denied that Israel is an ethno-state, and that many Africans and other non-Jewish immigrants have been expelled. And yet Israel is a liberal-democratic state. Can the liberals

---

26   Alexander Yakobson, "The prince of Denmark facing mass immigration – from Germany" Verfassungsblog (2016), http://verfassungsblog.de/the-prince-of-denmark-facing-mass-immigration-from-germany/

27   Anna Su, "The Nation Strikes Back" *The New Rambler* (May 2, 2016).

28   This is what Yakobson said to me in an email exchange when I asked why he calls Israel a liberal state despite its ethnocentric policies, while insisting that it would be illiberal for Europeans to affirm their ethnic identity.

in this debate, as well as Yakobson and Orgad, tell us, why Israel is deemed to be liberal, whereas European states that care about their ethnic identity are deemed to be illiberal and Nazi-like?

Ultimately Yakobson takes mass immigration into Europe as an unquestioned reality, as if it is somehow a natural outcome of liberalism, of the liberal endorsement of minority rights, logically embedded to the principle of individual rights. He does not say this openly for the very reason I just stated: he takes it for granted, as every liberal in this debate. He says:

> I accept the right of European peoples – as all other peoples – to preserve their national identity. I think that it should be accepted that this consideration is highly relevant to a country's policies as regards immigration and integration of immigrants.[29]

Does he really accept the right of Europeans to stop immigration altogether for the sake of preserving their national identity? And since demographic trends in some countries in Europe are already set to result in a situation in which the majority cultures will be reduced to majority-minority status, or greatly marginalized, does he agree that Europeans have a right to take measures to avoid this from happening? Yakobson's answer is that Muslims will likely assimilate into Europe's majority culture, even though the evidence is daily pointing in the opposite direction. Just Google "Muslim rape gangs in England", "Migrant sexual assaults spiral out of control in Germany", "Sweden rape epidemic", and so on. Google, too, welfare costs, educational attainments of Muslims or third generation Turks in Germany, and you will find, even from mainstream news sources, they have not assimilated.

Moreover, when we talk about assimilation, we need to understand that the majority cultures of the nations of Europe have been radically transformed to make them suitable to diversification, with huge penalties inflicted on those who disagree with this transformation. Therefore, we must realize that those who are assimilating, are assimilating to nations that are increasingly diversified, with multiple ethnic enclaves, cultural Marxists in power. Why would Muslims find it hard to assimilate to

---

29   See his reply to a comment in Alexander Yakobson, "The prince of Denmark facing mass immigration – from Germany" Verfassungsblog (2016), http://verfassungsblog. de/the-prince-of-denmark-facing-mass-immigration-from-germany/

a majority culture full of Mosques, a multicultural curriculum, and European males who have no sense of pride and identity?

George Fletcher

George Fletcher, Cardozo Professor of Jurisprudence at Columbia Law School. Fletcher, regarded as "one of the leading scholars in the United States in the fields of torts and criminal law", takes on the attitude of someone settled to a life in which liberals have pretty much solved everything and Western countries are doing great with hordes of immigrants enriching them without limits. He thinks that majority cultural rights should be restricted to "linguistic self-defense".[30] Any culture, both minority and majority, should have a right to defend their language in the face of threats. He lauds the ability of the Quebecois in Canada to protect their French language, from which point he deduces that the Quebecois "have held on well to their culture". What culture? Fletcher is prominently ignorant of the ways in which the Quebecois elites have redefined their people in linguistic terms over the last few decades. The very ethnic term "French Canadian", which in the past described a people of French-racial descent, has come to be seen as any Canadian speaking French without any reference to culture, ethnicity or religion.[31] The French Canadian elites have promoted the notion of multicultural immigration as a healthy thing to do for Quebec as long as immigrants are French speaking.[32] Everyone takes it as self-evidently true that a French speaking immigrant from Haiti is the same as a Quebecois with deep ancestral roots.[33]

The result has been that French speaking immigrants in Quebec have

---

30   George Fletcher, "Linguistic Defense and Offense" Verfassungsblog (2016), http://verfassungsblog.de/linguistic-defense-and-offense/

31   Rudy Fenwick, "Social Change and Ethnic Nationalism: An Historical Analysis of the Separatist Movement in Quebec" *Comparative Studies in Society and History* (vol. 23, no. 2, 1981).

32   Remi Tremblay, "The Failure of the French Canadian Immigration Strategy", (Council of European Canadians, November, 29, 2015), http://www.Euro-Canadian.ca/2015/11/failure-of-french-canadian-immigration-strategy.html

33   The rare few who voice some concerns about the effects of mass immigration on Quebec are immediately condemned, prompting articles with titles, "Quebec's ugly ethnic nationalism. A culture of intolerance and racism has been allowed to fester in the province of Quebec" (CBC News, February 1, 2017), requiring more indoctrination and totalitarian controls.

gained priority over Anglo Canadians with long lineages in Quebec. We thus have a situation in which Haitians in Quebec, for example, have started acting as the true representatives of the French heritage in Canada, while pushing aside the Anglo-Europeans who also played a role in Quebec and Canada's foundation. Indeed, the situation is now quite comical with the Académie Française, the exclusive and ancient institution tasked with safeguarding the French language, awarding Haitian novelist Dany Laferrièrem, on May 2015, the honor of being one of the "immortals" of French Canadian culture for publishing his novel *How to Make Love to a Negro Without Getting Tired*.

Christian Joppke

Finally, let's see if there is anything worthwhile about Christian Joppke's commentary.[34] Joppke, professor in "General Sociology" at the University of Bern, Switzerland, who self-describes himself as "a reactionary liberal" merely because he is a critic of multicultural group rights, may have been taken aback by Orgad's more edgy counter endorsement of group rights for the majority. Without much to say, this "author of more than one hundred publications", which barely anyone cares to read or cite, huffs and puffs about his "realistic" evaluation of the impossibility of limiting immigration "in a world of global mobility and flux, especially that consisting of or conditioned by people moving across borders". But, as I have noted here in varying ways, this immobility is typical for the vast majority of the world's population, except for massive mobility to the West.

Joppke is right that Orgad's "case for liberal majority rights" does not "go much beyond liberal constitutionalism". Yet, Joppke thinks that Orgad's theory can be used as a way of defusing populist resentment against immigration, by tricking voters into believing this theory is a defense of the actual culture of Europeans. Beyond this, the traitorous deceiver Joppke does not see much use for this theory. The individual rights Europeans currently enjoy are already consistent with the protection of the culture of Europeans and there is no reason to have a special theory that addresses their collective rights. In this

---

34   Christian Joppke, "Majorities Need No Rights: A Commentary on Liav Orgad's 'The Law of Majorities'" Verfassungsblog (2016), http://verfassungsblog.de/majorities-need-no-rights-a-commentary-on-liav-orgads-the-law-of-majorities/

respect, Joppke is closer to Jürgen Habermas's argument that there is no need for special cultural rights for either minorities or majorities. The theory of individual rights has been already constructed to deal adequately with the cultural identities of minorities and Europeans. Just as lesbians, gays and women do not need a separate culture but are to be treated legally like anybody else, so Europeans and immigrants can be like anybody else as long as the government does not impose assimilation, or institutes special cultural protections for Europeans.[35] Ensuring equal opportunities for success for everyone should be the only role of the government.

Obviously this argument is flawed in dismissing collectivist inclinations among humans and projecting the individualism of Europeans onto the world. However, the fundamental error of all the arguments proposed by liberals from left to right flows out of their unexamined presumption that liberalism requires Western nations to diversify their cultures through mass immigration. The entire liberal establishment has been deceiving Europeans for decades now into believing that diversification is intrinsic to the liberal cultural expectations of the West. It is not. To the contrary, diversification has resulted in the absurd situation we have today in which a theory of majority cultural rights has been developed to protect the culture of Europeans inside their own homelands! This is the context in which to understand Liav Orgad's theory.

---

35   On Habermas's view, see Ricardo Duchesne, "Germany Abolishes Itself" *Salisbury Review* (September 2015).

Part Four

Canada Spiraling Out of Control

The enemy is not merely any competitor or just any partner of a conflict in general. He is also not the private adversary whom one hates. An enemy exists only when, at least potentially, one fighting collectivity of people confronts a similar collectivity. — Carl Schmitt

Tell me who your enemy is, and I will tell you who you are. — Carl Schmitt

12

Liberal Nations Have No
Concept of the Political

Before World War II liberal rights were understood among Western states in a libertarian and ethno-nationalistic way. Freedom of association, for example, was understood to include the right to refuse to associate with certain members of certain ethnic groups, even the right to discriminate in employment practices. This racial liberalism was still institutionalized right up until the 1960s. The settler nations of Australia, Canada, United States, and New Zealand enjoyed admission and naturalization policies based on race and culture, intended to keep these nations "white". This liberal racial ethos was socially accepted with a good conscience throughout Western society. As Robert H. Jackson has observed:

> Before the war prevailing public opinion within Western states — including democratic states — did not condemn racial discrimination in domestic social and political life. Nor did it question the ideas and institutions of colonialism. In the minds of most Europeans, equality and democracy could not yet be extended successfully to non-Europeans. In other words, these ideas were not yet considered to be universal human rights divorced from any particular civilization or culture. Indeed, for a century or more race had been widely employed as a concept to explain the scientific and technological achievements of Europeans as compared to non-Europeans and to justify not only racial discrimination within Western states but also Western domination of non-western peoples. Racial distinctions thus served as a brake on the extension of democratic rights to people of non-European descent within Western countries as well as in Western colonies.[1]

---

1   Robert H. Jackson, "The Weight of Ideas in Decolonization: Normative Change in International Relations", In Goldstein and Keohane (Eds.), *Ideas and Foreign Policy: Beliefs, Institutions and Political Change* (Cornell University Press, 1993), 135).

Even in the case of de-Nazified Germany, governments after 1945 endorsed, as a matter of common sense, and well into the 1970s, an ethnic conception of German nationality, accepting migrants only as temporary "guest workers" on the grounds that Germany was "not an immigrant country", as Helmut Kohl, the chancellor of Germany from 1982 to 1998, observed.[2] European nations took for granted the ethnic cohesion of their cultures and the necessity of barring the entry and incorporation of people from different cultures categorized as a threat to the "national character".

Why, then, did the entire Western liberal establishment come to the view that European ethnocentrism was fundamentally at odds with liberal principles a few decades after WWII?

I will argue in the next chapters that a new set of normative claims with an in-built tendency for further radicalization suddenly came to take a firm hold over Western liberal nations in response to the Nazi experience, and that once these norms were accepted, and actions were taken to implement them institutionally, they came to "entrap" Westerners within a spiral that would push them into ever more radical policies that would increasingly create a situation in which Western nations would come to be envisioned as places always intended to be progressing toward a future utopia in which multiple races would co-exist in a state of harmony. These four norms may be summed up for now as follows:

---

2   Sara Miller Llana, "A new, unlikely 'nation of immigrants': Germany". *The Christian Science Monitor* (December 12, 2014). Of course, the German Federal Republic carefully avoided the slightest insinuation that it had not eliminated every remnant of the Nazis' citizenship laws, as it struggled with the exact status and naturalization possibilities of "guest workers". At first, through the 1950s, they managed to avoid confronting squarely with this issue since quite a few guest workers returned home, but during the 1960s their numbers started increasing again and fewer were returning, both because they realized the standard of living back home was not comparable (in Turkey from which most migrants had come), and because they had brought their wives and family members and basically had settled in ethnic enclaves. Consequently, by the 1980s, the government started to implement formal policies for the integration of what were still viewed as "foreign" workers. But through the 1990s and after, the concept of German citizenship underwent a dramatic change from an ethnic-oriented conception, which did not grant citizenship to persons who were not born in Germany, to a purely civic conception, which granted citizenship to persons who had lived in Germany for at least 15 years, with further changes introduced thereafter, principally, automatic citizenship to children of foreigners born on German soil as long as the parent has been in Germany for at least eight years as a legal immigrant. See Triadafilos Triadafilopoulos, *Becoming Multicultural: Immigration and the Politics of Membership in Canada and Germany* (UBC Press, 2012).

1. Westerners came to believe that racism was the worst evil of modern times because of its association with Nazism, and that, accordingly, it was immoral and illiberal for Western nations to identify themselves in terms of a particular race or even a particular ethnic group.

2. The immediate years after the defeat of Nazism saw the "outlawing of race" and the discrediting of "scientific racism" across the West.

3. Western colonialism was totally discredited at the same time that the old notion of the noble savage was revived with ever more infantile meanings about how Third World peoples embodied the innate goodness of humanity in their "naturalness" and "authentic traditional lifestyles".

4. The immediate intensification of a human rights discourse in which the principles of equality, dignity, and self-determination were extended to all humans as humans, resulting in the extension of Western citizenship rights to foreigners.

Carl Schmitt

Was there something within the ethnocentric liberalism of the pre-WW II era, including the Tory-oriented cultural liberalism of Canada, which made it susceptible to the promulgation of these norms and their rapid radicalization thereafter? Why did Western leaders succumb to the radicalization of these norms so easily? The answer may be found in Carl Schmitt's argument that liberal states lack a strong concept of the political.[3] I take this to mean that liberal leaders have an inherent weakness as political beings due to their inability to think of their nation states as a collectivity of people laying sovereign claim over a territory that distinguishes between friends and enemies, who can belong and who cannot belong in the territory.

Clearly, the way I will be employing Schmitt is not to argue that liberals have always been utterly devoid of any sense of collective identity,

---

3   Carl Schmitt, *The Concept of the Political*. Expanded Edition. Translated and with an Introduction by George Schwab. With a Foreword by Tracy B. Strong and Notes by Leo Strauss (The University of Chicago Press, 2007).

otherwise they would not have endorsed the ethnic nationalism I just outlined. As it is, humans have a natural in-group preference for their ethno-cultural community. No ideology can eradicate this tendency absolutely. What I have taken from Schmitt is that liberalism is inherently a way of thinking that prioritizes the liberty of the individual above all else without fully appreciating the uniquely European communitarian basis of liberal ideals themselves. Liberals have an imaginary conception of their nation states as associations formed by individuals for the purpose of ensuring their natural right to life, liberty, and happiness, even when they emphasize the importance of community standards. They have an imaginary view of their liberal states as associations created by isolated individuals reaching a covenant, a contract or agreement, amongst themselves in abstraction from any prior community. They have a predilection to whitewash the fact that their liberal states, like all states, were forcibly created by a people with a common language, heritage, racial characteristics, religious traditions, and a sense of territorial acquisition involving the derogation of out-groups.

For this reason, according to Carl Schmitt, liberals have an undeveloped sense of the political, an inability to think of themselves as members of a political entity that was created with a clear sense of who can belong and who cannot belong in the community. Having a concept of the political presupposes a people with a strong sense of who can be part of their political community, who can be friends of the community and who cannot be because they pose a threat to the existence and the norms of the community.

Liberals tend to deny that man is by nature a social animal, a member of a collective. They think that humans are all alike as individuals in wanting states that afford them with the legal framework that individuals need in the pursuit of liberty and happiness. They hold a conception of human nature according to which humans can avoid deadly conflict through a liberal state which gives everyone the possibility to improve themselves and society through market competition, technological innovation, and humanitarian works, creating an atmosphere in which political differences can be resolved through peaceful consensus by way of open deliberation.

They don't want to admit openly that all liberal states were created violently by a people with a sense of peoplehood laying sovereign rights over an exclusive territory against other people competing for the same territory. They don't want to admit that the members of the competing outgroups are potential enemies rather than abstract individuals seeking a universal state that guarantees happiness and security for all regardless of racial and religious identity. Humans are social animals with a natural impulse to identify themselves collectively in terms of ethnic, cultural and racial markers.

But today Europeans have wrongly attributed their unique inclination for states with liberal constitutions to non-Europeans. They have forgotten that liberal states were created by a particular people with a particular individualist heritage, beliefs, and religious orientations. They don't realize that their individualist heritage was made possible within the context of states or territories acquired through force to the exclusion of competitors. They don't realize that a liberal state if it is to remain liberal must act collectively against the inclusion of non-Europeans with their own in-group ambitions.

Hegel, Hobbes, and Schmitt

But I think that Schmitt should be complemented with Hegel's appropriation of the ancient Greek concept of "spiritedness". [4] Our sense of honor comes from our status within our ethnocultural group in our struggle for survival and competition with other groups.[5] This is the source of what the ancient Greeks called "spiritedness", that is a part of the soul comprising, in Plato's philosophy, pride, indignation, shame, and the need for recognition. Plato believed that the human soul consisted of three parts:

- a physically desiring part that drives humans to seek to satisfy their appetites for food, comfort, and sensual pleasure;

- a reasoning part that allows humans to calculate the best way to get the things they desire; and

---

4   For an extended examination of "spiritedness", see Ricardo Duchesne, *The Uniqueness of Western Civilization* (2011).

5   Jack Donovan, *The Way of Men* (Dissonant Hum, 2012)

- a "spirited" part that drives humans to seek honor and renown amongst their people.

Liberal theory developed in reaction to the destructive tendency inbuilt into the spirited part which was exemplified with brutal intensity during the Thirty Years War (1618-1648) and the English Civil War 1642-1651). Thomas Hobbes devalued the spirited part of man as just another appetite for power, for riches, and adulation. At the same time, he understood that this appetite was different from the mere natural appetites for food and sensual pleasure, in that they were insatiable and conflict-oriented.

Hobbes emphasized the destructive rather than the heroic character of this aspect of human nature. In the state of nature men are in constant competition with other men for riches and honor, and so enmity is a permanent condition of the state of nature, killing, subduing, and supplanting competitors. However, Hobbes believed that other aspects of human nature, namely, the instinct for self-preservation, fear of death and desire for "commodious living", were more powerful passions among humans, and that it was these passions, the fear of death in particular, which eventually led men to agree to create a strong central authority that would end the war of competing megalomaniacs, and maintain the peace by monopolizing the means of violence and agreeing to ensure the secure pursuit of commodious living by all. The insatiable desire and ambition of man for power and adulation would henceforth be relegated to the international sphere.[6]

But by the second half of the seventeenth century Hobbes's extreme pessimism about human nature gradually gave way to more moderate accounts in which economic self-interest in the market place, love of money, as calculated and contained by reason, would come to be seen as the main passion of humans.[7] The ideal of the spirited hero striving for honor and glory was thoroughly demeaned if not denounced as foolish. By the eighteenth century money making was viewed less as avaricious or selfish and more as a peaceful passion that improves peoples' manners and "makes for all the gentleness of life". As

---

6   Thomas Hobbes, *Leviathan*. Edited by Noel Malcolm (Oxford University Press, 2013).

7   The following paragraphs draw on Albert Hirschman's much talked about book, *The Passions and the Interests. Political Arguments for Capitalism before Its Triumph* (Princeton University Press, 1977).

Montesquieu worded it, "wherever there is commerce, there the ways of men are gentle". [8] Commerce, it was indeed anticipated, would soften the barbaric ways of human nature, their atavistic passions for glorious warfare, transforming competition into a peaceful endeavor conducted by reasonable men who stood to gain more from trade than the violent usurpation of people's property.

Eventually, liberals came to believe that commerce would, in the words expressed by the Scottish thinker William Robertson in 1769, "wear off those prejudices which maintain distinction and animosity between nations". [9] By the nineteenth century liberals were not as persuaded by Hobbes's view that the state of nature would continue permanently in the international relationships between nations. They replaced his pessimistic argument about human nature with a progressive optimism about how humans could be socialized to overcome their turbulent passions and aggressive instincts as they were softened through affluence and greater economic opportunities. With continuous improvements in the standard of living, technology and social organization, there would be no conflicts that could not be resolved through peaceful deliberation and political compromise. [10]

The result of this new image of man and political relations, according to Schmitt, was a failure on the part of liberal nations to understand that what makes a community viable as a political association with sovereign control over a territory is its ability to distinguish between friends and enemies, which is based on the ability to grasp the permanent reality that Hobbes understood about the nature of man, which is that humans (the ones with the strongest passions) have an insatiable craving for power, a passion that can be held in check inside a nation state with a strong Leviathan ruler, but which remains a reality in the relationship between nations. But, whereas for Hobbes the state of nature is a war between individuals; for Schmitt one can speak of a state of war between nations as well as between groups within a nation. Friends and enemies are always groupings of people.

In our time of mass multicultural immigration we can see clearly how

---

8   Cited in Hirschman, 60

9   Cited in Hirschman, 61

10   As Schmitt argues drawing on liberal ideas of progress, see *The Concept of the Political*, 75-79.

enemy groups can be formed inside a national collectivity, groups seeking to undermine the values and the ethnic character of the national group. Therefore, to have a concept of the political is to be aware, in our multicultural age, of the possibility that enemy outgroups can emerge within our liberal nations states; it is to be aware that not all humans are equally individualistic, but far more ethnocentric than Europeans, and that a polity which welcomes millions of individuals from collectivist cultures, with a human nature driven by the passions for power and for recognition, constitute a very dangerous situation.

It was Hegel, rather than Hobbes, who spoke of the pursuit of honor instead of the pursuit of riches or power for its own sake, as the spirited part of human nature, which is about seeking recognition from others, a deeply felt desire among men to be conferred rightful honor by their peers. We can bring this Hegelian insight into Schmitt to argue that the spirited part of the soul is intimately tied to one's sense of belonging to a political community with ethno-cultural markers. Without this spirited part members of a community eventually lose their sense of collective pride, honor, and will to survive as a political people. It is important to understand that honor is all about concern for one's reputation within the context of a group.[11] It is a matter of honor for immigrants, the males in the group, to affirm their heritage regardless of how successful they may be economically. Immigrants arriving in large numbers are naturally inclined to establish their own ethnic groupings within Western nations rather than disaggregate into individual units, contrary to what liberal theory says.

Non-white ethnic groupings stand as "the other", "the stranger", to use Schmitt's words, in relation to nations where Europeans still constitute the majority.[12] The friend-enemy distinction, certainly "the Us versus Them" distinction, can be applied to the relation between non-white ethnic groupings and European national groupings in the degree to which the collective actions of non-European groups negates the heritage and overall way of life of the majority European population. Ethnic groupings that negate the way of life of European liberal nations must be repulsed if European nations are to preserve their "own way

---

11 A point Donavan makes effectively in *The Way of Men*.

12 Schmitt, 27

of life". [13] To be cognizant of this reality is what it means to have a concept of the political in our current age of mass immigration. It does not mean that alien groupings are posing an immediate physical threat. Enemy groupings may also emerge as a major force through sheer demographic growth in a seemingly peaceful atmosphere, leading to all sorts of differences over voting patterns, accumulation of wealth and resources, ethnic hierarchies, divergent customs and religious practices, that become so pervasive that they come to threaten the way of life of the founding peoples, polarizing the nation into US versus Them.

The Leftist Interpretation of Schmitt Is Wrong

But don't Western liberals have enemies? Don't they believe, at least many Republicans, that Islamic radicals, and nations openly opposed to "Western values", are enemies of liberalism, against whom military violence may be used when necessary, even if Republicans negate the political in the sense that they want to bring about a situation in which humans define themselves as economic agents, or as moral crusaders dedicated to "democratic" causes? Don't multicultural liberals believe that opponents of multiculturalism and mass immigration in Western countries are "deplorable" people who must be totally marginalized as enemies of humanity?

Academics on the left have indeed appropriated Schmitt to argue that right wing liberals have not negated the political but simply produced a highly effective smokescreen over the West's ambition to impose an American-led corporate order in the world nicely wrapped with human rights for everyone.[14] They see Schmitt as someone who can teach us how to remove the smokescreen of "democracy", "human rights", and "economic liberty" from Western hegemony, exposing the true power-seeking intentions behind the corporate liberal elites.[15]

---

13   Schmitt, 49

14   See Chantal Mouffe, *The Return of the Political* (Verso, 1993).

15   Leo Strauss, whose review, "Notes on Carl Schmitt, The Concept of the Political",
     is included in the "Expanded Edition" from University of Chicago Press I am using,
     steers in this direction. It is not that this interpretation is wrong; it just misses the most
     salient trait of liberal nations, which is that, even if they still play power politics under
     the cover of nice sounding phrases, they do imagine themselves as non-political, as
     nations created by "natural" individuals for the sake of peace and prosperity, dedicated
     to a world of cosmopolitan harmony, rather than as ethnic collectivities based on force
     to the exclusion of "enemy groupings".

It seems to me that this appropriation of Schmitt is seriously flawed. Of course, Schmitt did not say that liberal nations as such are utterly devoid of any political existence, and of a concept of the political, since the very existence of a state supposes a sovereign right over a territory. A complete denial of the political would amount to a denial of the existence of one's state. It is also true that for Schmitt "what has occurred [in liberal nations] is that economics has become political"[16] in the enormous power that capitalist firms have, and in the way liberal states seek to augment, through non-economic means, their market share across the world. More than this, Schmitt emphasized how liberal states have "intensified" the enemy-friend distinction by ostracizing as enemies any state or political group disagreeing with their conception of humanity and conceptualizing liberal aggression against illiberal nations as final wars to end all wars.

There is no question, however, that Schmitt's central thesis is that liberalism has no concept of the political and that it lacks a capacity to understand the friend-enemy distinction. Liberals believe that the "angelic" side of humans[17] can manifest itself through proper liberal socialization, and that once individuals practice a politics of consensus-seeking and tolerance of differences, both inside their nations and in their relationships with other liberal nations, they will learn to avoid war and instead promote peaceful trade and cultural exchanges through commercial contracts, treaties, and diplomacy. Even though liberal states have not been able to "elude the political", they have yet to develop theories of the political which apprehend this sphere of human life in terms of its defining aspect, the friend-enemy distinction. Rather, liberal theorists are inclined to think of the state as one pressure group among a plurality of political groups all of which

---

16   Schmitt, 78.

17   Reading Steven Pinker's *The Better Angels of Our Nature: Why Violence Has Declined* (2011) in light of Schmitt's insights, one can see that Pinker's much heralded seriousness about human nature is really one more liberal outlook without a concept of the political. The idea of man as a "dangerous animal" is lacking in Pinker's claim that with affluence the angelic side of our human nature has finally had a chance to flourish. A Schmittian would reply that affluence generates other vices long noted by the great conservative philosophers of the past, such as uncontrollable appetites, laziness, avariciousness, effeminacy, and the lack of survival and territorial instincts we observe among whites today in not realizing that millions of Muslims in their nations raping women and engaging in terrorism are absolute indications that an enemy grouping is operating right inside their nations rather than mere individuals who have not yet been able to develop their angelic side.

lack a concept of the political in thinking that differences between groups can be handled through institutions that obtain consensus by means of neutral procedures and rational deliberation.

The negation of the political is necessarily implicit in the liberal notion that humans can be defined as individuals with natural rights. It is implicit in the liberal aspiration to create a world in which groups and nations interact through peaceful economic exchanges and consensual politics, and in which, accordingly, the enemy-friend distinction and the possibility of violence between groups is renounced. The negation of the political is implicit in the liberal notion of "humanity". The goal of liberalism is to get rid of the political, to create societies in which humans see themselves as members of a human community dedicated to the pursuit of security, comfort and happiness.

Therefore, we can argue with Schmitt that liberals have ceased to understand the political insomuch as liberal nations and liberal groups have renounced the friend-enemy distinction and the possibility of violence, under the assumption that human groups are not inherently dangerous to each other, but can be socialized gradually to become members of a friendly "humanity" which no longer values the honor of belonging to a group that affirms ethno-cultural existential differences. This is why Schmitt observes that liberal theorists lack a concept of the political, since the political presupposes a view of humans organized in groupings affirming themselves as "existentially something different". [18]

Thus, using Schmitt, we can argue that while Western liberal states had strong ethnic markers before WWII/1960s, with immigration policies excluding ethnic groupings deemed to be an existential threat to their "national character", they were nevertheless highly susceptible to the enactment of norms promoting the idea of civic identity, renouncing the notion that races are real, romanticizing Third World peoples as liberators, and believing that all liberal rights should be extended to all humans regardless of nationality, because they lacked a concept of the political. The racial or ethnocentric liberalism that prevailed in the West, collectivist as it remained in this respect, was encased within a liberal worldview according to which, to use the words of Schmitt, "trade and industry, technological perfection,

---

18   Schmitt, 27

freedom, and rationalization...are essentially peaceful [and...] must necessarily replace the age of wars". [19]

They believed that their European societies were associations of individuals enjoying the right to life and liberty. The experience of WWII led liberals to the conclusion that the bourgeois revolutions of the seventeenth and eighteenth centuries, which had finished feudal militarism, and which then led the Allies to fight a world war against the new militarism of fascism, were still "unfinished revolutions". The liberal bourgeois nations were still not liberal enough, in their division and ranking of individuals along ethnic lines, with many individuals not enjoying the same rights that were "naturally" theirs. The project of the Enlightenment, "the universalist spirit of the political Enlightenment", in the words of Jürgen Habermas, was not yet completed.

What Western liberals in the 1960s, the ones who dismantled immigration laws that discriminated against non-whites, and intro-duced the notion that multiple cultures could co-exist within the same state, did not realize, including conservatives leaders, was that their sense of ethno-cultural identity was the one collectivist norm still holding their liberal nations safely under the concept of the political. Once this last bastion of collectivism was deconstructed, liberal nations would be caught up within a spiral of radicalization wherein liberal nations would find it ever more difficult to decide which racial groups may constitute a threat to their national character, and which groups may be already lurking within their nations ready to play the political with open reigns, ready to promote their own ethnic interests; in fact, ready to play up the universal language of liberalism, against ethnocentric Europeans, so as to promote their own collectivist interests.

---

19   Schmitt, 75

13

Ethnic Liberalism Versus Post-WWII Norms

White Canadians to this day are being harassed for lack of progress in dismantling institutional racism,[1] half a century after the complete redefinition of Canada as a multicultural nation in 1971, after the Canadian Human Rights Act of 1977, which called for "equal opportunity" for "victims of discriminatory practices", after the Employment Equity Act of 1986, which instituted, and still mandates, affirmative hiring for minorities, after the Multiculturalism Act of 1988, which provides billions in financial support to immigrant groups to enhance their cultural identity in Canada[2] while extolling Euro-Canadians to dismantle their "Anglocentric" heritage. What is more, and what is really threatening, is that this multicultural enforcement has come along with a dramatic demographic alteration in the ethnic character of Canada through the yearly arrival of an average of 250,000+ immigrants since the early 1990s, which has reduced Euro-Canadians to a minority, or close to it, in all the major cities of Vancouver, Montreal, Toronto, with projections announcing that within 15 short years, by "2031, 47% of second-generation Canadians could belong to a visible minority group".[3]

The demands keep getting more radical and suicidal. How did it come

---

1   Not a day goes by in Canada without radio episodes, TV news, and magazine articles holding whites to account for their racist past. Here is the title of a CBC radio episode this morning: "Trump win gives 'permission' to racists, but hate crimes are nothing new in Canada", http://www.cbc.ca/radio/thecurrent/the-current-for-november-16-2016-1.3852164/trump-win-gives-permission-to-racists-but-hate-crimes-are-nothing-new-in-canada-1.3852174 (November 16, 2016).

2   According to Dan Murray, who heads Immigration Watch Canada, the total amount of grants given by Citizenship and Immigration alone for fiscal year 2013/14 was about $920 million, and for fiscal year 2014/15 it was over $720 million. These totals, he says, "are only for grants that were over $25,000. If the totals included grants under $25,000, they would be substantially higher". See "Exploiting Canada All the Way to the Bank" Immigration Watch (October 30, 2015), http://immigrationwatchcanada.org/2015/10/30/exploiting-canada-all-the-way-to-the-bank/

3   "Projections of the Diversity of the Canadian Population, 2006 to 2031" Statistic Canada, http://www.statcan.gc.ca/pub/91-551-x/91-551-x2010001-eng.pdf

to be that conservative candidate Kellie Leitch was called "unCanadian" a few months ago simply because she considered asking supporters in a survey whether the Canadian government should screen potential immigrants for anti-Canadian values? This was deemed to be an extremist, intolerant question, even by some conservatives, and yet the values Leitch had in mind were equality of the sexes, tolerance, gay rights, diversity, and multiculturalism.

What is going on? Kymlicka and Taylor are celebrated as paragons of Canada's highest moral commitments even though their ideas are part of a program that is rapidly leading to the rise of powerful ethnic coalitions in Canada, demographic displacement of Euro-Canadians, combined with massive welfare costs and totalitarian newspeak in the halls of academia. How could historians trained to show the utmost respect for what the documents and the evidence say get entrapped into obvious logical fallacies and empirically baseless assertions about the history of their own ancestors?

The answer put forward in the next chapters is that a new set of norms came to take a firm hold over Western liberal democracies after WWII calling for the dissolution of ethno-nationalism in Western states and for the complete discrediting of racial identities among Europeans, on the supposition that ethnocentrism and racial identities were ultimately responsible for conflicts among humans, and that if future wars as deadly as WWII were to be avoided Western nations had to institute human rights, offer Western citizenship to peoples across the world, and create multiethnic and multicultural states.

I will argue that once these norms were accepted, and actions were taken to implement them institutionally, they came to "entrap" Westerners within a spiral of radicalization, because these norms have an in-built tendency for never-satisfied "solutions", because they inevitably entail ever more demands for equality in face of the stubborn reality of ethnocentric tendencies among humans and racial inequalities in talents and achievements. Moreover, since this drive for equality has been a planned experiment carried out, with ever more determination, by countries that were overwhelmingly white, it has entailed and involved the arrival of endless masses of immigrant minorities in need of continuous equalization programs coupled with ever more radical assertions in favor of the ethnic interests of minorities with a strong sense of the political, of collective identity, against every perceived form of "white privilege".

The West is stuck pursuing a utopia of racial harmony and diversity through mass immigration that nowhere can be fulfilled because it is premised on unattainable goals. Hostile ethnic elites inside the West have exploited, and continue to exploit, these universal norms of racial equality, human rights, and multicultural citizenship, which I will explain shortly, for their own particular ends, creating ever more tensions and calls for further radicalization by brainwashed Europeans with a weak sense of ethnic identity.

While liberal rights among Western states prior to WWII were understood in an ethnocentric manner, as testified by their pro-European immigration policies, these states were highly susceptible to the new norms of racial equality and human rights because liberal leaders, as I argued in the last chapter, lack a strong concept of the political in presuming that their nations were associations formed by individuals for the purpose of ensuring their natural rights to economic freedom, security, and happiness, which all humans regardless of race supposedly aspire to have, rather than viewing their nations as creations by a people with a strong ethno-cultural identity, a collective identity, claiming sovereign right over a territory to the exclusion of other people with different, and always potentially threatening, ethno-political interests.

Spiral Radicalization Model

What do I mean by spiral of radicalization, or spiraling out of control? Some time ago, while researching the origins of the ideology of human rights, after reading that the emergence of an international law of human rights was the most critical international influence in the emergence of the Charter of Rights and Freedoms in 1982, I came up with the term "spiral diffusion model", which has struck me as quite useful in understanding the incredible manner in which anti-white diversity spread throughout the West in a few decades.[4] This model is used differently by leftist human rights scholars; firstly,

---

4   Thomas Risse, Stephen C. Ropp, Kathryn Sikkink, eds., *The Power of Human Rights. International Norms and Domestic Change* (Cambridge University Press, 1999).

as far as I know, it has been used only to understand when human rights are likely to become "habitual" in the behavior of governments around the world, and the argument basically is that the first step in bringing about "sustained improvements in human rights practices" is to make sure that the respective nations already have the political system to establish the rule of law, and the judicial and educational capacities required to give human rights traction and enforceability. Of course, this is all rather obvious, and almost tautological; and one wonders why academics think they have made a major discovery in finding "quantitative evidence for the proposition that countries with more highly developed legal institutions...tend to have better civil rights protections". [5]

But here is the interesting idea; they found that a "spiral" can be launched by creating certain normative conditions both at the domestic and the international level, such as having governments sign human rights treaties, for example, the Convention on the Elimination of Discrimination Against Women, or showcasing major global socializing events that promote rights in Third World nations, such as international conferences and meetings, that can then "end up entrapping" state actors to make "tactical concessions" that can lead to further concessions and possibly "to unexpected consequences under conditions of turmoil and change". [6] They might get the government to release political prisoners on grounds that their rights are being violated, or sign international agreements as a condition for getting foreign aid or for ending international sanctions, or get them to allow alternative political parties and voices.

They found that the more states are "embedded" in international institutions, "the more likely they are to ratify international human rights agreements", [7] and the more agreements they ratify to improve domestic conditions, the more a spiral of further changes can develop pushing the nation to the "next" stage. Without "entrapping" the nation to certain agreements and human rights discourses, they

---

5   Beth A. Simmons, "From ratification to compliance: quantitative evidence on the spiral model" in Thomas Risse, Stephen C. Ropp, Kathryn Sikkink, eds., *The Persistent Power of Human Rights: From Commitment to Compliance* (Cambridge University Press, 2013), pp.43-60.

6   *Ibid*, p. 48.

7   *Ibid*, p. 51.

found that human rights agreements tend to "sputter and eventually fail". While governments may adjust their behavior to international pressures and treaties "without necessarily believing in the validity of the norms", or purely for the sake of economic gain, it has been observed that minor concessions aimed at calming critics, can create certain normative conditions and precedents, as well as domestic pressures, that encourage further concessions later on, and thus create a dynamic for additional human rights treaties and institutional changes, until substantive changes are introduced aligning the state with the "moral standards of the international community"[8] from which it is no longer possible for state actors to escape without experiencing the brunt of reprisals by domestic and international moral arbiters.

This spiral diffusion model can be used to answer the question posed in the opening paragraph. Remember that the starting point of the spiral model, in respect to the diffusion of human rights in Third World nations, is that certain human right norms or treaties had to be put in place first in order to get the spiral going. The spiral needs a starting point, say, a tacit agreement that the human rights of non-violent political dissenters will not be violated. Only when such footholds are in place can we expect a spiral insofar as these first steps make possible, or create a normative-institutional climate, for the diffusion of further changes in favor of human rights.

Ethnic Liberalism

So, what were the normative and institutional starting points in the Western world that served as a launching platform for a spiral of diversity to be diffused leading to the current situation? The starting point for this spiral emerged in the West after WWII. (The intellectual origins of the ideas at the base of this spiral, of course, go further back in time, as will be briefly pointed out later). Once this spiral took off it would gather ever more momentum pushing Western nations into ever more radical policies leading to the current situation where Europeans are expected to celebrate a new national identity created through mass immigration and race mixing.

---

8   "How the International Community can Support UN Efforts in Burma/Myanmar" Report of the conference held on March 27, 2008 at Château Frontenac in Québec City, https://www.csi.hei.ulaval.ca/sites/csi.hei.ulaval.ca/files/Burma_texte_et_couvert__2_.pdf

The Western nations that defeated Nazism, it should be noted, were self-declared liberal-democratic nations in which individuals enjoyed rights of free speech, freedom of religion, freedom of association, and the right to a fair trial. However, the way these liberal rights were understood among Western states generally, before WWII, before the spiral took off, was in a libertarian and ethno-nationalistic way. It should be noted, moreover, that in the 1940s/50s the Allied leaders, the ones who condemned Nazi racial policies, believed that the peoples of the world were divided into different races and that it was legitimate for them to rule over "inferior peoples": "subjects of empire were seen as unworthy of self-rule, as backward, as culturally inferior, and so forth". [9] Well into the 1940s, with strong challenges coming only from the 1960s onward, the Allied nations, in varying ways, had franchise laws that excluded certain minorities from voting, routine racial discrimination in employment opportunities, unequal access to public spaces, combined with assorted discriminatory practices in everyday private affairs.

In saying this I am not endorsing any ethnic ranking or European imperial rule. All ethno-national groups have a right to self-determination. The issue at hand is how did it come about that these ethnocentric liberal nations found themselves caught up within a spiral of radicalization the moment these norms were enunciated leading to the situation in which all Europeans are living today in which the most minimal form of white identity is totally suppressed as the worst form of evil and illiberalism at the same time as non-whites are encouraged to affirm their ethnic collective rights, in the name of liberalism.

Post WWII Normative Situation in the West

Below I will offer a list of the primary norms that I think set the spiral going. To be clear, I am not trying to explain the origins of the norms that brought the West into the present state of affairs. The goal is to understand why there was such a fast acceleration against the ethno-nationalistic norms that were so readily accepted before WWII.

---

9   Alan C. Cairns, "Empire, Globalization, and the Rise and Fall of Diversity", in Alain C. Cairns et al, eds., *Citizenship, Diversity, and Pluralism: Canadian and Comparative Perspectives* (McGill-Queen's Press, 1999), p. 38.

I will offer arguments about how these new post-WWII norms came to entrap Westerners within a spiral of radicalization, how each norm reinforced the other, how each norm came to acquire meanings and goals not intended in their initial conceptualizations, all of them reinforcing each other, leading Western peoples into a funnel with a seemingly irreversible logic of pro-diversity hysteria and a pathological death wish.

Right after WWII, four norms, attitudes and feelings, came to take a firm hold over Westerners against their preceding confidence and acceptance of their right to exist as ethno-national states. These norms were, from the beginning, interconnected, driven by similar principles, and therefore in a state of rapid reinforcement and radicalization.

1. Westerners came to believe that racism was the worst evil of modern times because of its association with Nazism and German supremacist beliefs. Western governments concluded that Nazis, including Fascist governments, had committed "crimes against humanity", and that the Holocaust was a demonstration of the inhumanity of racist ideas that divided the peoples of the world into "superior" and "inferior" races, "inside" and "outside" members. A nationalism in which a race or even a particular ethnic group lay a privileged claim over the nation state was, accordingly, thoroughly discredited as inherently inconsistent with the ideals of liberal democracy. Over and over again, Western leaders began to announce that a true liberal state must be civic in orientation, based only on liberal values, standing above all ethnic groups, "neutral" both on matters of religion and race.

2. The immediate years after the defeat of Nazism saw the "outlawing of race" and the discrediting of "scientific racism" across the West. Western elites systematically spread out the idea, which up until WWII was only held by a minority of scholars, that the very idea of a science of "race" is unscientific, an ideology that took off in the West during the nineteenth century as a way of "finding a moral justification" for their colonial rule over non-whites. The differences between different nationalities are primarily due to cultural and environmental factors; the differences of biology are superficially about skin color, hair texture, or facial features, not about deep genetic differences in behavior and intelligence.

Since there is no scientific basis for the claim that humans can be categorized in terms of different races, there can be no scientific justification for racial discrimination; rather, discriminatory policies are creations of pathological individuals with an "irrational" fear of groups that are different in appearance. These fears can be eliminated through "proper" socialization and education.

3. The post-WWII era also saw the total discrediting of Western colonialism coupled with the intensification of the noble savage notion that Third World peoples embodied the innate goodness of humanity when freed from the corrupting influence of Western imperialism. Western imperialism was not a "civilizing" force but a violation of the liberal ideal that all peoples should have a right to national self-determination. Alongside these anti-colonialist sentiments, there developed movements against the unequal status of people of color inside Western nations. Western elites thus began to push for an end to discrimination in hiring, in voting, and, concomitantly, for an end to the privileging of one ethnic group over another by society generally. These demands also came along with the spread of the idea that all cultures are equal and that whites rose to dominance by exploiting Third World peoples, blacks and indigenous peoples. White people are morally responsible for the unequal distribution of wealth in the world and inside their nations and for the subjugation of non-European cultures generally. They should feel guilty and do something to make up for past crimes.

4. It was in the aftermath of WWII that human rights really took off, the norm that all humans as humans are born with inalienable rights to life, security, equality, and dignity. These rights are not rights exclusive to a nation, or the citizens of Western countries; they are universal rights regardless of the nationality and legal status of the human in question. As the 1948 UN Declaration of Human Rights, Article 2, stated: "Everyone is entitled to all the rights and freedoms set forth in this Declaration, without distinction of any kind, such as race, color, sex, language, religion, political or other opinion, national or social origin, property, birth or other status. Furthermore, no distinction shall be made on the basis of the political, jurisdictional or international status of the country or territory to which a person belongs.". . The "right to

live, liberty, and security of the person" (Article 3), are inherent to humans, and not derived from citizenship in a nation, and thus humans are entitled to them wherever they are, including those who arrive in Western nations without rights of their own. Western states must extend citizenship right to foreigners, there should be no line between citizen and non-citizen.[10]

It is my view, and this is why the spiral model may be useful, that the elites promoting these normative forces were not calling for the complete transformation of white nations into Multiracial Nations. These norms in-themselves, when they were first articulated in earnest and with persuasion from the late 1940s on, were not interpreted to mean that European nations needed to become diverse racially. These norms, to be sure, were already a radical challenge to the traditional ethnic-oriented libertarian ethos of the Western world. They were a spring board for radical agendas. But it would be wrong to project immediately onto these norms the radicalizing ideas that emerge out of them later, say, in the 1980s and after, however much we may realize retrospectively that our current multicultic climate is a logical culmination of these norms.

It would be wrong, for example, to argue that the ideal enunciated in Article 15 of the UN Declaration (that "no one shall be arbitrarily

---

10   My summation of these norms is based on countless sources read over many years, about which Westerners are aware in one way or another, books, newspaper articles, videos, conversations. Multiple sources could have been cited under each of these normative claims. But if there is one source I like to single out it is the rather inconspicuous book, *Becoming Multicultural: Immigration and the Politics of Membership in Canada and Germany* (UBC Press, 2012), by Triadafilos Triadafilopoulos. He observes that "The Second World War marked a crucial watershed in attitudes towards race, ethnicity, state sovereignty, and human rights", and identifies "the Holocaust, decolonization, and the emergence of a global human rights culture" as "world-historical events" that "gave rise to a distinctive normative context in the post-Second World War", and then goes on to argue that it was this new global normative context that compelled Canada and Germany to dismantle their "racist" immigration and citizenship policies (pp. 52, 8). Triadafilopoulos's insights will be acknowledged in the following chapters. There is, however, a major flaw in the way Triadafilopoulos frames this normative changes as if they were "global" in nature, and not because of his predictably pro-mass immigration approach, but his odd claim that the leaders of Canada and Germany were compelled to dismantle the "racist" policies of their respective nations because of the power of a new "global culture", when in truth this normative climate was strictly a Western phenomenon that was exploited, in limited but effective ways, as we will see below, by non-Western leaders to advance their own national interests. In not realizing that these norms were strictly Western, Triadafilopoulos ultimately fails to understand what drove Canada and Germany to dismantle their "White supremacist" immigration systems.

deprived of his nationality nor denied the right to change his nationality") is equal in meaning to the idea that Western nations must be open to millions of immigrants because "no one is illegal" or because "Western nations are inherently immigrant nations". This holds true as well for later human rights documents such as the 1966 International Covenant on Civil and Political Rights, which states:

> In those States in which ethnic, religious or linguistic minorities exist, persons belonging to such minorities shall not be denied the right, in community with the other members of their group, to enjoy their own culture, to profess and practice their own religion, or to use their own language.[11]

This statement is now used in support of the expansion of immigrant minorities inside Western nations even though it merely states that minorities already inhabiting a nation should enjoy cultural group rights. There is an intellectual distance, a radicalizing distance in-between the principle of minority rights and the current notion that Canada must be committed to the continuous inclusion of immigrant minorities.

The norms outlined above, to repeat, were imbued with radicalizing tendencies. From the 1940s through to the 1960s, Western nations, in varying ways, would witness movements to end discriminatory employment practices and franchises, as well as race-based immigration regulations. These years would also witness the UN's 1951 convention on asylum mandating that people seeking asylum in one country due to fear of persecution for their religious beliefs or racial make-up can't be sent back to face arrest or torture. Still, despite these substantial changes in the nature of Western liberalism, politicians were not celebrating in the 1940s, and even in the 1970s, the transformation of Western nations into race-mixed societies. Only since about the 1980s have Westerners been made to believe that a truly liberal nation is one where diversity is the most cherished value and where the culture is no longer identified as uniquely European in history, literature, traditions, laws, and language. My goal is to trace the spiraling, radicalizing dynamic of these norms.

---

11   As cited in Joseph Eliot Magnet, "Multiculturalism in the Canadian Charter of Rights and Freedoms", in Beaudoin and Mendes, Eds. *The Canadian Charter of Rights and Freedoms* (Carswell, 1996), Chapter 18, p. 8.

These norms were more or less accepted across the West after WWII although their diffusion and implementation followed different lines and degrees of intensification in each Western nation. The focus of the following chapters, however, will be on Canada. This will allow for a substantive, more detailed documentation of this spiral, step by step.

14

A White Man's Country

Canada had strong collective ethnic markers before WWII/1960s, with immigration policies that excluded ethnic groupings deemed to be an existential threat to the "national character". But as a liberal nation, Canada had a weak sense of the political, in Schmitt's sense, a weak understanding of the actual way the nation was founded, by a people with a strong Anglo-Quebecois identity rooted in a territory set up against potential enemy groupings. Instead, Canadian leaders imagined their nation to be a contractual creation by individuals seeking security, comfort and liberty, notwithstanding the emphasis the Canadian Tory tradition assigned to community British standards. This is why they were highly susceptible to the new normative climate that emerged after WWII.

Immigration Act of 1910

The ethnically-oriented normative liberalism that prevailed in Canada before WWII was clearly embodied in the Immigration Act of 1910, the Immigration Act Amendment of 1919, and the Chinese Immigration Act of 1923. The norms contained in these acts, even as they came under heavy critical scrutiny after WWII, and confidence in their validity was weakened, prevailed in Canada until the 1962/67 Immigration Regulations, which eliminated selection of immigrants based on racial criteria. These Acts envisioned Canada as a "white man's country". The Immigration Act of 1910 reinforced the immigration restrictions based on race contained in the Immigration Act of 1906, and in all prior government statements and policies about immigration since Confederation. The 1910 Act gave Cabinet the right to enact regulations to prohibit immigrants "belonging to any race deemed unsuitable to the climate and requirements of Canada or immigrants of any specified class, occupation, or character". [1]

---

1   Ninette Kelley, Michael Trebilcock, *The Making of the Mosaic. A History of Canadian Immigration Policy* (University of Toronto Press, Second Edition, 2010), p. 139.

The Immigration Act Amendment of 1919 introduced further restrictive regulations in reaction to the economic downturn after WWI and the rising anti-foreign sentiments of Canadians after this war. Immigrants from enemy alien countries were denied entry as well as immigrants of any nationality, race, occupation and class with "peculiar customs, habits, modes of life and methods of holding property". The Chinese Immigration Act of 1923 imposed further restrictions on Chinese immigrants to the point that the only Chinese admissible in Canada were diplomats, government representatives, merchants, and children born in Canada who wished to return after leaving for educational purposes. An estimated 15 Chinese immigrants only were able to gain entry into Canada between 1923 and 1946.

Now, while a few million immigrants from Continental Europe had been welcomed to Canada as "agriculturalists" after 1867, there was considerable ambivalence among the mainstream British elite as to whether non-British immigrant wage workers would fit into the Anglo culture or whether such "strange" religious sects as the Hutterites, Mennonites, and Doukhobors, as well as the hardy Ukrainian farmers and assorted Eastern Europeans, would threaten Canada's Anglo-Saxon character, its tradition of political freedom and self-government. But with the government keen on laying claim over the vast wild lands to the West, and the need for additional hands to sustain Canada's industrialization drive, the consensus of Canadians was that, as long as Asians (and blacks) were excluded, and "Anglo conformity" was emphasized, ensuring that non-British Europeans were transformed into English-speakers with manners and habits in line with Canada's "Britishness", things would be alright.[2] The expectation was not that non-British Europeans would readily assimilate to British ways, but that they would at least contribute to the economy and become law-abiding English-speaking citizens. The continued influx of "continental" immigrants in the first decades of the twentieth century aroused widespread concerns that Canada would lose its "British identity and become a "mongrel" nation. Up until the 1940s, the dominant British in Canada saw themselves as the true representatives of Canadian culture. "Britishness" still remained intrinsic to Canada's identity. The old imperial heritage, the monarchy,

---

2   Howard Palmer, "Reluctant Hosts: Anglo-Canadian Views of Multiculturalism in the Twentieth Century", in Gerald Tulchinsky, *Immigration in Canada: Historical Perspectives* (Copp Clark Longman, 1994).

the parliamentary system, deference to law and order, and other cultural trappings, mannerisms, clothing, and customs, were still the standard of what it meant to be "Canadian". Non-British Europeans were not perceived as members of this British club, even if many had come to accept their role in Canada as farmers, construction workers and street sweepers. Some elite members actually welcomed the biological merging of Anglo-Canadians with continental Europeans into a new "Canadian race", while others saw positive qualities in a Canada with diverse ethnicities from Europe existing alongside each other. Only non-Europeans were identified as "unassimilable races" that would pose a threat, in large numbers, to the unity and cohesion of Canada's national character and economy viability.

The experience of WWII would result in a complete break with these pro-European racial norms. As each generation after WWII would go on to enact ever more radical policies against "Anglo-Saxon racism" and for the "human rights" of all humans, Canadian liberals would gradually forget that their British-European identity, was their one political concept still holding their liberal nation together. Once this last bastion of collectivism was degraded, Canadian leaders would be caught up within a spiral of radicalization unable to decide which racial groups might be their friends and which might be their enemies, which groups might be already lurking within and outside the nation ready to play up the political with open reigns, ready to promote their own ethnic interests under the cover of the universal language of the new norms.

Mackenzie King's 1947 Speech and New Normative Pressures

The takeoff of the spiral was already evident in a speech that Prime Minister Mackenzie King gave before Parliament on May 1947:

> The policy of the government is to foster the growth of the population of Canada by the encouragement of immigration. The government will seek by legislation, regulation and vigorous administration, to ensure the careful selection and permanent settlement of such numbers of immigrants as can advantageously be absorbed in our national economy... With

regard to the selection of immigrants, much has been said about discrimination. I wish to make quite clear that Canada is perfectly within her rights in selecting the persons whom we regard as desirable future citizens. It is not a "fundamental human right" of any alien to enter Canada. It is a privilege. It is a matter of domestic policy... There will, I am sure, be general agreement with the view that the people of Canada do not wish, as a result of mass immigration, to make a fundamental alteration in the character of our population. Large-scale immigration from the Orient would change the fundamental composition of the Canadian population. Any considerable Oriental immigration would, moreover, be certain to give rise to social and economic problems of a character that might lead to serious difficulties in the field of international relations.[3]

Reading this speech from today's radicalized situation, the speech seems very strong in its racial orientation, but the discrediting of racial identity is already evident, never mind notions of racial hierarchy. The word "race" is absent from this famous speech, and there is nothing about "Asiatics" being "unsuitable" or being "an alien race", and not an inkling about Canada "being a white man's country", never mind anything about the rightful duty of English peoples to "rule over less civilized races". These phrases were common in the pre-WWII period. King's justification for not making any major alterations in Canada's immigration policies was that it was within the sovereign right of the Canadian government to select "the persons whom [it] regards as desirable future citizens".

However, while he is aware of the ideology of human rights, he still holds on to the norm that "it is not a 'fundamental human right' of any alien to enter Canada... It is a matter of domestic policy". He adds that "large scale immigration from the Orient would change the fundamental composition of the Canadian population". The Canadian government had a right to affirm its national cultural interests rather than submit to extra-national human rights norms.

Yet the spiral could not be appeased. Pressure soon began to mount over

---

3   William Lyon Mackenzie, "Statement of...Canada's Immigration Policy", 1947, in Howard Palmer, ed., *Immigration and the Rise of Multiculturalism* (Copp Clark Publishing, 1975).

the actually existing, racially-oriented, immigration acts of Canada. In the same year of 1947, the minister of external affairs suggested that the Chinese Immigration Act of 1923, could not be justified "under the UN Charter which Canada had signed and which called for an end to discrimination based on race, religion, and sex". [4] Diplomatic pressure from the Chinese government then led the Canadian government, in the same year, to terminate this Act. Moreover, the province of BC, in 1947, gave Asians the right to vote in federal elections and to enter professions from which they had been hitherto discriminated from entering; and in 1949 the federal government also gave Japanese Canadians the right to vote in federal elections.

The issue is not whether we disagree or not with these policies. It is to identify the take off point of the spiral, and indeed how fair minded it all seemed at first. No one in these days was calling for the total diversification of Canada through mass immigration in a state of hostility against the founding Euro-Canadians.

It is worth noting that Canada at this time was caving in to pressure from foreign countries and the UN generally, which was made up mostly of non-Western countries without any individual rights but with a strong concept of collective political identity, and, therefore, undisturbed by any norms expecting them to give up their sovereign right to determine the racial character of their nations, even though they, too, were signatories of the UN Charter. Canada, having played an important role in the creation of the UN in 1945, and in the creation of a multi-racial Commonwealth following the granting of independence to India, Pakistan, and Burma in 1947-48, felt morally obligated to the new anti-racist and pro-Third World norms.

The pressure to abide by the new norms was also coming from domestic groups in Canada with a weak sense of the political, business groups believing that what matters in human life is economic growth and prosperity, liberal nations are places in which abstract individuals enjoy the right to economic liberty and the pursuit of affluence regardless of their collective ethnic identity. It was also coming from leftist liberals who felt that Canada was not living up to its ideals of individual freedom and equality under the law and elimination of any form of

---

4   Patricia Roy, *The Triumph of Citizenship: The Japanese and Chinese in Canada, 1941-67* (UBC Press, 2011), p.

discrimination based on non-economic, racial and sexual criteria.

In a Standing Committee of the Senate on Immigration and Labour, which was active from 1946 through to 1953, and which went about collecting the views of multiple groups, ethnic lobby groups, civil servants, organized labour, humanitarian organizations and churches, it was recommended that the Immigration Act of 1910 be revised. The influence of organized labour was felt in this recommendation in its expression that immigration numbers should take into account level of unemployment and the ability of the economy to absorb new immigrants without threatening wages. However, the Canadian Congress of Labour openly recommended an end to racial criteria in immigration policy: "race ought not to be considered at all". Still, the Standing Committee at large, while concluding that racial wording should be avoided in a new immigration act, voiced approval of "Canada's traditional pattern of immigration and her strong European orientation". [5] A most interesting statement of this Committee was its assertion that Canada was a nation based on a mixture of white European peoples, not just Anglo-French, but Italians, Greeks, Slavs, Jews, Ukrainians. All these ethnic groups were deemed to be assimilable "into the national life of Canada". The consensus around these years, then, was that Canada would not discriminate against non-whites who were already citizens in Canada, would avoid using racial language in its immigration act, but would nevertheless affirm the British-European national character of the nation and its wish to maintain this character. The spiral, however, was just beginning to gather momentum.

Immigration Act 1952

Most Canadians in the 1950s continued to accept the essentials of the principles contained in the Immigration Act of 1910, as these principles came to be expressed by Mackenzie King in his speech of 1947, without any words about "less civilized races" and about Canada being a "White man's country". The Act of 1952 simply held the principle that Canada had a sovereign right to choose immigrants that were economically and culturally suitable to the British/European character of the nation. As has been noted by historians:

---

5   As cited in Triadafilos Triadafilopoulos, *Becoming Multicultural: Immigration and the Politics of Membership in Canada and Germany* (UBC Press, 2012), p. 62.

The Immigration Act of 1952 was not a significant departure from prior legislation as it largely codified existing practices...As in previous legislation, the governor-in-council was authorized to make regulations prohibiting immigrants based on their nationality, ethnicity, occupation, peculiar customs, unsuitability to the Canadian climate and probable inability to assimilate.[6]

However, it should be qualified that this Act was a significant departure in not making any references to the racial character of immigrants. What had changed, and this should be understood in its own right rather than as a change that inevitably foreshadowed our current hysteria about the blessings of diversity, is that, by 1952, Canadians were no longer comfortable with the term "race" as per the new norms of the post WWII era.

The new term mandated by social scientists was "ethnic group", and Canadian officials had come to accept this term. In the first UNESCO statement on race titled "The Race Question", issued on July 18, 1950, drafted by Ashley Montagu, it was declared that there was no scientific basis for theories of racial hierarchies.[7] From this declaration, it soon became commonplace among social scientists in the West to avoid the term "race" in preference of the term "ethnic groups". At first, the term "ethnic group" tended to include the notion that there were biological, though not hierarchical, differences between ethnic groups, but, from the 1960s on, this term came to acquire a meaning that was mostly cultural, about the language, beliefs, and institutions of peoples, with only a superficial emphasis on the physical appearances of ethnic groups. Differences in the social standing of races came to be explained, in textbooks used across Western universities, strictly in terms of social and cultural factors.

This discrediting of the term "race" was accepted by the Canadian government, and this is why the Immigration Act of 1952 used the term "ethnic group". The government and the British elites were eager to paint a picture of Canada as a race-mixed nation of Europeans rather than a nation of pure Anglos. At the same time, they sought to avoid

6   "Immigration Act of 1952" Canadian Museum of Immigration at Pier 21, http://www. pier21.ca/research/immigration-history/immigration-act-1952

7   There is an entry on the "Race Question" in Wikipedia, https://en.wikipedia.org/wiki/The_Race_Question

language that would make explicit their preference for members of the European race and their belief that non-whites, as a race, would not assimilate. Instead they spoke of the greater difficulties people from tropical and southern climes would have adapting to Canada's harsh winters, and the greater difficulties they would have in assimilating to Canada's culture. Walter Harris, Citizenship and Immigration Minister, in response to some queries about black immigrants coming to Canada from the West Indies, had this to say in a 1952 letter:

> One of the conditions for admittance to Canada is that immigrants, should be able readily to become adapted and integrated into the life of the community. In the light of experience it would be unrealistic to say that immigrants who have spent the greater part of their life in tropical and subtropical countries become readily adapted to the Canadian mode of life which, to no small extent, is determined by climatic conditions...They are more apt to break down in health and persons from tropical and subtropical countries find it more difficult to succeed in the highly competitive Canadian economy.[8]

Other government officials and publications of the day insisted that limiting immigrants from tropical (Commonwealth) countries was not a matter of prejudice but of avoiding racial tensions in the future. They said that "massive immigration" from tropical countries would create a "colour problem where none exists". As Ellen Fairclough continued to say in 1960s, when she was immigration minister, "Canada has no racial problem, nor Canada has a racial policy. And that is the way it is going to stay".[9]

These were sensible arguments. But the radicalizing logic of the norms was too strong to be limited to the values of 1952.

Third World Nations: Moral Arbiters of Western Countries

With the decolonisation of the British Empire, and the formal creation in

---

8   Clayton James Mosher, *Discrimination and Denial, Systematic Racism in Ontario's Legal and Criminal Justice Systems, 1892-1961* (University of Toronto Press, 1998), p. 95.

9   *Ibid.*

1949 of the Commonwealth of Nations "free and equal", and the growing influence of the UN, and the fact that, by 1961, African, Asian, and Latin American nations made up two-thirds of the UN General Assembly and that these nations, together with Western liberal elites, were pushing for more radical anti-racist resolutions, Canada could not escape the dynamic of a spiral contained in its own declared commitment to the promotion of human rights. The most obvious target of criticism was South Africa's apartheid. Through the 1950s the newly independent states of Asia and Africa complained about the refusal of the South African government to accord the same rights to citizens of black Commonwealth countries as citizens of white Commonwealth countries.[10] But South Africa was not the only target. Gaining ever more confidence in themselves as the moral judges of Westerners looking for redemption for their past imperial crimes, these new nations began to criticize the immigration policies of the Canadian government. Jamaica, Barbados, Trinidad, and other members of the Commonwealth, were, in the words of Triadafilopoulos, "the most vocal critics of Canadian immigration policy", demanding (in a report in 1957) complete equality for the residents of these nations in migrating to Canada as the citizens of England.[11]

But while the South Africa government affirmed its sovereign right to decide who could and could not belong within its dominant national culture, ignoring UN calls and continuing with its apartheid policies, the Canadian Prime Minister, John Diefenbaker, endorsed with conviction the principle of racial equality within the Commonwealth and the idea that all residents of the member states of the Commonwealth should be viewed equally "without regard to race or any other consideration". [12] It was hoped among Canadian officials that by taking a strong stand against racism in international bodies, and increasing immigration quotas from India and the British West Indies, Canada might compensate for its continued discriminatory policies in immigration. Thusly, the Minister of Immigration and Citizenship happily told critics that 22,000 immigrants from Asia had been welcomed to Canada between 1955 and 1959.

---

10 Nancy L. Clark, William H. Worger, *South Africa: The Rise and Fall of Apartheid* (Routledge, 2016), p. 5.

11 Triadafilos Triadafilopoulos, *Becoming Multicultural: Immigration and the Politics of Membership in Canada and Germany*, p. 65.

12 *Ibid*, p. 67.

But these gestures merely signaled to other members of the Commonwealth that Canada's sovereignty could be challenged by outgroups willing to take advantage of the new normative climate. Nazism, the racial ranking of the peoples of the world, coupled with the past imperial practices of Western powers, were attributed singularly to Western peoples by Westerners themselves. Third World nations would take on the role of progressive fighters for racial justice alongside leftist domestic groups in Western countries. The discipline of Anthropology played a very significant role in spreading the norm that Third World peoples were innocent, well-meaning, nature-loving, egalitarian humans. "Greedy", "individualistic", "materialistic" Westerners should learn to emulate them. The Pakistani government thus demanded a doubling of its immigration quota, and Canada agreed. Then, in 1960, the government announced that it would seriously work on a new immigration policy that would eliminate all discriminatory regulations. The spiral was starting to accelerate.

15

Human Rights and Immigration Legislation

The spiral was driven by a set of norms with an in-built radicalizing tendency. This tendency was contained in the supposition that the ethnic inequalities of the world, the wealth of European nations and the poverty of non-European nations, the impoverished status of blacks and aboriginals in the United States and the West generally, were a result of the discriminatory policies, the colonizing and under-developing activities of Europeans, rather than a result of cultural backwardness, differences in aptitudes or geographical lack of resources. If only all humans were granted the same rights to life, liberty, and economic success, the world could be improved drastically in a more egalitarian and prosperous direction.[1]

Fair Employment and Fair Accommodation Practices Acts (1951-1954)

Beginning in the 1940s and through the 1950s, a growing network of groups, academics, media, ethnic associations, and trade unions, operating within a liberal atmosphere, and endorsing a pluralist view of politics, in which the state was seen as just one actor among many others engaged in politics, rather than as the actor in charge of ensuring the collective identity of the nation, pushed for "equal citizenship" and for legislation that would protect the "human rights" of citizens against discrimination. Basing themselves on

---

1   It cannot be underestimated how influential the theory of "the development of underdevelopment", together with all the "dependency" theoretical variations thereof, as well as world systems theory, have been in blaming whites for their enrichment at the cost of the impoverishment of non-white nations. I refute at length these theories in *The Uniqueness of Western Civilization* (2011). For a recent, quick demonstration, of the absurdity of these theories, which refuse to recognize the incredible role of European science and institutions in the making of the industrial revolution, and the eventual responsibility of European for giving non-whites a chance to escape their poverty, see my article, "The Underdevelopment of European Pride" *Salisbury Review* (August 2016).

the UN Charter declaration that every human should have equal rights "without distinction as to race, sex, language, or religion", the groups worked tirelessly in the late 1940s and early 1950s, with the Canadian Jewish Congress and the Jewish Labor Committee playing the key roles, to bring legislation in Ontario, then in Canada generally, aimed at ending discrimination in employment, access to public spaces, housing and property ownership.[2]

At first, in the early 1940s, the Canadian Jewish Congress was preoccupied with fighting domestic antisemitism and encouraging toleration and understanding between Jews and Christian groups. But after WWII, Jewish groups decided to go beyond fighting against the perception that they were unassimilable aliens, and instead designed a grand strategy against discrimination generally, through alliances with other liberal and minority organizations. With racism now tied to the actions of Nazis, these groups successfully instilled upon politicians, and the Canadian Anglo elite at large, the view that discriminatory practices were "fascist" and had no place in a liberal nation. By the early 1950s, these liberal groups managed to bring about the Fair Employment and Fair Accommodations Practices Acts (1951-1954), which declared Ontario's allegiance to the principles of the UN Charter and the UN Declaration of Human Rights in rendering illegal any discrimination in employment and in access to public spaces in Ontario on grounds of race or creed.

These Acts, and other similar legislative measures, culminated, firstly, in the Canadian Bill of Rights enacted by Parliament on August 10, 1960, which is seen as the earliest expression of human rights law at the federal level, in declaring that all persons in Canada have "right to life, liberty and security". Secondly, it culminated in the Ontario Human Rights Code, passed June 15, 1962, which prohibited discrimination on the grounds of race, ancestry colour, ethnic origin, creed, sexual orientation, age and family status.

---

2   James Walker, "The 'Jewish Phase' in the Movement for Racial Equality in Canada" *Canadian Ethnic Studies Journal* (Spring 2002).

The End of "British Liberties"

Now, while it can be reasonably argued that these human rights laws were within the bounds of classical liberal discourse in affording minorities the same legal status, in accordance with the principle that all citizens of a nation should be guaranteed equal rights in the eyes of the law, these acts and codes constituted a dramatic alteration in the traditional language of "British liberties" that had prevailed in Canada before WWII. Before the Second World war, as Ross Lambertson has observed, "there was scant mention of human rights" not just in Canada but in international law.[3] The idea behind the concept of human rights is that all humans enjoy equal natural rights by virtue of belonging to the human race, which is very different from the "British liberties" idea, which emphasizes one's membership in a British national culture. These liberties included the principle of parliamentary supremacy, as the very keystone of the law and constitution, meaning that matters involving individual rights would be left to Parliament, which is to say that courts would defer to Parliament regarding issues about individual rights. (In Canada, be it noted, there was a plurality of parliaments within the federal-provincial division of powers).

The "British liberties" ensured by Parliament included such principles as fair play, which meant both fairness in the right of Canadian individuals to freedom of speech, freedom of association, freedom of religion, and in being treated equal under the law, "no man is above the law", everyone is subject to the same laws. However, as has been argued by James Walker, such British liberties in Canada as freedom of speech and association "were interpreted to mean the right to declare prejudices openly, to refuse to associate with members of certain groups, including to hire them or to serve them".[4] Equality under the law did not mean that individuals were obligated to include within their free associations members regardless of race. Freedom of association was understood to include the right to discriminate on grounds of ethnicity, religion, and sex.

But I disagree with the standing argument that the human rights legislation constituted a break with libertarian liberalism,

---

3   Ross Lambertson, *Repression and Resistance: Canadian Human Rights Activists, 1930-1960* (University of Toronto Press, 2004)

4   James Walker, "The 'Jewish Phase' in the Movement for Racial Equality in Canada".

or classical liberalism. The standing argument says that Canadian liberalism before WWII emphasized individual freedoms rather than equal rights of citizenship. However, in my view, it was not simply that minorities were discriminated in their exclusion from restaurants, barber shops and many other public spaces. It was not simply, as Lambertson says, that the "ideal of freedom was accorded a higher importance than the ideal of equality". [5] It was that the liberalism of this day was still ethnocentric, and this is why there were franchise laws that kept aboriginals in reserves and excluded them from the dominant British nation-state, as well as people of other races, through immigration laws that openly declared Asians and blacks to be unsuitable members of an official Canada intended to be a British community within which another national community existed, the Quebecois, with its own collective traditions.

One does not have to agree with discriminatory measures to understand that it is wrong to project the libertarianism of today, devoid as it is of any appreciation for the importance of ethnic identity with its notion that we are all the same as individuals with rights,[6] to understand that Canada's emphasis on its British collective identity was crucial to the making of Canada and indeed to the differentiation of Canada from the more libertarian and "Lockian" culture of the United States, as George Grant would put it.[7] Today Canada stands open to millions

---

5   Ross Lambertson, *Repression and Resistance: Canadian Human Rights Activists, 1930-1960*, p. 377.

6   This is a standard argument among autistic libertarians like Caleb McMillan who thinks that there should be no immigration controls, for such controls are "socialistic", see "Immigration Controls are Still Socialist" Mises.ca (February 6, 2016).

7   If I may bring up again the much used concept of "imagined communities", which the left embraced as a major revelation in social science, one does not have to deny that humans inescapably construct their realities at the epistemological level through the use of concepts, words, theories, and at the level of their everyday social lives, in the way they imagined themselves and their societies, to be very skeptical of the way this term has been used to make Europeans think that their sense of national identity, their very collective identities, are mere constructs of racist elites, imaginations which should be discarded to make way for new "liberating" constructs fabricated in academia with the funding of corporations. Our dishonest academics simply want Europeans to accept the reconstruction of the West into the grand Mongrel Civilization of the world. Paula Hastings correctly observes that Protestant Canadians of British descent overemphasized and embellished the Britishness of Canada to promote their "collective self-interest" as the true Canadians, with much intensity in the late 19th century, neglecting the role of other European peoples, most saliently the Quebecois. But as is typical with academics, all of whom are conformist extremists, it does not follow that this Britishness was purely imagined, an "artificial construct", considering that Canada was a nation heavily British in institutions and values, and that it was also overwhelmingly English. What is a total construct is the notion that European nations

of immigrants encouraged to claim this nation as their own, and, therefore, encouraged to impose their own sense of the political, their own collective tendencies upon a Euro-Canadian people prohibited to have any collective identity. The libertarianism of Canada before WWII, paradoxical as this may seem to us now, was collectivist in its belief that individual rights were rights which emerged from the British people, not from individuals as members of the human race, but from a particular British race, to which other ethnic groups that were white could assimilate but not people from very different races and cultures.

What made the acts and codes revolutionary was not simply that they were supportive of "equality of rights of minorities, at the expense of the libertarian rights of those wanting to exclude them". [8] What made them revolutionary was that a new liberalism was being advocated in direct challenge to the ethnocentric liberalism that prevailed in the past, a more civic-oriented conception of the Canadian nation, based on universal values, was emerging wherein membership in the nation was defined purely in terms of values of equal rights rather than shared heritage, a common faith, and a common ethnic ancestry. The traditional ethnic nationalism of Canadians was being discredited as racist and illiberal.

In the degree to which this ethnic identity was de-legitimatized, the concept of the political in Canada would be weakened, with Canadians of British and European descent having less recourse to the older argument that it is perfectly within Canada's political right to decide its ethno-cultural character. Indeed, these legislative changes, which I have only outlined, were the beginning of an accelerating spiral that would bring about ever more radical legislative changes, the end of all immigration restrictions by 1967, the complete redefinition of Canada as a multicultural nation in 1971, and much more.

---

are immigrant nations! See Paula Hastings, "'Our Glorious Anglo-Saxon Race Shall Ever Fill Earth Highest Place': The Anglo-Saxon and the Construction of Identity in Late-Nineteenth-Century Canada" in Philip Buckner and R. Douglas Francis, eds. *Canada and the British World* (University of British Columbia Press, 2006).

8   Ross Lambertson, *Repression and Resistance: Canadian Human Rights Activists, 1930-1960*, p. 213.

Immigration Regulations 1962

The 1962 Immigration Regulations constituted a radical break with the immigration policies Canada had followed throughout its history in replacing racial criteria with a "skill's based" immigrant admissions criteria. These Regulations, however, were not intended to bring about a radical change in the racial composition of Canada. They were intended to meet the new post-WWII normative requirements against "racism". These Regulations were implemented without a proper ascertaining of their radicalizing implications and certainly without anyone actually desiring a non-Anglo Canada with a totalitarian climate that would only allow the celebration and affirmation of non-white identities. Lacking a concept of the political, of the essential importance of a group ethnic identity for the survival of a people within its own nation state, Canadian Anglo politicians unknowingly took a delirious step down the path of cultural suicide when they implemented these Regulations.

Economic motivations were very important in this radical change. Canada's economy had been expanding rapidly since WWII and in the 1960s Canadians generally were very optimistic about future economic prospects. Meanwhile, the economies of Europe were also growing rapidly in the 1950s and the number of immigrants interested in coming to Canada was declining sharply, though Italy and Eastern Europe still remain important sources of immigrants. There was strong pressure from business elites on politicians to find new sources of immigrants.[9]

Yet, what is striking is that the main reason offered for these Regulations was that Canada no longer believed that immigration policy should be determined by racial criteria. Many of the politicians who legislated these changes may not have been keen on opening Canada's economy to races that were "unsuitable" to Canada's climate and national character, but they were certainly responding to the pressures generated by the new normative climate of the post-WW decades, which made racial discrimination in the West unacceptable.

Domestic and international groups and diplomats were holding

---

9   Ninette Kelley, Michael Trebilcock, *The Making of the Mosaic. A History of Canadian Immigration Policy*, pp. 337-351.

Canada to account regarding its obligations to live up to the protocols of human rights, the notion that true liberal states could not be based on any form of ethnic nationalism, and that racial distinctions were fascistic. As the Canadian Museum of Immigration at Pier points out in assessing the cultural climate behind these Regulations:

> Following the Second World War and the Holocaust, there was increased awareness and sensitivity to matters of racial discrimination. Prime Minister John Diefenbaker introduced the Bill of Rights in 1960, which rejected discrimination on the basis of race, colour, national origin, religion or sex. As such, the selection of immigrants on the basis of ethnicity and national origin became difficult to justify.[10]

But could not the government make a distinction between discrimination against minorities residing in Canada with citizenship and extending citizenship rights to non-European foreigners wanting to migrate to Canada? Today, no one makes this distinction, but assumes, as this article at the Canadian Museum of Immigration at Pier, that discriminating against Canadian citizens on the basis of race is the same as employing racial criteria against potential immigrants without citizenship. More than this, today the entire establishment assumes that Canada must welcome immigrants and eagerly strive for racial diversification if it is to live up to its "liberal ideals".

The politicians who legislated the 1962 Regulations were not as pathological. In fact, a central immigration reformer during this time, W.R. Baskerville, felt comfortable admitting that despite the abolition of racial criteria, Canada would "still give preference" in the selection of immigrants "to those countries which have traditionally supplied [its] immigrants".[11] Moreover, in official but not publicized papers, it was specified that immigrants from non-European countries would only be allowed to sponsor members of their immediate family, whereas European immigrants would be allowed to sponsor relatives as well. Canadian officials also voiced the view that there was nothing in the

---

10   "Immigration Regulations, Order-in-Council PC 1962-86, 1962", http://www.
      pier21.ca/research/immigration-history/immigration-regulations-order-in-
      council-pc-1962-86-1962

11   As cited in Jonathan Tepperman, *The Fix: How Nations Survive and Thrive in a World
      of Decline* (Duggan Books, 2016), p. 59.

Regulations prohibiting Canada from focusing on the recruitment of immigrants from European created nations.

Overall, no one envisioned these Regulations as a way of transforming Canada away from its Anglo-European heritage. The emphasis on skills, it was expected, would limit immigrants from Third World nations lacking modern educational facilities and industrial skills. The Canadian government still had a concept of the political, a sense that Canada was in charge of deciding which group of immigrants would suit the interests of British Canada. While it no longer voiced its right to decide its racial character, it did interpret these Regulations as consistent with the right of the government to refuse "immigrants whose presence would cause severe disruptions or drastic change". [12]

However, the spiral of radicalization built into the norms of racial equality, civic nationalism, human rights for everyone, could not be appeased. External governments with a strong sense of the political, heavily ethnocentric, were only too pleased to request answers from the Canadian government as to why the Regulations of 1962 were sill discriminatory in their exclusion of non-Europeans from sponsoring family relatives. Accordingly, governments in the West Indies, in South America, in Africa, Pakistan and China, demanded to know why Canadian officials were not eagerly seeking immigrants outside Canada's European sources of immigration. Accepting this pressure, in November 1965, Prime Minister Lester Pearson promised to remove all remaining barriers in the acceptance of immigrants of colour. Canada's government wanted to avoid "strong resentments in international relations". [13] This same year the majestic Canadian Red Ensign and Union Jack flag was replaced when Parliament approved the Maple Leaf flag. This was a symbolic break with the British past and with Canada's Britishness. The Maple Leaf would be a flag without any ethno-Anglocentric nationalistic symbolism.

The 1962 Regulations and the Maple Leaf flag both reflected the inherent weakness of the concept of the political among liberal politicians, and the further weakening of this concept, making it ever more difficult for Canadian leaders to affirm their ethno-cultural

---

12 As cited in Triadafilos Triadafilopoulos, *Becoming Multicultural: Immigration and the Politics of Membership in Canada and Germany*, p. 94.

13 *Ibid*, p. 98.

identity, and thus to stop the spiral of radicalization. Instead, the weaker Canada's political identity became, the stronger the spiral would become. Once these Regulations were passed, immigration would be judged strictly in terms of skilled versus unskilled immigrants, educated versus uneducated immigrants, and the overall benefits they could bring to Canada's economy.

Immigration Regulations 1967

Canada was a wonderful country in 1967, an idyllic and naively happy country, oblivious to the dark spiralling clouds gathering momentum on the horizon. For the Anglo elites Canada was not yet humanitarian enough. Caught up with the norm that progress required the obliteration of any sense of collective identity among Euro-Canadians, they decided to dismantle the last remaining "racist" trait in the 1962 Immigration Regulations, the exclusion of non-Europeans from sponsoring family relatives.

The Immigration Regulations of 1967 were enacted in the face of mounting pressure from both domestic groups, and from Commonwealth "freedom loving" countries in Africa, the Caribbean, and Asia. These countries demanded that Canada live up to its international advocacy of human rights and its membership within a Commonwealth of nationalities deemed to be equal and racist-free.

The 1967 Regulations were purely liberal in the economic sense, without any reference to the cultural needs and character of Canada, based solely on "a points system" in which immigrant applicants were given a score according to education and training, personal character, occupational demand, occupational skill, age, pre-arranged employment, knowledge of French and English, the presence of a relative in Canada, and employment opportunities in their area of destination.

Those with a score showing they could be beneficial to Canada's economic requirements would be accepted. Immigrants from white nations would now enjoy the same rights of sponsorship as immigrants from any other part of the world. The immediate family members of all accepted immigrants could be sponsored, while distant relatives would undergo the same points system evaluation. Immigration processing facilities would be opened outside Europe.

Kelley and Trebilcock observed that the Regulations of 1962 and 1967 "quickly led to a dramatic change in the composition of Canada's immigration intake, with Asia becoming the leading source of immigrants by the end of the period". They note that after these Regulations the proportion of immigrants coming from Asia and the Caribbean "increased dramatically, from 10 percent in 1965-6 to 23 percent in 1969-70". [14] The 1967 Regulations were soon felt in a very significant increase in the total number of immigrants, with approximately 525,000 arriving just between 1972 and 1974.

The apprehension among Canadians about this sudden arrival of people from very different cultures was such that in 1975 the government decided to organize public hearings, which led to the tabling of the so-called Green Paper in the House of Commons. The key message of the Green Paper was that Canadians were "concerned about the consequences for national identity that might follow any significant change in the composition of the population". [15] They wondered whether the arrival of "new racial groups into the population [might] outstripped the ability" of Canadians with each other in a harmonious way.

When the Green Paper was released, a Special Joint Committee received close to 2,000 letters of opinion, formal briefs, and oral testimonies from Canadians, with a high majority, 83 percent, demanding firmer controls on immigration from the "Third World". In what seems like a very different age, writers during this consultation process were unafraid to state openly that Third World immigration would alter "Canada's racial composition" and destroy Canada's "distinct national identity". Some even demanded the deportation of all non-whites and the restriction of immigrants to Anglo and Nordic countries only.

These were not the opinions of marginal individuals out of touch with the majority of Canadians. Gallup polls in the 1960s, let me repeat to readers again, showed that two thirds of Canadians were

---

14   Ninette Kelley, Michael Trebilcock, *The Making of the Mosaic. A History of Canadian Immigration Policy*, p. 354.

15   Triadafilos Triadafilopoulos, *Becoming Multicultural: Immigration and the Politics of Membership in Canada and Germany*, p. 111.

against bringing any immigrants, and thought that the levels of Asian immigration at the time were already too high. In the 1970s, Canadians were still holding these views. Relentless brainwashing of our children was not yet a reality. This would happen with incredible acceleration from about the mid-1980s, or during the 1990s, pushing the spiral ever more in a truly pathological, self-hating direction.

Ethnic Group Interests and the Discovery of the Ethnic Vote

The views expressed in these polls should hardly surprise us. Current research abundantly shows that ethnic groups throughout history have exhibited a preference for their own kind, and a disposition to judge other ethnic out-groups by their own in-group standards. This preference is a healthy and practical evaluation of one's ethnic identity and interests consistent with evolutionary theory. Now, this disposition is less marked among Northern Europeans. As Kevin MacDonald has written, Europeans evolved cultures with a strong individualist orientation, monogamous nuclear families, less emphasis on kinship relations and more on contractual relations. This individualism encouraged a "relatively low ethnocentrism" and a high level of "moral universalism". [16]

This European culture, particularly with the emergence of modern liberalism, the Enlightenment with its universal credo about the "rights of man", followed by the spread of the norms examined earlier, has been inclined to be less in-group oriented. It has also been inclined to the universal notion that members from highly collectivist cultures will relinquish their millennial, genetically-based heritage, once they get socialized within European individualist cultures. Liberals with a weak concept of the political think that all humans have a natural disposition to act as individuals in open markets, carry contractual relations based on trust with members outside their extended families, so long as they are given the opportunity to do so.

They don't realize that non-Europeans, as MacDonald shows, evolved in ecological contexts that "supported large tribal groups based on

---

16 Kevin MacDonald, "What Makes Western Cultures Unique?" http://www. kevinmacdonald.net/WesternOrigins.htm

extended kinship relations" where individualism was suppressed.[17] They don't realize that non-Europeans never developed liberal institutions based on the equal application of the law regardless of one's social rank, separation of church and state, and freedom of expression and association. Non-Europeans developed cultures with a strong ethnocentric disposition, extended family units, and far stronger in-group behaviors and out-group derogation. Still, the general Euro-Canadian public did have ethnocentric dispositions in the 1970s, did have a sense that "British liberties" could not be assimilated by non-Europeans, even as human rights and "anti-racist" norms were starting to spread rapidly from the top down, pushed by "progressive" elites and legislated by politicians.

What reveals how far the Canadian state had moved away from the concept of the political by the 1970s is the fact that the only individuals the political elites took seriously during the consultations carried by the Special Joint Committee were the members of the organized delegations of ethnic groups against "racists and bigots in Canada". Twenty-nine East Indian associations, the "Immigration Policy Action Community of the Vancouver Chinese Community", among others, defended the 1967 Regulations, and went beyond in calling for the expansion of sponsorship rights, while insisting that Canada was no longer a nation of two founding peoples, the English and French, but a nation of multiple cultures and races.

While the Special Joint Committee recommended that immigration be reduced to about 100,000 per year, as a way of appeasing critics for the time being, it not only emphasized the continuation of the 1967 Regulations, but called for the re-education (read, re-engineering of the souls) of Canadians, backed by funding of community programs to promote "inter-cultural understanding", as well as amplification of human right's legislation in order to "protect Canadians and immigrants from racial and ethnic discrimination". What is even more revealing about the radicalizing effects of the spiral during these years, and the ever weakening of any collective ethnic identity among Canadian elites, was the way MPs serving on this Joint Committee were impressed by the "vote-mobilizing ability of minority ethnic

17   Ibid.

organizations"[18] and the fact that ethnic groups represented the largest percentage of the groups that appeared before the Committee. Instead of pondering over the stronger sense of political grouping and identity among non-white immigrants, the liberal elites, the Liberal Party in power during these years, concluded the opposite: Canada should not impose tighter immigration controls, but should exploit the support of these groups by promoting mass immigration, never mind what the founding peoples were expressing in polls about their cultural dispossession. This was the beginning of what would become a major force in its own right accelerating the spiral: the rise, and the promotion by Canada's parties, of ethnic voting blocs against the ethnic interests of Euro-Canadians.

Nevertheless, we are getting ahead of ourselves. It is important to understand that the Immigration Regulations of 1967, notwithstanding their complete abolition of any racial traces in their stipulations, were not conceived with a view to bringing about a radical alteration in the ethnic composition of Canada. The expectation among politicians then was that it would be very difficult, from a practical sense, for Third World nations to generate immigrants with the skills and points necessary to apply for admission to Canada. The leaders of all the major parties agreed with these Regulations, and their state of mind was that Canada had met its obligations to the human rights expectations and non-racist norms of the times.

The radicalizing spiral, however, would gain more intensity as the sixties came to an end and the 1970s began, leading to the 1971 declaration that Canada was a multicultural nation.

---

18   Triadafilos Triadafilopoulos, *Becoming Multicultural: Immigration and the Politics of Membership in Canada and Germany*, p. 116.

16

Pierre Trudeau's Assault on Bicultural Nationalism

Between 1963 and 1969 the Royal Commission on Bilingualism and Biculturalism organized hearings across the nation

> to inquire into and report upon the existing state of bilingualism and biculturalism in Canada and to recommend what steps should be taken to develop the Canadian Confederation on the basis of an equal partnership between the two founding races, taking into account the contribution made by the other ethnic groups to the cultural enrichment of Canada and the measures that should be taken to safeguard that contribution". [1]

The current establishment view about this Commission's goal is that it was intended "to convince English-speaking Canadians that full-fledged recognition of French-Canadian cultural and linguistic rights was desirable". [2] However, rather than this bureaucratic interpretation, which says that the aim was to promote better cultural relations between the Anglophone and Francophone communities, help Canadians become bilingual in English and French, and, in this way, work out a solution to the threat of separatist nationalism in Quebec, I would emphasize the spirit of Canadian bicultural nationalism embodied in the Commission's work. Unfortunately, despite the Commission's recommendation for a bicultural identity, the increasingly globalized elites of the late 1960s and early 1970s decided to ignore this recommendation in the name of an artificially constructed multicultural identity open to branch-plant American capitalism. The corporate globalized establishment, together with leftists enamored with Expo and a world without strong

---

1   *A Preliminary Report of the Royal Commission on Bilingualism and Biculturalism.* 1965. (Ottawa: Queen's Printer). This report is archived in Government of Canada Publications, http://publications.gc.ca/site/archivee-archived.html?url=http://publications.gc.ca/collections/collection_2014/bcp-pco/Z1-1963-1-5-1-1-eng.pdf

2   Howard Palmer, "Reluctant Hosts: Anglo-Canadian Views of Multiculturalism in the Twentieth Century", in Gerald Tulchinsky, *Immigration in Canada: Historical Perspectives* (Copp Clark Longman, 1994), p. 317.

national identities, ignored the wishes of the Commission's expression of the majority opinion of a Canadian public that was still nationalistic in the 1960s, not in a nationalism based on Anglo conformity but in a bicultural nationalism unafraid to declare that Canada was made up of two "dominant" cultures.

The Quebecois were still quite ethnocentric in their national identity, but English Canadians did hope that, by emphasizing the founding dominance of both French and English peoples, a bicultural solution to Quebec separation could be found. Prominent French-Canadian critics of Trudeau's multiculturalism, such as Claude Ryan and Guy Rocher, agreed that biculturalism was an accurate reflection of the bilingual and bicultural reality of Canada. The bicultural recommendation, however, would never come to fruition. The spiral of radicalization was in full swing between 1963 and 1969, not only were non-Europeans arriving in numbers higher than ever, but the Anglo elites were more interested in American branch-plant capitalism than in accentuating Canada's bicultural heritage. Trudeau understood this, and so in 1971 he rejected Canada's bicultural identity in the name of a civic multicultural identity.

Cultural Nationalism Versus Ethnic and Civic Nationalism

What is cultural nationalism? Wikipedia, notwithstanding its leftist orientation, provides a short and efficient conceptual mapping in stating that cultural nationalism occupies "an intermediate position between ethnic nationalism on one hand and liberal nationalism on the other". [3] Cultural nationalism focuses "on a national identity shaped by cultural traditions and by language", unlike ethnic nationalism, which focuses on common descent, blood or kinship; and unlike liberal (or civic) nationalism, which focuses on the "Western" values of freedom, tolerance, and equality.

In the standard literature to which Wikipedia subscribes, civic nationalism is seen as the most "inclusive" nationalism for its claim that a nation can be liberal only if it advocates the inclusion of multiple ethnicities and cultures. But if I may play around with

---

3   "Cultural Nationalism", https://en.wikipedia.org/wiki/Cultural_nationalism

leftist pretensions, ethnic nationalism is the most inclusive since a nation that focuses on ethnic ancestry will automatically focus on the cultural traditions of those ethnic group(s) which have a true historical ancestry in the nation; and, if this nation happens to be liberal in its values and institutions, it will also emphasize equal individual rights in its national identity. In contrast, cultural nationalism does not tolerate ethnic nationalism, though it does tolerate civic nationalism insomuch as liberal values may be part of the nation's culture. Civic nationalism, on the other hand, is intolerant against both ethnic and cultural nationalism.

Earlier I defined Canadian nationalism up until the early 1960s using the term "ethnic liberalism". With the 1962/1967 Regulations, every remaining trace of ethnic nationalism was officially discarded in Canada, though it should be noted that the Quebecois then were a people with a strong sense of ethnic identity, even as the Immigration Regulations, and other human rights legislation, were demanding that Quebec, as a province, forego its "racist" nationalism. Unlike the rather homogeneous race of French Canadians, what still stood out among English Canadians in the 1960s, though in a diluted way, socially and institutionally, was their sense of cultural nationalism, a sense of Britishness made up of English ethnicities from the British Isles. This cultural nationalism was quite accepting of Quebec's foundational role, as well as open to continental European immigrants. In the 1950s and 1960s a wave of Mediterranean immigrants were welcomed. It was also a nationalism which, in the words of George Grant, saw in Canada a "stronger sense of the common good and of public order than was possible under the individualism of the American capitalist dream". [4] This Canadian cultural nationalism came out of a tradition of British Tory conservatism, a tradition that was barely existent in Britain by the 1960s, but which the Canadian Anglo majority still subscribed to, in combination with a host of unique traits nurtured in the cold soil of Canada, folkways, songs, amusements, historical experiences. This Anglo nationalism recognized that Canadians included other European ethnic groups rooted in Canada, and that in Canada there was another founding people, the Quebecois, with a very different culture in the province of Quebec.

---

4   George Grant, *Lament For A Nation. The Defeat of Canadian Nationalism* (Carleton Library Edition, [1965] 1970), p. x.

American Globalism and the Defeat
of Canadian Nationalism

The Royal Commission reflected this bicultural nationalism in its Report. However, during the years these hearings were conducted, from 1963 to 1969, the spiral was gaining much ground under the auspices of American global capitalism. Conservative Prime Minister John Diefenbaker was utterly defeated early in 1963, after winning a solid majority in 1957, along with his folksy prairie sentiments, or what remained of his cultural nationalism, always confusedly weak, as testified by his passage of the Canadian Bill of Rights of 1960, which undercut further Canada's historic allegiance to British liberties, the idea that Canadians had liberties as members of a British Canada, not as member of the human race.

Under Prime Minister Lester Pearson (1963-1968), the Canadian nationalist Red Ensign flag was replaced by the generic Maple Leaf in concert with the submission of Canada's economy under American globalism. Hitherto Canada's identity had been able to manifest itself co-extensively with British rule and cultural ties. In 1900, while 85 per cent of foreign capital invested in Canada was owned in Great Britain, this capital, and British investments generally through the 19th century, came largely "in the form of debt that was paid back and concentrated in railways, construction of utilities and funding of governments". [5] In other words, British capital served the making of Canada as a nation across a huge landmass. American investments in the 20th century, in contrast, were directly controlled by American companies, "allowing permanent ownership and control of enterprises". While the British share in 1955 had declined to 17 per cent, the US share had mushroomed to 77 per cent. A report of the Task Force on the Structure of Canadian Industry, the Watkins Report, published in 1968, the year Pearson ended his tenure, concluded that "the extent of foreign control of Canadian industry is unique among the industrialized nations of the world». [6]

---

5 "Canada-US Economic Relations" *The Canadian Encyclopedia*, http://www. thecanadianencyclopedia.ca/en/article/economic-canadian-american-relations/

6 As cited in Mel Watkins, *Staples and Beyond: Selected Writings of Mel Watkins*, edited by Hugh Grant and David Wolfe (McGill-Queen's Press, 2006), p.110. See also Kari Levitt, *Silent Surrender: the multinational corporation in Canada (McGill-Queen's Press, 2002)*. Chapter 1, "The Recolonization of Canada", covers the early 1960s and Pearson's capitulation to American corporate capital.

Through the 1950s and with intensity during the 1960s Anglo Canadian elites willingly bought into the "progressive" nature of American corporate internationalism and its agenda of consumerism and abstract individual rights without a nationalistic sense of the common good. Much as the conservatives tried to fight for a sense of Canadian identity and public good, by creating Ontario Hydro, the Canadian National Railway, and the Canadian Broadcasting Corporation, they could not withstand American globalism. Instead, the socialist liberals in Canada appropriated the concept of the common good while depriving it of any cultural content. The common good was reduced to progressive taxation for the purpose of promoting working class internationalism and human rights in a Canada open to the whole world.

At the same time, the 1962 and 1967 Regulations were having immediate effects in the ethnic composition of the immigrants as the hearings on biculturalism were being conducted, making Canada multi-cultural. This Commission, in fact, underwent some crucial changes in its use of language and in its objectives, during and after the regional and public hearings held across Canada in 1964 and 1965. By the time the full report of the commissioners was assessed and deliberated upon between 1969 and 1971, the Commission's starting objective was radically transformed from an effort to acknowledge the "Bicultural" character of Canada into an announcement by Prime Minister Trudeau that Canada was a "Multicultural" nation.

Royal Commission on Bilingualism and Biculturalism

Reading the *Report of the Royal Commission on Bilingualism and Biculturalism, General Introduction, Book I, The Official Languages*, published in 1967, we find that it takes issue right from the start with the use of the term "founding races", a term long used by historians and by government officials since Confederation, in reference to the British and French founding peoples, not in order to differentiate these two groups in biological terms but used interchangeably with "nationality". Canadians were always aware that the French and the English were two strong national peoples constantly fighting each other, though both Christian and original members of the European continent. But by the time this Report was written, the term "race" had been discredited, and so the Report was signalling to its audience that it was abandoning this term, clearly stating that in its terms of reference "there is no mention of race, people, or ethnic group but 'of the basically bicultural character of our country and of the subsequent contribution made by other cultures.'"[7]

The *Report*, in other words, was saying that it preferred to use the term "culture" to distinguish different peoples. However, at the same time, the *Report* does not discard altogether the term "ethnic group", not only because it is a term used "in both popular and academic language" but also a term that "expresses a sense of identity that a group has in terms of common origin and mainly in the biological sense, whether this origin is real or imaginary". This term, the *Report* ads, corresponds to certain realities of heredity and ancestry and "the feeling of belonging to an ethnic group", although this feeling "varies significantly from one group to another". [8]

Yet, as one reads carefully between the lines of the section entitled "The Key Words of the Terms of Reference", the transpiring message is that the term "ethnic group" will be used in reference to groups that are not Anglophone or Francophone. There is a section on the "the contribution of other ethnic groups" to Canada, with the implicit awareness that besides the English and French, there are "other ethnic groups" in Canada, and that the members of these groups have a strong sense of ethnic lineage.

In contrast, the *Report* identifies Anglophone and Francophone communities as "cultures», and calls Canada "bi-cultural" on the grounds that these are the two founding cultures, the "two great, distinct cultures in our country...the two dominant cultures in Canada...embodied in distinct societies". To its credit, the *Report* takes seriously the meaning of culture, the way in which culture affects "the group's manner of thinking and acting», and the fact that both the French and the English possess distinct institutions, languages, and traditions. A truly bicultural Canada is one in which members of both founding cultures enjoy equal

---

7   *Report of the Royal Commission on Bilingualism and Biculturalism, General Introduction, Book I, The Official Languages*, (Queen's Printer and Controller of Stationary, Ottawa, Canada, 1967), pp. xxi-lii.

8   *Ibid.*

partnership in participating in the nation. The commissioners were aware that the Quebecois did have a stronger sense of ethnic ancestry than English Canadians, but the hope was that by including Quebec as an equal partner in the making of "bicultural" Canada, this ethnic and separatist nationalism would be mitigated.

Liberalism lacks a concept of the political, of the idea that a political state is a collectivity of people with similar ancestry. In the face of the new norms of human rights, race is a construct, and ethnic nationalism is bad, British and French Canadians were expected to forego their ethnic attachments. On the other hand, we have just seen that the *Report* implicitly recognized that non-British and non-French groups were still strongly attached to their ethnicity. Herein we have in embryo a justification for our current policy of multiculturalism, embodied in the theory of Kymlicka, which recognizes the ethnic group identities of non-Europeans, as well as their individual rights, but only the individual rights of Euro-Canadians. The *Report*, however, did emphasize the collective and "dominant" bicultural identity of Canadians.[9] But this emphasis was short-lived, soon to be discarded in the name of multiculturalism.

During these hearings, when Canada's European population constituted about 97% of the total population, and when ethnic groups consisted of other Europeans, the commissioners had no idea they were in the midst of a spiral acquiring ever more momentum, one that was about to question even the "bicultural" character of the nation. They could not even anticipate that a mere few years after the release

---

9 Some interpreters, distracted by views expressed in Book IV of the Commission's Report on the "other ethnic groups", have concluded that "rather than support biculturalism, the Commission supported the recognition of a multiplicity of ethnic and cultural communities as part of a larger Canadian public". See John von Heyking and Elise Ray working paper, "Multiculturalism and Problems of Canadian Unity", University of Lethbridge, https://www.uleth.ca/dspace/bitstream/handle/10133/3268/Multiculturalism-Bavaria-Paper-2%200.pdf?sequence=1. I side with Howard Palmer's view that Book IV, which I cited in Chapter 3, "was commissioned as something of an afterthought" in response to an "ethnic backlash" against the commissioner's supposition that "other ethnic groups" were not as important. And, as Palmer adds, they took account of other ethnic groups "within the framework of biculturalism: ethnic minorities maintaining their cultural identity within the context of two dominant societies". Howard Palmer, "Reluctant Hosts: Anglo-Canadian Views of Multiculturalism in the Twentieth Century", pp. 317-18. The full citation, again, for Book IV is: "*Report of the Royal Commission on Bilingualism and Biculturalism, Book IV, The Contribution of the Other Ethnic Groups (Queen's Printer for Canada, 1970)*", which can be found in Government of Canada Publications, http://publications.gc.ca/site/eng/472354/publication.html

of the recommendations, under Pierre Trudeau's leadership, Canada would be redefined as a nation by and for individuals from all the cultures of the world.

Trudeau's Anti-Nationalism

Among current efforts to explain Pierre Trudeau's adoption of multiculturalism we have the following claims:

- Trudeau saw a multicultural Canada as a way to defuse French Canadian nationalism by making the Quebecois no more than one ethnic group among many others;

- Trudeau was responding and agreeing with the arguments mobilized by ethnic minorities, particularly the Ukrainians, that a Canada defined as a "bicultural" nation relegated other ethnic groups to a secondary status;

- It was a strategy devised by the Liberal Party to gain the ethnic vote from a Canada that had opened its borders to the world after the Immigration Regulations of 1962 and 1967.

What is missing here is Trudeau's determination to weaken the cultural domination Anglo Canadians had over the national identity of Canada. In rejecting the "biculturalism" recommended by the Royal Commission, and announcing in October 1971 that Canada's official identity was multicultural, Trudeau was rejecting both the French Canadian claim that they had a collective right to a unique nation, and the English Canadian identification of the rest of Canada with "Anglo culture".

Coming to intellectual maturity in the late 1940s and 1950s, Trudeau absorbed the strong animus in Western societies against the racial nationalism of Germany, and, by extension, against any form of nationalism. In their biography, *Trudeau and Our Times, Vol. 1: The Magnificent Obsession*, Stephen Clarkson and Christina McCall sum up well his anti-nationalism:

For him, nationalism was historically regressive, a force that was responsible for the worst wars in history. It was unacceptable, in his view, to exalt collective political claims at the cost of individual human rights.[10]

Clarkson and McCall, however, limit their understanding of Trudeau's anti-nationalism to his opposition to French-Canadian nationalism. He certainly directed most of his energies against French nationalists because they were the ones agitating during these days for a separate Quebec, but Trudeau's multicultural vision was also meant to undercut the identification of the Canadian nation state with Anglo-Canadians.

For Trudeau, the atrocities of the Second World War were inherent to the very nature of nationalism itself. The "very idea of the nation state is absurd", he wrote in possibly his best essay, "The New Treason of the Intellectuals", published in *Cité Libre* in 1962.[11] While Trudeau acknowledged that "nationalism was...the child of liberal democracy and the mystique of equality", he observed that an inescapable reality in the creation of nation states was the identification of the nation with an ethnic majority to the exclusion of other ethnic groups. This identification resulted in a situation in which minorities would always be striving to carve out their own states against the majority, and indeed against other minorities within their own lands, leading to constant tension and divisions.

Moreover, history had also shown that once nation-states were created, the ideals of freedom and equality tended to be pushed to the side by a state authority claiming to be the sovereign agent in charge of the interests of the nation. In this situation, it was only natural for those leaders with strong nations "to seek to rule over weaker peoples", in the name of their people.

For Trudeau, this history was apparent in the English conquest of Quebec, and the way the English, "the most nationalist of nationalists", imposed their "Anglo-Saxon language and customs"

---

10   Stephen Clarkson and Christina McCall, *Trudeau and Our Times, Vol. 1: The Magnificent Obsession* (McClelland & Stewart, 1990), p. 82.

11   This essay is available online, all the following citations from Trudeau come from this essay: https://docs.google.com/document/d/1CChvPQwRJWj02WN3nur7jKr9nwj8a BgPKzSliSIbMpY/edit?pli=1#heading=h.gwl098qh9ien

on the Quebecois, expecting them to assimilate, treating them with condescension, inventing "all kinds of stratagems by which democracy was made to mean government by the minority" in French speaking lands. Then, as the English grew in numbers, and the rest of Canada became populated with English speakers through immigration laws that "favour[ed] immigrants from the British Isles over those from France", the English "took to hiding their intolerance behind acts of majority rule", suppressing "bilingualism in the Manitoba legislature, violating "rights acquired by separate schools in various provinces", and "savagely" imposing conscription in 1917, and much more.

This aggressive Anglo-Canadian cultural nationalism was responsible for the emergence of French-Canadian nationalism. Canadians had to make up their minds, according to Trudeau, either accept a Canada incessantly divided by Anglo and French nationalisms, or reject both these two parochial choices and strive instead to make Canada into a "multi-national state". Much as he understood the historical roots of Quebecois anger against Anglo cultural arrogance, Trudeau condemned French-Canadian nationalism as another form of cultural arrogance bedevilled by similar flaws as Anglo nationalism, "an emotional and prejudiced" movement that would close-off Quebec from other nationalities, privilege the Quebecois above other ethnic minorities within, and destroy the chance of creating the first democratic "polyethnic" state in Canada.

The conclusion Trudeau reached was that Canadian leaders "must separate once and for all the concepts of state and nation". The meaning of this statement cannot be underestimated. He meant that no one ethnic group, neither the Anglo in Canada at large nor the Quebecois in Quebec, must lay claim over Canada's cultural identity. Just as religion was separated from the state, so must culture be separated from the state. Canada must be identified as a "polyethnic society" and in this way Canada will truly become a liberal-democratic society.

Trudeau was very vague as to how this polyethnic society would govern itself, other than to say that within a federal government:

> different regions within the country must be assured of a wide range of local autonomy, such that each national group, with an increasing background of experience in self-government, may be able to

develop the body of laws and institutions essential to the fullest expression and development of their national characteristics.[12]

What exactly does it mean to say that "each national group" in Canada (just French and English, or also Aboriginals and other ethnic nationalities?) "must be assured of a wide range of local autonomy", jurisdictions where they will be able to develop "laws and institutions" "essential to the fullest expression of their national characteristics"? We will see in future parts that to this day no one is sure what multiculturalism entails as far as jurisdictional powers and local autonomy are concerned.

The point I like to highlight here is what Trudeau says about Anglo-Canadians, his expectation that:

> English Canadians, with their own nationalism, will have to retire gracefully to their proper place, consenting to modify their own precious image of what Canada ought to be. If they care to protect and realize their own special ethnic qualities, they should do it within this framework of regional and local autonomy rather than a pan-Canadian one.[13]

Rejection of Bicultural Nationalism

We can see why Trudeau's vision for Canada was inconsistent with the recommendations of the Royal Commission. These recommendations aimed to defuse French Canadian nationalism within a federal Canada that was multiethnic with all Canadians enjoying the same individual rights, and Trudeau could work with that; but not with the notion that Canada was "bicultural".

It was not only, as many have argued, that Trudeau viewed Quebec nationalism as a greater collectivist threat to Canada than the commissioners believed it to be. For him both this nationalism and Anglo nationalism would continue to plague Canada if this nation was identified as a bicultural nation consisting of "two dominant cultures". Although

---

12   *Ibid.*

13   *Ibid.*

he did not advocate multiculturalism in the early 1960s, he did say that any nation that prioritizes the ethno-culture of the dominant group, and thereby establishes a nationalism that elevates the interests of this group (the French Canadians in Quebec, or the English and the French in Canada) above the interests of minorities, cannot be truly polyethnic and democratic. As he wrote in "New Treason of the Intellectuals",

> A truly democratic government cannot be nationalist because it must pursue the interest of all its citizens, without prejudice to ethnic origin.

There is no question that in announcing that Canada was "multicultural", Trudeau was voicing the views of a "multicultural movement" that was already percolating its ideas into the Canadian political discourse, what Lee Blanding has referred to as a "loosely organized group of activists who pushed the Federal Government to recognize that Canada was 'multicultural,' rather than 'bicultural,' between 1960 and 1971", with Ukrainian Canadians acting as "the driving force behind [this] multicultural movement". [14] While it is difficult to detect a coherent ideology from this movement, it would not be off the mark to say that during the 1960s certain members of the Canadian intellectual elite were of the view that a Canada that privileged the two "founding peoples" was a Canada that saw other ethnic groups as less Canadian, a Canada that underestimated the contributions of other ethnic groups, and a Canada that was no longer accurately describing the multiethnic character of the nation.

Trudeau was voicing these ideas, using the term "polyethnic", in a more intellectually developed manner already in the early 1960s, and then in a more politically direct way as the Prime Minister in 1971, when he responded to the Royal Commission that "biculturalism does not

---

14   Lee Blanding, "Re-branding Canada: The Origins of Canadian Multiculturalism Policy, 1945-1974", A Dissertation Submitted in Partial Fulfillment of the Requirements for the Degree of Doctor of Philosophy (University of Victoria, Department of History, 2013), https://dspace.library.uvic.ca:8443/bitstream/handle/1828/4736/Blanding_Lee_PhD_2013.pdf Miriam Verena Richter observes that almost simultaneously, Charles Hobart, a sociology professor at the University of Alberta, and Paul Yuzyk, professor of Slavic Studies at the University of Manitoba, began to speak of Canada as a multicultural society in a number of meetings in 1964 and 1965. See *Creating the National Mosaic. Multiculturalism in Canadian Children's Literature from 1950 to 1994* (Editions Rodopi B.V. Amsterdam, 2011), p. 36.

properly describe our society; multiculturalism is more accurate".[15] In calling Canada a multicultural state, he was saying that the Canadian nation should not be identified with the culture of either the English or the French ethnic group. Beyond the official languages of English and French, Canada should be seen as a nation based on liberal-democratic values, rather than as a nation founded and dominated by the cultural values and traditions of English Canadians and French Canadians.

The contributions of "other ethnic groups" would not just be acknowledged; Canada would henceforth cease to identify itself as an Anglo nation, and Quebec too would be encouraged to see itself as culturally diverse. Trudeau's point was not that multiple cultures would compete to claim Canada's identity or to claim territories within Canada as theirs. It was that individuals would be free to choose their cultural identity; the only expectation on the part of the government would be to ensure that all Canadians learned the official languages and accepted the values of multicultural liberalism. There would be two official languages but no official culture and therefore no privileging of the culture of any ethnic group.

Although he never defined the terms, the meanings of ethnic, cultural, and civic nationalism, and to this day no one has adequately drawn any distinctions between these terms in relation to Trudeau's writings and policies, it can be safely stated that he envisioned a Canada that was based on civic values, not values associated with the culture of a particular people, but political values deemed to be universal and acceptable by all humans regardless of race and religion. Trudeau thus pushed the spiral beyond a rejection of the ethnic nationalism already rejected in the Immigration Regulations of 1962/67. Not only race (the "White man's country" of the pre-WWII years) and ethnicity (Canada is a British/ Quebecois nation) would be separated from the concept of the political, from the identity of the nation, so would culture (Canada is a nation populated by people with a shared French and Anglo culture).

This constituted a further breakdown in the concept of the political in Canada, since the political hinges fundamentally on a sense of grouping by a people claiming a territorial state as their homeland on

---

15   Hugh Donald Forbes, "Trudeau as the First Theorist of Canadian Multiculturalism", in Stephen Tierney, *Multiculturalism and the Canadian Constitution* (UBC Press, 2007), p. 30.

grounds of ethnic and cultural ancestry. The only remaining concept of the political was a liberal ideas-based conception. Canada would henceforth be a nation with a core constitutional identity, official languages, coupled with certain holidays, symbols, and institutional procedures. And yet the spiral would not stop but would gain more momentum in the coming years.

17

The Trudeau Years and the Charter of Rights

Whenever Canadians, from politicians to academics, are asked what makes their nation unique, they invariably answer "Canada's multiculturalism and diversity". Don't they know this is increasingly the same answer coming out of most nations in the West? Canada is now a dime a dozen. But it cannot be denied that Canada produced the first Western leader, Pierre Trudeau, who envisioned a constitutional framework, however vague, for the integration of multiple cultures within one nation-state. As early as 1962, in "The New Treason of the Intellectuals", he insisted that Canada was already in possession of a federal constitutional framework, two major nationalities each with their own legal systems and representative bodies, together with other ethnic groups, for the further development of a consciously intended multicultural order in which the government would forego any association with a particular culture and make culture a private affair, much as religion had already become a personal choice across the West.

He further argued that creating a Canada without a collective cultural identity, an Anglo-Quebecois identity, would make this nation a model for the solution of ethnic strife and nationalist aggrandizement across the world:

> Canada could offer an example to all those new Asian and African states...who must discover how to govern their poly-ethnic populations with proper regard for justice and liberty... Canadian federalism is an experiment of major proportions...a brilliant prototype for the moulding of tomorrow's civilization.[1]

It was with this idea in mind that in 1971 he rejected bicultural nationalism for a multicultural identity. Trudeau, we have already noted, was imprecise in his writings and policy announcements about

---

1   "Treason of the Intellectuals", https://docs.google.com/document/d/1CChvPQwRJWj 02WN3nur7jKr9nwj8aBgPKzSliSIbMpY/edit?pli=1#heading=h.gwl098qh9ien

the nature of the powers that different cultural groups would enjoy within the federation. Would culture really be a personal choice, or would it entail giving "every ethnic group" the right to develop its own collective culture within the federation? He did say in his 1971 announcement:

> We believe that cultural pluralism is the very essence of Canadian identity. Every ethnic group has the right to preserve and develop its own culture and values within the Canadian context.[2]

Did he mean that the Canadian federation would allow each province of Canada, with their respective ethnic mixtures, the local autonomy it needed to achieve its cultural and economic goals, with Quebec using its provincial powers to maintain its linguistic and cultural characteristics, without imposing Quebecois culture upon all its residents? Or did he mean that each ethnic group, Muslims, Sikhs, Hindus, would be given the constitutional right to enjoy, in the language of New Treason of Intellectuals, a "wide range of local autonomy", or territorial powers?

We know that he did recognize "two official languages" in Canada, but insisted there was "no official culture". Believing that the acceptance of an official culture would entail the "precedence" of the English and the Quebecois "over" other ethnic groups, he concluded that the properly liberal way was to decouple culture from the state and the nation's historical identity. The liberal democratic institutions of Canada would be envisioned as purely civic in character rather than as creations of particular cultures. In affirming the right of every ethnic group to "develop its own culture and values" he could not possibly have been calling upon all ethnic groups to develop themselves as nationalities. He was likely saying that the government of Canada would institute policies to protect immigrants from discrimination by the existing majority cultures, avoid a melting pot in which immigrants and minorities would be compelled to assimilate to a majority Anglo or Quebecois culture, and instead allow minorities to express their distinctive identities, while encouraging them to blend into a larger liberal multicultural nation in which everyone's cultural identity would eventually become a private choice.

---

2   This is a regularly cited statement.

Multiculturalism: A Program for the Future

We shall return later to the varying, conflicting meanings inside the word "multiculturalism". What I like to challenge now is the widespread belief that in calling Canada "multicultural" Trudeau was describing a factual reality about Canada. When he said "biculturalism does not properly describe our society; multiculturalism is more accurate", he was not describing Canada as it was then, a nation with a population that was 74 percent British and French, and 96 percent European. The Aboriginal and the Asian population combined stood at only 2.6 percent. The entire nation was Anglo and French in its institutions: the legal system with its common and civil laws; the political system with the Parliament and the Assemblée nationale du Québec, the Protestant and Catholic religions and churches, everything, the entire English and French educational systems, based on subjects and books created and written by whites, was, from top to bottom, Anglo-French in character.

He did say in his 1962 essay that creating a polyethnic Canada would be an "experiment of major proportions". He was envisioning multiculturalism as a project for the future against the past. Canada was not going to become "a brilliant prototype for the moulding of tomorrow's civilization" merely by acknowledging its intra-European diversity or by fighting discrimination against a small number of minorities. The goal was to create a new Canadian identity based on the cultures of the world. By creating a Canada based on liberal ideas separated from any founding culture, Canada would showcase itself to the world as "a brilliant prototype" for the solution of ethnic conflict within nation states.

Trudeau blamed nationalism for having created "the scene of the most devastating wars, the worst atrocities and the most degrading collective hatred the world has ever seen". [3] He inherited and accepted the normative climate of the post-WWII era against ethnic nationalism and racism. He also accepted the notion that liberal rights should be seen as human rights extendable to all humans in the world. But he took the spiral one step further in believing that cultural nationalism, no less than ethnic and racial nationalism, was a major source of

---

3   "Treason of the Intellectuals", https://docs.google.com/document/d/1CChvPQwRJWj
     02WN3nur7jKr9nwj8aBgPKzSliSIbMpY/edit?pli=1#heading=h.gwl098qh9ien

human conflict and degradation of the human rights of individuals. The way to break cultural nationalism, he concluded, was to populate the nation with different cultures.

Hugh Forbes, a supporter of Trudeau's dream, has observed that it was clear from the moment official multiculturalism was instituted in 1971 that its success would "obviously depend on the deliberate diversification of the Canadian population". Accordingly, during the 1970s, Forbes notes:

> Canadian immigration offices were opened in various Third World countries to facilitate processing of applications, and the number of immigrants coming from these 'non-traditional sources' increased dramatically.[4]

Trudeau viewed these immigrants from "non-traditional sources" as members of "vibrant ethnic groups", and, in full acceptance of the notion that Third World peoples were more substantively cultural than Westerners, he actually said that they:

> would give Canadians of the second, third, and subsequent generations a feeling that they are connected with tradition and with human experience in various parts of the world and different periods of time.[5]

Canadians on their own, apparently, lacked a real culture other than a set of modern conveniences and a liberal constitution intended for all citizens.

In pursuance of this prototype vibrancy, the Trudeau administration increased Third World immigration immediately after 1971. There was already a crescendo in Third World immigration after the 1967 Regulations, with the proportion of immigrants from Asia and the Caribbean increasing from 10 percent in 1965-6 to 23 percent in 1969-70.[6] The 1970s saw an acceleration of this trend; of the 1.5 million immigrants who came to Canada between 1971 and 1981, 33

---

4   "Trudeau as the First Theorist of Canadian Multiculturalism", in Stephen Tierney, editor, *Multiculturalism and the Canadian Constitution*, p. 38.

5   *Ibid,* p. 29.

6   Ninette Kelley and Michael Trebilcock, *The Making of the Mosaic*, p. 354.

percent came from Asia, 16 percent from the Caribbean and South America, and 5.5 percent from Africa. Contrast this to the fact that in 1961 only 2 percent of immigrants were from Asia, and 0.6 from "other" non-European countries.[7]

Along with these numbers, the Trudeau government took some decisive measures to push Canada in a multiracial direction.[8] An estimated $200 million was set aside in the 1970s (which would equal 1.25 billion dollars today) to assist cultural groups to "retain and foster their identity", to overcome "barriers" to the full participation of immigrants in Canadian society, to promote "creative exchanges among all Canadian cultural groups", and to promote among immigrants at least one of the official languages. A "Directorate" within the Department of Secretary of State was created in 1972 to assist in the implementation of these initiatives. A particular task of this Directorate was to protect the human rights of ethnic minorities, to combat racial discrimination by white Canadians, and to persuade Canadians that immigrant diversity was really good for them. Then, in 1973, an entire "Ministry of Multiculturalism" was created "to monitor the implementation of multicultural initiatives within government departments". This was soon followed by another bureaucratic body, "Canadian Ethnocultural Council", to encourage ethnic organizations to participate in Canada's government. Plans were also put in place for the housing and educating of immigrants, and the removal of "racially discriminatory barriers" across Canadian society.

Between 1971 and 1982, there was an "explosion of academic research into ethnicity". [9] Eighty-eight scholarly works on cultural minorities were published, numerous collections of papers, and many symposiums on Canadian ethnic groups were held, the beginning of a "bonanza of remarkable proportions" in the study of multiculturalism during the 1980s and 1990s. Multiculturalism, as we will see next, would be further consolidated by Trudeau with a new Immigration Act in

---

7   "A Hundred Years of Immigration to Canada 1900-1999 (Part II), Canadian Council for Refugees, http://ccrweb.ca/en/hundred-years-immigration-canada-part-2

8   Michael Dewing and Marc Leman, "Canadian Multiculturalism", Parliamentary Research Branch. Library of Parliament (March 16, 2006), http://www.lop.parl.gc.ca/Content/LOP/ResearchPublicationsArchive/pdf/cir1000/936-e.pdf

9   Freda Hawkins, *Critical Years in Immigration: Canada and Australia Compared*, p. 227.

1976, a Human Rights Act in 1977, and a whole new constitution, The Charter of Rights, in 1982.

Trudeau, and the liberal establishment, believed that this nullification of Anglo-Quebecois cultural nationalism was necessary to create a "brilliant prototype" for the overcoming of human divisions and the creation of Utopia on earth. Whites were guilty for colonizing the magnificently egalitarian and humanitarian peoples of the Third World. But now they would be redeemed by creating a multicultural order that would allow the Third World to flourish inside Canada. As Forbes happily put it:

> Canadian multiculturalism now promises a way of incorporating the Third World into the First World without domination or oppression.[10]

But why would it have been illiberal for Canada to affirm its actual bicultural heritage since the overwhelming majority of its citizens in 1971 were Anglo-Quebecois, and all the institutions and values came from this majority? Because Trudeau, as a member of the immediate post-WWII generation, had inherited the normative climate of his generation. He sincerely believed that Western nations should be based on civic values alone, rather than any form of collective identity prioritizing one cultural group over another. He also believed that Third World peoples were victimized humans in need of human rights and a great source for the making of Canada into a prototype polyethnic nation. In the language of Carl Schmitt, Trudeau endorsed the post-WWII idea that human conflict was a result of racial and cultural divisions. He took it upon himself to be the first Western leader to make a nation, Canada, into a prototype for the harmonious co-existence of multiple cultures without relations of dominance. By making culture a private choice, he thought that Canada would get rid of the friend-enemy distinction, and thus abolish human conflict forever. The key was to decouple Canada from its historic Anglo-Quebecois traditions by populating it with peoples from multiple cultures and races and making cultural identity a private affair. Cultural nationalism, not just ethnic nationalism, was inconsistent with liberalism. Only a multi-racial population, not

---

10 "Trudeau as the First Theorist of Canadian Multiculturalism", in Stephen Tierney, editor, *Multiculturalism and the Canadian Constitution*, p.39.

a European population, would allow Canada to stand as a "brilliant prototype" for the future of humanity.

We just saw that Trudeau accentuated the Third World immigration trends that began with the 1962 and 1967 Immigration Regulations. However, it should be noted that immigration policy in Canada prior to the 1990s was still sensitive to labour-market considerations, with a tap on/tap off approach depending on levels of economic activity in Canada. The spiral had not yet thrown out the needs of the native working classes. For this reason, when it comes to absolute numbers, the 1970s recession decade saw low and high years of immigration, with the annual intake of immigrants reduced by about 60 percent from 1974 to 1978 (201,000 to 86,000), rising again in subsequent years, then falling again in the 1980s.[11] The difference in the 1970s was in the ethnic composition of immigrants, and in the legal-constitutional preparation of a future multiracial Canada.

Immigration Act of 1976, Human Rights Act of 1977

The passing of the Immigration Act of 1976 was one of the main legislative measures in the consolidation of Trudeau's multicultural agenda. According to Kelley and Trebilcock, this Act "marked a bold directional shift".[12] One component that stands out for me is that this Act did not concentrate on who should be restricted from Canada, as previous acts, but instead focused on who should be permitted into multicultural Canada. It created four new classes of immigrants: refugees, families, assisted relatives, and independent immigrants. This was the first time refugees were included as a distinct class and it established Canada's commitment to human rights to consider as immigrants not only refugees but "persecuted and displaced persons" that may not qualify as refugees under international convention. This

---

11   Ninette Kelley and Michael Trebilcock, *The Making of the Mosaic*, pp. 380-85.

12   *Ibid*, p. 381.

Act was also committed to "generous family reunification policies". [13] Distant relatives were no longer obligated to take part in the points system, as long as those sponsoring their relatives demonstrated their ability to provide sustenance for up to 10 years. From this point on, the proportion of immigrants coming to Canada from Third World nations would increase consistently.

The Canadian Human Rights Act, passed by Parliament in 1977,[14] was another measure initiated by the Trudeau government to promote equal opportunity to individuals deemed to be "victims" of discrimination on grounds of race, sexual orientation and beliefs. This Act, together with other legislative measures, increased the responsibility and power of judges and lawyers, and thereby reduced the power of elected representatives in the articulation of the cultural norms of the nation. Human rights imposed from above and formulated by cosmopolitan elites would trump, from now on, the rooted cultural norms of Canadians, if those norms were deemed to be inconsistent with these (elite created) rights. As Hugh Donald Forbes enthusiastically put it, the role of these judges and courts would be "to suppress the negative or discriminatory reactions of the dominant or majority group to the increasing presence of Others". [15] Accordingly, this Act contained a "hate speech provision" criminalizing the expression of statements categorized as "hateful" toward identifiable groups, the purpose of which was to promote acceptance of mass immigration and diversification among Euro-Canadians, by threatening imprisonment against those expressing views against mass immigration.

The Charter of Rights and Freedoms, 1982

The foremost legal experts in Canada view the Charter as a "transformative" constitution that elevated "to the status of supreme law" "a coherent body of substantive norms" that embodied the "traditional core values of liberal democracy, as adapted to the *reality*

---

13   *Ibid.*

14   Canadian Human Rights Act (R.S.C., 1985, c. H-6), Government of Canada, Justice Laws Website, http://laws-lois.justice.gc.ca/eng/acts/h-6/fulltext.html

15   "Trudeau as the First Theorist of Canadian Multiculturalism", in Stephen Tierney, editor, *Multiculturalism and the Canadian Constitution*, p. 36.

of the post-WWII pluralist and multicultural nation state". [16] These words come from Lorraine E. Weinrib, Professor at the Faculty of Law, University of Toronto. She is the most assertive in viewing the Charter as a document that emerged out of the determination of Western nations, after the violent experiences of WWII, to ensure "higher law guarantees" of the core values of liberal democracies strengthened by human rights standards. Brian Dickson, Former Chief Justice of the Supreme Court of Canada, also views the Charter as a document that "puts Canada in the mainstream of the post-World War II movement toward conscious recognition of, and protection for, fundamental rights". He goes on:

> The Charter is the logical culmination of Canadian developments in the field of human rights — it builds on provincial and federal human rights codes and the Canadian Bills of Rights. At bottom, the Charter protects those basic values, which most Canadians share and cherish. [17]

Similarly Joseph Eliot Magnet, Professor of Law at the University of Ottawa, interprets those aspects of the Charter dealing with minority rights in terms of the international preoccupation with human rights after WWII, citing a number of key documents including the 1966 International Covenant on Civil and Political Rights. [18]

It is Weinrib, however, who offers the more sweeping, and revealing assertions, about the "transformative aspirations" of the Charter as a document that was *not* "chained to Canadian legal history", but was really "transnational", the "hallmark of liberal democracy in the aftermath of the Second World War" in the Western world generally. This Charter, according to her, embodied aspirations that were growing in "many national settings, nurtured by the development and operation of supra-national human rights-protecting instruments".

---

16   Lorraine E. Weinrib, "The Canadian Charter's Transformative Aspirations", in Magnet et al. *The Canadian Charter of Rights and Freedoms: Reflections on the Charter After Twenty Years* (Butterworths, 2003), p. 18.

17   Brian Dickson, "The Canadian Charter of Rights and Freedoms: Context and Evolution", in Beaudoin and Mendes, Eds. *The Canadian Charter of Rights and Freedoms* (Carswell, 1996), chapter 1, p.19.

18   Joseph Eliot Magnet, "Multiculturalism in the Canadian Charter of Rights and Freedoms", in Beaudoin and Mendes, Eds. *The Canadian Charter of Rights and Freedoms* (Carswell, 1996), Chapter 18.

She traces, in passing, these aspirations to the "rationality and transnationalism of the Enlightenment", but her focus is on the post-WWII effort "to build and rebuild liberal democracies under the umbrella of the international instruments that protect human rights". [19] With the victory of Western democracies "over racist despots who destroyed democracy, debased the rule of law and flagrantly denied the most basic respect for human dignity and equal citizenship",[20] there emerged a movement determined to expand the role of the judiciary in guaranteeing the fundamental rights of citizens through the creation of new constitutions with instruments aimed at ensuring diversity and pluralism, with judges standing as guardians of these fundamental rights, ready to repudiate existing (traditional) practices deemed to be inconsistent with these rights. Weinrib is quite blunt, and correct, in stating:

> [T]he Charter does not encapsulate or work to perpetuate a distinctively Canadian legal legacy based on traditional, shared cultural norms. Nor did the Charter merely crystalize the protection of rights already protected by law at the time of its entrenchment. To the contrary: the Charter took Canada away from a repudiated history that had failed to respect liberty and fairness. The Charter introduced into the Canadian constitutional system the post-WWII approach to public law. Accordingly, normative analysis and comparative study, not recourse to history and tradition, were to be the appropriate methodology.[21]

The other legal experts cited above imply the same argument in their analysis of the Charter, although they are not as forceful, and sometimes they muddled the waters, or do not belabor the point about how the Charter was heavily influenced by supranational human rights principles detached from Canada's "shared culture, history, religion, or ethnicity". They do not see as clearly, or do not want to openly admit it, that the Charter was precisely about creating a new Canada based on post-WWII human rights principles, respect for diversity and minority rights, against a Canada in which liberal principles were

---

19   Lorraine E. Weinrib, "The Canadian Charter's Transformative Aspirations", p. 35.

20   *Ibid,* pp. 20-3.

21   *Ibid,* p. 22.

still encased within a wider set of community standards, customs, historical memories. The "transformative aspiration" was to promote diversity and human rights in Canada in contradistinction to any "traditional conservative moral code based on shared culture, history, religion, or ethnicity". Every remnant of "Tory" Canada had to go, including the way we understood the history of Canada as a nation founded by two races.

The "transformative" character of the Charter tends to be clouded when emphasis is placed on continuities between the Charter's commitment to the "preservation and enhancement of Canada's multicultural heritage" and the BNA accommodation of certain denominational communities, linguistic minorities in provinces, tribal rights, and the national minority of Quebec. The Charter is confounded as well when continuities are established between it and "such historic documents as the Magna Carta, the Bill of Rights of 1689…and the British North America Act of 1867". [22] This is not to deny that important continuities exited between these past historical documents and the Charter. Dickson is not wrong when he observes that "the entrenchment of rights and freedoms in the Constitution was…part of an ongoing process of ancient origin for the protection of fundamental rights and freedoms". [23] But he well knows, however, that "the Charter is the logical culmination of Canadian developments *in the field of human rights*". [24] He knows, too, that the West's profound commitment to human rights after the Second World War would "usher in a new period of human history". [25]

Yet, in the same vein as Weinrib and Dickson affirm the radical novelty of the Charter, they want to avoid the impression that the Charter is some abstract document enacted by legal experts with transnational minds out of touch with the wishes of the Canadian demos. Weinrib thus writes of the Charter as if it were a codification of the "substantive norms" already accepted by Western peoples in the decades after WWII. But it is clear that she envisions judges, and legal philosophers, citing Jürgen Habermas, as "guardians" of

---

22   Brian Dickson, "The Canadian Charter of Rights and Freedoms: Context and Evolution", chapter 1, p. 3.

23   *Ibid*, p. 2.

24   *Ibid*, p. 19.

25   *Ibid*, p. 5.

the "reconstruction" of Western polities employing rights principles "to correct shortcomings that are obvious, such as the barbarities of WWII, as well as those so embedded in our customs and traditions as to appear proper, acceptable". [26] Similarly, Dickson says that the Charter is "no more than a codification" of the "country's basic values", and that the role of the judiciary is not to impose new values but to ensure that Canadians "remain true to those values". [27]

Yet, these same experts tell us that the Charter, section 15 in particular, the equality provisions, "represents one of the most important and dynamic forces on the road to social justice". Section 15 affirms the right of all Canadians to be treated equally regardless of race, national or ethnic origin, religion, sex or any disability. By "dynamic" they mean that Canadians will be able to draw on equality provisions to eliminate every remaining inequality, as defined by current and future elites educated in our cultural Marxist universities. They take it as given that Canadians are a people marching to a future time when there will be equal social justice. They never define what they mean by "social justice" but simply take for granted that the equality provisions are a "dynamic force" intended to ensure social change and "equality". I will discuss section 15, combined with section 27, which deals with multiculturalism, in the next chapter. Suffice it to say now that I am aware of surveys showing that a majority of Canadians agree with the Charter, the equality provisions, and other sections of the Charter that affirm treaty rights for aboriginal peoples, gender equality, together with the sections that address "fundamental freedoms", "democratic rights", and "legal rights". [28] There are also some surveys showing that Canadians generally, when asked vaguely, agree with a multicultural Canada that recognizes group rights for minorities. Let's assume that these surveys really reflect what Canadians' think about the Charter rather than what they are expected to say after a lifetime of brainwashing. The point that is missing in these surveys, and in the idea that the Charter is a "dynamic force", with "transformative aspirations" reflecting the "substantive norms" of the majority of

---

26   Lorraine E. Weinrib, "The Canadian Charter's Transformative Aspirations", p. 36

27   Brian Dickson, "The Canadian Charter of Rights and Freedoms: Context and Evolution", p. 19.

28   "The Charter: Dividing or Uniting Canadians" Centre for Research and Information on Canada (April 2002), https://library.carleton.ca/sites/default/files/find/data/surveys/pdf_files/cric-crf-02-not.pdf

Canadians, is the way the Charter is being used to justify the truly "dynamic force" that mass immigration is, and whether Canadians have ever consented to the radical alteration of the racial and cultural composition of Canada.

It is beyond comprehension that in all the sources I have examined, including the multi-article editions on the Charter I am citing right now, there are no discussions of mass immigration, no open awareness that masses of immigrants have been arriving since the early 1990s, even though these books and articles are heavily about the constitutional aspects of Canadian multiculturalism, its implications for the future, and group rights. I have seen only two references to mass immigration in the chapter/article I cited above by Joseph Eliot Magnet. One, when he admits that section 27 of the Charter "was the result of intensive lobbying by Canada's ethno-cultural communities for greater respect, and a larger share of power in Canada's political system". [29] Two, when he admits that the Multiculturalism Act of 1988, which I will be discussing in the next chapter, was formulated in response to "Canada's requirement for high immigration", right after stating that "Canada absorbs roughly 250,000 immigrants each year". [30] Clearly, he is noticing that the two major legal documents on Canadian multiculturalism were formulated in direct relationship to mass immigration, and yet he seems oblivious to the ways in which mass immigration may well be (I have no doubt it is) the truly "dynamic force" in section 15 (and section 27) of the Charter. More on this in the next chapter.

I gather that one of the key shortcomings Weinrib would like to see transformed, in need of "rebuilding", is the notion that Canada is a nation with a bicultural heritage, a nation with people who are still attached to customs which experts have come to associate with the exclusionary immigration laws of the past and the Anglo conformity model. She would like to see English Canadians reconstructed in such a way that they forego their in-group attachments in the

---

29   Joseph Eliot Magnet, "Multiculturalism in the Canadian Charter of Rights and Freedoms", in Beaudoin and Mendes, Eds. *The Canadian Charter of Rights and Freedoms* (Carswell, 1996), Chapter 18, p. 4.

30   "What Does 'Equality Between Communities' Mean?" in Magnet et al. *The Canadian Charter of Rights and Freedoms: Reflections on the Charter After Twenty Years* (Butterworths, 2003), p. 281.

name of universal values that encourage a "broader sense of 'we'".[31] The expectation is that, in the same breath as the majority English population "corrects" its "shortcomings" by diluting its communitarian norms, under the guidance of supra-national principles, minority groups will do likewise in their gradual allegiance to the principle of individual rights. But there are some fundamental tensions here between this expectation and the multicultural right (encoded in the Charter) afforded to minorities to express their cultural particularity and pride, in a nation in which members of the majority culture are expected to forego their cultural particularities.

We have a situation in which the "dominant society", the dominant English culture, or Euro-Canadian population, is under the obligation of reconstructing its culture according to transnational values formulated by anonymous international human rights experts, who, in the same breath, mandate whites to "understand" the "human need" minorities have to belong in a cultural group and to have their customary values recognized. In his discussion of multiculturalism in the Charter, Joseph Magnet actually appeals to findings in social psychology to show how important it is for individuals to belong in a group of people with a similar culture. First, he says that "social psychologists have demonstrated that the individual self is incomplete without integration into a social group". Then he adds:

> The ethnic individual completes a significant aspect of personality – forms of self – by voluntary identification with *an ethnic group*...Attacks on cultural heritage are thus attacks on the individual selves of the ethnic group's members...Practices which restrict autonomy of ethnic communities to develop their own distinctive way, or to manifest freely their community experiences in daily rituals, institutions and social interaction with others, choke the self-development of the individual members of ethnic communities.

These are the same Western experts that never care to use the word "ethnic", "group interests", "collective interests", "autonomy of ethnic

---

31   These words come from Robert Putnam, the researcher who was taken aback upon discovering that diversity destroys the social capital of cities. His answer was to call for more brainwashing to force whites to believe it increases social trust. See "E Pluribus Unum: Diversity and Community in the Twenty-first Century. The 2006 Johan Skytte Prize Lecture" *Scandinavian Political Studies* vol. 30, no. 2 (June 2007).

communities", "cultural heritage" in reference to English Canadians or Euro-Canadians generally! Any insinuation by Euro-Canadians that they have their own collective interests is painted in negative terms and in need of eradication. Only English Canadians, and only they, must define their culture strictly in transnational civic terms, in terms of abstract, universal phrases such as "fundamental freedoms", "democratic rights", "mobility rights", "legal rights", "equality rights", and "language rights". This Charter, which took priority over every other legislative act in Canada's past, as part of the "supreme law of Canada", understands Canada to be a nation without any collective-national identity other than the collective minorities, aboriginals, Quebecois, and immigrant groups.

Instead of any objections about the "transformative aspirations" of the Charter against Canada's heritage, the standard "conservative" criticism about this Charter is that it decisively broke with the "historic tradition of parliamentary supremacy" embodied in the preamble to the Constitution Act of 1867, in which, to use the words of former Premier of Alberta, Peter Lougheed (1971 to 1985), "the role of the courts was to give effect to the political choices made by the legislators...bound by the idea that Parliament was supreme and the court's role of judicial review was limited". [32] These critics argue that, in spite of the notwithstanding clause (which gives the legislature the power to override rights in the Charter in exceptional circumstances and without affecting the guarantee of some rights and freedoms such as Democratic Rights, Mobility Rights, and Minority Language Educational Rights), the Charter brought a dramatic shift in authority from democratic representatives to judges and lawyers. Today one still hears conservatives complaining about unelected judges afforded "with the means to override the majority views represented by elected parliamentarians". The replies liberals have offered to these conservative criticisms reveal much about the meta-political forces that brought this Charter. The following defence of the Charter by Julius Grey, a well-known scholar in constitutional and human rights law, is worth citing:

It is unfortunate that many Canadians swallow the populist

---

32   Peter Lougheed, "Why a Notwithstanding Clause?" Archived - Building a Just Society: A Retrospective of Canadian Rights and Freedoms, Library and Archives Canada, https://www.collectionscanada.gc.ca/rights-and-freedoms/023021-1400-e. html

line even though polls indicate that they generally agree with the court decisions. An examination of the American experience can help us understand this. It has become a dogma of modern American conservatism that judicial activism is nefarious for democracy. In fact, the naming of judges who believe in "restraint" has become a Republican mantra. Yet when one seeks to discover what the courts have done to provoke this reaction one finds only two major matters, the integration of Afro-Americans and the facilitation of abortion. This illustrates a remarkable paradox. The American public is ready to prevent future judicial innovations, yet it appears to support the judiciary's past successes. When we consider that no political party could have easily achieved integration or liberalized abortion because this would have offended powerful lobbies, the contradictory nature of the opposition to judicial innovation becomes obvious. No one questions integration and the anti-abortion lobby is clearly a minority but today's politicians have made similar developments in the future highly unlikely.[33]

Even though he does not use the clearest expressions of admittance, what Grey is saying is that we cannot allow the demos to decide the major questions of a nation, such as whether Canada should cherish its bicultural character, or become a multiracial nation. He is saying that when one examines such legislative measures in America as integration of blacks and whites[34] and facilitation of abortion, one finds that the majority of the public did not support these measures until much later. When he writes that "even though polls indicate that they generally agree with the court decisions", he is referring to polls taken years after the decision, not before, and this is why he calls it a "remarkable paradox".

Gray thinks it is great to have courts, judges and legal scholars decide "major matters" for an entire people because they are the ones, apparently, carrying the march of human improvement ahead, the

---

33   Julius Grey, "The *Charter*: Its Achievements and its Detractors" Archived - Building a Just Society: A Retrospective of Canadian Rights and Freedoms, Library and Archives Canada, https://www.collectionscanada.gc.ca/rights-and-freedoms/023021-1400-e. html

34   Jared Taylor, "Integration has Failed", *American Renaissance* (February 2008), https://www.amren.com/news/2008/10/integration_has/

progressive ones, whereas the majority are mentally behind. The demos on their own are backward and cannot be trusted to bring major progressive changes. The elites need to take charge, enact the progressive changes, through manipulation if need be, for once these changes are enacted, the mob will go along with them, as polls later show.

This reliance on courts to settle "major" political questions began in Canada with the enactment of the Fair Employment and Fair Accommodation Practices Acts (1951-1954), and, one could add, the 1960 Canadian Bill of Rights, though I agree with Hugh Forbes that this Bill was "largely symbolic", and that it was the Charter that took the decisions concerning the fundamental rights of Canadians "out of the hands of elected officials [into the hands] of highly trained legal experts appointed by the politicians". Forbes thinks it has been a great change to have "highly trained experts" decide the character of Canada rather than the majority of the population, and he is quite open in stating that this had to be done in a "society striving to become genuinely multicultural...a future home for all the world's peoples". [35] Canadians, as the polls of the 1960s showed, could not be trusted to bring about Trudeau's "experiment of major proportions".

However, these liberal observations don't dig far enough into the metapolitical dynamic behind the imposition of multiculturalism across the West. The norms of human rights, race is a social construct, Third World peoples are benevolent, and ethnic nationalism is illiberal, which spread after WWII, were not norms originated by Canadians out of their traditions, folkways, and natural predispositions. They were norms with intellectual antecedents going back to the Enlightenment, or more precisely, to what has been identified as the "radical Enlightenment movement" that evolved after the 1750s, in the minds of such philosophers as D'Holbach, Helvetius, Condorcet, and Godwin. [36] These thinkers believe that the nature of humans was moulded entirely by the social and moral environment. This nature could therefore be remoulded through changes in the moral and institutional environment. New humans could be created, through

---

35 "Trudeau as the First Theorist of Canadian Multiculturalism", in Tierney (2007), p. 37.

36 Jonathan Israel, *Philosophy and the Making of Modernity, 1650-1750* (Oxford University Press, 2001).

a proper education and a proper alteration of the hierarchical and prejudicial institutions of the past.[37] That is, new humans without prejudices and without parochial attachments to their particular locality, country, or race. These new humans would be able to live in harmony with each other away from the wars and religious divisions of the past.

Since these humans were not yet born, but only a small elite of intellectuals were enlightened enough to know what it meant to be a new human, this elite decided it was their role to bring about this new humanity; some used forced, leading to the very violent French and Bolshevik revolutions, but the ones employing gradual steps gained the upper hand after the experience of WWII, laying the groundwork for the Fabian and cultural Marxist strategy of marching gradually and steadily through the institutions, taking them over, and in this way moulding the character and nature of Western peoples.[38] What was new after WWII, and this is why I have emphasized these norms, is that this elite came to the conclusion that white racial identity, European nationalism, and lack of universal human rights, were the remaining stumbling blocks in need of elimination in search of a perfected society. It is with this background in mind that we can make sense of what has been going on in Canada and the West since WWII.

The Charter is an expression of this radical transformation of Western civilization under the guidance of academics, administrative, legal, and business elites, all of whom have gradually accepted the idea that the peoples of the West must be remoulded to accept racial diversification through "education" and institutional changes.[39] The demos in the Charter is not the people of Canada, the majority of

---

37   J. Bury, *The Idea of Progress: An inquiry into its growth and origins* (Dover Publications [1932] 1960).

38   Clare Ellis, "The Socialist-Capitalist Alliance: the Fabian Society, the Frankfurt School, and Big Business" *Council of European Canadians*. This article has three parts posted in June 23, June 26, and July 8, 2014, http://www.Euro-Canadian.ca/2014/06/socialist-capitalist-alliance-fabian-society-frankfurt-school-and-big-business-part1.html

39   My understanding of the role of human rights experts, and professional elites generally who pretend they are speaking for "humanity", while lacking democratic consent and misleading their own people, benefitted from Andrew Fraser's "A Marx for the Managerial Revolution: Habermas on Law and Democracy". *Journal of Law and Society*, Vol. 28, No. 3 (2001).

Euro-Canadians who never asked for mass immigration; rather the demos is "humanity" and the human rights our elites have ascribed to this humanity. The spiral was now far away from any concept about the collective rights and liberties of the Anglo and Quebecois people.

18

Multiculturalism in the Charter

The identification of Canada as "multicultural" is a panoply of conceptual tensions, factual deceptions, and legal obfuscations. One would think that with the enactment of the Charter in 1982 (and the Multiculturalism Act of 1988, which we will discuss in the next chapter) the exact way in which Canada was officially multicultural would have been settled conceptually and legally.[1] Section 27 of the Charter tries to translate into a precise legal principle what multiculturalism means; it states that this Charter "officially recognizes" multiculturalism as "a Canadian value", and that:

> This Charter shall be interpreted in a manner consistent with the preservation and enhancement of the multicultural heritage of Canadians.

The seemingly obvious way of interpreting this statement is that everything else that is contained in the Charter, "Fundamental freedoms", "Democratic rights", "Equality Rights", for example, should be interpreted in a way that is "consistent with the preservation and enhancement" of multiculturalism. But how can such freedoms as freedom of thought, or such rights to equality as equal protection of the law without discrimination, be interpreted in ways that are consistent with the "enhancement" of cultures that may have different understandings of the meaning of these freedoms and rights?

Some have made light of Section 27 saying that it will have no impact on the way the fundamental freedoms of Canadians are interpreted. They argue that this statement about multiculturalism is "more of a rhetorical flourish than an operative provision".[2] Joseph E. Magnet,

---

1   Robert J. Sharpe and Kent Roach, *The Charter of Rights and Freedoms* (Irwin Law; 3rd edition, 2005).

2   These words are from Peter Hogg, as cited by Joan Small, "Multiculturalism, Equality, and Canadian Constitutionalism: Cohesion and Difference" in Stephen Tierney, ed., Multiculturalism and the Canadian Constitution (UBC Press, 2007), p. 198.

for his part, thinks that section 27 "reveals no coherent principle which courts can apply".

> There is no readily apparent meaning to be gleaned from the words of the text – no intelligible or agreed upon content for the multiculturalism principle...Instead, one discovers a vast heterogeneity of meanings or ideologies, not one of which is sufficiently developed that it can form a principled approach to section 27. These difficulties are compounded by the fact that section 27 is not a free standing provision, but only an interpretational guide.[3]

However, other legal scholars think that section 27 does reflect a "constitutional value" of the Canadian people, and that taken together with section 15, which guarantees equality rights to "every individual", it means that members of minority cultural groups have a right to be treated equally, not suffer discrimination, enjoy equal human dignity, and full membership in society. The "equality of rights" are said to be "at the core of the Charter",[4] and since they include the right of individuals from different cultures and religions to express their cultural identities, then section 27, it is argued, is about ensuring that the rights of members of minority cultural groups are not violated by the majority culture.

Other experts, however, wonder whether these two sections conflict, because, for one, section 15 does not apply to groups but to individuals. It has also been noted that the pursuit of equal rights for all Canadians works to reduce the cultural differences and thus conflicts with the idea of group identity and preservation. On the other hand, in the same paragraph of section 15 where it is stated that "everyone should be treated equally by laws or government policies", it is also stated that "the Charter does not require that government always treat people in exactly the same way", because Canadians come from different cultures and, accordingly, they have an individual right, for example, to "observe different religious holidays without losing their job". It is

---

3   Joseph E. Magnet, "Multiculturalism in the Canadian Charter of Rights and Freedoms", in *The Canadian Charter of Rights and Freedoms*, eds. Gerald Beaudoin and Errol Mendes (Toronto: Carswell, 1996), chapter 18, p. 23.

4   "Rights and freedoms in Canada", Government of Canada, Department of Justice, http://www.justice.gc.ca/eng/csj-sjc/just/06.html

argued by some interpreters that this is an example of what the Charter means when it says that its rights and freedoms "shall be interpreted in a manner consistent with the preservation and enhancement of the multicultural heritage of Canadians".

This same section 15 of the Charter, sub-section 15 (2), also says that the government has the constitutional right "to create special programs aimed at improving the situation of individuals who are members of groups that have historically experienced discrimination in Canada". This implies that ensuring equality of rights in a way that is "consistent with the enhancement of multiculturalism" allows the government to provide special assistance (extra funding for minority cultural programs, and antidiscrimination programs) to members of ethnic groups that have been historically discriminated by Euro-Canadians, and that continue to be discriminated. Therefore, it appears that the Charter grants "special" rights to non-European cultural groups that can claim there was, and continues to be, discrimination against them. Legal scholars have argued indeed that section 27, in light of what section 15 says about "equality", could be used to encourage the government to give financial support to members of minority cultures in Canada, if it can be demonstrated that said members were discriminated in the past, and if it can be demonstrated that said members are still experiencing discrimination on grounds of their cultural identity.

Before looking at what legal effects section 27 (in combination with section 15) have had in recent Canadian court decisions, a distinction should be made between a) the special constitutional status which the Canadian Constitution accords Aboriginal peoples, the national minority of Quebec, denominational communities, and English and French linguistic minorities, and b) what these sections say about the enhancement of cultural diversity. The Constitution grants these four groups the right to survive as distinct communities within Canada's federation. It would be misleading to think that section 27 (along with section 15) grants every immigrant minority group in Canada the same special constitutional status. Legal experts argue that this is not the case. We should not worry, they reason, about the rise of multiple cultural groups demanding the same constitutional status as the Quebecois, Aboriginals, and denominational communities. According to Magnet, such a claim would be "at the outer extremes (or perhaps beyond the limits) of section 15 of the Charter". [5]

The guarantee of equality of rights of section 15 relate to the right of every individual to be treated equally under the law, the right to equal protection and benefit without discrimination based on race, national origin, sex, religion, age or mental or physical disability. But, as Joan Small then asks, what is the effect of section 27 upon this equality principle of section 15?

> How does, or should, the fact that Canada's is a multicultural society affect understanding of equality law? What sorts of claims, if any, can persons or groups who are not given special constitutional status make?[6]

For Magnet, the antidiscrimination principle of section 15 is based on ideals of individual equality, rather than on ideals applicable to groups, which section 27 tends to be about; these two ideals should not be confused.[7] Yet, as Small is aware, and so is Magnet as he navigates through these slippery concepts, there is no question that the principle that all individuals should have the same rights stands in tension with the principle of multiculturalism, which is about the enhancement of collective cultural pluralism as a Canadian value.

While the principle of equal rights for every individual says that it is unfair to give special rights to one group, the principle of multiculturalism, in combination with principle of equality in section 15, as we just saw above, may be interpreted as calling for equal respect and opportunities for minority immigrant groups in Canada vis a vis the "dominant" majority culture through special government initiatives.

---

5   As cited by Joan Small, "Multiculturalism, Equality, and Canadian Constitutionalism: Cohesion and Difference", p. 199.

6   *Ibid.*

7   Joseph E. Magnet, "Multiculturalism in the Canadian Charter of Rights and Freedoms", in *The Canadian Charter of Rights and Freedoms*, ed. Gerald Beaudoin and Errol Mendes (Toronto: Carswell, 1996), chapter 18, p. 25. He notes elsewhere: "Section 15 guarantees equality of rights, to "every individual". It is the rights of individuals, not of groups, that has powered the Supreme Court of Canada's sophisticated equality jurisprudence". See "What Does 'Equality Between Communities' Mean?" p. 277.

Court Cases Since the 1980s about Section 27

Joan Small carefully examines various recent Court cases that have invoked section 27. This section was invoked by the Supreme Court in the landmark Charter case R. v. Big M Drug Mart Ltd. (1985), in which the guarantee of freedom of religion in section 2 of the Charter was used to invalidate a federal statute requiring businesses to be closed on Sundays for religious reasons, in the name of a particular religion, the religion of the majority culture which calls for a Sabbath. The Court noted that requiring Canadians to observe "the day of rest preferred by one religion" contradicted "the preservation and enhancement of the multicultural heritage of Canadians".[8]

Section 27 has also been invoked in R. v. Keegstra (1990) in the name of supporting the goal of restricting activity that goes against the enhancement of multiculturalism by promoting hatred among groups in Canadian society. It was stated that multiculturalism cannot be enhanced if promotion of hatred is allowed against identifiable cultural groups. In another case, (Human Rights Commission) v. Taylor (1990), Chief Justice Brian Dickson argued that section 27 could reinforce limits on freedom of expression, specifically hate speech. Taking section 27 together with section 15, he argued that fighting racial and religious discrimination would be a sufficient objective for limiting free expression. Said differently, since section 15 encourages Canadians to fight racial and religious discrimination, and section 27 identifies cultural plurality as a value of Canadians, it can be argued that speech that is overtly critical of the values of other cultures would be inconsistent with the "enhancement of multiculturalism".

Examining these cases and others, Joan Small reasons that the invocation of section 27 has been mainly about accommodating individual rights within the context of multiculturalism "without drawing a sharp distinction between group rights and individual rights", or "pitting one group against another". These cases, she thinks, have illustrated that, for the Court, section 27 should inform the principles of section 15, and that there is "nothing in section 27 that precludes an interpretation that supports interests that individuals

---

8   For this and the following cases mentioned here, see Joan Small "Multiculturalism, Equality, and Canadian Constitutionalism: Cohesion and Difference, pp. 200-209. See also Peter W. Hogg, *Constitutional Law of Canada*, 2003 (Thomson Canada Limited, 2003), pp. 742-743.

have – in association with group membership – that originate from their ethnocultural identity". [9]

But she then struggles through all sorts of legal and conceptual complications; after confidently stating that the Court is developing a reasonable contextual approach that accommodates individual rights with the enhancement of diversity, Small acknowledges that "a contextual approach" that invokes the importance of diversity coupled with the need "to determine whether there has been a violation of the 'essential human dignity' of individuals from different cultures" is riddled with tensions and diverging interpretations. This becomes all the more confounding when one considers the "notion of group dignity":

> How does a group feel self-respect or self-worth? Is the Court concerned with the feelings of the totality of the members or of the group as a group? If the latter, how does one determine who speaks for the group or how group feeling is to be measured? The Court has never said. And the Court has not been asked to consider the possibility of the dignity of a group pitted against that of an individual member, yet, it is in precisely these circumstances that the legal conception of dignity would be crucial. [10]

Small's suggestion about how courts are handling this reminds me of the communitarian liberalism Kymlicka and his supporters have envisioned at the level of political theory. She says that the way the Court appears to be reasoning about these matters is by thinking of dignity in a "relational" way, by situating individuals within "the context" of a cultural community. For individuals, dignity is in part defined by community or group membership; and for groups, dignity is arguably the totality of attributes that are constitutive of the group identity.

Likewise, as Kymlicka says, the rights of individuals cannot be taken in isolation, since individuals are members of groups and their sense of identity and dignity is tied to their membership in a cultural group.

---

9   Joan Small, "Multiculturalism, Equality, and Canadian Constitutionalism: Cohesion and Difference", p. 204.

10   *Ibid*, p. 205.

Kymlicka also insists that immigrant groups are not asking for their own separate, self-governing nations or provinces within Canada. They typically are not calling for ethnic-group rights that limit the rights of individuals within their group; and if some are, the Charter of Rights precludes them from getting such rights, since section 27 has to be seen in the context of the other fundamental freedoms protected by the Charter. Coerced marriages, female circumcision, or any practice that is inconsistent with integration into a liberal society are excluded. Section 27 merely endorses in principle group rights that afford immigrant minorities "external protections" against majority decisions and that provide minorities with the cultural resources to enhance their opportunities for individual success including policies that end discrimination, affirmative action, exemption from some rules that violate immigrant religious practices.

This liberal communitarian view is apparent in what Small says about the Multani v. Commission Scolaire Marguerite-Bourgeoys case (2006). The Court decided that an outright prohibition of the wearing at school of a kirpan would have been contrary to the guarantee of freedom of religion in section 2(a) of the Charter, and while no reference was made to section 27, according to Small, the court did imply adherence to Canada's protection of the need of immigrants to have their group dignity protected within the context of liberalism when it said that "…accommodating Gurbaj Singh and allowing him to wear his kirpan under certain conditions demonstrates the importance that our society attaches to protecting freedom of religion and to showing respect for its minorities". [11]

Ethnic Demography is Destiny

It seems to me that this view, for all its "contextual" talk, is seriously flawed in offering a strictly legalistic account of the meaning of multiculturalism and group rights, without the slightest awareness of the "dynamic force" of mass immigration and the rapidly changing ethnic balance of power in Canada and what the science of evolutionary psychology says about ethnic group interests. The standard position is roughly that Canada's multiculturalism is merely designed to overcome discrimination against historically disadvantaged minority groups,

---

11   *Ibid,* p. 208.

eradicating barriers against the integration of immigrant minorities, assisting immigrants in learning Canadian languages and norms, and fostering respect for Canada's cultural pluralism. Immigrant groups do not want, and are not guaranteed, in the words of Magnet, "maintenance claims", by which he means group rights to "maintain intact, indefinitely into the future, the distinguishing features of identity that bind them together as a distinctive society". [12]

In answer to the question, "do groups have equality rights?", Magnet thus notes that the constitution recognizes that only "certain denominational communities, English and French linguistic groups, Aboriginal peoples, and the national minority in Quebec", have "special entitlements". Certain denominational communities have rights to segregation in education "to perpetuate their religious communities". English and French linguistic communities have the right to certain services, schools systems, and equitable shares in the federal public sector workforce. Aboriginals have guarantees to preserve their own distinctive communities, and the national minority in Quebec is "granted substantial powers of self-government to control their destiny of their community in their own particular way". [13] Magnet's answer, then, is that immigrant minorities don't have the same equality rights as these four constitutional groups, which is similar to what Joan Small says.

However, in the other article by Magnet we have been referencing here, "Multiculturalism in the Canadian Charter of Rights and Freedoms", he brings up in his discussion of section 27 the concept of "structural ethnicity, "which refers to the capacity of a collectivity to perpetuate itself, control leakage in its membership, resist assimilation, and propagate its beliefs and practices". [14] He then says that "to the extent the structural ethnicity principle inheres in section 27, a dramatic impact on Canada's Charter system results". [15] This principle may seem to be akin to the "maintenance claim" but Magnet uses it differently to

---

12   "What Does 'Equality Between Communities' Mean?" in Magnet et al. *The Canadian Charter of Rights and Freedoms: Reflections on the Charter After Twenty Years* (Butterworths, 2003), p. 282.

13   *Ibid*, p. 286-88.

14   "Multiculturalism in the Canadian Charter of Rights and Freedoms", chapter 18, p. 28. Both articles by Magnet are excellent, the best ones I have read on the legal meaning of multiculturalism.

15   *Ibid*, chapter 18, p. 32,

examine whether one can say that this principle "inheres" in section 27, in the words to "preserve" and "enhance" Canada's cultural pluralism.

He notes that section 27, after all, "fell into place at the insistence of the 'third force'—immigrant minorities".[16] Section 27 was not called for by Canada's historic minorities. Section 27, then, "must be taken [as] claims for greater power welling up from ethnic minorities unprotected by historic constitutional provisions", about minorities looking for something closer to "maintenance claims". While Magnet says that it would be "absurd" to infer that the "structural ethnicity principle" possibly implied in the words "preserve" and "enhance" "goes so far as to guarantee to every sub-national group its own provincial government", this principle "may nevertheless encourage creation of quasi-autonomous administrative structures…under the control of particular groups[as] a powerful means of insuring that these groups have the capacity to maintain themselves, and to develop according to their particular perception of their own special requirements". [17] This argument is analogous to Charles Taylor philosophical concept of "deep diversity" expressed in a more precise legalistic fashion.

It is worth citing here some more passages from Magnet on this matter:

> [D]emographic considerations, as well as the wishes of the groups involved, may make the claims of some communities to such structures stronger than others.[18]

> The language of section 27 – "preservation and *enhancement*" – is conducive to establishment of doctrines presupposing an affirmatively acting constitutional law, at least with respect to cultural groups.[19]

Since section 27 says that the Charter as a whole should be interpreted in light of Canada's commitment to multiculturalism, Magnet says that this section:

---

16   *Ibid*, p. 33.

17   *Ibid*.

18   *Ibid*, p. 35.

19   *Ibid*, p. 41. His italics.

could alter the minimum standards of respect for personal liberty…in favour of the special needs of semi-autonomous groups to preserve their special characteristics…[I]t may well come to mean that groups exercising semi-autonomous power may be less respectful of individual rights than government proper, if this is necessary to preserve the essential features of the group' identity.[20]

While Magnet praises the "advantage of section 27" in permitting "a balancing of individual and collective values",[21] he notes that there is no "readily apparent doctrine" to regulate the incipient "conflict" between the "systems of individual and group rights in the Charter". [22]

It is amazing that in this carefully grafted discussion about the meaning of section 27, the contemporary "dynamic force" of mass immigration and the rapidly changing ethnic demography of Canada, never comes up, even though Magnet writes about "claims for greater power" by "immigrant minorities". He wants to determine the meaning of section 27 as if it were only about words rather than about how these words will be interpreted in the coming decades as immigrant-ethnic groups continue to grow exponentially. I will repeat that he does not have a word to say about the groups rights of the majority population. There is not a word about how the historic founding peoples of Canada, and this is true of the Quebecois since this province is also experiencing mass immigration, will "preserve", never mind "enhance", their cultural heritage.

Since WWII the elites in control of Western culture have been teaching to impressionable white students that emotional attachments to in-groups are not only backward and illiberal, but "a personality disorder, a public health pathogen". [23] This is the same establishment that has laboriously tried to "legitimize and acknowledge" the ethnic group identities of minority groups even at the price of limiting individual rights. While the expectation is that second generation immigrants

---

20   *Ibid*, p. 44.

21   *Ibid*, p. 46.

22   *Ibid*, p. 44.

23   Carl C. Bell and Edward Dunbar, "Racism and Pathological Bias as a Co-Occurring Problem in Diagnosis and Assessment", in Thomas A. Widiger, ed. *The Oxford Handbook of Personality Disorders* (2012).

will not cling to their past collective identities but will be satisfied with the expression of softer identities consistent with liberal values, the arguments of Magnet and Taylor make a lot more sense when we (truly) contextualize this debate in terms of the truly "dynamic force" that is mass immigration and in terms of the (truly) contextual reality we are witnessing in Europe regarding lack of integration by second and third generation Muslims in Europe.[24] The fact that Kymlicka has never offered any time-limits as to how long immigrants will require special group rights is inseparable from the more pertinent fact that he has never offered any limits on the number of immigrants that should come every year and on the number of years that Canada should have open borders. To the contrary, Kymlicka is an advocate of increasing immigration numbers across the West and looks forward to the day when Canada and the whole Western world can "never again" be identified as "White and Christian".

Given these realities, it is necessary to go beyond a mere legalistic and static account of the nature of multiculturalism in Canada. We need a proper scientific grasp of ethnic group interests. We have already referenced recent research showing that organisms as diverse as amoebas, elephants, and humans survive inside in-groups in competition with out-groups. In-group cooperation and preference is an evolutionary strategy consistent with the survival, enhancement, and protection of one's own herd, family, or people. In-group preference is not an immoral form of behavior that must be eradicated as "xenophobic". What the science says is neither that in-groups needlessly seek to attack any out-group nor that in-groups have an inborn disposition to hate others. In-group members concentrate on the performance of altruism within the group rather than aggression towards outsiders unless the competing out-group comes to be seen as a threat. Conflict escalation between ethnic groups is lower when physical barriers exist between them. Japan, Korea, and many other countries today have a high degree of homogeneity, but none of them are engaged in wars of exclusion and violence against other ethnic groups in other places. Why then is everyone presuming that if Western countries decided to end mass immigration they are thereby

---

24   To cite one of numerous studies, a report authored by Munira Mirza, Abi Senthilkumaran, and Zein Ja'far, *Living apart together: British Muslims and the paradox of multiculturalism* (London: Policy Exchange, 2007), revealed that members of the younger generation of Muslims in England were actually more orthodox than their fathers and grandfathers.

engaged in acts of exclusion and violence? The evidence is clearly pointing in the opposite direction: violence and rapes against out-groups have increased dramatically in those Nordic countries that decided to "enrich" themselves with diversity.

When all is said, the meaning of multiculturalism, and what the Charter means by multiculturalism, will be determined by the proportion of non-Europeans in Canada. The demographic displacement of Europeans by immigrants will result in new readings of the Charter leading to ever stronger interpretation of the words "consistent with the preservation and enhancement of the multicultural heritage of Canadians". When the Charter was enacted in 1982, the spiral of radicalization in Canada was still in its early stages, and the interpretation of this phrase in the next few years was relatively soft, because the proportion of cultural groups that were not Euro-Canadian was still relatively small. While the proportion of non-European immigrants did increase dramatically in the 1970s, in absolute terms, however, total immigration numbers were not that high. The annual intake was reduced by about 60 percent from 1974 to 1978 (201,000 to 86,000 immigrants), rising again in subsequent years, but then falling again in the 1980s. In 1985, the total inflow was only 84,000, the lowest number since 1962.[25] If we look at the 1981 Census, one year before the Charter, we find that, in terms of ethnic origins, only 3% of the population declared an "Asian and African" origin, and 1.7% declared a "Far East Asian" origin, and 2% a "North and South American" origin. True mass immigration, on a continuous basis, year after year, is a phenomenon that began in the second half of the 1980s/early 1990s.

Sharia Law in Ontario

We should not be surprised at new, and much harder cases to come up in the coming years, over the meaning of section 27. Let me make reference, finally, to a particularly relevant case, though it was at the provincial level, which occurred during a period of 20 months between 2004 and 2005 over the introduction of sharia law in Ontario.[26]

---

25   Ninette Kelley and Michael Trebilock, *The Making of the Mosaic*, p. 380.

26   L. Clarke, "Asking Questions about Sharia: Lessons from Ontario", in Anna C. Korteweg, Jennifer A. Selby, eds. *Debating Sharia: Islam, Gender Politics, and Family Law Arbitration* (University of Toronto Press, 2012).

It really began in 2003 when the Islamic Institute of Civil Justice said it intended to establish family faith-based tribunals for the 400,000 Muslim Ontarians similar to the tribunals which had been established by Catholic and Jewish communities, in accordance with the province's Arbitration Act in 1999. During the debates, a former attorney general, Marion Boyd, was asked to evaluate the workings of this Arbitration Act to determine whether it adversely affected women in particular. In her report, which came out in 2004, Boyd recommended that the "Arbitration Act should continue to allow disputes to be arbitrated using religious law". The gist of her argument was that since Christian and Jewish tribunals were working, perhaps it would only be fair, and consistent with the principle of enhancing multiculturalism in Canada, to allow Muslim tribunals. But there was a lot of opposition headed by Western-centric feminist legal experts associated with the Liberal Party, arguing that such tribunals were incompatible with the principle of equality of rights for women. Irfan Syed, chairman of the Toronto-based Muslim Lawyers Association, countered these arguments saying:

> In truly multicultural countries, this is quite common. It's a legitimate way to give religious communities some autonomy within the scope of our law. The two can exist because the Canadian courts have an ultimate supervisory capacity.

However, the Western-centric feminists won. In September 2005, Dalton McGuinty, who was Ontario Premier at the time, turned against religious arbitration, announcing that there would be "no sharia law in Ontario" and "no religious arbitration". "There will be one law for all Ontarians". While some saw this case as an indication of the ways in which multiculturalism discourages assimilation and encourages "illiberal" legal practices, others greeted the results as an indication of the ways in which Canadian multiculturalism is flexible enough in its detection of "illiberal activities" and its acceptance of cultural practices that do not violate fundamental freedoms. But what cannot be ignored in these legalistic assessments of the Charter is the simple demographic question: what proportion of Ontario's population was Muslim during this period. In 2001, the percentage of Muslims in Ontario was 3.1 and in 2011 it was 4.6. In Canada the proportion of Muslims was 3.2 in 2011. That's not a large proportion. The future ethno-demographic context will determine the meaning of multiculturalism. The context we have is one in which the population growth between 2001 and 2011 by religious association in Canada was 72% for Sikh, 69% for Hindu, 65% for Muslim, and -3 for Christian,[27] with Islam declared to be Canada's "fastest growing religion" in 2013.[28] It is a rapidly changing context, with projections pointing to a situation in which, by 2031, "one third of Canada's population and nearly two thirds of Toronto's population will be members of a visible minority group". [29]

Already, the dominant *academic* feminist establishment has rejected the "Western-centric" feminist position, arguing that Western multicultural societies (Western constitutional democracies per se) need to be "more flexible" in the incorporation of the values of minority cultures. Focusing on the sharia law experience in Ontario, a number of females recently put together a volume with the title, *Debating Sharia: Islam, Gender Politics, and Family Law Arbitration*, concluding that the "challenge now" for Western societies is "to include Islam within its dominant narrative".[30] Westerners, they argue, need to calm down and understand that Muslims are not trying to institute sharia law in exclusion of Western liberal values, but within the context of these values. Muslims are not seeking to impose sharia as a separate legal system based exclusively on the Koran. Westerners commit "the error of essentialism" when they view Islam as having an essence that is fixed. When sharia principles are transferred to Europe they take a different meaning within the context of democratic constitutionalism. As sharia principles are debated and enacted within a multicultural liberal setting, they will be "constructed" differently. This is already evident, multicultural feminists argue, in the way Muslims utilize liberal procedures in their efforts to bring sharia law to the West. They

---

27   "The Times They Are A Changin': Implications of Ontario's Changing Demographics", Presented by Dr. Doug Norris Senior, Vice President and Chief Demographer, Environics Analytics, at Conference of Ontario Association of Cemetery and Funeral Professionals Alliston, Ontario (October 9, 2014), (https://oacfp.com/assets/uploads/content/pdf_upload/Doug_Norris_presentation_on_demographics.pdf   Jordan Press, "Survey shows Muslim population is Canada's fastest growing religion in Canada" National *Post* (May 8, 2013).

28   Jordan Press, "Survey shows Muslim population is Canada's fastest growing religion in Canada" *National Post* (May 8, 2013).

29   "The Times They Are A Changin': Implications of Ontario's Changing Demographics".

30   Anna C. Korteweg, Jennifer A. Selby, eds. *Debating Sharia: Islam, Gender Politics, and Family Law Arbitration* (University of Toronto Press, 2012).

are trying to incorporate sharia law in ways consistent with "ideals of tolerance and pluralism". In the same vein, Westerners need to contextualize their own Western legal values in such a way that the "principle of equality between cultures" is taken at its true value to mean the giving of equal respect to Islamic ideals. That is, not equality in the sense that two separate systems are encouraged to co-exist alongside each other, but equality in that both sides learn to interact with each other in a state of mutual respect. Westerners need to understand that, just as Sharia principles are being influenced by Western values, so will Western values be influenced by sharia and Islamic values. This is what multiculturalism is all about: the bringing together of multiple cultures in a state of mutual enrichment for everyone. Muslims just want to rely on "Islamic principles and legal rules to guide or structure their daily lives", rather than on imperious liberal values that are closed to multicultural rethinking.[31]

This feminist take on the transformation of Western legal traditions through the incorporation of sharia principles is a more accurate rendition of how the meaning of multiculturalism is being determined by the actual "dynamic force" of mass immigration. Thus, in England proper, where Muslims are about 5 percent of the population, according to a 2011 census, and, more importantly, where a large percentage of the Muslims, ranging between 35 percent to 20 percent of the population, are already found in a number of cities, sharia law is no longer a debate about whether it should exist; it "has already become quite entrenched in Britain", according to Denis MacEoin's book, *Sharia Law Or 'one Law for All?*, which observes that:

> The Muslim Arbitration Tribunal claims to deal with family, inheritance, mosque and commercial disputes and has courts in London, Birmingham, Bradford, Nuneaton and Manchester. In truth there are many more courts.[32]

MacEoin argues plainly but effectively that the problem with sharia law is that it does not recognize the equal status of male and females

---

31 These passages come from L. Clarke, "Asking Questions about Sharia: Lessons from Ontario", and Jocelyne Cesari, "Foreword: Sharia and the Future of Western Secularism", in Anna C. Korteweg, Jennifer A. Selby, eds. *Debating Sharia: Islam, Gender Politics, and Family Law Arbitration*

32 Denis MacEoin, *Sharia Law Or 'one Law for All?* (Civitas: Institute for the Study of Civil Society, 2009), p. 2.

but "reflects" a "male-dominated" culture. Islam does not accord an equal hearing to a woman's opinion but holds that her voice is only half a man's voice. Sharia law also goes against the principle of Western liberalism that religious precepts should not partake in legal decision making, such as "remaining in good standing with Muslim ideals", or "acting in accordance with Islamic duty". Nevertheless, supporters of sharia law have already persuaded members of the British elite that multicultural tolerance should include accepting some form of sharia decision making, not necessarily a "parallel legal system", but at least "semi-autonomous social fields" of Islamic jurisprudence, to use the more acceptable language of pro-sharia activists.[33] The most notable convert is the Archbishop of Canterbury, who spoke sympathetically about sharia law in 2008, and most recently the incoming Prime Minister Theresa May, who sparked a controversy when she said British people could "benefit a great deal" from sharia teaching while calling for a review which will last up to 18 months to investigate whether sharia courts are discriminating against Muslim women and whether there are cases in which British law is being broken by sharia court decisions. Currently there are an estimated 100 sharia Law courts operating throughout the UK. What will determine the place of sharia in Britain is not what the PM says, decides, or what any review announces for the moment. The proportion of Muslims in Britain, which are projected to keep growing in the indefinite future, will be the deciding dynamic force.

---

33   Samia Bano, *Muslim Woman and Sharia Councils: Transcending the Boundaries of Community and Law* (Palgrave Publishers, 2012). Bano notes that "sharia councils have existed in Britain since the 1970s and 1980s" as unofficial legal bodies providing advice in family and marital disputes.

19

The Rise of Multicultural Globalism

George Grant's Lament for Canada

When George Grant lamented the "defeat of Canadian nationalism" in light of the inept failures of Diefenbaker's government to withstand continentalism and the American imposition of its "Lockian" corporate consumer culture in the early 1960s, he was simultaneously lamenting the defeat of Tory conservatism. For Grant the only force capable of sustaining the independence of Canada was Tory conservatism. This conservatism was "grounded in the wisdom of Sir John A. MacDonald, who saw plainly more than a hundred years ago that the only threat to nationalism was from the south, not across the sea".

> To be a Canadian was to build, along with the French, a more ordered and stable society than the liberal experiment in the United States.[1]

Liberals such as Frank Underhill had it backwards in thinking that Canada could only become a true nation by breaking off with its British heritage. It was Canada's Tory heritage, Grant insisted, along with the communitarian nationalism of the French in Quebec, which lay at the foundation of Canada's unique character and independence. This Tory conservatism recognized that the Canadian nation was predicated on both the rights of individuals and the "right of the community to restrain freedom in the name of the common good". [2] By the time Diefenbaker came along, this Tory conservatism had been thoroughly diluted, the British stock minimized, the pull of the "American way of life" irresistible, English-speakers looked "dull" and "stodgy".

Diefenbaker's nationalism came from his small town life in the

---

1   *Lament of a Nation: The Defeat of Canadian Nationalism*, (The Carleton Library, [1965] 1970, pp. 3-4.

2   *Ibid*, p. 64.

prairies. The old WASP elites of Montreal and Toronto were no longer interested in Canada's heritage, "most of them made money by being the representatives of American capitalism and setting up the branch plants". [3] Profit-making was their preoccupation, and the way to maximize profits was through continentalism. Diefenbaker was confused. In endorsing in the same vein the "free enterprise assumptions" that were now well ensconced within his party, along with the populist concerns of small town and rural Canadians, while never realizing that the survival of English Canadian nationalism required cooperation with French Canadians and acceptance of their rights as a people with communitarian rights, Diefenbaker's nationalism came to nothing more "than rhetoric and romance".

Grant came to the pessimistic conclusion that the "Lockian" liberalism of the Americans, "the freedom of the individual to use his property as he wishes, and for a limited government which must keep out of the market place", was unflappably tied with corporate capitalism, with the promotion of science and technology, testimony of a "dynamic society" in which "it is impossible to conserve anything for long", and in which, therefore, conservatism is impossible, and Canadian nationalism. "The impossibility of conservatism in our era is the impossibility of Canada". [4]

What Grant could not have envisioned was that the very years he was writing *Lament for A Nation* were the beginnings of the end of the two founding races of Canada, not just the consolidation of "Lockian" American capitalism, but the onset of Global Multicultural Capitalism against any form of cultural nationalism. He could not have foreseen the immensely despairing reality that Canadian conservatism would not only sell out to corporate capitalism, abandon its Tory nationalism, but would endorse the Liberal's celebration of the communitarian identities of non-whites and immigrants in opposition to any form of cultural and ethnic expressions by Anglo and Quebecois Canadians.

There was another development Grant could not have foreseen: the convergence of the Left and the Right across the Western world, both in their abandonment of so-called "rigid" ideological stances on economics and in their common support for mass immigration,

---

3   *Ibid*, p. 47.

4   *Ibid*, p. 68.

globalism, together with their common hatred of European ethno-national identities. Just as Canadian conservatives rejected Toryism, and American conservatives moved away from what would later come to be identified as "Paleoconservatism", in the name of what is now known as "Neoconservatism", so did formerly left-wing political parties began to advocate, from the late 1970s on, a "centre-left" politics, known in Britain as the "Third Way", involving a rejection of "rigid" government interventionism, commitment to balanced budgets, emphasis on personal responsibility, encouragement of public-private partnerships, coupled with the provision of equal opportunity through investment in "human development", education, and protection of social capital.[5]

It has been, however, in their endorsement of globalism (masquerading as globalization) that the left and right have really converged in a state of amicable reinforcement, notwithstanding their varying emphasis on different aspects of globalism. The right's main interest has been the promotion of policies that augment the expansion of global capitalism, deregulation, freer mobility of capital and information at low cost between borders, as well as international labour migration. Corporate globalists want goods with a generic identity for consumers across the globe. They prefer niche markets without clear national boundaries, "globally standardized products that are advanced, functional, reliable—and low price". They don't want consumers with "deeply ingrained local preferences of taste". They want to sell "in all national markets the same kind of products sold at home or in their largest export market...on the basis of appropriate value—the best combinations of price, quality, reliability, and delivery". They want "products that are globally identical with respect to design, function, and even fashion". National identities are inefficient, slow moving, inconsistent with the new technologies of communications. They want humans without national identities endlessly seeking pleasures in a "homogenized world market" in which every person in the globe "wants products and features that everybody else wants". Different cultural preferences, national tastes, production standards and technologies are "vestiges of the past". [6] Globalists don't want consumers and producers who will

---

5   Anthony Giddens. *Beyond Left and Right: The Future of Radical Politics.* (UK: Polity Press, 1994).

6   The cited words in this paragraph come from an article published back in 1983, now seen as quite original, by Theodore Levitt, "The Globalization of Markets", *Harvard Business Review* (May 1983).

care about the national economy, national jobs, and resent corporations who move in and out of towns without caring for the effects these movements have on the communities.

The Left's globalist narrative is more complicated and goes something like this: Humans are members of the same species; the racial differences between them are superficial, cultures should not be viewed in "essentialist" terms, but as constructs in a state of continuous change. To be a true liberal, one must allow individuals to express themselves without being tied to pre-given identities, be they cultural, national, or sexual identities. With the "freeing" of humans from identities "constructed" by "white males" and the emergence of new gender and racial identities, humans will learn to become global citizens, identifying themselves as members of an "international community" devoid of hierarchies of dominance and the divisions generated by "exclusive" national identities. These new humans will be morally sensitive to the suffering of "strangers", quick in their responses to violations in the human rights of everyone, assist those threatened by famines in Africa, tsunamis in Asia, floods and earthquakes, while celebrating trans-sexuality and pan-sexuality in an orgiastic state of happiness. With the spread of transnational corporations, IGOs and INGOs, the European Union and other supranational organizations and trade blocs, power has become "deterritorialized" and so there is a need for global governance and the breakdown of nationalism. As members of this increasingly transnational world, Europeans must think of their cosmopolitan responsibility rather than their national interests.[7]

The right may not be as keen with leftist demands for "global social justice", but corporate globalists have come to realize that the seemingly humanitarian concerns of the left serve as an excellent moral umbrella for the spread of global capitalism. Corporations love the way leftist causes adorned the narcissistic consumerist culture they promote with humanitarian concerns about transsexual rights, "discriminated minorities" and "suffering refugees". The left and the right have

---

7   The literature on these issues is massive. For some samples, see Mikhail Epstein, "Transculture: A Broad Way Between Globalism and Multiculturalism". *The American Journal of Economics and Sociology* vol. 68, no. 1 (2009). One much cited article is Inderpal Grewal and Caren Kaplan, "Global Identities: Theorizing Transnational Studies of Sexuality" *A Journal of Lesbian and Gay Studies* vol. 7. No. 4 (2001). The whole project of breaking apart identities, and they really mean European identities, fascinates the left, see in particular the many publications of Zygmunt Bauman; for example, *Culture in a Liquid Modern World*. (Polity Press, 2011).

actually reached a new consensus on the supposed *economic* benefits of mass immigration. The dominant pro-immigration argument today is really a combination of right and left economic concerns about how the populations of Western countries are set to decline dramatically in the next decades due to continuing below-replacement fertility rates, which is resulting in a shrinking labour force, at the same time as the population is aging, which will bring a decline, so they argue, in both economic growth and in the possibility of financing socialist programs. A decline in population, both sides say, will bring a "massive" crisis which, left to its own, without mass immigration, will result in widespread labour shortages, lower tax receipts, declining welfare supports and lower consumption levels.[8]

Only now has this convergence come to be well understood with Brexit, the election of Donald Trump, and the persistent growth of populist nationalist parties in Europe with platforms that stray between (and away from) traditionally left and right positions. As a recent mainstream article announced: "Forget left and right—the new divide in politics is between nationalists and globalists". My aim in this chapter, however, is not to explain the convergence of the right and left, but to continue my argument on the radicalizing normative climate in Canada by focusing on some of the ways in which conservatives in the 1980s and after came to endorse, sometimes with even stronger commitment, the outlook of multiculturalism, diversity, including the anti-racist hysteria of the left. The result of this was that the only party that had occasionally argued, in the spirit of Toryism, in favor of the political, of the group rights of Euro-Canadians, capitulated by the 1980s.

Brian Mulroney's Globalist "Post Fordist Regime" of Accumulation

One of the most talked about books in Canadian politics is Stevie Cameron's *On the Take: Crime, Corruption and Greed in the Mulroney Years*, which came out in 1994. Written from a partisan leftist view, this book accused Mulroney's government of rampant corruption and backroom deals with powerful lobbies. Cameron attributed

---

8   Ricardo Duchesne, "There is no Capitalist or Socialist Economic Rationale for Mass Immigration" Council of European Canadians (March 11, 2016), http://www. Euro-Canadian.ca/2016/03/no-capitalist-or-socialist-economic-rationale-exists-for-mass-immigration.html

this to Mulroney's right wing, "open for business" attitude, in which everything was "for sale" and corporate values prevailed above social democratic concerns. Critics of this book have either questioned some of Cameron's charges, or have said there was nothing particularly unusual about Mulroney's corruption, as the subsequent government of Jean Chrétien would demonstrate with its own corruption scandals. What this perspective on Mulroney's "right wing" administration misses is that Mulroney, Conservative Prime Minister of Canada from 1984 to 1993, was the most ardent promoter of multiculturalism, mass immigration, and a global identity for Canada. It was under his government that mass scale immigration from non-European sources on a continuous basis irrespective of the economic needs of the Canadian working class was fully implemented. It was under his insistence that multiculturalism would be enforced into "all aspects of Canadian society" and that Canada would be sold to the world as a business place with a global, not a national, identity dedicated to the enhancement of racial diversity. The Conservatives had come to realize that cultural Marxism was conterminous with global capitalism and that selling Canada to the world for its humanitarian diversity was a great image to solidify global capitalism in Canada.

In June 1984, Mulroney told a cheering crowd, right upon his election, that his party now stood for multiculturalism and would not allow itself to be called "the Party of White Anglo-Saxon Protestants". Multicultural diversity, he said, was an absolutely obligatory part of Canada's national identity and to reject it was to reject Canada. He then outlined future changes his party intended to implement in the hiring policies of the federal government, services in non-official languages, funds for the preservation and advancement of non-European cultures and greater efforts to "stamp out racism wherever it rears its ugly head". [9]

Mulroney was part expression of a worldwide realization among conservative politicians that New Left ideas, with their focus on cultural politics, opposition to patriarchal and nationalist working classes, were not incompatible with capitalist accumulation but could function instead as "humanitarian" superstructural supports. During the late 1970s, and with ever more serious gravity in the 1980s, the international capitalist elites had come to the realization that the Keynesian regime of accumulation, which had brought effective

9   Freda Hawkins, *Critical Years in Immigration, Canada and Australia Compared* (1991), p. 240.

demand and economic stability from the late 1940s to the early 1970s, and which involved a "class compromise" between the white working class and the business elites, together with husband-supporting wages, job protection, and rising incomes across the board, was no longer suitable for the more globalizing imperatives of capitalism.

This regime of accumulation, identified by French Marxist Regulation Theory as a "Fordist regime of accumulation"[10] in reference to Henry Ford and the creation of a new form of capitalism in the 20th century based on mass production and mass consumption, was exhausted; it could no longer generate high profits in the 1970s as Western economies were experiencing slow growth, stagflation, or inflation combined with unemployment, with no Keynesian solutions in sight. The elections of Thatcher (1979), Reagan (1980), and Mulroney facilitated the ability of the capitalist elites to develop a new regime of accumulation, which has come to be known as "Post-Fordist".

This Post-Fordist regime involves globalized financial markets and free trade zones allowing businesses to move across national borders in search of lower wages and unregulated standards. It involves an emphasis on service industries rather than manufacturing, including pursuit of niche markets without national characteristics, new communication technologies for up to the minute financial information and investments decisions, in and out of nations, as well as intensification of a feminized workforce with stagnant wages and double-income families.[11]

Conservative politicians were themselves pawns within the wider web of global capitalist forces. Their role was to create a political climate that would facilitate the introduction of this Post-Fordist regime. Playing up to usual conservative tropes of "limited government", "self-reliance", "private property", "traditional values" worked well for right wing journalists seeking moral comfort. These values were all the more wondrous when combined with the new norms of racial equity, Third World dignity, human rights for all, gender equality, and a form of civic nationalism open to the world's peoples.

---

10   Robert Brenner and Mark Glick, "The Regulation Approach: Theory and History" *New Left Review* (Number 188, 1991). Bob Jessop, "Twenty Years of the (Parisian) Regulation Approach: the Paradox of Success and Failure at Home and Abroad" *New Political Economy*, vol. 2, no. 3, 1997.

11   Michael Porter, "The Competitive Advantage of Nations" *Harvard Business Review* (March-April 1990).

For the secure jobs of the past, which allowed men to be the breadwinner of the family, the Post-Fordist regime provided temporary work with "flexible scheduling" in the service sector at low wages, with no benefits or security, and little opportunity for mobility, while maximizing the efficiency and productivity of businesses. Regulation Marxists analyzed these changes well but failed to appreciate how capitalists managed to incorporate the New Left's cultural critique of Western patriarchy and racism. Under Mulroney's "Progressive Conservatives" Canada was showcased to the world as a nation successfully integrating the norms of multiculturalism, mass immigration and human rights while playing up its "realistic" appreciation of economic matters.

My point is not the economic policies of the Mulroney administration were necessarily a "failure". They were "required" to keep the process of accumulation going. One can argue that NAFTA and other multilateral agreements that transformed GATT into the World Trade Organization increased the competitiveness of Canadian firms, pressuring companies to become more specialized and integrated into globally based supply and distribution networks, while affording consumers with a greater variety of goods at cheaper prices. One can also make a good case about the benefits of converting the federal sales tax into the goods and services tax, the reduction of investment controls, privatization of many crown corporations, as well as sound efforts to cut government spending to levels closer to government's revenues.[12] My critical observations concern the ways in which these right wing economic policies were framed within the ideology of immigrant multiculturalism, and the degree to which the radicalizing momentum of the post WWII normative climate had taken over Canadian conservatism.

There were three key legislative and policy measures pushed by the Mulroney administration to bring about the integration of right wing economics with immigrant multiculturalism:

• Employment Equity Act of 1986

• Multiculturalism Act of 1988

---

12   Michael Hart and Bill Dymond, "Six Stewards of Canada's Economy – History by the Numbers Favours Mulroney and Chretien While Trudeau Leaves a Legacy of Deficits and Debts" *Policy Options* (2003).

- Five Year Immigration Plan, 1990-1995, to bring at least 250,000 immigrants per year in recessionary times, regardless of fluctuations in the unemployment rate.

Employment Equity and Multiculturalism Act

The Employment Equity Act of 1986[13] had nothing to do with closing the gap between the rich and the working classes. The Act, targeted to federally regulated employees, mandated employers to eliminate "barriers" limiting employment opportunities to historically disadvantaged Aboriginals, women and visible minorities. Formal legal equality in hiring (treating everyone equally regardless of race and gender) was not enough; it was also "necessary to amend historic wrongs and ameliorate the economic differences among groups". "Positive" policies for the hiring, training, retention, and promotion of members of "disadvantaged" groups would be encouraged. Since everyone was lumped together, visible minorities, Aboriginals, rich non-white immigrants, women from every class and colour, and people with disabilities, historic wrongs applied to any of these groups, except white males. Rich non-white immigrants just off the plane were to be given preference over poor white males born in Canada.

In passing the Multiculturalism Act of 1988, Canada became the first country in the world to pass a law designating itself as a nation committed to "preserve and enhance multiculturalism" and allow immigrants and minorities to "keep their identities without the fear of official persecution". The aim of the Act was to effectively "multiculturalize" every aspect of Canadian life, starting with the administrative practices of the executive branch, in the areas of hiring, promotion of non-discrimination, and, in the words of Joseph Magnet, "sensitization of the federal public workforce to the multicultural principle". [14]

The preamble to the Act established the connection between the 1982 Charter's objective of "preserving and enhancing the multicultural

---

13   Brenda Cardillo, "Defining and measuring employment equity" *Perspectives* vol. 5, no. 4 (1993), http://www.statcan.gc.ca/pub/75-001-x/1993004/38-eng.pdf

14   Joseph Eliot Magnet, "Multiculturalism in the Canadian Charter of Rights and Freedoms", in Beaudoin and Mendes, eds. *The Canadian Charter of Rights and Freedoms* (Carswell, 1996), Chapter 18, p. 21.

heritage of Canada", "while working to achieve the equality of all Canadians in the economic, social, cultural and political life of Canada". This reference to equality meant both that there would be no discrimination in terms of race, national origin and religion, and that Canada was committed to the equality of members of all ethnic groups to preserve, enhance, and share their cultural heritage. It needs to be emphasize that the aim of the Act was not merely to ensure equal treatment and respect for all Canadians regardless of ethnicity; it was also to ensure, in the words of Magnet, "freedom from discrimination and *group survival*". [15]

The Act specifies that the following objectives should be taken into account in the development of policies and programs: recognition of the historic contribution to Canadian society of different ethnic communities, the equal value of the diversity of all individuals, the assurance that all individuals will be treated equally under the law at the same time that their diversity will be respected and valued equally, the promotion of interaction among different cultural communities as a way of enhancing understanding and creativity. [16] In 1991, a Department of Multiculturalism and Citizenship was created with a mandate to promote "appreciation, acceptance and implementation of the principles of racial equality and multiculturalism". This Department was also entrusted with the promotion of non-Anglo-European "cultures, languages and ethnocultural group identities".

Starting in the 1990s, more than ever, Canadians would be told that what made them distinctive as a people was their multicultural identity, not the many centuries that went into the creation of the nation, the Quebecois and Acadians who were born as a new people in the soil of New France and created all the institutions and cultures of Acadia and Quebec, without hardly any immigrants arriving until the 1960s; or the Anglo pioneers and settlers who created the rest of Canada's political institutions and culture, along with the settlers and immigrants from the British Isles and from Europe; no, this was a past to be overcome in the name of a new vision of Canada as a nation of diverse peoples. Citizenship and Immigration Canada would provide

---

15   *Ibid*. Italics added.

16   Jack Jedwab, "To Preserve and Enhance: Canadian Multiculturalism Before and After the Charter", in Magnet et al. *The Canadian Charter of Rights and Freedoms: Reflections on the Charter After Twenty Years* (Butterworths, 2003).

"strategic direction for implementing the Canadian Multiculturalism Act", by "helping federal and public institutions to respond to the needs of a diverse society", by supporting "public education programs and outreach initiatives such as Black History Month, Asian Heritage Month", as well creating a "Federal-Provincial-Territorial Multiculturalism Network".[17] A key component of the "education programs" was the teaching of a new revised history of Canada's heritage that would accentuate the role of Aboriginals and "diverse" immigrants rather than the British heritage.

In a 2002 publication released by Citizenship and Immigration Canada, *A Newcomer's Introduction to Canada*, "for new immigrants", it was announced that "Canada is a land of many cultures and many peoples". Other than the Aboriginal people, identified as the "First Nation", everyone was identified as an immigrant: "We have all come from somewhere else". "Through Canada's history, millions of immigrants have helped to build this country". [18] Minorities would stand for authentic cultural traditions to be celebrated for their colour and vibrancy. This stamping out, promoted both in multiple government publications and integrated into the curriculum across Canada, was directed singularly against the British people and their legacy in Canada.

The French in Quebec had successfully managed to portray themselves, from the 60s onward, as an oppressed minority within Canada with its own legitimate identity seeking a new constitutional deal framed against Anglo Canada. It was the British, and then the Europeans who

---

17   ARCHIVED – Annual Report on the Operation of the Canadian Multiculturalism Act, 2012-2013", http://www.cic.gc.ca/english/resources/publications/multi-report2013/3.asp

18   This publication is no longer available; the old link now redirects you: "The publication 'A Newcomer's Introduction to Canada' is no longer available. Please refer to the 'Welcome to Canada: What you Should Know' for information on settling in Canada", http://www.cic.gc.ca/English/pdf/pub/welcome.pdf This new publication, published in 2013, is differently focused on providing basic information about "settling" in Canada, and, actually, to its credit, has a section, "Diversity and its Limits", with the following words: "Canada's openness and generosity do not extend to barbaric cultural practices that tolerate spousal abuse, honour killings, female genital mutilation, forced marriage or other gender based violence. Those guilty of these crimes are severely punished under Canada's criminal laws". Of course, this should be obvious; nevertheless, it is worth noting that this is a publication expressing the "assimilationist" conservative argument. The older "A Newcomer's Introduction to Canada" is referenced in some books and articles, with cited words: Shauna Wilton, "Official Literature for New Canadians. Images and Perceptions of Canada" in Pierre Anctil and Zila Bernd, eds. *Canada from the Outside In: New Trends in Canadian Studies* (Peter Lang 2006), pp. 241-242.

had assimilated to English Canada, who would be asked to relinquish any sense of culture deeply grounded in ethnic bonds, ancestry, and cultural habits. The ethnicity of Native peoples would be viewed in primordial terms as deeply rooted in their lands, communities, histories, and customary identities. But normal British and English Europeans would be prohibited from binding themselves to a geographical and cultural "homeland". There was no such thing as a Canadian identity that could be linked primordially to the British. The British-Canadian identity was to be witnessed only in multicultural tolerance, pluralist values, democracy, and diversity. Asians, Blacks, and Latinos would have hyphenated identities such as "I am really Chinese, but I live in mosaic Canada", or "I have ethnic Chinese roots, but I identify with Canadian diversity and democracy". [19] Indeed, in the degree to which the British were identified historically as the agents of racist and exclusionary immigration practices, whereas the immigrants (including the millions who were not yet in Canada) were the victims of such practices, multiculturalism would promote a state of mind in which the agents of Canadian diversification, the immigrants and minorities, would be automatically viewed as progressive, whereas the Canadians who opposed this diversification would be seen as xenophobic and intolerant, and therefore as people to be investigated for hate speech violations.

We can only offer an overview of the thousands of acts, events, changes, and policies implemented during this period at the federal, provincial, and local levels to create a multicultural Canada, involving integration into the labour market, into the electoral process, into civil society.

Writing about these programs and changes would take too much space. Suffice it to make this last point: the introduction of multiculturalism into the education of children would not be a matter of adding a course here and there in the curriculum, but would become a pervasive and defining feature of schooling. The central component of this new schooling would be a curriculum focused on fighting "racism", "anti-Black and anti-Asian prejudices", not just "structural and institutional" forms of racism, but the "sometimes subtle" forms implicit in Canadian culture and in the psychology of

---

19   On "ethnic identity", "hybridity" and "ethnic formation processes in Canada", see Alan Simmons, *Immigration and Canada. Global and Transnational Perspectives* (Canadian Scholar's Press, 2010), pp. 196-207.

white children.[20] Students would be taught about the "inequities in education in schools and universities, as well as in media, policing and law and the courts; in the provisions for health care; and in many other areas in communities from business to voluntary organizations". They would be taught how the concept of human rights was critical "to support anti-racism" and how this concept had been progressively expanded over the years as a weapon to fight any perceived form of discrimination in Canada.[21]

Immigration During the Harper Years

The third major change brought by Mulroney, under the Five Year Immigration Plan, 1990-1995, was a commitment to bring at least 250,000 immigrants every year in opposition to the long standing link between annual immigration intakes and existing economic conditions in Canada. To quote Kelley and Trebilcock:

> For the first time in Canadian history, the government — supported by most of the major political parties [actually by all] — committed itself to a longer term view of immigration less influenced by current stages in the business cycle, and to a significant increase in immigration at a time of serious economic recession. This policy represented a sharp departure from the Department of Labour's view in the 1950s and 1960s that immigration levels should reflect the current state of the economy". [22]

Those who argue that the moment a nation has a capitalist economy,

---

20   The promotion of a "multicultural education" skyrocketed in the 1990s, and is now a massive industry, possibly the biggest industry ever in education and curriculum reform, backed by continuous flows of funding from the government. For endless, incessant propaganda on the benefits of breaking Canada away from its European heritage and cultivating a diverse curriculum and race mixing, see the website of the "Canadian Multicultural Foundation", http://www.cmef.ca/

21   Keith A. McLeod and Eva Krugly-Smolska, eds. "Multicultural Education: A Place To Start. Guideline for Classrooms, Schools and Communities. Diversity in Canada" (Published by the Canadian Association of Second Language Teachers, 1997), http://www.caslt.org/Print/rep5ep.htm   Among the many coded-words and mandates produced by "multicultural education" are "cultural responsiveness" in teacher attitudes and beliefs, "resisting resistance to cultural diversity in teacher education and classroom instruction", see Geneva Gay, "Teaching To and Through Cultural Diversity" *Curriculum Inquiry* vol. 43, no. 1 (2013). This is a journal associated with The Ontario Institute for Studies in Education of the University of Toronto.

22   *The Making of the Mosaic*, p. 385.

the pressures for globalization and for mobile labor across borders will be unstoppable, forget that throughout Canada's history the economic argument for immigration was embedded to the idea that Canada was and must remain a "white man's country". It is true that during the early 1900s, business leaders were able to recruit cheap immigrant labourers from Asia for mining, logging, and railway construction, but the Vancouver Riot of 1907, among other events, led to the stringent Immigration Act of 1910 and the Immigration Act Amendment of 1919, with the end result that only continental Europeans were allowed as wage labourers. After WWII as well, businesses made arguments in favour of bringing immigrants from non-European nations using the rationale that Europeans were no longer as interested in coming to Canada by the late 1950s, at a time when Canada's economy was booming and short of manpower. But the goal then was to bring in a few thousand in response to the economic needs of Canadians, while also making sure that the cultural character of Canada was not changed. As Kelley and Trebilcock have noted, up until Mulroney's time, there was a tap on tap off immigration policy, which Trudeau used during the recession years of the 1970s.

It was really from Mulroney's time that Canada's historical ethnic identity would start to undergo a dramatic alteration. From 1981 to 2001, the number of visible minorities (excluding Aboriginals) increased more than threefold from 1.1 million people, or nearly 5% of the population, to 4.0 million people, or 13% of the population. This growth was primarily a result of rapidly rising immigration intakes after the mid-1980s. As Jason Kenney, the Immigration and Multiculturalism Minister (2008-2013) during Stephen Harper's conservative government, proudly told *Maclean's* magazine:

'[T]he Mulroney government ran the most, quote, 'progressive' immigration policy in Canadian history.' Over his nine years in office, Mulroney tripled immigration levels from 85,000 in 1983 to more than 260,000. 'He brought in the Multiculturalism Act. He brought in more generous family reunification policies, which are the most popular element of immigration policy. Entire communities were founded under Brian Mulroney, like the Hong Kong immigrants pre-'97 who came in through a special investor program.' [23]

23 See *The Canadian Encyclopedia* article, "Jason Kenney Reinventing the Conservative

Kelley and Trebilcock point out that from Mulroney through to Stephen Harper's years, there was "broad political and public consensus" or "a widely shared commitment to a relatively high and constant level of immigration" across the political spectrum. Even Bob White, president of the Canadian Labour Congress, argued in 1992 that large scale immigration did not take jobs from native workers but created new ones. Almost everyone came to believe that "a dramatically more diverse, multi-ethnic, multicultural immigrant intake" was good for Canada.[24]

There was an exception, however, by way of the Reform Party. Although this party began as a Western Canada-based protest movement, it became a federal political party from 1987 to 2000. Apart from its populist demands for democratic reforms and its strict social conservative views, what stood out about this party, and what brought it down eventually, was its opposition to the consensus on high level immigration. In 1991, it issued a statement stating its opposition to "any immigration...designed to radically or suddenly alter the ethnic makeup of Canada". The Reform Party was forced to back off from this statement after intense accusations that it was harboring racist and xenophobic ideas. These types of accusations continued to plague the Reform Party through the 1990s, with a Toronto-area candidate forced to withdraw his candidacy in 1993 after making "anti-immigrant" remarks. Despite the efforts of the leader, Preston Manning, to eliminate any ethnic-based language from the Party's immigration proposals, and despite selecting minority candidates to run as candidates in the 1997 federal election, the party could not escape the relentless media campaigns against its "intolerant" and bigoted" views. Eventually, this party was replaced in 2000 by a more palatable party, the Canadian Alliance, which combined about half of the Progressive Conservative policies, and half of Reform's policies, minus the immigration card. From this alliance the "new" Conservative Party was born in 2003.

As the Reform movement was defeated, ethnic and refugee groups, together with their legal and academic advocates, grew in power, ready to pounce at the slightest indication that the reigning government might consider stricter selection criteria or a more restrictive refugee

Party", http://www.thecanadianencylcopedia.ca/en/article/jason-kenney-reinventing-the-conservative-party/

24   *The Making of the Mosaic*, p. 416.

admissions approach. During the Liberal government of Jean Chretien (1993-2003), for example, a huge controversy followed the publication of a report in 1997, *Not Just by Numbers: A Canadian Framework for Future Immigration*, simply because this report recommended the introduction of standardized admission tests to prove fluency in English or French. The government was forced to change tune, though after 9/11, with everyone concerned about security, the Immigration and Refugee Protection Act was passed in June 2002 designed to stop criminals and illegal immigrants from getting into the country as well as enhance the power of security to prosecute people smuggling. While there was some optimism about immigration reforms, with the election of Stephen Harper in 2006, particularly with the appointment of Jason Kenney in 2008 as Immigration and Multiculturalism Minister, the end result of Harper's reign was the reinforcement of the new consensus favouring a continuously high level of immigration. Kenney did play up the assimilationist side, Canadian identity, raising concerns over the language abilities of immigrants, over ethnic enclaves, and the "radicalization" of immigrants. And he did introduce a few changes, very modest, but which nevertheless instigated outcries from the left, such as the 2012 Faster Removal of Foreign Criminals Act, new rules against conferring citizenship on children who were born outside of Canada to parents also born outside of Canada, and protections against marriage fraud. Yet, in the end, Kenney, and the Harper government, more than ever, would make a habit of boasting about how their conservative government had sustained immigration levels that made "Canada the largest per capita receiver of new immigrants in the entire world", and how the immigrants it brought deserved to be admired as truly Canadian for having "a much higher incidence of post-secondary degrees than the Canadian population at large". [25]

This is true: under Harper, the admission of immigrants into Canada reached its highest levels ever since the early 1900s, with immigration numbers ranging from 240,000 to 265,000 between 2003 and 2012. The government also increased the total number of temporary foreign workers, steadily, from 102, 932 in 2003 to 213, 573 workers in 2012. The effects of these numbers on the ethnic composition of Canada were substantial: In 2011, Canada had a foreign-born population of about 6,775,800 people, which represented 20.6% of the total

---

25 Josh Visser, "Jason Kenney lashes out angrily after Bob Rae blames 'anti-immigration bias' for troubled temporary foreign worker file" *National Post* (April 30, 2014).

population, the highest proportion among the G8 countries.[26] The Conservative Party, in fact, turned the concerns of the Reform Party on its head, committing itself to the cultivation of ethnic voters as a way of enhancing Canada's conservative values. Kenney, who spent most his days as MP donning ethnic attire in countless ceremonies, put it this way:

> If we are honest, Canadians have much to learn from our newest arrivals. The foundation of strong families, the value of faith, the necessity of excellence in education. To the extent that those values need to be renewed in every generation if Canada is to remain strong and free, immigrants are our allies.[27]

Instead of satisfying them, these acts embittered leftists lest they lose the ethnic vote, with some hysterically accusing Harper of an "abhorrent record on refugees and immigration". But beyond differences about who was the most "open" and "compassionate" towards immigrants, these years saw the consolidation, across the West, of a new consensus expressing the view that high rates of immigration were "necessary" if the Western world was to avert economic decline and a collapse of the welfare state. Countless studies were commissioned arguing that Westerners had no choice but to welcome millions of immigrants due to persisting low fertility rates among whites, a shrinking domestic labour force, and an aging population in need of health care and pensions. While the leftist side emphasized the supports new immigrants offered to the maintenance of the welfare state, the right emphasized the overall economic benefits of labour-force growth. Mind you, some leftists philosophers, Emmanuel Levinas and Jacques Derrida, did not want anything to do with such hedonistic concerns, and emphasized instead the nurturing of a new cosmopolitan ethics, beyond the still Eurocentric perspective of Immanuel Kant, a cosmopolitan community

---

26 Statistics Canada, https://www12.statcan.gc.ca/census-recensement/2006/ref/info/immigration-eng.cfm

27 "Jason Kenney Reinventing the Conservative Party", http://www.thecanadianencyclopedia.ca/en/article/jason-kenney-reinventing-the-conservative-party/ The "objective" of Kenney is well described in Alec Castonguay, "The inside story of Jason Kenney's campaign to win over ethnic votes" *Maclean's* (February 2, 2013): "His objective: understanding, seducing and attracting ethnic communities to the Conservative party, an electorate once taken for granted by the Liberal Party of Canada. He has shaken thousands of hands, put away hundreds of very spicy meals and pulled off his shoes an incalculable number of times in entering mosques, temples or integration centres to give speeches".

based on an all-inclusive morality, "unconditional hospitality" towards the Other, "goodness, mercy, charity", with white families educated enough to welcome "strangers" (who turned out to be rapists) into their homes, standing above the insidious parochial values of the past.[28] These concerns were sometimes voiced by "compassionate" conservatives, though, on the whole, they preferred to talk about data oriented studies "demonstrating" the ways in which trade liberalization fuelled economic growth, brought higher incomes and less poverty in the world, and eased the diffusion of technologies across borders.

The Left and Right are two sides of the same coin promoting globalism and identifying nationalists as the enemy. In the language of Carl Schmitt, both sides believe that the friend-enemy distinction can be abolished in a world in which there is a consensus on basic human rights and economic interdependency. The one obstacle standing in the way of this abolition, they hold, is the tribalism of nationalism and white identity. Mass immigration will result in the mixing of races inside white created countries, and this will result in eternal happiness and endless prosperity. This view was encapsulated in a recent *New York Times* article:

> [B]eing mixed makes it harder to fall back on the tribal identities that have guided so much of human history, and that are now resurgent. Your background pushes you to construct a worldview that transcends the tribal...President Trump has answered this challenge by reaching backward — vowing to wall off America and invoking a whiter, more homogeneous country...The point is that diversity — of one's own makeup, one's experience, of groups of people solving problems, of cities and nations — is linked to economic prosperity, greater scientific prowess and a fairer judicial process.[29]

---

28 Mustafa Dikec, Nigel Clark, Clive Barnett, "Extending Hospitality: Giving Space, Taking Time" *Paragraph*, vol 32, no. 1 (2009).

29 Moises Velasquez-Manoff, "What Biracial People" *New York Times* (March 4, 2017). This article, as is the case with other similarly argued articles I have seen, suffers from a sequence of monumental contradictions. First, it argues against the racist "homogeneity" of whiter America, while insisting that race-mixed individuals are superior in intelligence and overall ability to create better nations. Secondly, it says that increasing racial diversification in the United States has been behind its prosperity, while informing us that "multiracials" today make up only "an estimated 7 percent of Americans". What about the making of the United States into the wealthiest and most innovative nation in the world by the 1950s when the nation was whiter, and when non-whites were not partaking in the nation's creative genius? Thirdly, the studies it cites about the superiority of mixed individuals amount to nothing more than

What the globalists fail to realize is that only Europeans are relinquishing the political, their tribal identity, whereas non-European nations and ethnic groups inside the West are globalizing and playing up to cosmopolitan values while maintaining their ethno-national identities. In the end, non-Europeans, if current trends continue, will win since the political ultimately exists in the context of a national community, and can never become universal. The US versus Them distinction cannot be abolished, for it is part of human nature, human creativity, the very energy that makes life meaningful, gives it colour and real diversity.

Refuting the Economic Argument for Immigration

I have already presented some arguments against the widespread claim that constant high level immigration is beneficial to Canadians. Kelley and Trebilcock cite mostly the pro-immigration economic arguments according to which immigrants "bring net benefits, not only because they supply labour but also because they require goods and services, thus increasing the demand for locally supplied labour". They cite other studies claiming that immigrants compete "for different types of jobs" than natives and so they "complement" rather than "replace one another". They also bring studies claiming "that increased immigration [has] tended to generate a net fiscal surplus, playing little observable role in reducing wages".

The only studies these two leftists mention countering these claims are about how recent immigrants have not fared as well as earlier immigrants, resulting in a "widening gap between the earnings of the Canadian born and the foreign born". This latter finding, of course, is not a counter argument, but is actually an observation the promoters of immigration love to bring up to argue that more needs to be done to overcome the "racist inequities" in the earnings of Canadians and immigrants. Kelley and Trebilcock footnote *The Effects of Mass Immigration on Canadian Living Standard*, edited by Herbert Grubel (which I consulted in my empirical refutation of Kymlicka's claims),

---

"demonstrating" that race mixed individuals tend to be stronger believers in "diversity", and thus they are better for the nation's wellbeing. This is the trashy reasoning they teach at American Ivy Leagues.

but they don't bring any of the arguments of this book. *The Making of the Mosaic* is supposed to be a comprehensive assessment of the history of immigration and its role in shaping Canada, with a focus on the role of economic factors, "meticulously documented", and yet the benefits of the current "constant high level of immigration" is taken as a given, which should not surprise us, since the entire left-right establishment is committed to this policy; all the funding goes to research pre-packaged in "demonstrating" that immigration is good.

Since Kelley and Trebilcock frame some of their claims in relation to the benefits of immigration generally for Western nations, and since I have already addressed the Canadian situation,[30] with some minor statements concerning the disastrous situation in Europe, I will close this chapter by highlighting the situation in Sweden, with some references to Germany. This is not irrelevant to Canada. Diversification and mass

---

30 I will add here that there is a major study by Ellen Russell and Mathieu Dufour on the very complicated question of Canadian living standards since the 1970s, with the title "Rising Profit Shares, Falling Wage Shares", published in 2007 by The Canadian Centre for Policy Alternatives, showing that during the years in which the policy of a "high and constant level of immigration" was effected, "despite a prolonged period of economic expansion...Canadians' average real wages—which are wages adjusted for inflation—have not increased in more than 30 years...Canada's economy grew by 72% between 1975 and 2005, in real per capita terms. Over the same time period, labour productivity (measured as GDP/hour) grew by 51%. A growing economy with rising labour productivity seems like it would translate into rising real wages. But this has not been the case...Real wages have been stagnant for 30 years running. This 30-year stagnation of Canadian workers' real wages is dramatically at odds with previous historical experience...From 1961 until the late-1970s, it was the norm for workers' real wages to rise continuously...The stagnation of workers' real average wages is remarkable, given that Canadian workers are increasingly productive...[M]ost economic models would predict that real wages rise as productivity rises. But it is evident that rising productivity is not generating a commensurate rise in real wages. A stagnation of workers' real average wages despite their rising productivity is a powerful indictment of the promise that a growing economy—and increased productivity—will produce benefits widely shared by the majority of Canadian workers. It simply isn't happening...Canadian workers' wage share increased between 1961 and the late-1970s, then it started a steady decline that continues today... In 1961 workers' wage share was 64.61% of the remaining economic pie, while by 2005 their wage share had fallen to just over 60%—the lowest level we've seen in workers' wage share since 1961". So, who benefited from this new regime of accumulation? Answer: "Corporate profit shares follow the opposite path...Corporate profit shares dropped in the 1960s, through the late-1970s and early-1980s. After that the profit share rose steadily— dramatically so in the last several years. (In terms of yearly data, the small dips in the early-1980s and early- 1990s were associated with recessions.) Corporate profit shares went from 28.91% of the remaining economic pie in 1961 to 33.68% by 2005—the highest level we've seen in profit share since 1961...[C]orporations' profit share has been persistently increasing while workers' wage share has been persistently decreasing since the late-1970s". See Ellen Russell and Mathieu Dufour, "Rising Profit Shares, Falling Wage Shares", http://policyalternatives.ca/sites/default/files/uploads/publications/National_Office_Pubs/2007/Rising_Profit_Shares_Falling_Wage_Shares.pdf

immigration are a Western-wide phenomenon, and only when we approach it as such, can we fully understand that the arguments made for diversification in Canada are part of a wider package of arguments for diversification of all white nations, and part of a program to destroy white identity.

Sweden is lauded by immigration advocates as the one nation that is "weathering the demographic storm" with its high acceptance of asylum seekers and economic migrants in the past two decades. The Right/Left propaganda is that Sweden has been "expanding" since 2010 with "high private consumption and investment underpinning economic growth", that GDP expanded by 3.6 percent in 2015 and that "employment is rising and unemployment is falling". But beyond these isolated facts, the evidence is otherwise. Keep in mind that Swedes are not allowed to voice critical views about immigration, so we have to rely on the observations of the few who dare to question the government's allegations. Tino Sanandaji, perhaps because he is a Kurdish immigrant, currently a researcher at the Institute of Economic History at the Stockholm School of Economics, is the one academic who has questioned the establishment. These are his key findings:

- In the age group between 20 and 64 years, 82 percent of native born Swedes are employed compared to only 58 percent of immigrants. This gap "has remained constant going back to 2000, and even slightly increased compared to 1990".

- 30 percent of immigrants don't qualify to go to high-school after 9th grade, as compared to only 9 percent of Swedes.

- Immigrants are not filling the skills-jobs economists claimed they would, which is why on average they earn 40 percent less than Swedes.

- While a 3.6 GDP growth for 2015 may seem reasonably good, the GDP growth per capita has not been impressive at all: since 2006, it has been next to zero, somewhere around 0.6 percent per year on average.

- The media would have us believe that most of the migrants are women and children, but about 70% are males, and an estimated

92 percent of those unaccompanied migrants were male in 2015. In contrast, when Sweden took refugees from Finland during World War II, 90 percent were below the age of 10. "But now almost all of them are late teenagers – supposedly; we know many are older for a fact". "The media created this taboo where because they are officially supposed to be children we can't question it, and you are fascist if you do. Yet most people can see that many are adults".

- In the mid-1990s, Sweden had "one of the highest performances in international test scores". But today Sweden's test scores "are already second last after Greece. Swedish policies played the major role here, but immigration may explain about 30% of that decline".

- The media likes to paint a picture of a Swedish majority happily supporting mass immigration. But the media is totally biased; there are scientific polls "that clearly state that the majority or plurality of Swedes support reducing refugee immigration, even going back as far as the 1980s" One recent poll shows very high opposition, with only 8% saying we are not taking enough immigrants, 58% saying we are taking too many. "It's the elite opinion that forms the consensus that Sweden should take many more immigrants – it's almost like a religion, but it is not the popular view". [31]

- Most important of all, the true Swedish population is being demographically replaced by Near Eastern and African ethnic peoples. The immigrant population has been increasing steadily from 14.5% in 2000, to 19.1% in 2010 to 21.5% in 2014. The non-ethnic Swedish group "might perhaps reach 35-40% within 30 years. In Malmo, Sweden's third largest city, it's already almost 50% of the total. So that's where Sweden could be going to be in a generation because Malmo started to take immigrants earlier".

I could go on about the rapidly growing "exclusion areas" (ghettoes inhabited primarily by non-Swedes), rampant vandalism, the incessant

---

31   For these numbers I have drawn from an excellent recent interview, "Sweden on the Brink? – An Interview with Dr. Tino Sanandaji" posted February 21, 2016, https://www.linkedin.com/pulse/sweden-brink-interview-dr-tino-sanandaji-erico-matias-tavares Margaret Wente had an article with some similarly revealing statistics, "Sweden's ugly immigration problem" *The Globe and Mail* (September 11, 2015). On the steep decline in Sweden's ranking in test scores, see Tino Sanandaji, "Sweden Has an Education Crisis, but it Wasn't Caused by School Choice" *National Review Online* (June 21, 2014).

sexual assaults against Swedish women, the fact that immigrants consume most of the nation's government financial assistance, and much more.[32] It is easy to come up with economic facts showing that businesses stand to gain from cheaper supplies of labour, more consumers, and the multiplier effects of welfare spending. A proportion of the immigrants do find lower paying jobs in services and other informal sectors, and a percentage of the "growth in employment" can be accounted for by the hiring of immigrants. But these are economic benefits to migrants and economic costs to the natives of Sweden as whole. It can also be argued generally that growing economies need growing populations, increasing supplies of both workers and consumers, and that the growth of Western economies in the last two centuries has been associated with population growth. Yet, it is also the case that population growth has been a negative factor in instances in which it has outpaced productivity increases, and that economies with very high populations, despite strong economic growth, tend to have lower GDP per capita than countries with similar growth rates but low population densities. The precise nature of the relationship between population growth and economic wellbeing is not unidirectional but varies from country to country.[33]

The Right/Left argument should be seen as suspect in the way it speaks about foreign labour as if it were merely a matter of attracting immigrant workers to solve labour shortages on the assumption that a) immigrant labour is equal in quality, or equally suitable to the skill-needs of European economies, and b) the resident labour supply is insufficient to meet labour demand as if there was no unemployment in the host nation. This is less true for Canada, but in Europe, for over a decade now, it has been apparent that there is a horrendous mismatch between the quality of immigrant labour and the needs of the European economy. The vast majority of Muslim and African immigrants have the wrong education. Too few engineers, scientists, and skilled labourers have come or have been able to be educated in the host nation. This is why there is an employment gap in Europe between natives and non-natives.

---

32 Spencer P. Morrison, "Migrants Responsible For 95% Of Sweden's Crime Increase—Justice Costs Surge By $8.7 Billion" *The American Revenant* (February 19, 2017).

33 Richard A. Easterlin, "Effects of Population Growth on the Economic Development of Developing Countries" *The Annals of the American Academy of Political and Social Science* vol. 369 (1967).

To this day, Turks in Germany, even after 50 years and three generations, remain poorly educated, some 30 percent don't have a school leaving certificate,[34] and only 14 percent do a degree from Germany's top-level high schools, half the average of the German population. Only 20 percent of Turks have a regular job; the other 80% live on state social benefits. The Bertelsmann Foundation calculated that immigrants in Germany generally, before the massive migrant invasion of 2014 and 2015, were costing the government up to $20 billion per year.[35] Germany could have learned from the Swedish case, but instead it brought in over a million migrants in 2015, with economists celebrating this as a "great step" in solving Germany's labour scarcity. However, according to an article from February 2, 2016, the costs so far, for the shelter, welfare and integration of these migrants was €22 billion for 2016 and an expected €27.6 billion for 2017.[36] Professor for Finance Bernd Raffelhüschen, has calculated a fiscal burden of 17 billion Euro per year provided that the refugees integrate quickly into the labour market. Assuming that the migrants are integrated into the labour market within six years, an unrealistically positive scenario by Raffelhüschen's own admission, he has estimated that the total costs of the refugees will amount to a staggering 900 billion Euro.[37]

Given this reality of unused immigrant labour, how could economists in Germany argue about labour shortages? Something other than economics is motivating them. Unemployment rates in Europe have been quite high for some time; Spain's unemployment rates have stood above 20 percent since 2008. Portugal, Italy, Ireland, Greece, and other countries have masses of unused labour supplies. There is no way around the fact that this unused resident labour supply would be sufficient to solve the present and future labour shortages. It is also the case that, in economic terms alone, the percentage of unused labour is a function of whether the country educates its own young population

34 Katrin Elger, "Survey Shows Alarming Lack of Integration in Germany" Spiegel Online (January 26, 2009), http://www.spiegel.de/international/germany/immigration-survey-shows-alarming-lack-of-integration-in-germany-a-603588.html

35 *Ibid.*

36 "Migrant crisis to cost Germany €50 billion by 2017" *The Telegraph* (February 2, 2016).

37 This German article, "Flüchtlingskrise könnte fast eine Billion Euro kosten" (November 25, 2015) was translated for me by PhD German student, Holger Michiels, working under my supervision. An article on Raffelhüschen's estimations in English announces: "Migrant Crisis to cost Merkel's government over a TRILLION pounds". Express (July 21, 2016).

to acquire the skills demanded by the economy. In short, the argument that the needs of Europe's far more advanced economies can be met by the poorest, least educated populations in the world is clearly a poorly conceived idea that could only have come from economists totally subservient to cultural Marxist precepts, not from economists abiding by the principles of economics as a science.

20

Canada: The First Post-National State in History?

The only words from Justin Trudeau that may be remembered after he is gone are the ones he expressed in an interview with the *New York Times Magazine* on Nov. 10, 2015, six days after he was sworn in: that Canada is "the first postnational state". The journalist who interviewed him wrote an article, "Trudeau's Canada, Again", with some additional quoted words in-between his own:

> Trudeau's most radical argument is that Canada is becoming a new kind of state, defined not by its European history but by the multiplicity of its identities from all over the world. His embrace of a pan-cultural heritage makes him an avatar of his father's vision. 'There is no core identity, no mainstream in Canada,' he claimed. 'There are shared values — openness, respect, compassion, willingness to work hard, to be there for each other, to search for equality and justice. Those qualities are what make us the first postnational state.'[1]

Everyone knows that Justin Trudeau is a man without ideas. He had a mediocre education, a bachelor's degree with average grades and an easy-to-get teaching degree. He was a high school drama teacher before he was persuaded to run for a parliamentary seat. There is no denying, however, that in these words Justin Trudeau captured something unique about contemporary Canada. Canadians are indeed imagining their nation as a post-nation. We have met the concept "imagined communities" and "social imaginary" a few times in this book. It refers to the ways in which people imagine their social existence, the values and beliefs they think embody their nation's existence, the deep-seated modes through which they understand themselves as a collectivity of people. The Canadian people do imagine themselves as a nation that has no core identity because they believe that being "Canadian" today is being "multicultural", inclusive of many identities from all

1 Guy Lawson, "Trudeau's Canada, Again", *New York Times* (December 8, 2015).

over the world. They have been brainwashed to believe that insistence on one cultural identity, even a "Western", or a "Christian" identity, is exclusionary. But why "post-national"?

It is tempting to use the term "postnational", as Wikipedia does, in reference to processes "by which nation states and national identities lose their importance relative to supranational and global entities". [2] The immense power of multinational corporations, the internationalization of financial markets, together with the growth of such supranational political entities as the United Nations, the European Union, and NATO, as well as the spread of global media and the ongoing migration of millions of individuals and groups across national borders, are all factors that have weakened the sovereignty of nations and thus contributed to postnationalism. It is also true, and consistent with the emphasis we have placed on human rights, that postnationalism, as Wikipedia says, "is linked to the expansion of international human rights law and norms...reflected in a growing stress on the rights of individuals in terms of their 'personhood,' not just their citizenship".

But there is a deeper meaning in the current use of "post-national", and it is the one that Justin was alluding to, which goes to the heart of a nation's identity, and which points to the emergence of a totally new identity in Canada, a product of the dynamics of multiculturalism, diversity, and mass immigration. One of the earlier uses of the term "posnationalism" can be found in a heavily cited article published in 1999 with the title "Challenging the Liberal Nation-State? Postnationalism, Multiculturalism, and the Collective Claims Making of Migrants and Ethnic Minorities in Britain and Germany". [3] This article investigates the merits of the claim that mass immigration, "and the resulting presence of culturally different ethnic minorities", are bringing about a fundamental challenge to the national liberal model of citizenship. It identifies two approaches making this claim, the postnational and the multicultural approaches, which can be identified as one approach for our purposes here. This postnational-multicultural school claims that

---

2   https://en.wikipedia.org/wiki/Postnationalism

3   Ruud Koopmans and Paul Statham, "Challenging the Liberal Nation-State? Postnationalism, Multiculturalism, and the Collective Claims Making of Migrants and Ethnic Minorities in Britain and Germany" *American Journal of Sociology*, vol. 105, no. 3 (1999). The term "postnational" really took off in the 1990s.

Western "nation-state's legitimacy, authority, and integrative capacities are being weakened from within by the increasing pluralization of modern societies"brought on primarily by the arrivals of high numbers of immigrants from multiple cultures. The liberal, universal values that underpin Western nation states "are being challenged by claims for special group rights (or exemptions from duties) by a multitude of collective actors who emphasize their cultural difference from the rest of society". Ethnic minorities and native born Western majorities are increasingly clashing "over such issues as language rights, regional autonomy, political representation, education curriculum, land claims, immigration and naturalization policy, even national symbols, such as the choice of national anthem or public holidays". Immigrants are also eroding the cultural and political boundaries of Western states by "transcending" their frontiers through the regular and dense communication links they maintain with their homelands. "Migrant communities increasingly take on the character of transnationally linked diasporas and are well equipped for taking advantage of the new opportunities of postnational citizenship". [4]

But according to the evidence collected by the authors of this article, which is based essentially on surveys of immigrants and ethnic minorities in Britain and Germany for the period 1990–95, there is "very little support" and "mixed results" for the postnational-multicultural model, and "strong support for the continuing relevance of national models of citizenship". There is "very little evidence" that transnational migrant organizations are playing a role in national politics, and that immigrants are appealing to supranational institutions, and that minorities are "making demands on national governments in the name of international legal conventions and rights". Rather, the nation-state "continues to be by far the most important frame of reference for the identities, organizations, and claims of ethnic minorities". [5]

The authors of this article are wrong. There are major flaws in their conception of the term post-nationalism in their otherwise professionally written, seemingly "scientific" paper. Simply on grounds of common sense, the thesis of the paper should strike readers as evidentially true: immigrant minorities are inhabiting states, Germany

---

4   *Ibid*, pp. 653-696

5   *Ibid*.

and England, which do still have territorial sovereignty, citizenship requirements, and institutional networks, bureaucracies, political parties, legal and educational institutions, which immigrants cannot but participate within if they are to function within those states. Strictly speaking, the political, in Carl Schmitt's sense, which presupposes a government with a monopoly over the means of violence coupled with ultimate legal authority, cannot be eradicated altogether as long as a government proper exists. But what this article is missing altogether is the incredible weakening of the political that has been transpiring in the Western world in the last decades, in varying degrees, since WWII with the radicalizing spread of civic nationalism, opposition to any form of white racial identity, romantic notions about the naturally good intentions of non-European peoples, and the evolution of new forms of citizenship based on universal human rights. The authors themselves are products of this radicalizing logic and so it should come as no surprise that the very evidence they rely upon to invalidate the post-national-multicultural approaches point to the emerging reality of a post-national situation in Western states. The authors use as evidence for the continued viability and relevance of Western nation states the fact that immigrant groups are striving for "equal opportunity and multicultural rights" using the institutional procedures afforded by these states. Post national should not refer only to the presence of minorities appealing to international or supra-national authorities and the maintenance of cultural links with homelands. The authors fail to realize that the post-national-multicultural approach is validated in the degree to which minorities exert ever stronger pressures upon liberal states "for the recognition of cultural identities and special group rights". This is evidence that they are integrating to a state committed to multiculturalism and diversity and which immigrants are using for their own interests in a postnational direction.

Charles Foran, CEO of the Institute for Canadian Citizenship, is correct in stating that Justin Trudeau was "outlining, however obliquely, a governing principle about Canada in the 21st century". [6] Justin said what no other head of state has ever said. This is a reflection of Canada's status as the first official multicultural state, the first nation with the first leader, Pierre Trudeau, to conceive a constitutional framework for the creation of "polyethnic" nation to be showcased as a model for

---

6   Charles Foran, "The Canada experiment: is this the first 'postnational' country? *The Guardian* (January 4, 2017).

the nations of the world. His son is expressing the current state of an experiment pushed in earnest by his father. As Foran gushes out: "postnationalism is a frame to understand our ongoing experiment in filling a vast yet unified geographic space with the diversity of the world".

> Our government believes in the value of immigration, as does the majority of the population. We took in an estimated 300,000 newcomers in 2016, including 48,000 refugees, and we want them to become citizens…The greater Toronto area is now the most diverse city on the planet, with half its residents born outside the country; Vancouver, Calgary, Ottawa and Montreal aren't far behind.[7]

But what is it about the term "postnational" that makes it so new? Was Justin not saying what his father had already implied many decades before? None of the articles I have read on this topic make a distinction. Foran thinks it has to do with the stronger identification Canadians have today with multiculturalism. He gets a bit confused observing that Canada is still a nation-state, "Canada has borders, where guards check passports, and an army".

My view is that postnationalism is an attack on civic nationalism, the last remaining vestige of white national identity. It is the last step in the radicalizing logic of the post-WWII normative climate. It signals the end of the political for Western peoples. The eradication of Canadian ethnic and cultural nationalism is not enough; civic nationalism, the notion that Canada is based on universal ideas with roots in Western liberal principles, is still ethnocentric, conceived by "privileged white males". We met in chapter 8 the arguments of Sunera Thobani calling for a new Canada that is truly multicultural in allowing minorities to play an equal role in the shaping Canada's identity without having to shred their traditional values in terms set by liberal political concepts. Academia is now full of teachers expecting their students to understand that the "Western liberal discourse" still draws an Us versus Them dichotomy in separating "good Muslims" who are "moderate" or more Westernized, and "bad Muslims" who follow Islam more strictly. Leftists have long been calling for a new "radical multicultural" discourse in which the "homogenizing, essentialist, and chauvinist" side of liberal

---

7   *Ibid.*

multiculturalism is "exposed". They claim that multiculturalism is still burdened with discriminatory tendencies, driven by a "binaristic" logic wherein foreigners or future immigrants are divided into those who are fully "human" and can be accepted into Canada, according to a points system, and those who cannot be afforded such rights because they lie outside the supremacist narrative of liberalism.[8] As Richard Day put it, how can the "equal worth of others" be acknowledged without recognizing in principle the equal worth of other cultures in the making of Canada? Radical multiculturalism teaches that cultures are in a state of constant flux, and that in a multicultural setting no culture sets the terms; rather, each should be seen in "borderline negotiations of difference and identity" with each other in a state of mutuality. The English maple leaf, the Quebec *fleurs-de-lis*, the RCMP uniform, and Christian religious oaths and holidays should eventually give way to hybridization and coexistence with the symbols of other cultures. A postnational Canada requires making a final step in eradicating not only the remaining vestiges of cultural nationalism but the presumption that Canada is a nation with civic values that are specifically "Western".

These are no longer ideas hidden in the halls of academia. They are everywhere.[9] Immigrant minorities understand their force as weapons to "enhance" their ethnic interests. The recent widespread opposition to conservative candidate Kellie Leitch when she simply considered putting a question in a survey to her supporters asking: "Should the Canadian government screen potential immigrants for anti-Canadian values?" was an attack on civic nationalism. This question was deemed to be an extremist, intolerant question, even by some conservatives. Yet by "anti-Canadian" Leitch mean values that are contrary to leftist values like equality of the sexes, tolerance, gay rights, diversity, and multiculturalism. How can this be "unCanadian"?[10] It is because this

---

8   For the use of the terms I just cited, see: David Bennett, ed. *Multicultural States: Rethinking Difference and Identity* (Routledge, 1998). This is a collection of articles by academics from around the world pushing radical multiculturalism.

9   Simply Google the words "radical multiculturalism" or "radical democratic multiculturalism", and you will see what I meant. It is a plague.

10   The outcry against Leitch came from across the political spectrum: Althia Raj, "Deepak Obhrai: Kellie Leitch Acting 'Un-Canadian' With Immigrant Values Proposal" *Huff Post Canada* (September 29, 2016), Jagdeesh Mann was particularly insulted that Leitch would insinuate that some cultures are somehow less intolerant than others: "This absurdity cuts to the heart of the flaw with Ms. Leitch's proposal. Placed under a microscope, every culture across the globe will reveal underlying streaks

question still presupposes the concept of the political, "us versus them", those who are "more" Canadian" and those who are "less" Canadian. The spiral of radicalization has reached a point in which the separation of peoples in terms of whether they are more or less likely to assimilate to liberal multiculturalism is seen as a form of exclusionary discrimination, an inability to show hospitality toward those who belong to cultures that are not liberally-minded.

But should not Westerners protect the values of liberal multiculturalism and exclude those who don't abide by these values? This is what some conservatives are saying, sheepishly begging Leftists to understand that civic nationalism is not racist just because this nationalism is Western in origins. But these attacks are seen for what they are, weak efforts by conservatives holding on to the last vestiges of the political. The Left wins every time, for every argument one makes for the exclusion of some Muslims has to draw on the political, which is seen to violate the principle of equality. Civic nationalism prioritizes "Western values" and thus excludes "others" no matter how much it claims that these values are "for humanity". The only consistent argument is that of including all Muslims and calling for more programs to assimilate them into a radical multiculturalism that recognizes their right to sharia law and their collective nature. In the end, the only group that can be consistently excluded are those Europeans who want to retain the concept of the political through the affirmation of their particular cultural and ethnic identity. Muslims are agents for the diversification of Western cultures and, therefore, for the negation of the European concept of the political and the creation of universal states in which the US versus Them distinction is abolished. Ethno-nationalist Europeans are the last enemy that must be eliminated in order to bring an end to the political.

There are other words Justin Trudeau has expressed for which he may be remembered, although everyone else repeats them as much: "tolerance", "compassion", "inclusive diversity is a strength and a force that can vanquish intolerance and hate". Justin Trudeau has the mind of a 12 year old child, and this is the basis of his political success, his ability to be sincerely in favor of an ideology that is fundamentally infantile in its notion that it can rid the world of the Us versus Them distinction. His feel-good,

---

of intolerance". Even multicultural Canada is no better than monocultural Saudi Arabia. This is the meaning of radical multiculturalism! *Globe and Mail* (September 20, 2016).

selfie-like, easy-to-follow beliefs don't require any effort to understand, but they do give our pampered elites and snow flake generation a laid-back yet seemingly solid sense of self-righteousness. It is a wonderful world accepting multiple cultural outlooks, sexual lifestyles, and religious practices, without having to endorse any one in particular and without having to think through their inconsistencies, while living a narcissistic life well disguised with compassionate bromides about diversity.

Justin is voicing a generalized normative state of affairs with mass support. It is a feeling that is impermeable to self-examination. Terrorist acts, recurring sexual assaults, massive welfare dependency, are but "challenges" demanding more inclusiveness and tolerance, which are the values of a postnational state, not Western, but generically human. Canada is a place for global citizens. Its values are shared by humanity. A postnational state promises to bring a complete end to human conflict and exclusions, an end to the friend enemy struggles that have prevailed through human history. Justin is the man who will finally bring this reality onto humanity.

Across Canada, in every town and city, in every school and university, in businesses and government offices, in advertisements, books, movies, newspapers, magazines and internet sites, the same phrases about inclusiveness, diversity, and tolerance are announced. Everywhere one goes, even in one's own home, the Multicultural Party is watching you; everywhere one looks, one sees the face of Diversity's omniscience. The Party controls everything in Canada, even the history of Canadians, by academics who work in the Ministry of Truth, where they are dedicated to the alteration of historical records to fit the needs of a post national state.

The only force that can destroy this totalitarian spiral is the affirmation by Euro-Canadians of their historical heritage and ethnic interests, without qualification, in a complete state of certainty that Canada is their nation and that they have every right to determine its future against the deception of an elite welcoming white demographic displacement by other ethnic groups without any sense of loyalty to its ancestors and basic dignified pride.

About the Author

Ricardo Duchesne, a professor at The University of New Brunswick for 25 years, took early retirement in 2019 after experiencing an "academic mobbing". The bestseller status of *Canada in Decay* and its favourable reviews were a major instigator in this mobbing. It corroborated Duchesne's claim in this book that Canadian universities do not tolerate critical reflection over the issue of mass immigration and the demographic marginalization of Euro-Canadians. The so-called "critical thinking" academics love to talk about consists in nothing more than brainwashing students to believe that questioning immigrant diversity is an expression of "white supremacy".

Professor Duchesne is the only academic in the history of Canada who decided to take on the lies academics and journalists have been spreading about the imposition of diversity, and he paid the price for this courageous act with the loss of his academic position.

He is happy to say, however, that he does not regret writing *Canada in Decay*. He hopes that reading this book will convey to students why it is morally wrong to accept without self-questioning and rational deliberation the conventional points of view imposed by those in power.

His first book, *The Uniqueness of Western Civilization* (2011), is recognized as a landmark book in tracing the origins of the West back to the aristocratic warlike culture of prehistoric Indo-Europeans, and demonstrating that the West has been the most creative civilization in history in all the endeavours of human life, in philosophy, art, science, architecture, technology, institutional innovations, exploration, and more. Uniqueness was reviewed extensively, including six full review essays.

His second book, *Faustian Man in a Multicultural Age* (2017), is the first book to address the racial aspects of Western uniqueness, the origins

369

of the European race, the importance of Oswald Spengler' concept of "Faustian Soul" in comprehending the incredible dynamism of European peoples, together with an assessment of the ways in which cultural Marxists are seeking to destroy this Soul through immigrant diversification.

Professor Duchesne is the founder and one of the chief contributors to the Council of European Canadians website (www.Euro-Canadian.ca). He is currently writing his fourth book on the psychological uniqueness of the European mind and personality. A key to understanding why Europeans accomplished far more culturally than all the other races combined lies in their apprehension of the mind as a faculty separate from the enveloping world of nature, customs, and bodily appetites. This separation of the mind from the surrounding world, of thought from sensory impressions and material objects, began with the pre-Socratics. The ancient Greeks, originally grounded in the aristocratic Indo-European culture of heroic striving for the highest, had a relatively keen sense of personal agency, which eventually led them to gain consciousness of their consciousness and identify the mind as the agency of knowledge and truthfulness.

Index